Computer Accounting

with

QuickBooks® Online

Second Edition

Donna Kay, MBA, PhD, CPA, CITP

McGraw Hill

COMPUTER ACCOUNTING WITH QUICKBOOKS® ONLINE, SECOND EDITION

Published by McGraw-Hill Education, 2 Penn Plaza, New York, NY 10121. Copyright © 2021 by McGraw-Hill Education.
All rights reserved. Printed in the United States of America. Previous edition © 2019. No part of this publication may be
reproduced or distributed in any form or by any means, or stored in a database or retrieval system, without the prior written
consent of McGraw-Hill Education, including, but not limited to, in any network or other electronic storage or transmission,
or broadcast for distance learning.

Some ancillaries, including electronic and print components, may not be available to customers outside the United States.

This book is printed on acid-free paper.

1 2 3 4 5 6 7 8 9 LMN 24 23 22 21 20

ISBN 978-1-260-88806-5 (bound edition)
MHID 1-260-88806-1 (bound edition)
ISBN 978-1-264-10813-8 (loose-leaf edition)
MHID 1-264-10813-3 (loose-leaf edition)

Executive Portfolio Manager: *Steve Schuetz*
Product Developer: *Sarah Sacco*
Marketing Manager: *Claire McLemore*
Content Project Managers: *Sherry Kane and Emily Windelborn*
Buyer: *Susan K. Culbertson*
Design: *Egzon Shaqiri*
Content Licensing Specialist: *Melissa Homer*
Cover Image: *©Alexander Spatari/Getty Images*
Design Elements: *QuickBooks® and QuickBooks® Online Plus are registered trademarks of Intuit Inc.*
Compositor: *SPi Global*

All credits appearing on page or at the end of the book are considered to be an extension of the copyright page.

Library of Congress Cataloging-in-Publication Data

Names: Kay, Donna, author.
Title: Computer accounting with QuickBooks Online / Donna Kay, MBA, PhD,
  CPA, CITP.
Description: Second edition. | New York, NY : McGraw-Hill Education, [2021]
  | Includes index.
Identifiers: LCCN 2019041940 | ISBN 9781260888065 (spiral bound)
Subjects: LCSH: QuickBooks. | Small business–Accounting–Computer
  programs. | Small business–Finance–Computer programs.
Classification: LCC HF5679 .K38 2021 | DDC 657/.9042028553–dc23
LC record available at https://lccn.loc.gov/2019041940

The Internet addresses listed in the text were accurate at the time of publication. The inclusion of a website does not
indicate an endorsement by the authors or McGraw-Hill Education, and McGraw-Hill Education does not guarantee the
accuracy of the information presented at these sites.

mheducation.com/highered

Preface

Computer Accounting with QuickBooks Online

Donna Kay

Welcome to Learning QuickBooks Online!

Gain a competitive advantage – learn a leading online financial app for entrepreneurs using *Computer Accounting with QuickBooks Online*. Designed using the most effective way to learn QuickBooks Online, this text streamlines learning QuickBooks Online because it focuses on you—the learner.

Proven instructional techniques are incorporated throughout the text to make your mastery of QuickBooks Online as effortless as possible. Using a hands-on approach, this text integrates understanding accounting with mastery of QuickBooks Online. Designed for maximum flexibility to meet your needs, *Computer Accounting with QuickBooks Online* can be used either in a QuickBooks Online course or independently at your own pace. *Good luck* with *QuickBooks Online and best wishes for your continued success,*

Donna Kay

Meet the Author

Donna Kay is a former professor of Accounting and Accounting Systems & Forensics, teaching both undergraduate and graduate accounting. Dr. Kay earned B.S. and MBA degrees from Southern Illinois University at Edwardsville before receiving a Ph.D. from Saint Louis University, where she conducted action research on the perceived effectiveness of instructional techniques for learning technology. Dr. Kay designs her textbooks to incorporate the most effective instructional techniques based on research findings, making your learning journey as effective as possible.

Named to Who's Who Among American Women, Dr. Kay holds certifications as both a Certified Public Accountant (CPA) and Certified Informational Technology Professional (CITP) and is an active member of the American Institute of Certified Public Accountants (AICPA).

Donna Kay is also the author of *Computer Accounting with QuickBooks*, a leading textbook for learning QuickBooks Desktop software.

Visit Dr Kay's websites www.my-quickbooks.com and www.my-quickbooksonline.com to learn more about her books and support materials for the texts.

What's New?

New, updated, and expanded features to make learning QuickBooks Online even easier include:

- Expanded Chapter coverage exploring the latest QBO features and functionality

- Expanded Payroll activities including Payroll setup

- Updated Time Tracking coverage

- Updated Sales Tax coverage

- Updated Reports coverage

- Expanded Customers List coverage

- Expanded Vendors List coverage

- Updated and expanded Chapter activities

- Updated Exercises and Projects that offer the most effective teaching and learning approach to minimize student carryforward QBO errors to subsequent chapters and assignments

- Enhanced formatting with bolded field names and field entries to highlight action steps

- New coverage for QBO free student access code to use with this text

- Streamlined way to stay up to date with ongoing QBO updates

- Expanded QBO SatNav, providing Satellite Navigation for QBO

- XPM Mapping for eXplore, Practice, Master pedagogy to enhance student understanding of the learning process

QuickBooks Online SatNav

How Do I Streamline Navigating QuickBooks Online?

QBO SatNav is your satellite navigation system for QBO. QBO SatNav breaks navigating QBO into three processes: QBO Settings, QBO Transactions, and QBO Reports. A QBO SatNav is provided with each chapter and project.

The portion of the QBO SatNav that is the focus of the chapter is highlighted. An expanded QBO SatNav gives additional detail about transactions covered in a chapter, such as the following Chapter 4 Banking SatNav.

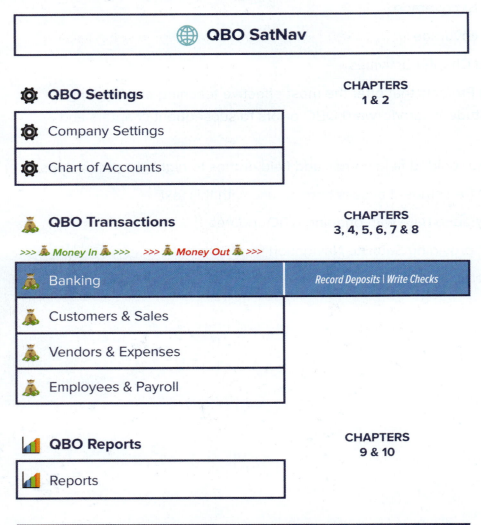

Faster, Smarter Learning with Smart Dots

How Can I Save Time While Learning QBO?

Make learning QuickBooks Online faster and smarter with Smart Dots. As demonstrated below, step-by-step instructions with coordinating Smart Dots on screen captures make learning QuickBooks Online faster and easier with increased focus.

1 From the Navigation Bar, select **Sales**

2 Select the **All Sales** tab

3 From the Sales Transactions window, select the drop-down arrow for **New transaction**

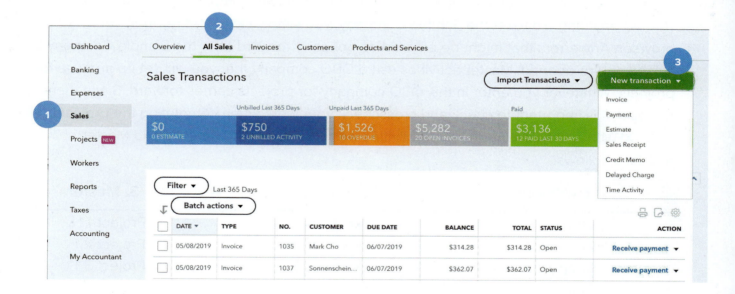

XPM Mapping

What is the Most Effective Way to Learn QuickBooks Online?

Use a highly effective, three-step XPM approach to streamline learning QuickBooks Online:

eXplore → Practice → Master

1. eXplore. Providing numerous screen shots and detailed instructions, chapters in *Computer Accounting with QuickBooks Online* are designed as tutorials for you to explore and learn QuickBooks Online features.

2. Practice. Designed with fewer instructions, the end-of-chapter exercises provide opportunities for you to practice and test your understanding.

3. Master. Virtual company projects provide mastery opportunities for you to apply and integrate your QuickBooks Online skills.

eXplore and Practice activities use a test drive Sample Company where you cannot "break" anything. To reset the Sample Company, you simply close and re-open your web browser. Any errors that might be entered do not carry forward after the Sample Company is closed and re-opened. Master activities use a QBO company that you will set up and use for projects. Whatever you enter in this QBO company for projects carries forward. Since there is no reset, it is important to check and crosscheck your work when completing the projects.

XPM mapping, listing eXplore activities with corresponding Practice and Master activities, follows.

1. eXplore	→	2. Practice	→	3. Master
Chapter 1		Exercises 1		Project 1.1
Chapter 2		Exercises 2		Project 2.1
Chapter 3		Exercises 3		Project 3.1
Chapter 4		Exercises 4		Project 4.1
Chapter 5		Exercises 5		Project 5.1
Chapter 6		Exercises 6		Project 6.1
Chapter 7		Exercises 7		Project 7.1
Chapter 8		Exercises 8		Project 8.1
Chapter 9		Exercises 9		Project 9.1
Chapter 10		Exercises 10		Project 10.1

Stay Up To Date with Ongoing QBO Updates

How Do I Stay Up to Date with QBO Updates?

QuickBooks Online is updated on an ongoing basis. So some QBO features may appear slightly different from what is shown in your text due to new rollouts from Intuit.

For your convenience in tracking QBO updates, two sources for update information and how the updates might affect your text are:

- www.my-quickbooksonline.com, select QBO Updates link
- www.mhhe.com/KayQBO2e, select QBO Updates

Online Learning Resources

Computer *Accounting with QuickBooks Online* is accompanied by two websites that offer additional resources for learning QuickBooks Online. Visit:

- www.my-quickbooksonline.com
- www.mhhe.com/KayQBO2e

Resources for students include:

- Presentation Slides for each chapter
- QuickBooks Online Updates
- How to obtain free QBO Student Access

Resources for instructors include:

- Instructor Resource Guide and Solutions
- Test Bank
- How to obtain free QBO Instructor Access
- Pre-Built Connect Course

Acknowledgments

To make this second edition possible, special thanks to:

- McGraw-Hill QuickBooks Online team Steve, Kevin, Sarah, and Marianne
- Sara Barritt for her accuracy checking and editing
- Brian Behrens for always being in my corner with greatly appreciated support
- Carolyn Strauch, Crowder College
- Karen May, New Mexico State University

All the QuickBooks educators who share ideas, comments, suggestions, and encouragement.

QuickBooks Online Certification

How Do I Learn More About QBO Certification?

QuickBooks Online Certification is certification that is obtained by passing the QuickBooks Online Certification Examination. The QBO Certification Exam consists of 4 sections and 95 questions, with an average time of 2 hours to complete. To pass the Exam, you must obtain a minimum score of 80% on each section. If you obtain less than 80% on a section, you receive 4 attempts to retake a section of the exam to obtain your certification. The QBO Certification Exam is updated each year so you are certified for one year. For more information about preparing for QuickBooks Online Certification, go to QBO Certification.

In preparing this publication, McGraw-Hill Education, its author(s), employees and representatives (collectively, the "Publisher") have taken every effort to ensure that the Computer Accounting with QuickBooks Online materials and related websites ("Materials") are as comprehensive as possible and designed to assist you in preparation of the QuickBooks User Certification examination. Your level of success in passing or achieving a particular score on any examination, however, is dependent upon a number of factors including your knowledge, ability, dedication and time spent preparing for such an examination. Because such factors differ among individuals, and changes may occur with respect to examinations after the publication of the Materials, the Publisher cannot and does not guarantee your success on any examination including, without limitation, the QuickBooks User Certification examination.

THE MATERIALS ARE PROVIDED "AS IS" WITH ANY FURTHER REPRESENTATIONS OR WARRANTIES, EXPRESS OR IMPLIED, UNDER NO CIRCUMSTANCES WILL THE PUBLISHER, ITS SUPPLIERS OR AGENTS BE LIABLE FOR ANY SPECIAL OR CONSEQUENTIAL DAMAGES THAT RESULT FROM THE USE OF, OR THE INABILITY TO USE, THE MATERIALS. IN NO EVENT SHALL THE TOTAL LIABILITY BY PUBLISHER TO YOU FOR DAMAGES, LOSSES, AND CAUSES OF ACTION (WHETHER IN CONTRACT, TORT, OR OTHERWISE) EXCEED THE AMOUNT PAIDBY YOU FOR SUCH MATERIALS. Applicable law may not allow the limitation or exclusion of liability or incidental or consequential damages (including but not limited to lost data), so the above limitation or exclusion may not apply to you.

Connect

What kind of study tools does Connect offer?

SmartBook 2.0. A personalized and adaptive learning tool used to maximize the learning experience by helping students study more efficiently and effectively. SmartBook 2.0 highlights where in the chapter to focus, asks review questions on the materials covered and tracks the most challenging content for later review recharge. SmartBook 2.0 is available both online and offline.

Assignment Materials. After completing assignments in *Computer Accounting with QuickBooks Online* students can enter key elements of their solution into Connect for grading. Based on instructor settings, they can receive instant feedback either while working on the assignment or after the assignment is submitted for grade. Assignable materials include: in chapter activities, exercises, projects, practice quizzes, and test bank materials.

Connect Insight. At-a-glance performance dashboards that use robust visual data displays that are each framed by intuitive question, to provide actionable recommendations and guide students towards behaviors that could increase class performance and enables instructors to give targeted tuition precisely when and where it is needed.

ReadAnywhere App. Using McGraw-Hill's ReadAnywhere app, you can access the *Computer Accounting with QuickBooks Online* eBook anywhere, both online and offline, data free, by signing in with your Connect login and password. Use simply download the entire textbook or only the chapters you needed. The app also provides the same tools available in the laptop version of the eBook, and any notes or highlights made to the text will sync across platforms so they're available both on the app and In Connect.

You're in the driver's seat.

Want to build your own course? No problem. Prefer to use our turnkey, prebuilt course? Easy. Want to make changes throughout the semester? Sure. And you'll save time with Connect's auto-grading too.

65%
Less Time Grading

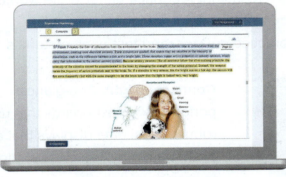

Laptop: McGraw-Hill; Woman/dog: George Doyle/Getty Images

They'll thank you for it.

Adaptive study resources like SmartBook® 2.0 help your students be better prepared in less time. You can transform your class time from dull definitions to dynamic debates. Find out more about the powerful personalized learning experience available in SmartBook 2.0 at **www.mheducation.com/highered/ connect/smartbook**

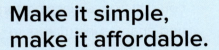

Make it simple, make it affordable.

Connect makes it easy with seamless integration using any of the major Learning Management Systems— Blackboard®, Canvas, and D2L, among others—to let you organize your course in one convenient location. Give your students access to digital materials at a discount with our inclusive access program. Ask your McGraw-Hill representative for more information.

Padlock: Jobalou/Getty Images

Solutions for your challenges.

A product isn't a solution. Real solutions are affordable, reliable, and come with training and ongoing support when you need it and how you want it. Our Customer Experience Group can also help you troubleshoot tech problems— although Connect's 99% uptime means you might not need to call them. See for yourself at **status. mheducation.com**

Checkmark: Jobalou/Getty Images

SUPPORT AT every step

FOR STUDENTS

Effective, efficient studying.

Connect helps you be more productive with your study time and get better grades using tools like SmartBook 2.0, which highlights key concepts and creates a personalized study plan. Connect sets you up for success, so you walk into class with confidence and walk out with better grades.

Study anytime, anywhere.

Download the free ReadAnywhere app and access your online eBook or SmartBook 2.0 assignments when it's convenient, even if you're offline. And since the app automatically syncs with your eBook and SmartBook 2.0 assignments in Connect, all of your work is available every time you open it. Find out more at **www.mheducation.com/readanywhere**

"I really liked this app—it made it easy to study when you don't have your text-book in front of you."

- Jordan Cunningham, Eastern Washington University

No surprises.

The Connect Calendar and Reports tools keep you on track with the work you need to get done and your assignment scores. Life gets busy; Connect tools help you keep learning through it all.

Calendar: owattaphotos/Getty Images

Learning for everyone.

McGraw-Hill works directly with Accessibility Services Departments and faculty to meet the learning needs of all students. Please contact your Accessibility Services office and ask them to email accessibility@mheducation.com, or visit **www.mheducation.com/about/accessibility** for more information.

Contents

Computer Accounting with QuickBooks Online

Donna Kay

Chapter 1 QuickBooks Online Navigation and Settings   1

Chapter 2 QBO Chart of Accounts   71

Chapter 3 QBO Transactions   128

Chapter 4 Banking   195

Chapter 5 Customers and Sales   243

Chapter 6 Vendors and Expenses   308

Chapter 7 Inventory   354

Chapter 8 Employees and Payroll   415

Chapter 9 QBO Adjustments   466

Chapter 10 QBO Reports   523

Appendix A QBO Apps: Mac, Windows, and Mobile   605

Appendix B QuickBooks Online versus QuickBooks Desktop   607

Index   614

Contents Overview

Designed as hands-on tutorials for learning QuickBooks Online, *Computer Accounting with QuickBooks Online* chapters provide screen captures with step-by-step, detailed instructions. To improve long-term retention of your QuickBooks Online skills, end-of-chapter learning activities are designed with fewer instructions to test your understanding and, when needed, to develop your skills to quickly seek out additional information to complete the task. The ability to find information as needed is an increasingly important skill in a rapidly changing business environment. The design of *Computer Accounting with QuickBooks Online* seamlessly facilitates your development of this crucial skill.

Chapter 1 QuickBooks Online Navigation and Settings

This chapter provides a guided tour of QuickBooks Online using QBO Navigation and QBO tools. Chapter 1 introduces the QBO Sample Company. Project 1.1 provides an opportunity to setup a new company, Mookie The Beagle Concierge, that will be used throughout the text.

Chapter 2 QBO Chart of Accounts

This chapter introduces how to customize the QBO Chart of Accounts to meet specific business needs. Chart of Accounts topics include adding accounts, adding subaccounts, editing accounts, and inactivating accounts.

Chapter 3 QBO Transactions

Chapter 3 provides an introduction to the various types of transactions entered in QBO, including banking, customer, vendor, and employee transactions.

Chapter 4 Banking

This chapter focuses on the Checking account and Check Register for a small business. Topics include making deposits, writing checks, and matching bank transactions.

Chapter 5 Customers and Sales

Chapter 5 demonstrates how to record customers transactions. Topics include how to create Invoices and record customer payments.

Chapter 6 Vendors and Expenses

Chapter 6 focuses on recording vendors transactions, such as recording expenses for services. Topics include recording vendor services paid by check and credit card.

Chapter 7 Inventory

Chapter 7 focuses on recording vendors transactions related to inventory, including creating purchase orders, entering bills for inventory, and paying bills. In addition, customers transactions related to inventory are also covered.

Chapter 8 Employees and Payroll

Chapter 8 covers tracking time and billing tracked time using QBO employee and payroll features.

Chapter 9 QBO Adjustments

Chapter 9 covers how to create a Trial Balance and enter adjusting entries using QBO.

Chapter 10 QBO Reports

Chapter 10 completes the accounting cycle, covering a variety of QBO reports, including financial statements and management reports.

Appendix A QBO Apps: Mac, Windows, and Mobile

Appendix A summarizes features of the QBO App for Mac and Windows. In addition, QBO Mobile app features are discussed.

Appendix B QuickBooks Online versus QuickBooks Desktop

Appendix B compares the different features of QuickBooks Online and Quickbooks Desktop for both the client versions and the accountant versions of each.

QuickBooks Online Navigation and Settings

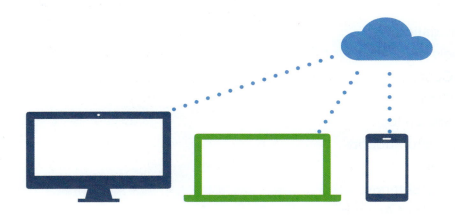

Your best friend, Cy Walker, has dreamed of owning his own business. Now Cy has an opportunity to launch his first entrepreneurial endeavor, a pet concierge service for young working professionals who need assistance balancing pet care and work commitments. Realizing he has many business decisions to make, Cy knows he needs good solid information to make those decisions. So building an accounting system that can capture that data and provide information and data analytics for decision making is crucial—if his business is to succeed.

Cy asks if you would research different financial system apps that could meet his business needs, make a recommendation, and then assist him in implementing the new system as soon as possible. After completing your review of various financial apps, you recommend that for Cy's specific business needs, QuickBooks Online (QBO) would be a good option since it uses accounting in the cloud. This permit both you and Cy to access QBO from different locations and devices. Cy concurs with your recommendation. Now your next step is to learn QuickBooks Online. Cy gifts you this book for learning QBO fast.

Chapter 1

LEARNING OBJECTIVES

Chapter 1 introduces QuickBooks Online. In this chapter, you will learn about the following topics:

- QBO Test Drive Sample Company
- QBO SatNav
- QBO Navigation
- QBO Tools
  - QBO Gear Icon
  - QBO Create (+) Icon
  - QBO Search Icon
- QBO Help and Support
- QBO Settings
  - Company Settings
  - QBO Chart of Accounts
- Accounting Essentials: Legal, Tax, and Financial Questions

Section 1.1

QBO TEST DRIVE

WHAT IS QUICKBOOKS ONLINE?

QuickBooks® Online (QBO) is a cloud-based financial system for entrepreneurs. We use a web browser to access QBO instead of using software installed on a computer like QuickBooks® Desktop (QBDT). So the advantage of QBO is that we can access QBO from any desktop or laptop computer that has an Internet connection. QBO also offers an accompanying mobile QBO app for use with smartphones and tablets.

> **QuickBooks Online (QBO)** refers to the QuickBooks system accessed through a web browser with data stored in the cloud. **QuickBooks Desktop (QBDT)** refers to QuickBooks software that is installed on your desktop or laptop computer.

QBO is updated on an ongoing basis. So some features on your screen may be slightly different from those shown here due to new, dynamic QBO updates.

> For your convenience, information about QBO updates that affect your text are posted at **www.My-QuickBooksOnline.com** > **QBO Updates** and at **www.mhhe.com/KayQBO2e.**

WHAT IS AN EASY WAY TO LEARN QUICKBOOKS ONLINE?

Learning QuickBooks Online requires integrating knowledge of accounting, financial systems, and financial technology. Don't become discouraged if you find that you need to go over the same material more than once. That is normal. Learning how accounting and financial technology is interrelated requires repetition.

QuickBooks® and QuickBooks® Online Plus are registered trademarks of Intuit Inc.

To make learning QBO easier, we will use the three-step XPM (eXplore, Practice, Master) approach:

1. **eXplore** QuickBooks Online using the chapter with step-by-step walk through screen captures. Don't worry about making mistakes or "breaking" QBO. Instead, focus on learning how to navigate and use QBO.
2. **Practice** entering information and transactions into QBO end-of-chapter exercises.
3. **Master** QBO with QBO projects. The projects cover QBO tasks from setting up a new QBO company and entering transactions to generating QBO reports.

First, we will eXplore using the Chapter illustrations, then we will Practice using Exercises at the end of the chapter, and finally we will Master QBO by completing the Project at the end of each chapter. The eXplore Chapter activities and Practice Exercises use a Sample Company that resets each time it is opened and closed. So you do not have to be stressed about errors that might carry forward to subsequent Chapters and Exercises. The Projects, however, provide an opportunity for you to demonstrate mastery of QBO and your QBO data does carry forward to subsequent Projects.

ACCESS QUICKBOOKS ONLINE SAMPLE COMPANY

To access the QBO Sample Company, complete the following steps.

1   Open a web browser. (Note: Intuit recommends using Google Chrome.)

2   Go to the Sample Company at https://qbo.intuit.com/redir/testdrive

3   Follow onscreen instructions for security verification. If a message about cookies or blocking pop-up windows appears, follow the onscreen instructions.

> **Note: Although the Sample Company link should work, if for some reason the previous link for the Sample Company doesn't work with your browser, using Google search, type in "qbo.intuit.com Sample Company". Select the link to Test Drive Sample Company.**

Craig's Design and Landscaping Services, the QBO Sample Company, should appear on your screen.

QBO SAMPLE COMPANY RESET

While you are using the Craig's Design and Landscaping Services Sample Company, the information you enter will be saved. *After you close* the Sample Company, automatically all the settings and data are reset to the original data and settings before you entered your work. The Sample Company repopulates with its original data.

Since we will be using the Sample Company to explore and practice with QBO, the reset will permit you to start over each time you enter the Sample Company. You do not have to worry about carrying forward errors that ripple through the remaining chapters.

The Sample Company default setting is to log out after one (1) hour of inactivity. Since the Sample Company then repopulates with the original data automatically, you will lose any work you entered. Therefore, it is important to plan accordingly so that you can complete all activities needed before closing the Sample Company.

To increase the amount of time from one (1) hour to three (3) hours before the log out for inactivity occurs:

1. From Craig's Design and Landscaping Services QBO Sample Company, select the **Gear** icon

2. Under Your Company section, select **Account and Settings**

3. Select **Advanced**

4. Select **Other preferences**

5. For the option Sign me out if inactive for, click on **1 hour**

6. From the drop-down menu, select **3 hours**

7. Select **Save**

8. Select **Done**

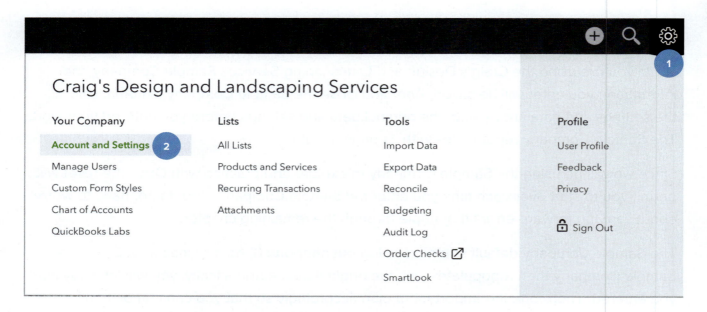

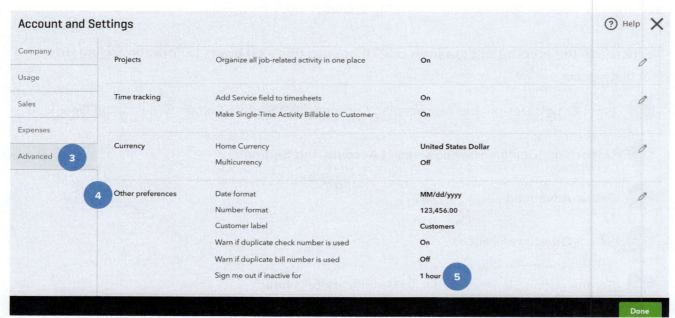

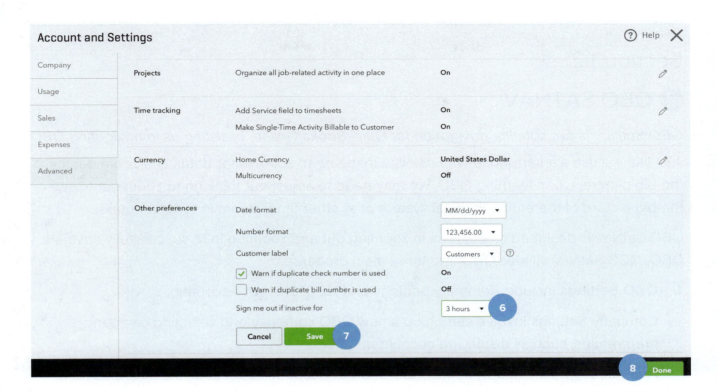

We use the Sample Company for practice throughout the chapter and exercises. For mastery projects at the end of each chapter, we will set up a new QBO company that does not reset automatically.

Section 1.2

🌐 QBO SATNAV

QBO SatNav is our satellite navigation for QuickBooks Online, assisting us in navigating QBO

Just like we use a smartphone with satellite mapping to zoom in for detail and zoom out for the big picture, when learning QBO, we may need to adjust our thinking to zoom out to see the big picture of the entire financial system or at other times zoom in to view details.

QBO SatNav is designed to assist us in zooming out and zooming in to successfully navigate QBO. QBO SatNav divides QBO into three main processes:

1. **QBO Settings** include Company Settings and QBO Chart of Accounts.

    Company Settings involve setting up a new QBO company and selecting company preferences, such as displaying account numbers.

    Another aspect of QBO Settings is the Chart of Accounts, a list of all the accounts for a company. Accounts can be used to sort and track accounting information. For example, a business needs one account for cash, another account to track amounts customers owe (Accounts Receivable), and yet another account to track inventory. QBO automatically creates a Chart of Accounts when we set up a new QBO company. QBO then permits us to modify the Chart of Accounts to customize it for specific company needs.

    QBO Settings are covered in Chapters 1 and 2.

2. **QBO Transactions** involve recording transactions as **input** into the financial system. Transaction types can be categorized as Banking, Customers & Sales, Vendors & Expenses, and Employees & Payroll. In basic terms, recording transactions involves recording money in and money out of the company.

    Transactions are exchanges between the QBO company and other parties, such as customers, vendors, and employees. Typically in a transaction, the company gives something and receives something in exchange. QBO is used to keep a record of what is given and what is received in the transaction. We can enter transaction information into QBO using the onscreen Journal or onscreen forms, such as onscreen Invoices and onscreen Checks.

    QBO Transactions are covered in Chapters 3, 4, 5, 6, 7, and 8.

3. **QBO Reports** are the **output** of the system. Reports typically provide information to decision makers. For example, accounting information is used to prepare:

- **Financial statements** for external users, such as creditors and investors. Internal users, such as managers, also may use financial statements. Financial statements are standardized financial reports that summarize information about past transactions. The primary financial statements for a business are:

  ‣ **Balance Sheet**: summarizes what a company owns and owes on a particular date.

  ‣ **Profit and Loss Statement** (or **Income Statement**): summarizes what a company has earned and the expenses incurred to earn the income.

  ‣ **Statement of Cash Flows**: summarizes cash inflows and cash outflows for operating, investing, and financing activities of a business.

- **Tax returns** for federal and state tax agencies.

- **Management reports** for company managers and owners to use when making business decisions. Such decisions include: Are we collecting customer payments when due? An example of such a report is an Accounts Receivable Aging report that summarizes past due customer accounts.

QBO Reports are covered in Chapters 9 and 10.

QBO SatNav will be used in each chapter to illustrate which aspect(s) of QBO the chapter will focus on. If you start to feel lost in QBO, return to the QBO SatNav to assist in navigating QBO.

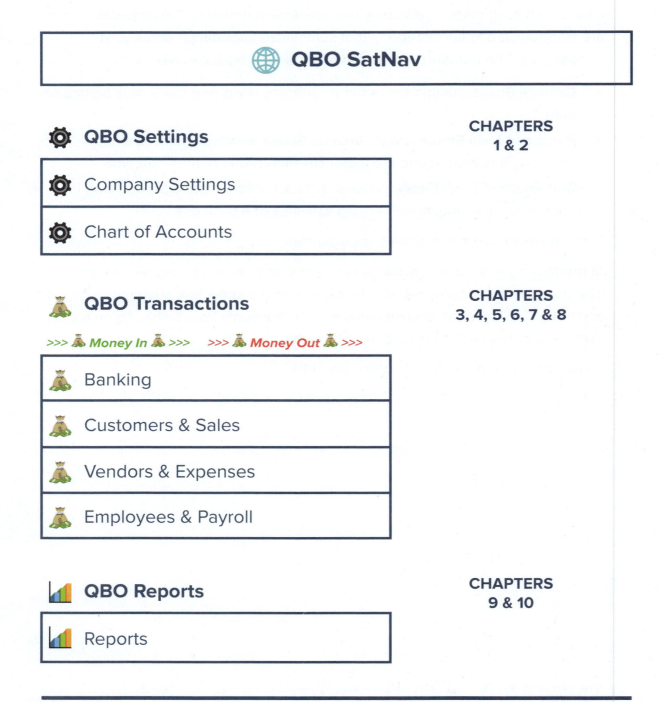

The portion of the QBO SatNav that is the focus of the chapter will be highlighted. For example, in this chapter the focus is on Company Settings, so Company Settings is highlighted in the following QBO SatNav.

QBO SatNav

QBO Settings

Company Settings

Chart of Accounts

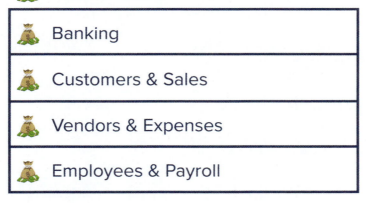

QBO Transactions

Banking

Customers & Sales

Vendors & Expenses

Employees & Payroll

QBO Reports

Reports

Section 1.3

QBO NAVIGATION

Taking a few minutes to learn QBO navigation will make learning QBO easier. The primary way to navigate QBO is using the QBO Navigation Bar, located on the left side of the screen. The Navigation Bar permits you to quickly access commonly used QBO screens.

As QBO is updated by Intuit, the items listed on the Navigation Bar may continue to change, so your Navigation Bar may appear slightly different from the one shown below.

1 **Dashboard** provides on overview and summary of key information for your QuickBooks Online company

2 **Banking** transactions relate to Bank and Credit Card accounts and transactions

3   **Sales** transactions relate to customers and sales transactions (money in)

4   **Expenses** transactions relate to vendors and expenses transactions (money out)

5   **Projects** is a QBO feature that organizes and tracks the timeline and profitability of projects

6   **Workers** transactions relate to employees and payroll transactions (money out)

7   **Reports** summarize the output of our QBO financial system

8   **Taxes** relate to sales taxes and, if QuickBooks Online payroll is used, payroll taxes

9   **Accounting** displays the Chart of Accounts

10   **My Accountant** is used to connect QBO to your accountant

DASHBOARD

Dashboard appears when you log into your QBO company. If the dashboard does not appear, click on Dashboard on the Navigation Bar to display it.

Like a car dashboard, this QBO Dashboard provides a digital overview. We can customize the dashboard to display information to meet our specific business needs and requirements. Note that the dashboard appearance may change over time as Intuit rolls out ongoing QBO updates, so your dashboard may appear differently from the dashboard shown here.

To view and explore the QBO Dashboard:

1   Select **Dashboard** on the Navigation Bar

2   The QBO Sample Company is **Craig's Design and Landscaping Services**

3   The Dashboard displays graphs of useful information in managing a company. The **Invoices** graph shows overdue and not yet due amounts from customers. This is useful in focusing attention on collecting overdue customer accounts.

4 The **Profit and Loss** graph displays Net Income, Income (Revenue) and Expenses for tracking profitability

5 The **Expenses** graph reflects the different categories of expenses, focusing attention on how money is spent

6 The **Sales** graph displays how sales vary over the month. Notice that the time period can be changed and the graph updates accordingly.

7 The Dashboard displays a **Bank account** summary, listing the company's Bank and Credit Card accounts including the bank balance and the QBO balance

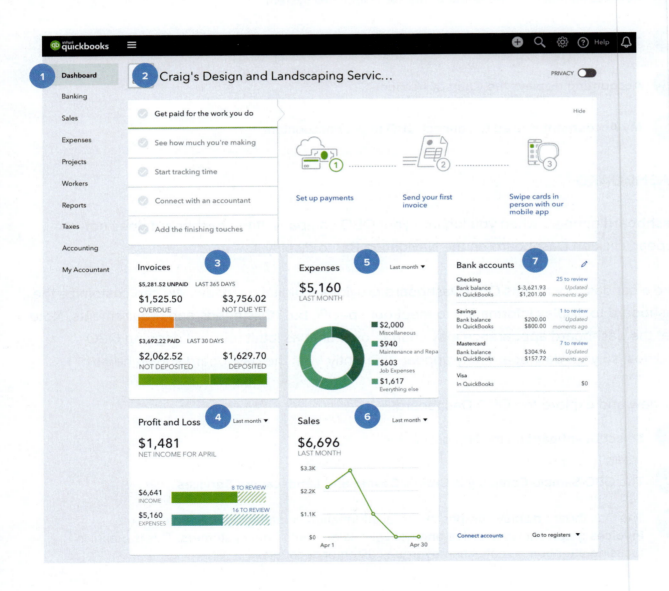

BANKING

Banking transactions relate to Bank and Credit Card accounts and transactions. QBO can be used to record transactions that affect Bank accounts, such as a Checking account, and Credit Card accounts, such as a VISA account.

To facilitate error detection, QBO permits the QBO Bank and Credit Card accounts to be connected directly to the related bank or credit card company. Once connected, you can download transactions from the bank or credit card company automatically and then match the downloaded transactions from the bank to your QBO data.

To explore the QBO Banking features:

1. Select **Banking** on the Navigation Bar

2. Select the **Banking** tab

3. To watch a video about QBO Banking, select **Take a tour**

4. The cards that appear at the top of the banking screen are **QBO Bank and Credit Card accounts** that are connected to the related bank accounts

5. The cards at the top summarize key information for the accounts including the **Bank Balance**. This is the balance that the bank shows for the Checking, Savings, or Credit Card account.

6. The card also shows the **Balance in QuickBooks** for the account. When there is a discrepancy between the balance per the bank and the balance per QuickBooks, the discrepancy may be due to an error or a timing difference (the bank has recorded it at a different time than when you recorded it in QBO). With a quick glance at the cards on the banking screen, you can see if there is a discrepancy. Some QBO clients use this approach instead of a monthly bank reconciliation to isolate and track any discrepancies.

7. QBO downloads transactions from the bank account. Then QBO attempts to match the downloaded transactions to transactions entered in QBO. In the Action column, **Match** will appear if QBO has found a possible match between the downloaded bank transactions and a transaction entered in QBO.

SALES

Sales transactions relate to customers and sales transactions (money in).

To explore the QBO Sales features:

1 Select **Sales** on the Navigation Bar

2 Select the **Overview** tab. This screen is a sales dashboard. The top graphic shows income over time. This provides insight into when sales are occurring. Another graphic shows unpaid and paid invoices. At a glance, you can see if there are overdue amounts due from customers.

3 Select the **All Sales** tab. This screen lists all sales that have already been recorded. You can filter the sales transactions to locate specific transactions. Also, you can email Invoices to customers, and they can pay online.

4 Select the **Invoices** tab. This screen lists Invoices, including the status of the Invoice as overdue, due, paid (not deposited), or deposited. At the top is the graph showing overdue Invoices and the total amount of unpaid Invoices.

5 Select the **Customers** tab. This tab may be labeled Clients depending upon the settings chosen when setting up the QBO company. The list of customers is shown in the lower section of the screen.

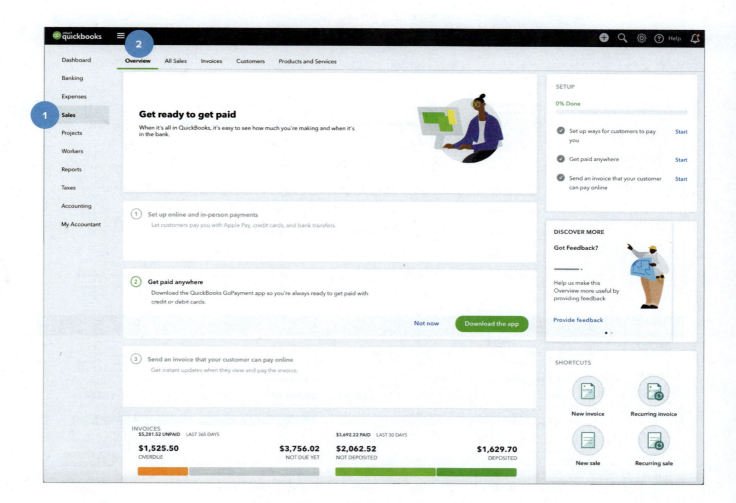

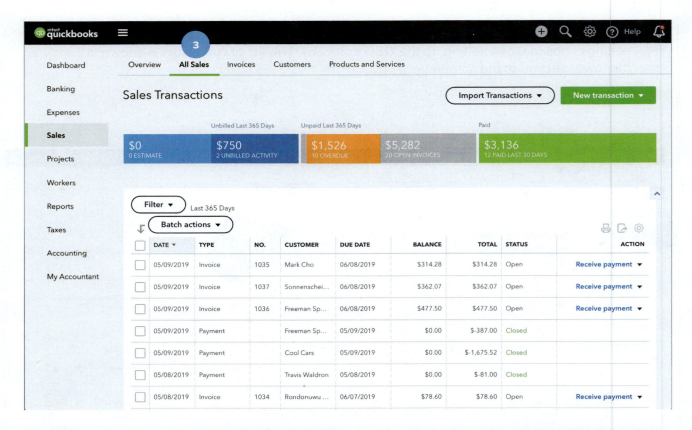

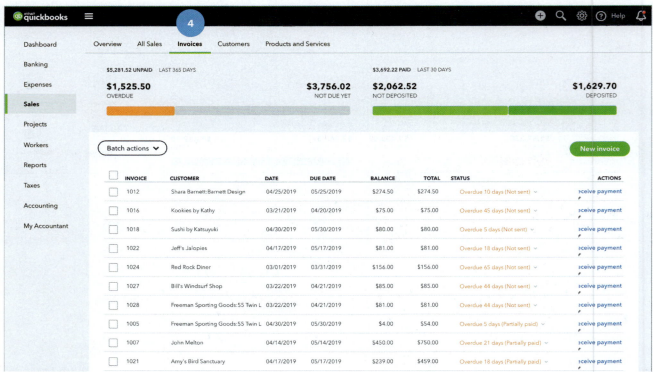

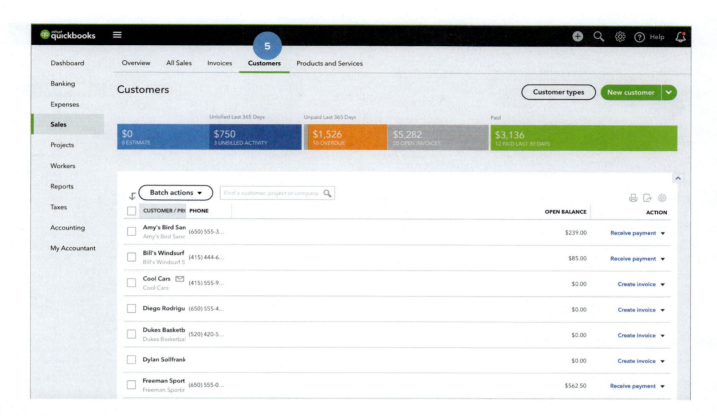

EXPENSES

Expenses transactions relate to vendors and expenses transactions (money out).

To explore QBO Expenses features:

1 Select **Expenses** on the Navigation Bar

2 Select the **Expenses** tab. This screen lists expenses that have already been recorded. You can filter the expenses transactions to locate specific transactions or select expenses that you would like to pay online through QBO.

3 Select the **Vendors** tab. Across the top of the Vendors screen is a useful dashboard feature, showing Overdue, Open Bills, and Paid. At a glance, you can see if you have overdue amounts due to your vendors. The list of vendors is shown in the lower section of the screen.

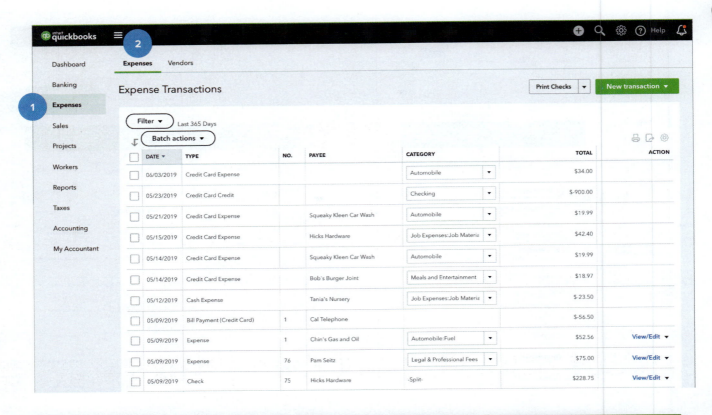

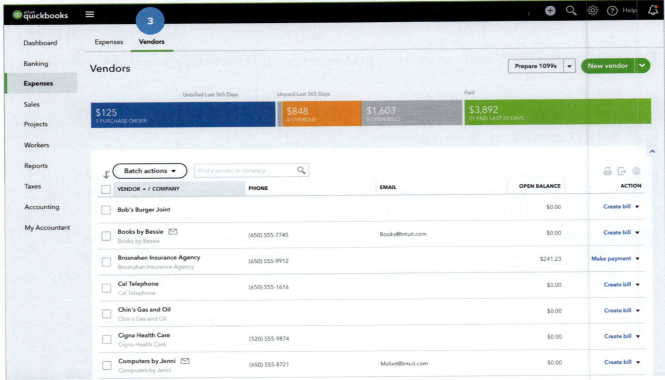

PROJECTS

Projects is a new QBO feature that may not appear on your Navigation Bar for the QBO company you set up in Project 1.1. Intuit tests and rolls out updates to different users of QBO at different times, so your screens may differ from those shown in this text.

To explore QBO Projects:

1   Select **Projects** on the Navigation Bar

2   To view a video on how to use QuickBooks Projects to track project income and costs, select **See how it works**

3   To set up a QBO project, select **Start a project**

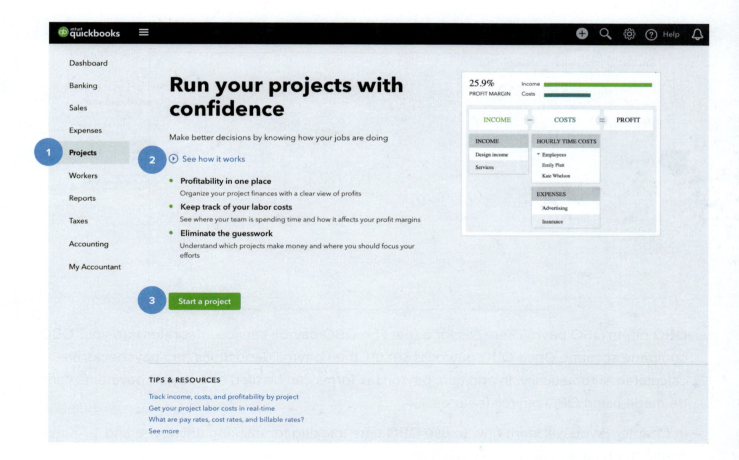

WORKERS

Workers transactions relate to employees and payroll transactions (money out). Until recently, Workers on the Navigation Bar was labeled Employees. When the Navigation Bar label was updated from Employees to Workers, it now includes employees plus contractors. Contractors are not employees, but are vendors that are paid without withholding and other payroll taxes. To be considered a contractor instead of an employee, Internal Revenue Service requirements must be met. For more information about the differences between employee status and contractor status, go to www.irs.gov.

To explore the QBO Workers feature:

1   Select **Workers** on the Navigation Bar

2   Select the **Employees** tab

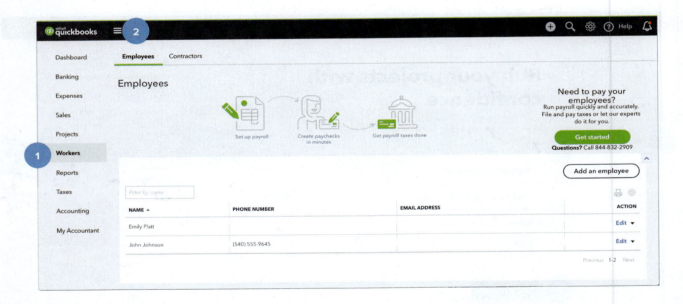

QBO offers QBO payroll services for a fee. The QBO payroll service integrates into your QBO company account. Once QBO payroll is set up, then payroll deductions and paychecks are calculated automatically. In addition, payroll tax forms can be filed and payroll payments can be made using QBO payroll features.

In Chapter 8 you will learn how to use QBO time tracking for tracking employee and contractor time and how to use QBO payroll.

REPORTS

Reports summarize the output of our QBO financial system.

To explore QBO Reports features:

1 Select **Reports** on the Navigation Bar

2 Select the **Standard** tab

3 Notice that you can designate reports as **Favorites** to appear in the section at the top of the screen to save time in the future

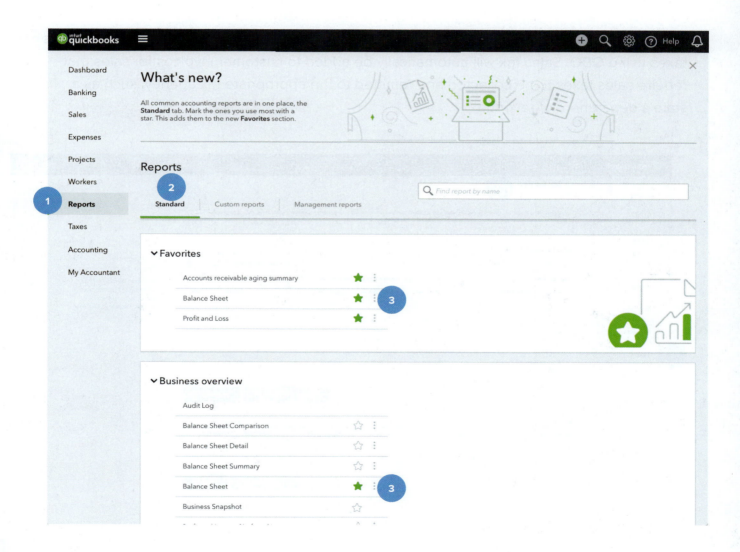

TAXES

Taxes relate to sales taxes and, if QuickBooks Online payroll is used, payroll taxes.

To explore QBO Taxes features:

1 Select **Taxes** on the Navigation Bar

2 If QBO Payroll is set up, you may have two tabs on your screen: Sales Tax tab and Payroll Tax tab. If necessary, select Sales Tax tab. If QBO Payroll is not set up yet, then your screen will display the **Sales Tax Center**.

From this screen you can set up sales taxes to streamline the collection and tracking of sales taxes using QBO. Sales tax will automatically be added to customer invoices for sales that require sales taxes to be collected and remitted to the appropriate tax agency, such as a state's department of revenue.

ACCOUNTING

Accounting displays the Chart of Accounts.

To explore the QBO Accounting features:

1 Select **Accounting** on the Navigation Bar

2 Select the **Chart of Accounts** tab

3 Select **See your Chart of Accounts**. From this screen you can add New accounts and Run reports listing the Chart of Accounts.

4 Select the **Reconcile** tab. Some QBO accounts can be connected to Bank accounts or Credit Card accounts. This make it easier to match your QBO accounts (your books) to the bank records. This streamlines reconciling your book balance to the bank balance. It also facilitates finding errors and oversights. You will learn more about how to match your QBO accounts to Bank and Credit Card accounts in Chapter 4.

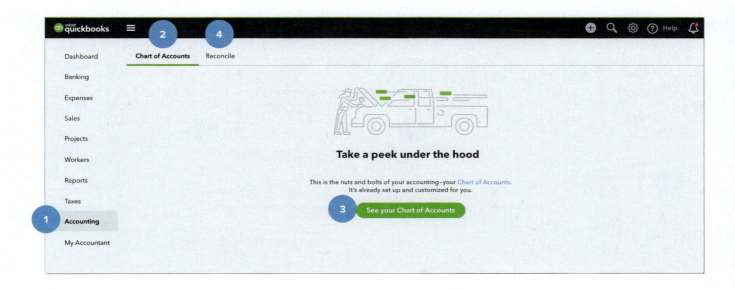

MY ACCOUNTANT

My Accountant is used to connect QBO to your accountant. Project 1.1 contains instructions on how you can connect your QuickBooks Online company with your instructor using My Accountant.

To explore the QBO My Accountant feature:

1 Select **My Accountant** on the Navigation Bar

2 To start the process to give your accountant administrative access to your QBO company data, you would enter the **Accountant's email**

3 After entering your accountant's email, you would select **Invite**

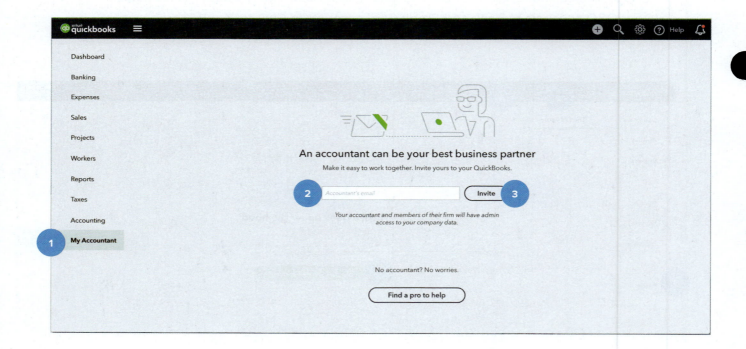

Section 1.4

QBO TOOLS

While the Navigation Bar is the primary way to navigate QBO, we can also access tasks using the following three useful QBO tools:

1 **Gear** icon

2 **Create (+)** icon

3 **Search** icon

GEAR ICON

The Gear icon located in the upper right of the QBO screen lists various tasks. The tasks are grouped into categories: Your Company, Lists, Tools, and Profile.

To explore the Gear tool:

1 Select the **Gear** icon to display the task options

2 Select **Account and Settings** to update company settings

3 Select **Chart of Accounts** to view and update the list of accounts our company uses

4 Select **All Lists** to view lists such as Chart of Accounts, Customers List, and Vendors List

5 Select **Recurring Transactions** to view the list of transactions that are saved for future reuse

6 Select **Audit Log** to view the list of transactions entered

CREATE (+) ICON

The Create (+) icon located in the upper right of the QBO screen lists various transactions we can create.

To explore the Create (+) tool:

1 Select the **Create (+)** icon to display options for entering transactions

2 **Customers** transactions include create an invoice, receive payment, create an estimate, create a credit memo, and create a sales receipt

3 **Vendors** transactions include create an expense, enter a check, create a bill, pay bills, create a purchase order, and create a credit card credit

4 **Employees** transactions include entering payroll and tracking time worked using single time activity and weekly timesheet

5 **Other** transactions include create a bank deposit, record a bank transfer, and create a journal entry

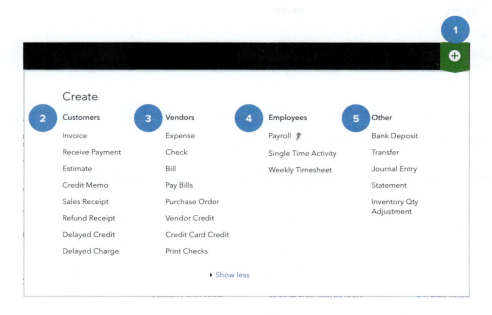

SEARCH ICON

The Search icon located in the upper right of the QBO screen permits us to search for amounts, dates, display names, and more to locate transactions. Advanced Search permits us to further define our search. The Search feature is useful if we want to review a transaction after it has been entered or we need to update a transaction.

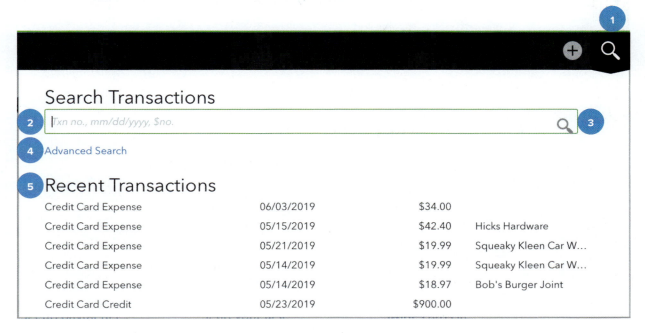

1 Select the **Search** icon

2 Enter **Search** criteria, such as $ Amount, Transaction No. or Date

3 Select **Search**

4 Select **Advanced Search** to enter more detailed search criteria

5 Notice the list of **Recent Transactions**. This is a convenient way to review transactions that were recently entered.

Section 1.5

QBO HELP AND SUPPORT

To use the QBO Help and Support feature:

1 Select the **? Help** icon

2 Enter the question

3 Select **Search**

4 For additional assistance, select **Contact us** and search for the question

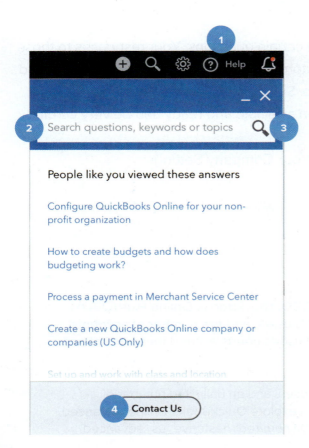

Section 1.6

QBO SETTINGS

When setting up a new QBO company, we want to align QBO with our company legal and tax information. During setup, we must specify the legal entity form used by our company, such as sole proprietorship, partnership, LLC, or corporation. In addition, the tax form that our company uses will affect the accounts we need in QBO. For more information about legal entity form and tax forms, see Accounting Essentials at the end of this chapter.

Two aspects of QBO settings are:
- Company Settings
- QBO Chart of Accounts

COMPANY SETTINGS

When setting up a new QBO company, you are asked certain questions. Your responses to those questions will determine some of the QBO settings automatically. Some settings can be changed later, but other settings cannot be changed after setup. So it is important when setting up a new QBO company to have all of your company information available and ready and be very careful.

After the QBO company has been setup, to access Your Company Settings:

1 Select **Gear** icon

2 Select **Account and Settings**

3 Select **Company** to review Company information

4 Select **Usage** to view usage limits information for QBO. QuickBooks Online Plus (QBO+) has usage limits. For example, QBO+ had a limit of 5 users, and the number of accounts in the Chart of Accounts is limited to 250. If a QBO user's needs exceed these limitations, Intuit offers QuickBooks Online Advanced.

QuickBooks Online Advanced provides for up to 25 users and an unlimited number of accounts in the Chart of Accounts. If you would like to explore QuickBooks Online Advanced, Intuit provides a test drive company at https://qbo.intuit.com/redir/testdrive_us_advanced.

5 Select **Sales** to review Company Sales preferences

6 Select **Expenses** to review Company Expenses preferences

7 Select **Advanced** to review Company Advanced preferences

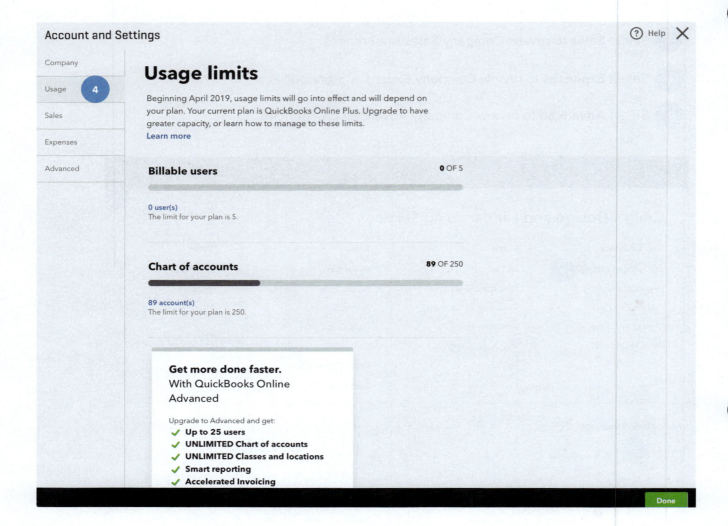

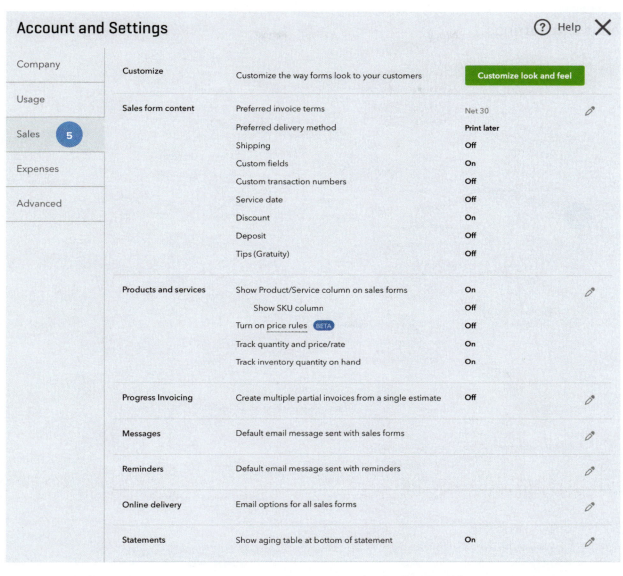

Account and Settings

(?) Help ✕

Company			
Usage	**Customize**	Customize the way forms look to your customers	**Customize look and feel**
Sales 5	**Sales form content**	Preferred invoice terms	Net 30 ✎
		Preferred delivery method	**Print later**
Expenses		Shipping	**Off**
Advanced		Custom fields	**On**
		Custom transaction numbers	**Off**
		Service date	**Off**
		Discount	**On**
		Deposit	**Off**
		Tips (Gratuity)	**Off**
	Products and services	Show Product/Service column on sales forms	**On** ✎
		Show SKU column	**Off**
		Turn on price rules BETA	**Off**
		Track quantity and price/rate	**On**
		Track inventory quantity on hand	**On**
	Progress Invoicing	Create multiple partial invoices from a single estimate	**Off** ✎
	Messages	Default email message sent with sales forms	✎
	Reminders	Default email message sent with reminders	✎
	Online delivery	Email options for all sales forms	✎
	Statements	Show aging table at bottom of statement	**On** ✎

Account and Settings

(?) Help ✕

Company	**Bills and expenses**	Show Items table on expense and purchase forms	**On** ✎
Usage		Track expenses and items by customer	**On**
		Make expenses and items billable	**On**
Sales		Default bill payment terms	
Expenses 6	**Purchase orders**	Use purchase orders	**On** ✎
Advanced	**Messages**	Default email message sent with purchase orders	✎

Account and Settings

(?) Help ✕

Company				
Usage	**Accounting**	First month of fiscal year	**January**	✎
		First month of income tax year	**Same as fiscal year**	
Sales		Accounting method	**Accrual**	
		Close the books	**Off**	
Expenses	**Company type**	Tax form	**Not sure/Other/None**	✎
Advanced ⑦	**Chart of accounts**	Enable account numbers	**Off**	✎
		Discount account	Discounts given	
		Tips account		
		Billable expense income account	Billable Expense Incom	
	Categories	Track classes	**Off**	✎
		Track locations	**Off**	
	Automation	Pre-fill forms with previously entered content	**On**	✎
		Automatically apply credits	**On**	
		Automatically invoice unbilled activity	**Off**	
		Automatically apply bill payments	**On**	
	Projects	Organize all job-related activity in one place	**On**	✎
	Time tracking	Add Service field to timesheets	**On**	✎
		Make Single-Time Activity Billable to Customer	**On**	
	Currency	Home Currency	**United States Dollar**	✎
		Multicurrency	**Off**	
	Other preferences	Date format	**MM/dd/yyyy**	✎
		Number format	**123,456.00**	
		Customer label	**Customers**	
		Warn if duplicate check number is used	**On**	
		Warn if duplicate bill number is used	**Off**	
		Sign me out if inactive for	**3 hours**	

QBO CHART OF ACCOUNTS

The Chart of Accounts is a list of all the accounts for a company. Accounts are used to sort and track information. For example, a business needs one account for cash, another account to track amounts customers owe (Accounts Receivable), and another account to track inventory.

QBO automatically creates a Chart of Accounts (COA) when we set up a new company. Then we may customize the COA, adding and editing accounts as necessary to fit our company's specific needs.

In the next chapter we cover how to customize QBO COA to meet company needs and specific business requirements. Since one of the primary reasons most businesses are using QBO is to organize financial information for tax return preparation, we want to customize the QBO COA to align with the company's tax return.

To view the Chart of Accounts:

1 From the Navigation Bar, select **Accounting** to display the COA <u>or</u>

2 From the **Gear** icon, select **Chart of Accounts** to display the COA

3 If necessary, select **See your Chart of Accounts**

4 To run the COA report, from the Chart of Accounts window, select **Run report**

5 To view more detail about a specific account in the COA, from the Chart of Accounts window, select **View register** for the specific account. A register shows every transaction for an account with the running balance.

6 This completes the chapter activities. **Close** the QBO Sample Company web browser window to reset the Sample Company before proceeding to the exercises at the end of this chapter.

Dashboard

Banking

Sales

Expenses

Projects

Workers

Reports

Taxes

(1) Accounting

My Accountant

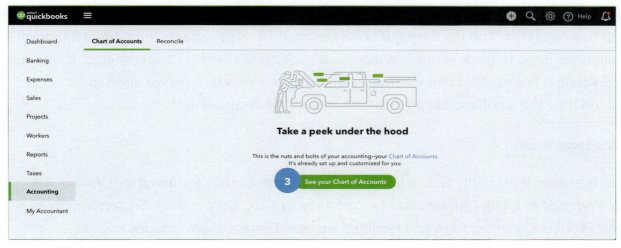

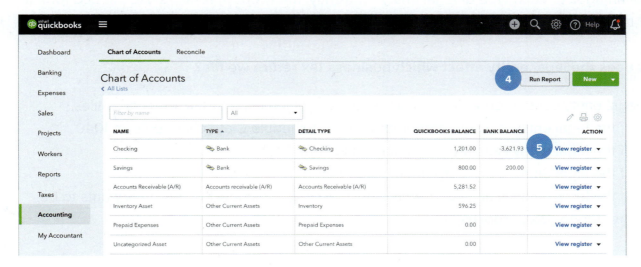

Section 1.7

ACCOUNTING ESSENTIALS
Legal, Tax, and Financial Questions

Accounting Essentials summarize important foundational accounting knowledge that may be useful when using QBO

Why do we care about the legal entity and tax form used by our business when setting up an accounting system?

The type of legal entity a business uses impacts the equity accounts we need and the tax form our business files. The tax form our business must file also impacts the type of financial information we need to track in our financial system. Bottom line: It's all interrelated. If we are going to set up a financial system that meets our business needs, then we need to understand how the legal and tax implications impact the financial system.

What is a legal entity?

How our business legal entity was organized (Sole Proprietorship, Partnership, Limited Liability Partnership (LLP), Limited Liability Company (LLC), C Corporation, S Corporation, or Nonprofit) affects which tax form and tax lines we use. There are advantages and disadvantages to each type of legal entity. Currently, many entrepreneurs use the LLC form to offer tax advantages and also limit liability of the owners.

How does the legal entity affect which business tax return we file?

The legal entity used to organize a business affects which tax return the business files.
- If the legal entity is a sole proprietorship, file Schedule C attached to Form 1040
- If the legal entity is a partnership (LLP), file Form 1065
- If the legal entity is a C corporation, file Form 1120
- If the legal entity is an LLC, then the business chooses how the business wants to be treated for tax purposes

What business tax return does an LLC file?

It depends. If a business is an LLC (Limited Liability Company), then the business has a choice to make regarding how the business wants to be treated for tax purposes. For tax purposes, assuming an LLC meets necessary tax requirements, an LLC can elect to be treated as:
- Sole proprietorship, filing Schedule C attached to owner's Form 1040
- Partnership, filing Form 1065
- S corporation, filing Form 1120S (See irs.gov for more information about requirements to elect the S corporation option for tax purposes.)

How do we know which business tax return needs to be filed?

Business tax returns to file are as follows:
- Sole proprietorships file Schedule C attached to owner's Form 1040
- Partnerships file Form 1065
- C corporations file Form 1120
- S corporations file Form 1120S

Business Type	Tax Form
Sole Proprietorship	Form 1040 Schedule C
Partnership	Form 1065
C Corporation	Form 1120
S Corporation	Form 1120S

How does our business tax return affect our financial system?

When setting up the financial system and accounts for our business, it is often helpful to review the tax form that our business files. Then our company's accounts can be customized to track information needed for our tax form. Basically, we can align our accounts with the tax return, so information in our accounts feeds into the lines on the tax return. This can reduce the amount of extra work needed at year end to obtain information for the business tax return. The tax form used by the type of organization is listed previously, and the forms and tax lines can be viewed at www.irs.gov.

Practice Quiz 1

Q1.1

Which of the following does not appear on the QuickBooks Online Navigation Bar?

a. Accounting
b. Expenses
c. Owners
d. Sales

Q1.2

Which of the following categories does not appear on the QuickBooks Create (+) screen?

a. Banking
b. Customers
c. Employees
d. Vendors

Q1.3

How do you access QBO Account and Settings?

a. Create (+) icon
b. Gear icon
c. Search icon
d. Help icon

Q1.4

What are two ways that we can access and view the Chart of Accounts in QBO?

a. From the Navigation Bar select Accounting
b. From the Create (+) icon select Other > Chart of Accounts
c. From the Gear icon select Chart of Accounts
d. From the Home Page select Chart of Accounts

Q1.5

Which of the following could be considered three main processes of the QBO SatNav for using QuickBooks Online?

a. QBO Settings, QBO Transactions, QBO Reports
b. QBO Sales, QBO Expenses, QBO Reports

c. QBO Chart of Accounts, QBO Exchanges, QBO Settings

d. QBO Sales Transactions, QBO Banking Transactions, QBO Reports

Q1.6

QBO transactions include which of the following?

a. Sales

b. Expenses

c. Banking

d. All of the above

Q1.7

Financial statements include which of the following two?

a. Income statement

b. Statement of cash flows

c. Cash flow forecast

d. Physical inventory worksheet

Q1.8

Which of the following legal entities can use QuickBooks Online?

a. Sole proprietorship

b. Partnership

c. S corporation

d. All of the above

Q1.9

Match the following legal entities with the federal tax return the entity files.

1. Form 1040 Schedule C

2. Form 1120

3. Form 1065

4. Form 1120S

a. Partnership

b. C Corporation

c. S Corporation

d. Sole Proprietorship

Q1.10

Which federal tax return does an LLC (Limited Liability Company) file?

a. Form 1040 Schedule C

b. Form 1065

c. Form 1120S

d. It depends upon how the LLC chooses to be treated for tax purposes

Q1.11

QuickBooks Online Settings to set up a new company include which of the following two?

a. Chart of Accounts

b. Reconciliation Settings

c. Company Settings

d. Tax Settings

Exercises 1

> We use the **QBO Sample Company, Craig's Design and Landscaping Services,** for practice throughout the exercises. The Sample Company will reset each time it is reopened. So make certain to allow enough time to complete exercises before closing the Sample Company. Otherwise, you will lose the work you have entered when you reopen the Sample Company.

To access the QBO Sample Company, complete the following steps.

1   Open a web browser. (Note: Intuit recommends using Google Chrome.)

2   Go to the Sample Company at https://qbo.intuit.com/redir/testdrive

3   Follow onscreen instructions for security verification. If a message about cookies or blocking pop-up windows appears, follow the onscreen instructions.

> **Note: Although the Sample Company link should work, if for some reason the previous link for the Sample Company doesn't work with your browser, using Google search,** type in "qbo.intuit.com **Sample Company". Select the link to Test Drive Sample Company.**

Craig's Design and Landscaping Services should appear on the screen.

⚠ Reminder: While you are using the Craig's Design and Landscaping Services Sample Company, the information you enter will be saved. After you close the Sample Company, automatically all the settings and data are reset to the original data and settings before you entered your work. When you close the web browser for the QBO Sample Company, your work is not saved.

The Sample Company default setting is to log out if inactive for one (1) hour. Since the Sample Company resets automatically, you will lose any work you entered. So it is important to plan accordingly so that you can complete all activities needed before closing the Sample Company.

To increase the amount of time from one (1) hour to three (3) hours before the log out for inactivity occurs:

1. From Craig's Design and Landscaping Services QBO Sample Company, select the **Gear** icon

2. Under Your Company section, select **Account and Settings**

3. Select **Advanced**

4. Select **Other preferences**

5. For the option Sign me out if inactive for, click on **1 hour**

6. From the drop-down menu, select **3 hours**

7. Select **Save**

8. Select **Done**

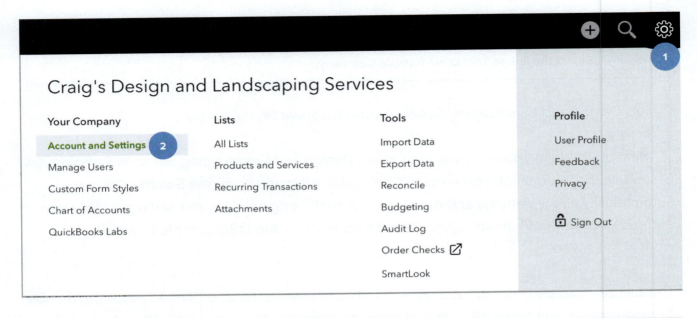

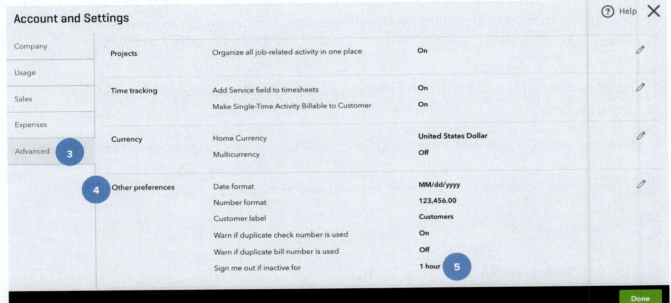

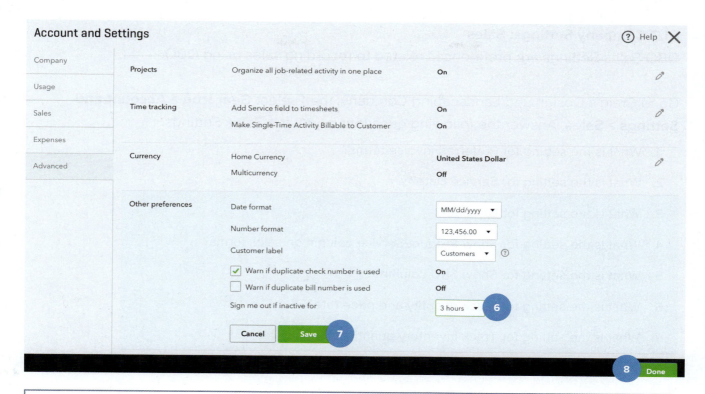

⚠️ **The Sample Company** will reset each time it is reopened. This allows you to explore and practice QBO without concern about carrying forward errors to later chapters. However, you will want to make certain to allow enough time to complete all chapter activities before closing the Sample Company. Otherwise, you will lose the work you have entered when you reopen the Sample Company.

E1.1 Company Settings: Company

QBO Company Settings are preferences for using QBO. When the QBO company is set up, some of the company settings can be automatically set up at that time. Some company settings can be changed at a later time after company set up.

Go to Craig's Design and Landscaping Company, then select **Gear icon > Account and Settings > Company**. Answer the following questions about the Company Settings.

1. What is the setting for Tax Form?

2. What is the setting for Company email?

3. What is the setting for Company address?

E1.2 Company Settings: Sales

QBO Sales Settings are preferences related to recording sales using QBO.

Go to Craig's Design and Landscaping Company, then select **Gear icon > Account and Settings > Sales**. Answer the following questions about the Sales Settings.

1. What is the setting for Preferred invoice terms?

2. What is the setting for Service Date?

3. What is the setting for Discount?

4. What is the setting for Show Product/Service column on sales forms?

5. What is the setting for Show SKU column?

6. What is the setting for Track quantity and price/rate?

7. What is the setting for Track inventory quantity on hand?

E1.3 Company Settings: Expenses

QBO Expenses Settings are preferences related to recording expenses using QBO.

Go to Craig's Design and Landscaping Company, then select **Gear icon > Account and Settings > Expenses**. Answer the following questions about the Expenses Settings.

1. What is the setting for Show Items table on expense and purchase forms?

2. What is the setting for Track expenses and items by customer?

3. What is the setting for Make expenses and items billable?

4. What is the setting for Use purchase orders?

E1.4 Company Settings: Advanced

QBO Advanced Settings are preferences related to advanced items that are not listed under the other preference settings.

Go to Craig's Design and Landscaping Company, then select **Gear icon > Account and Settings > Advanced**. Answer the following questions about the Advanced Settings.

1. First month of fiscal year?

2. First month of income tax year?

3. Accounting method?

4. Enable account numbers?

5. Pre-fill forms with previously entered content?

6. Automatically apply bill payments?

7. Add Service field to timesheets?

8. Make Single-Time Activity Billable to Customer?

9. Home Currency?

10. Warn if duplicate check number is used?

E1.5 Chart of Accounts

The Chart of Accounts is a list of accounts a company uses to track accounting information. QBO sets up a Chart of Accounts when setting up a new company. Then accounts can be edited, added, and inactivated as needed.

Go to Craig's Design and Landscaping Services, then from the Navigation Bar, select **Accounting**. Answer the following questions about the Chart of Accounts.

Account Types

- **Bank**
- **Accounts Receivable (A/R)**
- **Other Current Assets**
- **Fixed Assets**
- **Accounts Payable (A/P)**
- **Credit Card**
- **Other Current Liabilities**
- **Long Term Liabilities**
- **Equity**
- **Income**
- **Cost of Goods Sold**
- **Expenses**
- **Other Income**
- **Other Expense**

What is the Account Type for the following accounts?

1. Checking account

2. Visa

3. Accounts Receivable (A/R)

4. Advertising

5. Prepaid Expenses

6. Pest Control Services

E1.6 Chart of Accounts

The Chart of Accounts, a list of accounts, contains specific information about each account.

Go to Craig's Design and Landscaping Services, then from the Navigation Bar, select **Accounting**. Answer the following questions about the Chart of Accounts.

In the following Chart of Accounts, what is the name of each of the columns?

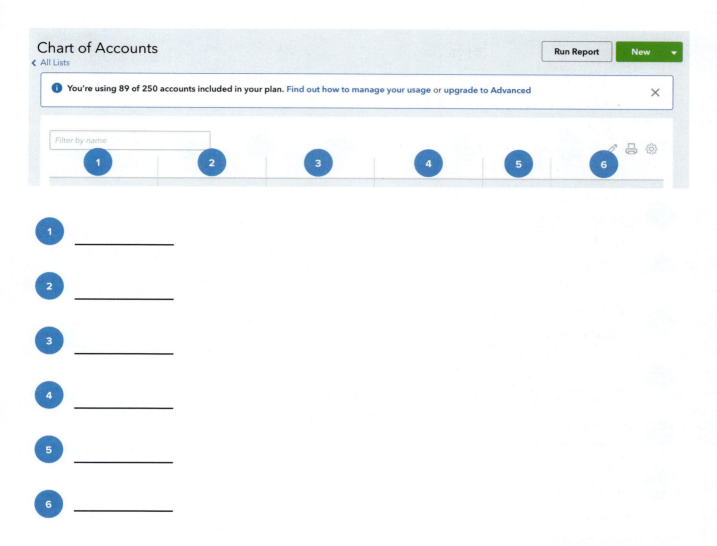

1 _____

2 _____

3 _____

4 _____

5 _____

6 _____

E1.7 Register

A Bank Register, also called a Check Register, contains specific information about transactions for the corresponding Bank account or Checking account.

Go to Craig's Design and Landscaping Services, then from the Navigation Bar select **Accounting > View Register** for the Checking account in the Chart of Accounts. Answer the following questions about the Bank Register for the Checking account.

In the following Bank Register, what is the name of each of the columns?

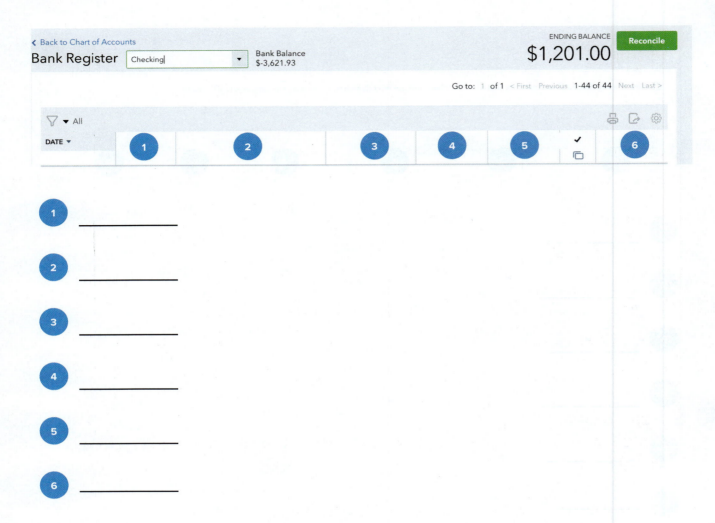

1 _____

2 _____

3 _____

4 _____

5 _____

6 _____

E1.8 Transactions

Transactions can be grouped into different types or categories of transactions.

Match the following categories found on the Create (+) window with the following transactions.

- **Customers**
- **Vendors**
- **Employees**
- **Other**

1. Bank Deposit

2. Single Time Activity

3. Expense

4. Sales Receipt

5. Payroll

6. Journal Entry

7. Purchase Order

8. Estimate

9. Pay Bills

10. Check

11. Receive Payment

12. Invoice

E1.9 QBO SatNav

The QBO SatNav provides an overview of QuickBooks Online and the various associated tasks and activities.

Match the three main QBO processes of the QBO SatNav with the following items.

- **QBO Settings**
- **QBO Transactions**
- **QBO Reports**

1. Income Statement

2. Create VISA Credit Card account

3. Exchange of cash for sale of product with customer

4. Statement of Cash Flows

5. Exchange of credit card payment for purchasing of product from vendor

6. Balance Sheet

E1.10 QBO Tools

QBO Tools are used to perform various QBO tasks.

Match the following two QBO tools with the following appropriate items.

- **Gear icon**
- **Create (+) icon**

1. Invoice

2. Recurring Transactions

3. Purchase Order

4. Settings

5. Check

6. All Lists

7. Bank Deposit

8. Audit Log

9. Credit Card Credit

10. Sales Receipt

11. Pay Bills

12. Receive Payment

13. Chart of Accounts

14. Weekly Timesheet

15. Manage Users

16. Journal Entry

Project 1.1

Mookie the Beagle™ Concierge

BACKSTORY

Mookie The Beagle™ Concierge, a pet care service, was founded by Cy Walker, a young professional who was searching for a way to meet his demanding work and travel commitments while caring for his pet beagle, Mookie.

Cy discovered that he was not the only working professional trying to balance pet care and work commitments. So Cy started Mookie The Beagle Concierge to provide caring staff who go beyond the typical doggie day care, providing water and food (even organic and home cooked), exercising the pet with scheduled walks and playtime, providing pet training, administering required medication, taking the pet to scheduled and unscheduled vet visits that often fall during the work day when a professional cannot take time off, and providing other pet wellness and support services as needed.

Drawing upon a local university veterinarian program, Cy hired vet students with pet care training and flexibility in their schedules. Working as independent contractors, the students were a good fit for providing high quality, relatively low cost pet care on a flexible basis. If intensive pet care is needed, such as when a client has out-of-town travel, two or three vet students rotate schedules to accommodate the pet's needs.

Cy designed and developed a Mookie The Beagle Concierge app which permits clients to schedule pet care service. Mookie The Beagle Concierge app also tracks complicated medication schedules, showing who administered the medication and when. The app permits the client to view and speak to the pet in real time. In addition, the app connects to the vet's office for followup questions, provides pet parent texting to Mookie The Beagle Concierge staff, and offers an on-call button to alert staff of urgent issues.

In short, Mookie The Beagle Concierge takes pet care to the next level, providing convenience and pet care support that permits professionals to maintain busy work and travel schedules while being assured their valued pet is receiving the best of care.

Based upon your recommendation, Mookie The Beagle Concierge selected QuickBooks Online to maintain its financial records and asks you to assist in setting up QBO. After reviewing Mookie The Beagle Concierge user requirements for a financial system, you agree to provide ongoing QBO consulting services. In addition, you will train Cy in QuickBooks Online so he can take over some QBO tasks in the future.

Complete the following for Mookie The Beagle Concierge.

🌐 QBO SATNAV

Project 1.1 focuses on QBO Settings, specifically the QBO Company Settings as shown in the following QBO SatNav.

QBO SatNav

QBO Settings

Company Settings

Chart of Accounts

QBO Transactions

Banking

Customers & Sales

Vendors & Expenses

Employees & Payroll

QBO Reports

Reports

HOW TO USE THE QBO+ ACCESS CODE

To use QBO with this project, you will need to sign up for a free QBO Access Code from Intuit. Then you set up your account using the Access Code. After that, you can log into QBO using your User ID and Password.

> ⚠️ **When setting up a QBO company,** it is important to complete the following steps as specified. QBO uses the steps you complete to create a QBO company with specific settings. If the specified steps are not completed, then the QBO company will not have the necessary settings to complete your assignment. The easiest approach is to take your time and stay focused while setting up the QBO Company.

> ⚠️ **A summary of steps to obtain and use the QBO Access Code follow. If for any reason these steps or links are not working properly, the Intuit links or process may have changed. In that case, for updated instructions go to www.my-quickbooksonline.com > select link: QBO 2E > scroll down to section entitled: Free QBO for Students > Select links for step-by-step Intuit instructions and video to obtain an access code. Or go to www.mhhe.com/QBOKay2e, the Online Learning Center, for updated instructions.**

1. Obtain your free QBO+ access code from Intuit at https://intuit.me/mh-online.

2. After obtaining your access code from Intuit, using a web browser go to the QBO sign up web page at https://quickbooks.intuit.com/signup/retail/.

3. Enter the **License number**

4. Enter the **Product number**

5. Select **I agree to the Terms of Service**

6. Select **Set Up Account**

7. Follow the onscreen instructions to set up your account. Keep a record of your **User ID** and **Password**. You will need this later.

8. Enter What's Your Business Called? **Mookie The Beagle Concierge [Your Name]**

9. Select How long have you been in business? **Less than 1 year**

10. Uncheck **I've been using QuickBooks Desktop and want to bring in my data**

11 Select **Next**

12 When the screen What would you like to do in QuickBooks? appears, select **Send and track invoices**

13 Select **Organize your expenses**

14 Select **Manage your inventory**

15 Select **Track your retail sales**

16 Select **Track your bills**

17 Select **Track your sales tax**

18 Select **Pay your employees**

19 Select **Track hours**

20 Select **All set**. The QBO Mookie The Beagle Concierge screen should appear.

21 When the Welcome window appears, select **Let's go** to take the QBO tour.

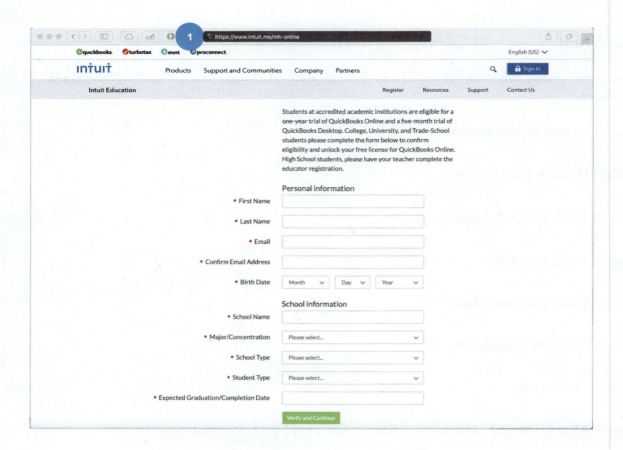

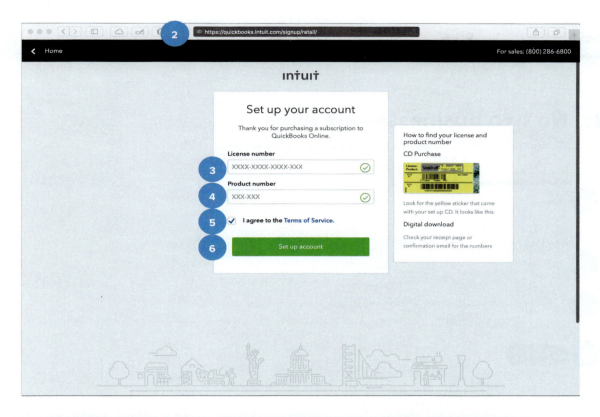

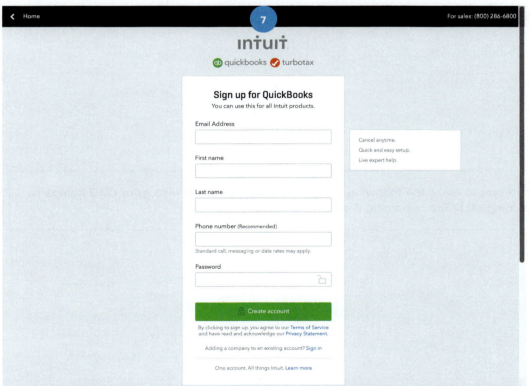

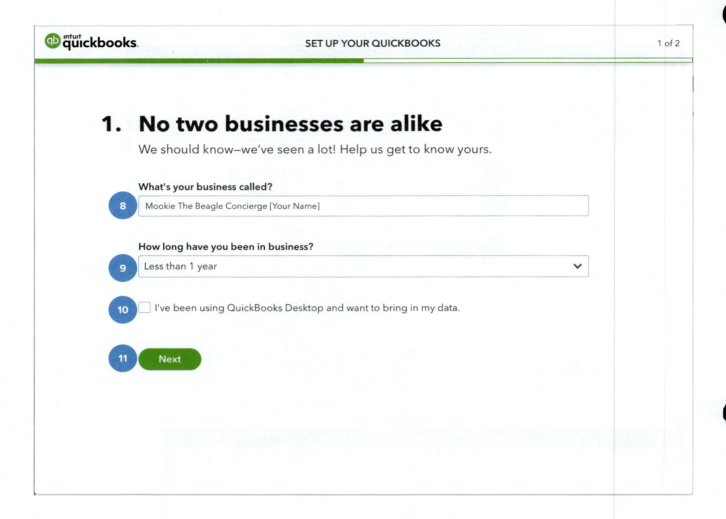

> ⚠ **Warning:** it is important to make the following selections as shown. Otherwise, your QBO company may be unusable for completing the remaining Project instructions.

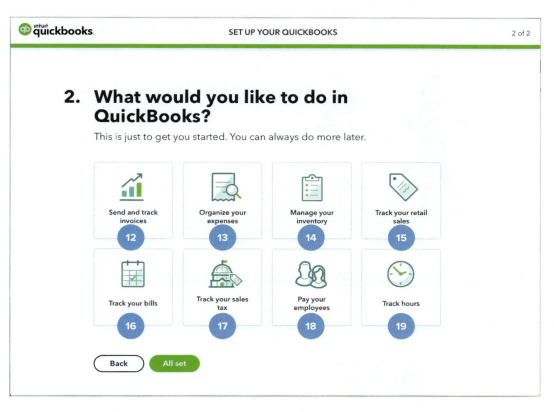

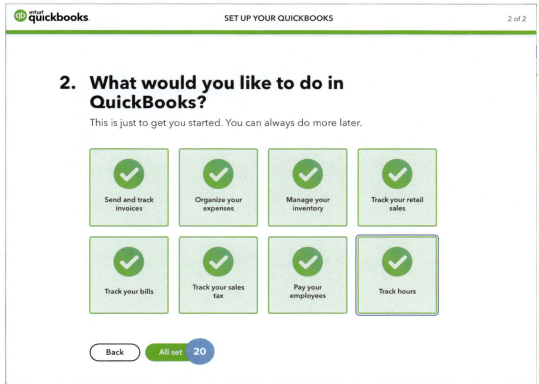

×

Welcome, Mookie The Beagle Concierge [Your Name]!

This 30-second tour will help you get down to business on QuickBooks.

Let's go 21

HOW TO LOG INTO QBO

After completing the steps to use the QBO Access Code, the next time we log into QBO, we will complete the following steps:

1 Using a web browser, go to qbo.intuit.com

2 Enter **User ID** (the email address you used to set up your QBO Account)

3 Enter **Password** (the password you used to set up your QBO Account)

4 Select **Sign in**

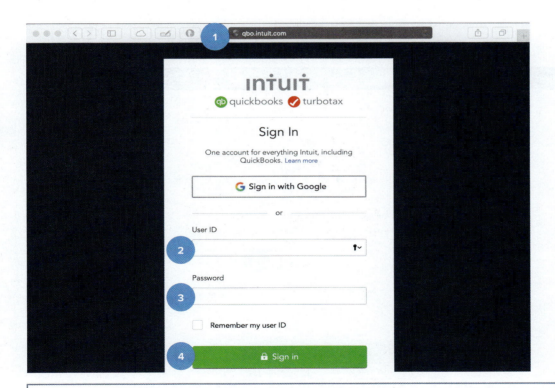

> **If you are not using a public or shared computer,** to speed up login you can save your login to your desktop and select Remember Me. If you are using a public computer or shared computer, do not save to the desktop and unselect Remember Me.

> ⚠️ **The new QBO company** we create in Project 1 will carry all work forward into future chapters and projects. So it is important to check and crosscheck your work to verify it is correct before clicking the Save button. Any uncorrected errors will be carried forward in your QBO company for text projects.

INVITE YOUR ACCOUNTANT (INSTRUCTOR)

Next, invite your accountant (in this case your instructor) to join your QuickBooks Online company. This permits your accountant (instructor) to view your QBO company when using QuickBooks Online Accountant. Basically, through QBO you will send your accountant (instructor) an email and the accountant (instructor) clicks on the link in the email to join your QBO company.

To invite your accountant (instructor) to join your QBO Company:

1 From the Navigation Bar, select **My Accountant**

2 Enter **your Instructor's email**

3 Select **Invite**

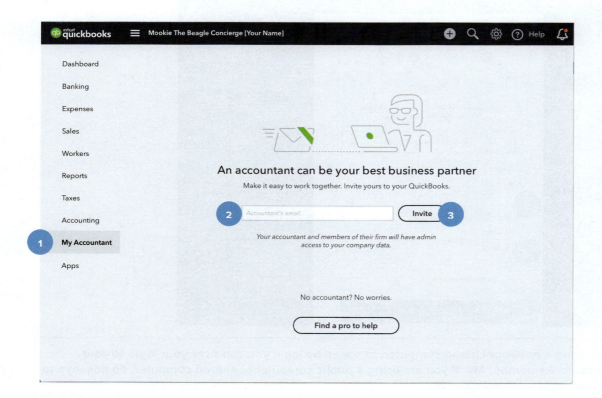

> **If your instructor receives an error message** when accepting your QBO Invite, completely Delete the invite from your QBO Company. (Do not click Resend). Then recreate the invite. Typically this fixes this known issue with invites. If it does not fix the issue after you delete the invite and recreate it, then contact your Instructor or Intuit Support.

QBO UPDATES

Be aware that when you first log in to your QBO Project Company, QBO update notices are posted on the opening screen. Pay attention to these update notices and look for how it may change QBO. Note that since QBO is updated on an ongoing basis, updates to QBO may result in differences between QBO and the instructions in your text. If it is a major update, we will have an update posted at www.my-quickbooksonline.com, QBO Update link to assist you. Updates are also posted at www.mhhe.com/KayQBO2e.

Also note that QBO updates are rolled out in phases, so different users may see different features as QBO tests and then rolls out updates to various users. Intuit releases a monthly update on QBO improvements. Use this link to access monthly summaries of updates and improvements: https://my-quickbooksonline.com/qbo-monthly-updates-and-improvements.

QBO DASHBOARD

When you log into your QBO Project Company, you will notice a QBO Dashboard. Like a car dashboard, this QBO Dashboard provides a digital overview. We can customize the dashboard to display information to meet our specific business needs and requirements. Note that the dashboard may change over time as Intuit rolls out new QBO updates.

P1.1.1 Set Up QBO

Complete QBO set up for Mookie The Beagle™ Concierge using the following information.

1. To select the Tax Form complete the following.
   a. Select **Gear icon > Account and Settings**
   b. Select **Company tab > Edit pencil** on the right in Company Type section
   c. Select **Tax Form: Small business corporation, two or more owners (Form 1120S)**
   d. Select **Save**
   e. What does the Legal name field display?

P1.1.2 Company Settings: Sales

QBO Sales Settings are preferences related to recording sales using QBO.

Answer the following questions about Mookie The Beagle Concierge's QBO Sales Settings.

Select **Gear icon > Account and Settings > Sales tab**.

1. What is the setting for Preferred invoice terms?

2. What is the setting for Service Date?

3. What is the setting for Discount?

4. What is the setting for Show Product/Service column on sales forms?

5. What is the setting for Show SKU column?

6. What is the setting for Track quantity and price/rate?

7. What is the setting for Track inventory quantity on hand?

P1.1.3 Company Settings: Expenses

QBO Expenses Settings are preferences related to recording expenses using QBO. Select **Gear icon > Account and Settings > Expenses tab**.

Answer the following questions about Mookie The Beagle Concierge's QBO Expenses Settings.

1. What is the setting for Show Items table on expense and purchase forms?

2. What is the setting for Track expenses and items by customer?

3. What is the setting for Make expenses and items billable?

4. Change the setting for Make expenses and items billable to **On**

5. What is the setting for Use purchase orders?

6. Change the setting for Use purchase orders to **On**

P1.1.4 Company Settings: Advanced

QBO Advanced Settings are preferences related to advanced items that are not listed under the other preference settings. Select **Gear icon > Account and Settings > Advanced tab**.

Answer the following questions about Mookie The Beagle Concierge's QBO Advanced Settings.

1. First month of fiscal year?

2. First month of income tax year?

3. Accounting method?

4. Close the books?

5. Tax form?

6. Enable account numbers?

7. Pre-fill forms with previously entered content?

8. Automatically apply bill payments?

9. Add Service field to timesheets?

10. Make Single-Time Activity Billable to Customer?

11. Home Currency?

12. Warn if duplicate check number is used?

P1.1.5 Chart of Accounts

The Chart of Accounts is a list of accounts a company uses to track accounting information. QBO sets up a Chart of Accounts when setting up a new company. Then accounts can be edited, added, and inactivated as needed.

Display Mookie The Beagle Concierge's Chart of Accounts that QBO automatically created by selecting **Navigation Bar > Accounting**. If necessary, select **See your Chart of Accounts**.

What is the QBO Account Type for the following accounts appearing in Mookie The Beagle Concierge's Chart of Accounts?

QBO Account Types

- **Bank**
- **Accounts Receivable (A/R)**
- **Other Current Asset**
- **Fixed Asset**
- **Accounts Payable (A/P)**
- **Credit Card**
- **Other Current Liabilities**
- **Long Term Liabilities**
- **Equity**
- **Income**
- **Cost of Goods Sold**

- **Expenses**
- **Other Income**
- **Other Expense**

> **QBO is continually** rolling out new features so it is possible your Chart of Accounts may not look the same as the accounts listed here. If an account is not listed in your Chart of Accounts, then just identify the appropriate account type.

1. Uncategorized Asset
2. Owner's Investment
3. Retained Earnings
4. Billable Expense Income
5. Sales
6. Uncategorized Income
7. Cost of Goods Sold
8. Advertising & Marketing
9. Bank Charges & Fees
10. Car & Truck
11. Contractors
12. Employee Benefits
13. Insurance
14. Interest Paid
15. Job Supplies
16. Legal & Professional Services
17. Meals & Entertainment
18. Office Supplies & Software
19. Other Business Expenses
20. Rent & Lease
21. Repairs & Maintenance
22. Salaries & Wages
23. Taxes & Licenses
24. Travel
25. Uncategorized Expense
26. Utilities

Chapter 2

QBO Chart of Accounts

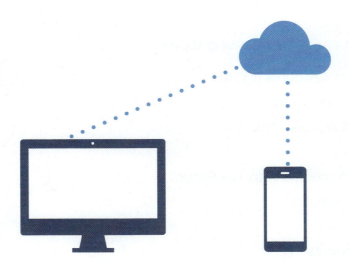

Cy Walker plans to use QBO to generate information for preparing tax returns for his new business, Mookie The Beagle Concierge. Cy has observed how chaotic and stressful it can be when a new business waits until it is time to file the tax return to start collecting the data needed. To streamline the process, Cy has discussed with you setting up QBO so it aligns with his business tax return. He would like to use QBO throughout the year to capture data about transactions, so that the information can be easily retrieved from QBO when it is time to file returns. Your next step is to learn more about the Chart of Accounts and how it can be customized in QBO so it aligns with the data needed to complete a business tax return.

Chapter 2

LEARNING OBJECTIVES

Businesses use QuickBooks Online for many reasons, but one of the main reasons is usually to track information for tax return preparation. To provide information the client needs to prepare a tax return requires customizing the QBO Chart of Accounts to align with the tax return.

In this chapter, you will learn about the following topics:

- QBO Sample Chart of Accounts (COA)
  - View QBO Chart of Accounts
  - Display QBO COA Account Numbers
  - View QBO Registers
- Align QBO Chart of Accounts with Tax Return
- Edit QBO Chart of Accounts
  - Add QBO Accounts
  - Add QBO Subaccounts
  - Edit QBO Accounts
  - Inactivate QBO Accounts
- Accounting Essentials: Chart of Accounts

Section 2.1
 QBO SATNAV

QBO SatNav is our satellite navigation for QuickBooks Online, assisting us in navigating QBO

Chapter 2 focuses on QBO Settings, specifically the QBO Chart of Accounts highlighted in the following QBO SatNav.

 **QBO Settings**
Company Settings
Chart of Accounts

 **QBO Transactions**

Banking
Customers & Sales
Vendors & Expenses
Employees & Payroll

 **QBO Reports**

Reports

Section 2.2

QBO SAMPLE COMPANY LOGIN

To log into the QBO Sample Company:

1 Open a web browser. (Note: Intuit recommends using Google Chrome.)

2 Go to https://qbo.intuit.com/redir/testdrive

3 Follow onscreen instructions for security verification

> **Note: Although the Sample Company link should work, if for some reason the previous link for the Sample Company doesn't work with your browser, using Google search type in "qbo.intuit.com Sample Company". Select the link to Test Drive Sample Company.**

The QBO Sample Company, Craig's Design and Landscaping Services, should appear on the screen.

While you are using the Craig's Design and Landscaping Services Sample Company, the information you enter will be saved. *After you close* the Sample Company browser window, automatically all the settings and data are reset to the original data and settings before you entered your work.

Since we will be using the Sample Company to explore and practice with QBO, the reset will permit you to start over each time you open the Sample Company. You do not have to worry about carrying forward errors that ripple through the rest of the chapters.

The Sample Company default setting is to log out if inactive for one (1) hour. Since the Sample Company resets automatically, you will lose any work you entered. So it is important to plan accordingly so that you can complete all activities needed before closing the Sample Company.

To increase the amount of time from one (1) hour to three (3) hours before the log out for inactivity occurs:

1 From Craig's Design and Landscaping Services QBO Sample Company, select the **Gear** icon

2 Under Your Company section, select **Account and Settings**

3 Select **Advanced**

4 Select **Other preferences**

5 For the option Sign me out if inactive for, click on **1 hour**

6 From the drop-down menu, select **3 hours**

7 Select **Save**

8 Select **Done**

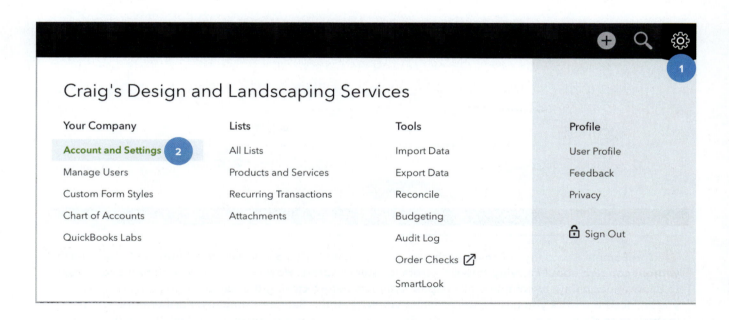

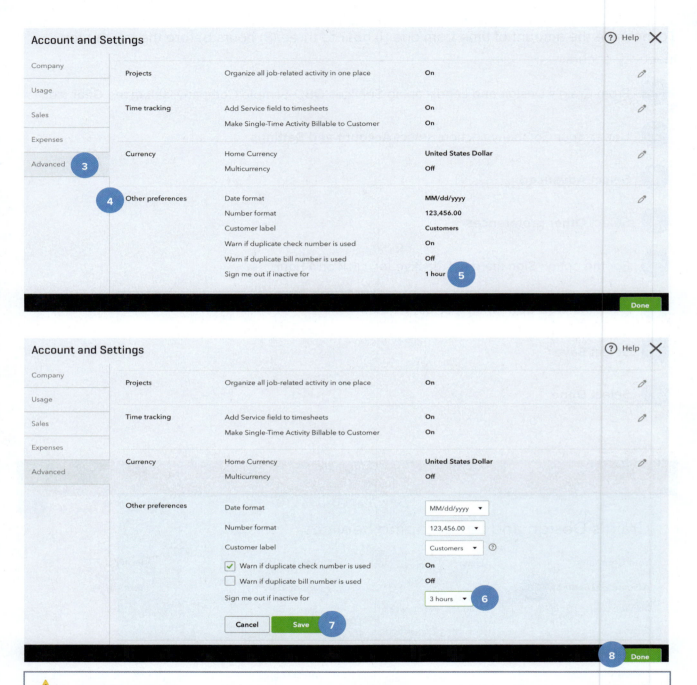

⚠️ **The Sample Company** will reset each time it is reopened. This allows you to explore and practice QBO without concern about carrying forward errors to later chapters. However, you will want to make certain to allow enough time to complete all chapter activities before closing the Sample Company. Otherwise, you will lose the work you have entered when you reopen the Sample Company. Furthermore, when instructed to close the browser to reset the Sample Company, it is important to follow the instructions precisely and close and reopen the browser so that your work results in the correct answers.

Section 2.3

QBO SAMPLE COMPANY CHART OF ACCOUNTS

The Chart of Accounts is a list of accounts and account numbers. A company uses accounts to record transactions in the accounting system. Accounts, such as a Checking account or Inventory account, permit us to sort and track information.

QuickBooks will automatically create a Chart of Accounts when we set up a new company. Then we can customize the Chart of Accounts, adding and editing accounts as necessary to suit our company's specific needs.

QuickBooks also permits us to use subaccounts. Subaccounts are useful in tracking additional detail. For example, a parent account might be Insurance Expense. The two subaccounts might be Disability Insurance Expense and Liability Insurance Expense. By having two subaccounts we can easily track how much a company spends on each type of insurance, as well as for insurance in total.

In Project 2.1, we will edit the Chart of Accounts for the QBO Company for Mookie The Beagle Concierge, but for now we will use the Sample Company to view and edit a sample Chart of Accounts.

Your text uses the Sample Company for practice throughout the chapter and exercises. The Sample Company will reset each time it is reopened. So make certain to allow enough time to complete all chapter activities before closing the Sample Company. Otherwise, you will lose the work you have entered. Furthermore, when instructed to close the browser to reset the Sample Company, it is important to follow the instructions precisely and close and reopen the browser so that your work results in the correct answers.

VIEW QBO CHART OF ACCOUNTS

To display the Chart of Accounts (COA):

1. Select **Accounting**

2. Select **Chart of Accounts** tab and the following Chart of Accounts should appear

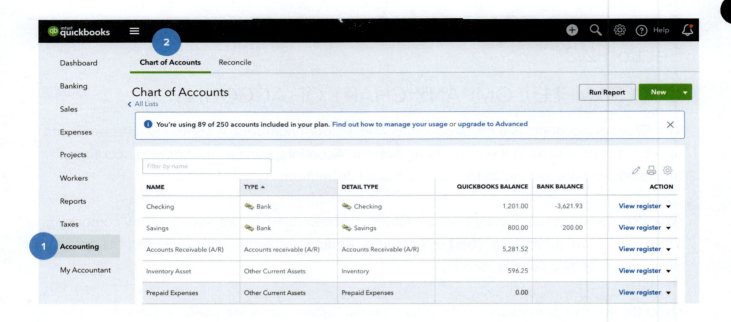

DISPLAY QBO COA ACCOUNT NUMBERS

Account numbers are used to uniquely identify accounts. Usually account numbers are used as a coding system to also identify the account type. For example, a typical numbering system for accounts might be as follows.

Account Type	Account No.
Asset accounts	10000 - 19999
Liability accounts	20000 - 29999
Equity accounts	30000 - 39999
Revenue (Income) accounts	40000 - 49999
Expense accounts	50000 - 59999

To display account numbers in the Chart of Accounts:

1 Select the **Gear** icon to display options

2 Select **Account and Settings**

3 Select **Advanced**

4 For Chart of Accounts, select the **Edit Pencil**, then select **Enable account numbers**

5 Select **Show account numbers**

6 Select **Save**

7 Select **Done** to close Account and Settings

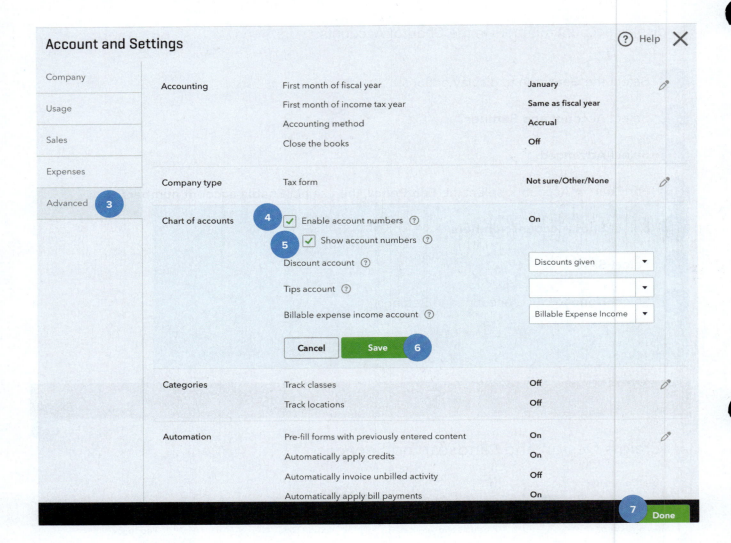

To enter account numbers in the Chart of Accounts:

1 Select **Accounting** in the Navigation Bar

2 If necessary, select the **Chart of Accounts** tab

3 If necessary, select See your Chart of Accounts. Notice that the Chart of Accounts now displays a **Number** column.

4 Select the **Edit pencil** icon

5 Enter **Account Numbers** in the Number column

6 Typically we would select Save. In this case, select **Cancel**.

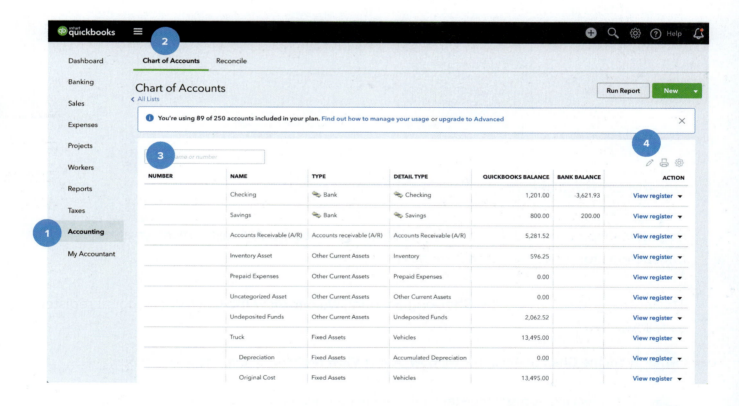

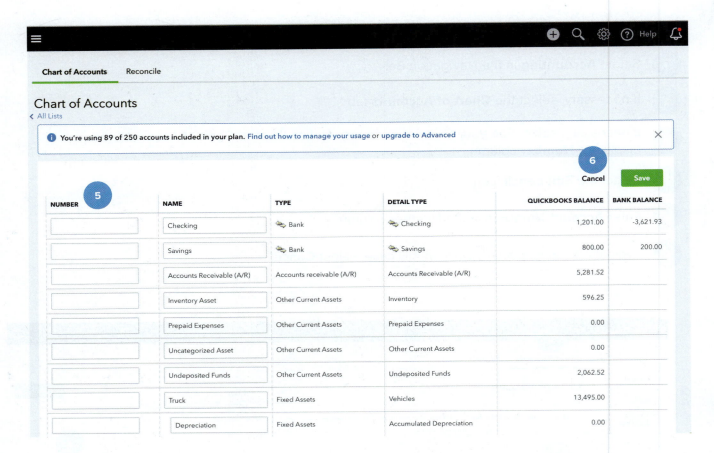

VIEW QBO REGISTERS

Registers display more detailed information about accounts. A register displays all transactions for an account and a running balance.

To view more detail about the Checking account, we can view the Checking account register as follows:

1. From the Chart of Accounts window, select **View register** for the Checking account

2. The Checking account register shows every transaction in the account and a running **Balance** is displayed on the right

3. Select **Back to Chart of Accounts** to close the Register and return to the Chart of Accounts

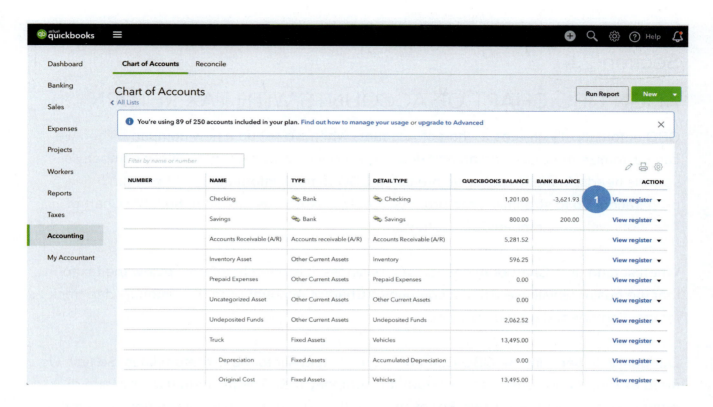

Section 2.4

ALIGN QBO CHART OF ACCOUNTS WITH TAX RETURN

QBO automatically creates a Chart of Accounts when we set up a new company. Then we can customize the COA, adding and deleting accounts as necessary to fit our company's specific needs. In many cases, we are using QBO to track information for tax return preparation. So to streamline the process, it only makes sense to align the QBO Chart of Accounts with our company's tax return.

When setting up a Chart of Accounts for a business, it is often helpful to review the tax form that the business will use. Then a company's Chart of Accounts can be customized to track information needed for the tax form.

Our goal is to see that the QBO Chart of Accounts feeds into the tax return lines. So first, we need to know which business tax return the company files. The tax form used by form of organization is listed as follows. For example, if the business is an S corporation, then for federal income taxes the business files Form 1120S.

Form of Organization	Tax Form
Sole Proprietorship	Form 1040 Schedule C
Partnership	Form 1065
C Corporation	Form 1120
S Corporation	Form 1120S

To view various tax return forms for businesses with the tax lines on each form, go to the Internal Revenue Service (IRS) website: www.irs.gov.

Section 2.5

EDIT QBO COA

We can customize the Chart of Accounts by adding, editing, and inactivating accounts as needed to meet a company's specific and changing needs.

ADD QBO ACCOUNTS

To add a new account to the Chart of Accounts:

1. From the Navigation Bar, select **Accounting**

2. If necessary, select the **Chart of Accounts** tab

3. From the Chart of Accounts window, select **New**

4. From the Account window, select **Account Type: Bank**

5. Select **Detail Type: Saving**

6. Enter **Name: Savings**

7. If not a subaccount, **uncheck Is sub-account**

8. Normally we would select Save and Close, but in this case select **Cancel**

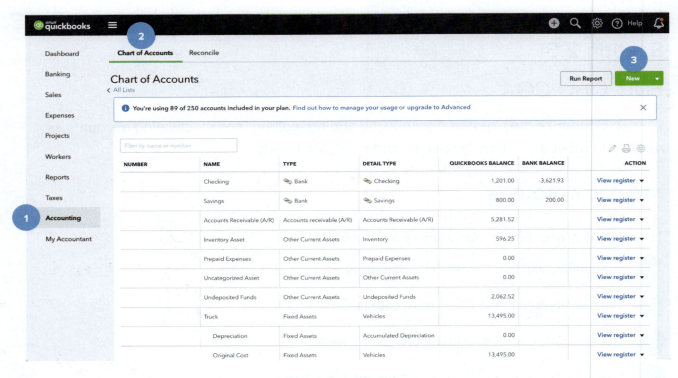

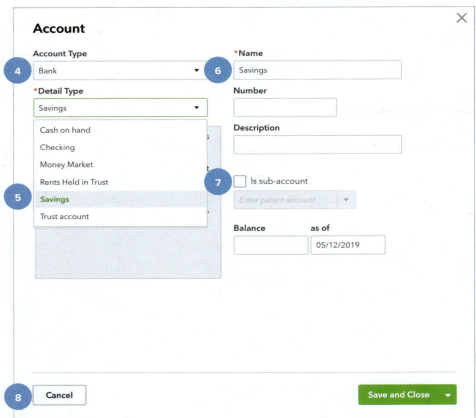

ADD QBO SUBACCOUNTS

Subaccounts are subcategories of an account. For example, the Sample Company has a Utilities Expense account with two subaccounts:

- Gas and Electric
- Telephone

To add a subaccount to an account:

1 From the Chart of Accounts window, select **New**

2 From the Account window, select **Account Type: Expenses**

3 Select **Detail Type: Utilities**

4 Enter **Name: Water Sewer and Trash**

5 Check **Is sub-account**

6 From the drop-down list, select **Utilities**

7 Select **Save and Close**

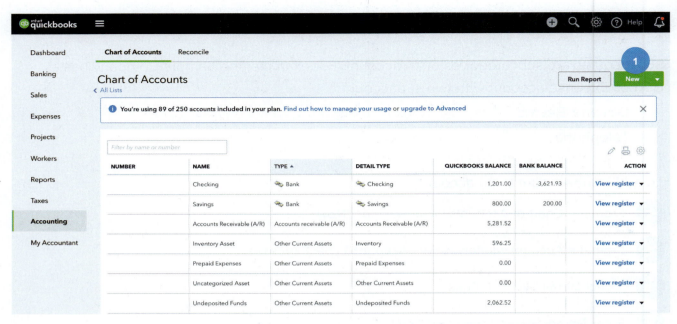

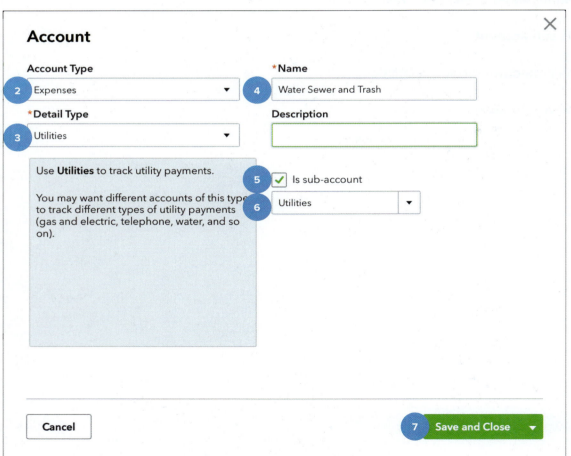

EDIT QBO ACCOUNTS

We can edit an account in QBO to update the account name. To change the name of an account:

1 From the Chart of Accounts window for the Utilities account, select the **drop-down arrow** next to Run Report

2 From the drop-down list that appears, select **Edit**

3 Update **Account Name: Utilities Expenses**

4 Select **Save and Close**

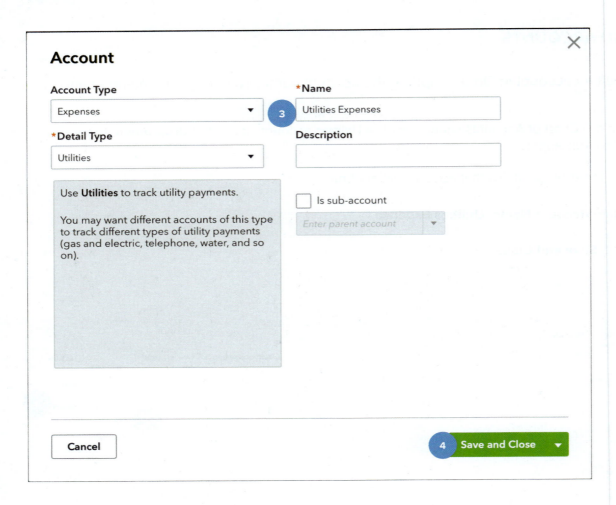

INACTIVATE QBO ACCOUNTS

Sometimes we no longer need to use an account. So QBO permits us to inactivate the account in the Chart of Accounts. If an inactivated account has been used to record transactions, then the transactions are still intact but the account is designated in reports as Inactive. If at a later time, we need to restore an inactive account, QBO will permit us to do so.

To inactivate an account:

1 From the Chart of Accounts window for the Water Sewer and Trash account, select the **drop-down arrow** next to Run Report

2 From the drop-down list that appears, select **Make inactive**

3 When asked Are you sure you want to inactivate this? select **Yes**

4 This completes the chapter activities. **Close** the QBO Sample Company web browser window to reset the Sample Company before proceeding to the exercises at the end of this chapter.

By adding, editing, and inactivating accounts, we can customize the QBO Chart of Accounts to align with the business tax return. This can save countless hours when preparing tax reports, reduce errors, and streamline tax return preparation.

Section 2.6

ACCOUNTING ESSENTIALS
Chart of Accounts

Accounting Essentials summarize important foundational accounting knowledge you may find useful when using QBO

What is the primary objective of accounting?

- The primary objective of accounting is to provide information for decision making. Businesses use a financial system, such as QuickBooks Online, to capture, track, sort, summarize, and communicate financial information.

How is financial information for decision making provided?

- Financial reports summarize and communicate information about a company's financial position and business operations.

What is the difference between financial reports and financial statements?

- Financial reports include financial statements, in addition to other reports, such as cash flow forecasts.
- Financial statements are standardized financial reports, typically consisting of a Balance Sheet, Profit and Loss Statement, and a Statement of Cash Flows, that summarize information about past transactions.
- Financial statements are provided to external users and internal users for decision making.
- External users include bankers, creditors, and investors.
- Internal users include managers and employees of the business.

What are the main financial statements for a business?

- The primary financial statements for a business are:
  - **Balance Sheet** summarizes what a company *owns* and *owes* on a particular date.
  - **Profit and Loss Statement** (also referred to as P & L Statement or Income Statement) summarizes the income a company has earned and the expenses incurred to earn the income.
  - **Statement of Cash Flows** summarizes cash inflows and cash outflows for operating, investing, and financing activities of a business.

What is a Chart of Accounts?

- Chart of Accounts (COA) is a list of all the accounts and account numbers for a business. Accounts are used to sort and track accounting information. For example, a business needs one account for cash, another account to track amounts customers owe (Accounts Receivable), and yet another account to track inventory.

Why Use Accounts?

- We use accounts to record transactions in our accounting system. Accounts, such as a Checking account or Insurance Expense account, permit us to sort, organize, summarize, and track information.
- We can add subaccounts for even better tracking. For example, we could add subaccounts Rental Insurance Expense and Liability Insurance Expense as subaccounts to our Insurance Expense account. We have additional detail provided by the subaccounts, Rental Insurance and Liability Insurance Expense, and the subaccounts roll up into the total for the parent account, Insurance Expense.

What are the Different Types of Accounts?

- We can group accounts into the following different account types:

Balance Sheet Accounts			Profit and Loss Accounts	
Assets	**Liabilities**	**Equity**	**Income**	**Expenses**
Bank account	Accounts Payable	Capital Investment	Sales	Supplies Expense
Accounts Receivable	Credit Cards Payable	Retained Earnings	Consulting Fees	Rent Expense
Equipment	Loans Payable		Interest Income	Utilities Expense

What are Balance Sheet Accounts?

- The Balance Sheet is a financial statement that summarizes what a company owns and what it owes.

- Balance Sheet accounts are accounts that appear on the company's Balance Sheet.

- Three types of accounts appear on the Balance Sheet:
  1. Assets
  2. Liabilities
  3. Owners' (or Stockholders') Equity

Assets		**Liabilities**		**Equity**
Everything your business **owns**		Everything your business **owes**		The residual of **Assets minus Liabilities**
	=		+	
• Cash • Bank accounts • Equipment • Accounts Receivable		• Credit Cards • Sales Tax Payable • Loans		• Capital Stock • Retained Earnings

1. Assets are resources that a company owns. These resources are expected to have future benefit.

Asset accounts include:
- Cash
- Accounts receivable (amounts to be received from customers in the future)
- Inventory
- Other current assets (assets likely to be converted to cash or consumed within one year)
- Fixed assets (property used in the operations of the business, such as equipment, buildings, and land)
- Intangible assets (such as copyrights, patents, trademarks, and franchises)

How Do We Know if an Account is an Asset?

Ask:
Will our enterprise receive a *future benefit* from the item?

Answer:
If we will receive *future benefit*, the account is probably an *asset*. For example, prepaid insurance has future benefit.

---

2. Liabilities are amounts a company owes to others. Liabilities are obligations. For example, if a company borrows $10,000 from the bank, the company has an obligation to repay the $10,000 to the bank. Thus, the $10,000 obligation is shown as a liability on the company's Balance Sheet.

Liability accounts include:
- Accounts payable (amounts that are owed and will be paid to suppliers in the future)
- Sales taxes payable (sales tax owed and to be paid in the future)
- Interest payable (interest owed and to be paid in the future)
- Other current liabilities (liabilities due within one year)
- Loan payable (also called notes payable)
- Mortgage payable (The difference between a note payable and a mortgage payable is that a mortgage payable has real estate as collateral.)
- Other long-term liabilities (liabilities due after one year)

How Do We Know if an Account is a Liability?

Ask:
Is our enterprise *obligated* to do something, such as pay a bill or provide a service?

Answer:
If we have an *obligation*, the account is probably a *liability*.

3. **Equity accounts** (or stockholders' equity for a corporation) represent the net worth of a business. Equity is calculated as assets (resources owned) minus liabilities (amounts owed).

Different types of business ownership include:
- Sole proprietorship (an unincorporated business with one owner)
- Partnership (an unincorporated business with more than one owner)
- Corporation (an incorporated business with one or more owners)

Owners' equity is increased by:
- Investments by owners. For a corporation, owners invest by buying stock.
- Net profits retained in the business rather than distributed to owners

Owners' equity is decreased by:
- Amounts paid to owners as a return for their investment. For a sole proprietorship or partnership, these are called withdrawals or distributions. For a corporation, they are called dividends.
- Losses incurred by the business

How Do We Calculate Equity?

Equity = Assets - Liabilities

* Assets*
- Liabilities
= Equity

What we *own* minus what we *owe* leaves equity.

What are Profit and Loss Accounts?

- The Profit and Loss Statement (also called the Income Statement or P&L Statement) reports the results of a company's operations, listing income and expenses for a period of time.

- Profit and Loss accounts are accounts that appear on a company's Profit and Loss Statement.

- QBO uses two different types of Profit and Loss accounts:
  1. Income accounts
  2. Expense accounts

1. Income accounts record sales to customers and other revenues earned by the company. Revenues are the prices charged customers for products and services provided.

Examples of Income accounts include:
- Sales or revenues

- Fees earned

- Interest income

- Rental income

- Gains on sale of assets

2. Expense accounts record costs that have expired or been consumed in the process of generating income. Expenses are the costs of providing products and services to customers.

Examples of Expense accounts include:
- Cost of goods sold (CGS) expense

- Salaries expense

- Insurance expense

- Rent expense

- Interest expense

How Do We Calculate Net Income?

Net Income = Income (Revenue) - Expenses (including CGS)

  Income (Revenue)
- Expenses (including CGS)
= Net Income (Net Profit or Net Earnings)

Net income is calculated as income (or revenue) less cost of goods sold and other expenses. Net income is an attempt to match or measure efforts (expenses) against accomplishments (revenues).

3 Names for the Same Thing: Net Income is also referred to as Net Profit or Net Earnings.

What are Permanent Accounts?

- In general, Balance Sheet accounts are considered **permanent** accounts (with the exception of the Withdrawals or Distributions account, which is closed out each year).
- Balances in permanent accounts are carried forward from year to year. Thus, for a Balance Sheet account, such as a Checking account, the balance at December 31 is carried forward and becomes the opening balance on January 1 of the next year.

What are Temporary Accounts?

- Profit and Loss accounts are called **temporary** accounts because they are used to track account data for a temporary period of time, usually one year.
- At the end of each year, temporary accounts are closed (the balance reduced to zero). For example, if a Profit and Loss account, such as Advertising Expense, had a $13,000 balance at December 31, the $13,000 balance would be closed or transferred to owners' equity at year-end. The opening balance on January 1 for the Advertising Expense account would be $0.

Practice Quiz 2

Q2.1

Select two from the following to display the Chart of Accounts (COA):

a.   From the Navigation Bar, select Accounting

b.   From the Navigation Bar, select Customers > Chart of Accounts

c.   From the Create (+) icon, select Chart of Accounts

d.   From the Gear icon, select Chart of Accounts

Q2.2

In QBO, the Chart of Accounts displays which of the following two?

a.   QuickBooks Balance

b.   Bank Balance

c.   All account transactions

d.   None of the above

Q2.3

The Chart of Accounts displays:

a.   Account Name

b.   Type

c.   Detail Type

d.   All of the above

Q2.4

Why would a company want to use account numbers on its Chart of Accounts?

a.   To be able to check the current account balance quickly

b.   To uniquely identify each account on the Chart of Accounts

c.   To confuse users of the Chart of Accounts

d.   None the above

Q2.5

To display account numbers on the Chart of Accounts in QBO:

a.   From the Navigation Bar, select Transactions > Chart of Accounts > Enable Account numbers > Show account numbers

b.   From the Create (+) icon, select Other > Chart of Accounts > Account Numbers

c.   From the Gear icon, select Chart of Accounts > Account Numbers

d.   From the Gear icon, select Account and Settings > Advanced > Enable account numbers > Show account numbers

Q2.6

Registers in QBO:

a.   Display more detailed information about accounts

b.   Display all transactions for the account

c.   Display a running balance for the account

d.   All of the above

Q2.7

To view a register:

a.   Display the Chart of Accounts, then select View Register

b.   From the Navigation Bar, select Register

c.   From the Gear icon, select Register

d.   From the Create (+) icon, select Register

Q2.8

Match the following legal entities with the federal tax return the entity files.

1. Form 1040 Schedule C

2. Form 1120

3. Form 1065

4. Form 1120S

a.   Partnership

b.   C corporation

c.   S corporation

d.   Sole proprietorship

Q2.9

To edit an account in the Chart of Accounts:

a. Display the Chart of Accounts, then select Edit

b. Display the Chart of Accounts, then select Run Report drop-down arrow, select Edit

c. From Create (+) icon, select Chart of Accounts, select Edit

d. None of the above

Q2.10

To inactivate an account in the Chart of Accounts:

a. Display the Chart of Accounts, then select Delete

b. Display the Chart of Accounts, then select Run Report drop-down arrow, select Make Inactive

c. From Create (+) icon, select Chart of Accounts, select Delete

d. None of the above

Q2.11

An example of an Asset account is:

a. Mortgage Payable

b. Sales Taxes Payable

c. Equipment

d. None of the above

Q2.12

Income accounts for a company are used to track:

a. Sales to customers and other revenue earned

b. Costs that have expired or been consumed

c. Cost of items sold to customers

d. Purchases from vendors

Q2.13

What are assets?

a. Net worth of a company

b. Amounts paid to owners

c. Resources that a company owns with future benefit

d. Amounts owed to others and are future obligations

Q2.14

Accounts used for only one year are called:

a.   Temporary accounts

b.   Short-term assets or liabilities

c.   Supply accounts

d.   Estimate accounts

Exercises 2

> **We use the QBO Sample Company, Craig's Design and Landscaping Services, for practice throughout the exercises. The Sample Company will reset each time it is reopened. So make certain to allow enough time to complete exercise before closing the Sample Company. Otherwise, you will lose the work you have entered.**

To access the QBO Sample Company, complete the following steps.

1   After closing any open web browser windows displaying the QBO Sample Company, open a new web browser window. (Note: using a new web browser window to access the QBO Sample Company, resets the Sample Company to its original settings for the exercises.)

2   Go to https://qbo.intuit.com/redir/testdrive

3   Follow onscreen instructions for security verification.

Craig's Design and Landscaping Services should appear on your screen.

E2.1 COA: Types of Accounts

The Chart of Accounts is a list of accounts used by a company. The accounts can be grouped into different categories.

Using the QBO Sample Company to Craig's Design and Landscaping Services, select **Navigation Bar** > **Accounting**.

Indicate the QBO Account Type for each of the following accounts appearing in Craig's Chart of Accounts.

QBO Account Types
- **Bank**
- **Accounts Receivable (A/R)**
- **Other Current Asset**
- **Fixed Asset**
- **Accounts Payable (A/P)**
- **Credit Card**
- **Other Current Liabilities**
- **Long Term Liabilities**
- **Equity**
- **Income**
- **Cost of Goods Sold**
- **Expenses**
- **Other Income**
- **Other Expense**

Account	QBO Account Type
1. Bank Charges	
2. Meals and Entertainment	
3. Accounts Receivable (A/R)	
4. Maintenance and Repair	
5. Landscaping Services: Job Materials	
6. Equipment Rental	
7. Accounts Payable (A/P)	
8. Mastercard	
9. Savings	
10. Loan Payable	
11. Inventory Asset	
12. Opening Balance Equity	
13. Retained Earnings	
14. Interest Earned	
15. Design Income	
16. Landscaping Services	
17. Landscaping Services: Labor	
18. Undeposited Funds	
19. Cost of Goods Sold	
20. Notes Payable	
21. Legal and Professional Fees	
22. Rent or Lease	
23. Utilities	
24. Billable Expense Income	

E2.2 Aligning COA and Tax Return

Typically when customizing the Chart of Accounts for businesses, we want to verify that the accounts on the Chart of Accounts correspond to expenses shown on the tax return the business files.

Assume that Craig's Design and Landscaping Services files the following IRS Schedule C Form 1040 for its business operations.

SCHEDULE C
(Form 1040)

Department of the Treasury
Internal Revenue Service (99)

Profit or Loss From Business
(Sole Proprietorship)

▶ Information about Schedule C and its separate instructions is at *www.irs.gov/schedulec.*
▶ Attach to Form 1040, 1040NR, or 1041; partnerships generally must file Form 1065.

Name of proprietor

Social security number (SSN)

A Principal business or profession, including product or service (see instructions)

B Enter code from instructions ▶

C Business name. If no separate business name, leave blank.

D Employer ID number (EIN), (see instr.)

E Business address (including suite or room no.) ▶
City, town or post office, state, and ZIP code

F Accounting method: **(1)** ☐ Cash **(2)** ☐ Accrual **(3)** ☐ Other (specify) ▶

G Did you "materially participate" in the operation of this business during 2016? If "No," see instructions for limit on losses . ☐ Yes ☐ No

H If you started or acquired this business during 2016, check here . . . . ▶ ☐

I Did you make any payments in 2016 that would require you to file Form(s) 1099? (see instructions) . . . . ☐ Yes ☐ No

J If "Yes," did you or will you file required Forms 1099? . . . . ☐ Yes ☐ No

Part I   Income

1	Gross receipts or sales. See instructions for line 1 and check the box if this income was reported to you on Form W-2 and the "Statutory employee" box on that form was checked . . . . ▶ ☐	1
2	Returns and allowances	2
3	Subtract line 2 from line 1	3
4	Cost of goods sold (from line 42)	4
5	**Gross profit.** Subtract line 4 from line 3	5
6	Other income, including federal and state gasoline or fuel tax credit or refund (see instructions)	6
7	**Gross income.** Add lines 5 and 6 . . . . ▶	7

Part II   Expenses. Enter expenses for business use of your home **only** on line 30.

8	Advertising	8	18	Office expense (see instructions)	18
9	Car and truck expenses (see instructions).	9	19	Pension and profit-sharing plans .	19
			20	Rent or lease (see instructions):	
10	Commissions and fees .	10	a	Vehicles, machinery, and equipment	20a
11	Contract labor (see instructions)	11	b	Other business property . . .	20b
12	Depletion	12	21	Repairs and maintenance . . .	21
13	Depreciation and section 179 expense deduction (not included in Part III) (see instructions).	13	22	Supplies (not included in Part III) .	22
			23	Taxes and licenses	23
			24	Travel, meals, and entertainment:	
14	Employee benefit programs (other than on line 19) . .	14	a	Travel	24a
15	Insurance (other than health)	15	b	Deductible meals and entertainment (see instructions) .	24b
16	Interest:		25	Utilities	25
a	Mortgage (paid to banks, etc.)	16a	26	Wages (less employment credits) .	26
b	Other	16b	27a	Other expenses (from line 48) . .	27a
17	Legal and professional services	17	b	**Reserved for future use** . . .	27b

For the following accounts from Craig's Chart of Accounts, identify the corresponding Line number on the Schedule C.

Craig's COA	IRS Schedule C
1. Cost of Goods Sold	Schedule C Line _____
2. Advertising	Schedule C Line _____
3. Legal and Professional Fees	Schedule C Line _____
4. Maintenance and Repair	Schedule C Line _____
5. Office Expenses	Schedule C Line _____
6. Rent or Lease	Schedule C Line _____
7. Taxes and Licenses	Schedule C Line _____
8. Utilities	Schedule C Line _____

E2.3 Display and Enter Account Numbers

Account numbers are used to uniquely identify accounts. The account number can also be used to identify the type of account.

Using the QBO Sample Company, Craig's Design and Landscaping Services, complete the following.

1. Turn on Account Numbers.
    a. To turn on account numbers, select **Gear icon** > **Account and Settings** > **Advanced** > **Check Enable account numbers** > **Check Show account numbers** > **Save** > **Done**
    b. To display COA, from the **Navigation Bar**, select **Accounting**
    c. On the Chart of Accounts, what is the name of the column displaying the account numbers?

2. Enter Asset Account Numbers.
    a. From the Chart of Accounts window, select **Edit pencil**
    b. Asset accounts will be numbered in the 1000s. Starting with 1001 for the first Asset account, **enter** accounts numbers consecutively for the following Asset accounts.
        - Checking
        - Savings
        - Accounts Receivable (A/R)
        - Inventory Asset
        - Prepaid Expenses

3. Enter Liability Account Numbers.
   a. If needed, from the COA window, select **Edit pencil**
   b. Liability accounts will be numbered in the 2000s. Starting with 2001 for the first Liability account, **enter** account numbers consecutively for the following Liability accounts.
      - Accounts Payable (A/P)
      - Mastercard
      - Visa
      - Arizona Dept. of Revenue Payable
      - Board of Equalization Payable
      - Loan Payable
      - Notes Payable

4. Enter Equity Account Numbers.
   a. If needed, from the COA window, select **Edit pencil**
   b. Equity accounts will be numbered in the 3000s. Starting with 3001 for the first Equity account, **enter** account numbers consecutively for the following Equity accounts.
      - Opening Balance Equity
      - Retained Earnings

5. Enter Income Account Numbers.
   a. If needed, from the COA window, select **Edit pencil**
   b. Income accounts will be numbered in the 4000s. Starting with 4001 for the first Income account, **enter** account numbers consecutively for the following Income accounts.
      - Billable Expense Income
      - Design Income
      - Fees Billed
      - Landscaping Services
      - Other Income
      - Pest Control Services
      - Sales of Product Income
      - Services

6. Enter Expense Account Numbers.
   a. If needed, from the COA window, select **Edit pencil**
   b. Expense accounts will be numbered in the 5000s. Starting with 5001 for the first Expense account, **enter** account numbers consecutively for the following Expense accounts.
      - Cost of Goods Sold
      - Advertising
      - Automobile
      - Bank Charges
      - Commissions & Fees
      - Disposal Fees
      - Dues & Subscriptions
      - Equipment Rental
      - Insurance
      - Job Expenses
      - Legal & Professional Fees
      - Maintenance & Repair
      - Meals and Entertainment
      - Office Expenses
      - Promotional
      - Purchases
      - Rent or Lease
      - Stationary & Printing
      - Supplies
      - Taxes & Licenses
      - Travel
      - Travel Meals
      - Utilities

E2.4 COA: Add Accounts

Using the QBO Sample Company, Craig's Design and Landscaping Services, complete the following.

In order to align better with the IRS Form 1040 Schedule C, Craig would like you to add accounts to its QBO Chart of Accounts.

To add accounts to the COA, from the Navigation Bar, select **Accounting > New**.

1. Add Interest Expense Account.
    a. Select **Account Type: Expenses**
    b. Select **Detail Type:** _____
    c. Enter **Name: Interest Expense**
    d. Leave **Number blank**
    e. Leave **Description blank**
    f. Leave **Is sub-account unchecked**
    g. Select **Save and New**

2. Add Other Expenses Account.
    a. Select **Account Type:** _____
    b. Select **Detail Type:** _____
    c. Enter **Name: Other Expenses**
    d. Leave **Number blank**
    e. Leave **Description blank**
    f. Leave **Is sub-account unchecked**
    g. Select **Save and Close**

E2.5 COA: Add SubAccounts

Using the QBO Sample Company, Craig's Design and Landscaping Services, complete the following.

In order to align better with the IRS Form 1040 Schedule C, Craig would like you to add 2 subaccounts to the Rent or Lease account in its QBO Chart of Accounts.

To add subaccounts to the COA, from the Navigation Bar, select **Accounting > New**.

1. Add Vehicles, Machinery, and Equipment Subaccount.
   a. Select **Account Type:** _____
   b. Select **Detail Type: Equipment Rental**
   c. Enter **Name: Vehicle, Machinery, and Equipment**
   d. Leave **Number blank**
   e. Leave **Description blank**
   f. **Check Is sub-account**
   g. Enter **Parent Account:** _____
   h. Select **Save and New**

2. Add Other Business Property Subaccount.
   a. Select **Account Type:** _____
   b. Select **Detail Type: Rent or Lease of Buildings**
   c. Enter **Name: Other Business Property**
   d. Leave **Number blank**
   e. Leave **Description blank**
   f. **Check Is sub-account**
   g. Enter **Parent Account:** _____
   h. Select **Save and Close**

E2.6 COA: Edit Accounts

Using the QBO Sample Company, Craig's Design and Landscaping Services, complete the following.

In order to align better with the IRS Form 1040 Schedule C, Craig would like you to edit 2 accounts in its QBO Chart of Accounts.

To edit account names in the COA, from the Navigation Bar, select **Accounting** > **Edit pencil**.

> **Another way to edit accounts when you need to update more than just the account name** is to select the specific account > drop-down arrow by View register or Run report > Edit.

1. Edit Name of Maintenance and Repairs Account.
   a. Edit the name of the Maintenance and Repairs account to Repairs and Maintenance. Select **Save**
   b. After saving, what 3 subaccounts are listed immediately after the Repairs and Maintenance account?

2. Edit Name of Legal and Professional Fees Account.
   a. Edit name of the Legal and Professional Fees account to Legal and Professional Services. Select **Save**.
   b. After saving, what 3 subaccounts are listed immediately after the Legal and Professional Services account?

E2.7 COA: Inactivate Accounts

Using the QBO Sample Company, Craig's Design and Landscaping Services, complete the following.

In order to align better with the IRS Form 1040 Schedule C, Craig would like you to inactivate two accounts in its QBO Chart of Accounts.

To inactivate an account in the QBO COA, from the Navigation Bar, select **Accounting** > select the **specific account** > **drop-down arrow by View register or Run report** > **Make inactive**.

1. Inactivate the Penalties and Settlements Account.
   a. Inactivate the Penalties and Settlements account. When asked Are you sure you want to inactivate this?, select **Yes**.
   b. Now what is the last account listed in Craig's QBO Chart of Accounts?

2. Inactive the Other Portfolio Income Account.

    a. Inactivate the Other Portfolio Income Account. When asked Are you sure you want to inactivate this?, select **Yes**

    b. Now what are the last three accounts listed in Craig's QBO Chart of Accounts?

E2.8 Definitions

Match the following Account Types with the appropriate definition.

Account Types

- **Assets**
- **Liabilities**
- **Equity**
- **Revenues**
- **Expenses**

Definitions	Account Type
1. What we own less what we owe equals this	
2. Prices charged customers for products and services	
3. Resources that we own that have future benefit	
4. Obligations or amounts that we owe to others	
5. Costs of providing products and services to customers	

E2.9 Account Types

For each of the following accounts on Craig's Design and Landscaping Services Chart of Accounts, identify Account Type and Financial Statement on which it appears.

Account Types

- **Asset**
- **Liability**
- **Equity**
- **Income**
- **Expense**

Financial Statements

- **Balance Sheet**
- **Profit and Loss**

Account	Account Type	Financial Statement
1. Design Income		
2. Savings		
3. Accounts Receivable (A/R)		
4. Rent or Lease		
5. Prepaid Expenses		
6. Notes Payable		
7. Inventory Asset		
8. Opening Balance Equity		
9. Utilities		
10. Undeposited Funds		
11. Accounts Payable (A/P)		
12. MasterCard		
13. Visa		
14. Loan Payable		
15. Sales of Product Income		
16. Legal and Professional Fees		
17. Advertising		
18. Meals and Entertainment		
19. Retained Earnings		
20. Checking		
21. Landscaping Services		
22. Pest Control Services		
23. Cost of Goods Sold		
24. Automobile: Fuel		
25. Bank Charges		
26. Interest Earned		

Project 2.1

Mookie the Beagle™ Concierge

> **Project 2.1 is a continuation of Project 1.1. You will use the QBO Company you created for Project 1.1. Keep in mind the QBO Company for Project 2.1 does not reset and carries your data forward, including any errors. So it is important to check and crosscheck your work to verify it is correct before clicking the Save button.**

BACKSTORY

Mookie The Beagle™ Concierge, a concierge pet care service, provides convenient, high-quality pet care. Cy, the founder of Mookie The Beagle Concierge, has asked you to customize the Chart of Accounts to assist in streamlining tax preparation. Mookie The Beagle Concierge, an S corporation, files U.S. Federal Form 1120S, which can be viewed at www.irs.gov.

Complete the following for Mookie The Beagle Concierge.

🌐 QBO SATNAV

Project 2.1 focuses on QBO Settings, specifically the QBO Chart of Accounts as shown in the following QBO SatNav.

🌐 **QBO SatNav**

⚙️ **QBO Settings**

⚙️ Company Settings
⚙️ Chart of Accounts

💰 **QBO Transactions**

💰 Banking
💰 Customers & Sales
💰 Vendors & Expenses
💰 Employees & Payroll

📊 **QBO Reports**

📊 Reports

HOW TO LOG INTO QBO

To log into QBO, complete the following steps.

1 Using a web browser go to qbo.intuit.com

2 Enter **User ID** (the email address you used to set up your QBO Account)

3 Enter **Password** (the password you used to set up your QBO Account)

4 Select **Sign in**

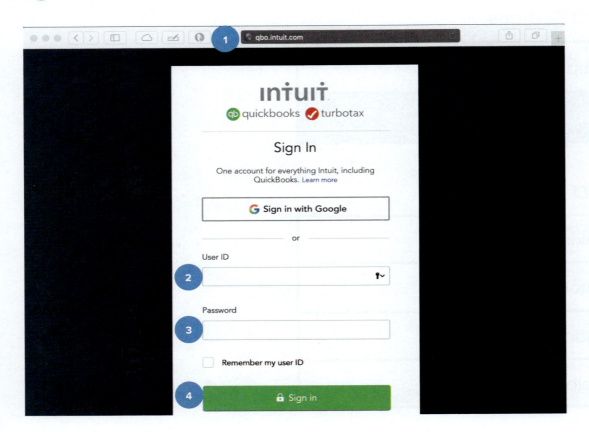

> **If you are not using a public or shared computer, to speed up login, you can save your login to your desktop and select Remember Me. If you are using a public computer or shared computer, do not save to the desktop and unselect Remember Me.**

> **The new QBO company** we created in Project 1.1 will carry all work forward into future chapters. So it is important to check and crosscheck your work to verify it is correct before clicking the Save button. Any uncorrected errors will be carried forward in your QBO company for text projects.

P2.1.1 Aligning the COA with the Tax Return

Typically when customizing the Chart of Accounts for a business, we want to verify that the accounts on the Chart of Accounts correspond to expenses shown on the tax return the business files.

Mookie The Beagle Concierge files the following IRS Form 1120S for its business operations.

Form 1120S

U.S. Income Tax Return for an S Corporation

OMB No. 1545-0123

Department of the Treasury
Internal Revenue Service

▶ Do not file this form unless the corporation has filed or is attaching Form 2553 to elect to be an S corporation.
▶ Information about Form 1120S and its separate instructions is at *www.irs.gov/form1120s.*

For calendar year

A S election effective date	**TYPE OR PRINT** — Name	**D** Employer identification number
B Business activity code number (see instructions)	Number, street, and room or suite no. If a P.O. box, see instructions.	**E** Date incorporated
C Check if Sch. M-3 attached ☐	City or town, state or province, country, and ZIP or foreign postal code	**F** Total assets (see instructions) $

G Is the corporation electing to be an S corporation beginning with this tax year? ☐ Yes ☐ No   If "Yes," attach Form 2553 if not already filed
H Check if: **(1)** ☐ Final return **(2)** ☐ Name change **(3)** ☐ Address change **(4)** ☐ Amended return **(5)** ☐ S election termination or revocation
I Enter the number of shareholders who were shareholders during any part of the tax year . . . . ▶

Caution: Include **only** trade or business income and expenses on lines 1a through 21. See the instructions for more information.

Income

1a	Gross receipts or sales **1a**	
b	Returns and allowances **1b**	
c	Balance. Subtract line 1b from line 1a	**1c**
2	Cost of goods sold (attach Form 1125-A)	**2**
3	Gross profit. Subtract line 2 from line 1c	**3**
4	Net gain (loss) from Form 4797, line 17 (attach Form 4797)	**4**
5	Other income (loss) (see instructions—attach statement)	**5**
6	**Total income (loss).** Add lines 3 through 5 . . . . ▶	**6**

Deductions (see instructions for limitations)

7	Compensation of officers (see instructions—attach Form 1125-E)	**7**
8	Salaries and wages (less employment credits)	**8**
9	Repairs and maintenance	**9**
10	Bad debts	**10**
11	Rents	**11**
12	Taxes and licenses	**12**
13	Interest	**13**
14	Depreciation not claimed on Form 1125-A or elsewhere on return (attach Form 4562)	**14**
15	Depletion (**Do not deduct oil and gas depletion.**)	**15**
16	Advertising	**16**
17	Pension, profit-sharing, etc., plans	**17**
18	Employee benefit programs	**18**
19	Other deductions (attach statement)	**19**
20	**Total deductions.** Add lines 7 through 19 . . . . ▶	**20**
21	**Ordinary business income (loss).** Subtract line 20 from line 6	**21**

For the following accounts from Mookie The Beagle Concierge's QBO COA, identify the corresponding Line number on Form 1120S.

QBO COA	IRS Form 1120S
1. Rents	Form 1120S Line _____
2. Advertising	Form 1120S Line _____
3. Repairs and maintenance	Form 1120S Line _____
4. Interest	Form 1120S Line _____
5. Bad debts	Form 1120S Line _____
6. Taxes and licenses	Form 1120S Line _____

P2.1.2 COA: Add Accounts

Complete the following steps to add Asset accounts to Mookie The Beagle Concierge's Chart of Accounts.

> **QBO is continually** rolling out new features, so it is possible your Chart of Accounts may not appear the same are your text. If your COA doesn't have the following accounts, add them to your COA as follows.

To add accounts to the COA, from the Navigation Bar, select **Accounting > New**.

1. Add Checking Account.
    a. Select **Account Type: Bank**
    b. Select **Detail Type: _____**
    c. Enter **Name: Checking**
    d. Leave **Description blank**
    e. Leave **Is sub-account unchecked**
    f. Select **Save and New**

2. Add Accounts Receivable Account.
    a. Select **Account Type: _____**
    b. Select **Detail Type: _____**
    c. Enter **Name: Accounts Receivable (A/R)**
    d. Leave **Description blank**
    e. Leave **Is sub-account unchecked**
    f. Select **Save and New**

3. If your COA does not have an Undeposited Funds account, add the Undeposited Funds account.
   a. Select **Account Type: Other Current Assets**
   b. Select **Detail Type:** _____
   c. Enter **Name: Undeposited Funds**
   d. Leave **Description blank**
   e. Leave **Is sub-account unchecked**
   f. Select **Save and New**

4. Add Prepaid Expenses Account.
   a. Select **Account Type: Other Current Assets**
   b. Select **Detail Type:** _____
   c. Enter **Name: Prepaid Expenses**
   d. Leave **Description blank**
   e. Leave **Is sub-account unchecked**
   f. Select **Save and Close**

P2.1.3 COA: Add Accounts

Complete the following steps to add Liability and Equity accounts to Mookie The Beagle Concierge's Chart of Accounts.

> QBO is continually rolling out new features, so it is possible your Chart of Accounts may not appear the same as your text. If your COA doesn't have the following accounts, add them to your COA as follows.

To add accounts to the COA, from the Navigation Bar, select **Accounting > New**.

1. Add Accounts Payable Account.
   a. Select **Account Type:** _____
   b. Select **Detail Type:** _____
   c. Enter **Name: Accounts Payable (A/P)**
   d. Leave **Description blank**
   e. Leave **Is sub-account unchecked**
   f. Select **Save and New**

2. Add VISA Credit Card Account.
   a. Select **Account Type:** _____
   b. Select **Detail Type:** _____
   c. Enter **Name: VISA Credit Card**
   d. Leave **Description blank**
   e. Leave **Is sub-account unchecked**
   f. Select **Save and New**

3. Add Unearned Revenue Account.
    a. Select **Account Type:** _____
    b. Select **Detail Type: Other Current Liabilities**
    c. Enter **Name: Unearned Revenue**
    d. Leave **Description blank**
    e. Leave **Is sub-account unchecked**
    f. Select **Save and New**

4. Add Owner Distributions Account.
    a. Select **Account Type: Equity**
    b. Select **Detail Type:** _____
    c. Enter **Name: Owner Distributions**
    d. Leave **Description blank**
    e. Leave **Is sub-account unchecked**
    f. Select **Save and Close**

P2.1.4 COA: Add Subaccounts

Complete the following to add subaccounts to Mookie The Beagle Concierge's Chart of Accounts.

> **QBO is continually** rolling out new features, so it is possible your Chart of Accounts may not appear the same as your text.

To add subaccounts to the COA, from the Navigation Bar, select **Accounting > New**.

1. After verifying your COA has a Prepaid Expenses account, add the subaccount: Prepaid Expenses: Supplies.
    a. Select **Account Type: Other Current Assets**
    b. Select **Detail Type:** _____
    c. Enter **Name: Supplies**
    d. Leave **Description blank**
    e. Check: **Is sub-account**
    f. Enter **Parent Account: Prepaid Expenses**
    g. Select **Save and New**

2. Add Subaccount: Prepaid Expenses: Insurance.
   a. Select **Account Type: _____**
   b. Select **Detail Type: _____**
   c. Enter **Name: Insurance**
   d. Leave **Description blank**
   e. Check: **Is sub-account**
   f. Enter **Parent Account: Prepaid Expenses**
   g. Select **Save and New**

3. Add Subaccount: Prepaid Expenses: Rent.
   a. Select **Account Type: _____**
   b. Select **Detail Type: _____**
   c. Enter **Name: Rent**
   d. Leave **Description blank**
   e. Check: **Is sub-account**
   f. Enter **Parent Account: Prepaid Expenses**
   g. Select **Save and Close**

P2.1.5 COA: Add Subaccounts

Complete the following to add subaccounts to Mookie The Beagle Concierge's Chart of Accounts.

> QBO is continually rolling out new features, so it is possible your Chart of Accounts may not appear the same as your text.

To add subaccounts to the COA, from the Navigation Bar, select **Accounting > New**.

1. After verifying your COA has an Insurance (Expenses) account, add the subaccount: Insurance: Renter Insurance Expense.
   a. Select **Account Type: _____**
   b. Select **Detail Type: _____**
   c. Enter **Name: Renter Insurance Expense**
   d. Leave **Description blank**
   e. Check: **Is sub-account**
   f. Enter **Parent Account: Insurance**
   g. Select **Save and New**

2. Add Subaccount: Insurance: Liability Insurance Expense.
    a. Select **Account Type: _____**
    b. Select **Detail Type: _____**
    c. Enter **Name: Liability Insurance Expense**
    d. Leave **Description blank**
    e. Check: **Is sub-account**
    f. Enter **Parent Account: Insurance**
    g. Select **Save and Close**

P2.1.6 Display and Enter Account Numbers

Complete the following for Mookie The Beagle Concierge.

> **QBO is continually** rolling out new features, so it is possible your Chart of Accounts may not have the same accounts as listed below. If your COA doesn't have the following accounts, add the appropriate accounts to your COA before adding the account numbers.

1. Turn on Account Numbers.
    a. To turn on account numbers, select **Gear icon > Account and Settings > Advanced > Check Enable account numbers > Check Show account numbers > Save > Done**.
    b. To display COA, from the **Navigation Bar**, select **Accounting**.
    c. On the Chart of Accounts, what is the name of the column displaying the account numbers?

2. Enter Asset Account Numbers.
    a. From COA window, select **Edit pencil**.
    b. Asset accounts will be numbered in the 1000s. Starting with 1001 for the first Asset account, **enter** accounts numbers consecutively for the following Asset accounts.
        - Checking
        - Accounts Receivable (A/R)
        - Inventory
        - Prepaid Expenses
        - Prepaid Expenses: Insurance
        - Prepaid Expenses: Rent
        - Prepaid Expenses: Supplies
        - Uncategorized Asset
        - Undeposited Funds

3. Enter Liability Account Numbers.
    a. If needed, from the COA window, select **Edit pencil**.
    b. Liability accounts will be numbered in the 2000s. Starting with 2001 for the first Liability account, **enter** account numbers consecutively for the following Liability accounts.
        *   Accounts Payable (A/P)
        *   VISA Credit Card
        *   Unearned Revenue

4. Enter Equity Account Numbers.
    a. If needed, from the COA window, select **Edit pencil**.
    b. Equity accounts will be numbered in the 3000s. Starting with 3001 for the first Equity account, **enter** account numbers consecutively for the following Equity accounts.
        *   Opening Balance Equity
        *   Owner Distributions
        *   Owner's Investment
        *   Owner's Pay & Personal Expenses
        *   Retained Earnings

5. Enter Income Account Numbers.
    a. If needed, from the COA window, select **Edit pencil**.
    b. Income accounts will be numbered in the 4000s. Starting with 4001 for the first Income account, **enter** account numbers consecutively for the following Income accounts.
        *   Billable Expense Income
        *   Sales
        *   Uncategorized Income

6. Enter Expense Account Numbers.

   a. If needed, from the COA window, select **Edit pencil**

   b. Expense accounts will be numbered in the 5000s. Starting with 5001 for the first Expense account, **enter** account numbers consecutively for the following Expense accounts.

      - Cost of Goods Sold
      - Shipping
      - Advertising & Marketing
      - Ask My Accountant
      - Bank Charges & Fees
      - Car & Truck
      - Contractors
      - Employee Benefits
      - Insurance
      - Insurance: Liability Insurance Expense
      - Insurance: Renter Insurance Expense
      - Interest Paid
      - Job Supplies
      - Legal & Professional Services
      - Meals & Entertainment
      - Office Supplies & Software
      - Other Business Expenses
      - Reimbursable Expenses
      - Rent & Lease
      - Repairs & Maintenance
      - Salaries & Wages
      - Taxes & Licenses
      - Travel
      - Uncategorized Expense
      - Utilities

P2.1.7 COA

Complete the following for Mookie The Beagle Concierge.

Display the COA by selecting **Navigation Bar > Accounting**.

Indicate the QBO Account Type for each of the following accounts appearing in Mookie The Beagle Concierge's Chart of Accounts.

QBO Account Types
- **Bank**
- **Accounts Receivable (A/R)**
- **Other Current Assets**
- **Fixed Assets**
- **Accounts Payable (A/P)**
- **Credit Card**
- **Other Current Liabilities**
- **Long Term Liabilities**
- **Equity**
- **Income**
- **Cost of Goods Sold**
- **Expenses**
- **Other Income**
- **Other Expense**

Account	QBO Account Type
1. Checking	
2. Accounts Receivable (A/R)	
3. Inventory	
4. Prepaid Expenses	
5. Prepaid Expenses: Insurance	
6. Prepaid Expenses: Rent	
7. Prepaid Expenses: Supplies	

8. Accounts Payable (A/P)

9. VISA Credit Card

10. Unearned Revenue

11. Owner Distributions

12. Owner's Investment

13. Retained Earnings

14. Sales

15. Advertising & Marketing

16. Bank Charges & Fees

17. Contractors

18. Insurance: Liability Insurance Expense

19. Insurance: Renter Insurance Expense

20. Interest Paid

21. Legal & Professional Services

22. Meals & Entertainment

23. Office Supplies & Software

24. Rent & Lease

25. Repairs & Maintenance

26. Travel

27. Utilities

P2.1.8 Account Types

The following accounts are from Mookie The Beagle Concierge's Chart of Accounts. For each account, identify Account Type and Financial Statement on which it appears.

Account Types

- **Asset**
- **Liability**
- **Equity**
- **Income**
- **Expense**

Financial Statements

- **Balance Sheet**
- **Profit and Loss**

Account	Account Type	Financial Statement
1. Sales		
2. Checking		
3. Accounts Receivable (A/R)		
4. Rent & Lease		
5. Prepaid Expenses		
6. Prepaid Expenses: Supplies		
7. Office Supplies & Software		
8. Prepaid Expenses: Insurance		
9. Insurance: Liability Insurance Expense		
10. Undeposited Funds		
11. Accounts Payable (A/P)		
12. VISA Credit Card		
13. Prepaid Insurance: Rent		
14. Interest Paid		
15. Contractors		
16. Legal & Professional Services		
17. Advertising & Marketing		
18. Meals & Entertainment		
19. Retained Earnings		
20. Owner's Investment		
21. Owner Distributions		
22. Inventory		
23. Utilities		

Chapter 3

QBO Transactions

Cy Walker's business, Mookie The Beagle Concierge, needs to track all its business transactions and record the transactions in an organized way. Cy knows that he will also need to be able to sort and retrieve the transaction information at a later time. QuickBooks Online provides an easy way to enter and retrieve transaction information. So your next step is to learn more about how to record transactions using QBO.

Chapter 3

LEARNING OBJECTIVES

One objective of our QBO financial system is to collect information about transactions. Transactions are simply exchanges between our business and other parties, such as customers, vendors, and employees. We need to keep a record of all transactions, and QBO offers us a streamlined way to keep track of those transactions.

After we set up QBO Company Settings and the QBO Chart of Accounts, we're ready to enter transactions into QBO. Transactions increase and decrease accounts so that's why it's important for us to have our Chart of Accounts created before we enter transactions.

When working with clients, we have to determine the types of transactions that the client will need to record. Then we plan how to save time and minimize errors when entering those transactions, especially ones that are recurring.

Chapter 3 introduces different types of transactions, and later chapters will look at each type of transaction in greater detail. In this chapter, you will learn about the following topics:

- QBO Lists
  - Chart of Accounts
  - Customers List
  - Vendors List
  - Employees List
  - Products and Services List
- Update QBO Lists
  - Update QBO List Before Entering Transactions
  - Update QBO List While Entering Transactions
  - Create QBO Products and Services List
- What Forms To Enter Transactions in QBO
  - Enter Transaction Using Onscreen Form
  - Enter Transaction Using Onscreen Journal
- How to Enter Transactions in QBO
  - Navigation Bar
  - Create (+) Icon
  - Gear Icon and Recurring Transactions

- Types of QBO Transactions
  - Banking and Credit Card Transactions
  - Customers and Sales Transactions
  - Vendors and Expenses Transactions
  - Employees and Payroll Transactions
  - Other Transactions
- Banking Transactions
  - Make Deposit
- Customers and Sales Transactions
  - Create Invoice
- Vendors and Expenses Transactions
  - Create Expense
- Employees and Payroll Transactions
- Other Transactions
- Recurring Transactions
- Accounting Essentials: Double-Entry Accounting

Section 3.1

 QBO SATNAV

QBO SatNav is your satellite navigation for QuickBooks Online, assisting you in navigating QBO

Chapter 3 provides an overview of QBO transactions, shown in the following QBO SatNav.

 QBO SatNav

 QBO Settings

Company Settings
Chart of Accounts

 **QBO Transactions**

Banking	Record Deposits | Write Checks
Customers & Sales	Create Sales Receipts > Record Deposits
Vendors & Expenses	Enter Bills > Pay Bills
Employees & Payroll	Enter Time > Pay Employees > Payroll Liabilities

 QBO Reports

Reports

Section 3.2

QBO SAMPLE COMPANY LOGIN

To log into the QBO Sample Company:

1 Close any web browser windows that already display the QBO Sample Company. Open a new web browser window. (Note: Intuit recommends using Google Chrome.)

2 Go to https://qbo.intuit.com/redir/testdrive

3 Follow onscreen instructions for security verification.

> **Note: Although the Sample Company link should work, if for some reason the previous link for the Sample Company doesn't work with your browser, using Google search type in "qbo.intuit.com Sample Company". Select the link to Test Drive Sample Company.**

The QBO Sample Company Craig's Design and Landscaping Services should appear on the screen.

While you are using the Craig's Design and Landscaping Services Sample Company, the information you enter will be saved. *After you close* the Sample Company, automatically all the settings and data are reset to the original data and settings before you entered your work.

Since we will be using the Sample Company to explore and practice with QBO, the reset will permit you to start over each time you enter the Sample Company. You do not have to worry about carrying forward errors that ripple through the rest of the chapters.

The Sample Company default setting is to log out if inactive for one (1) hour. Since the Sample Company resets automatically, you will lose any work you entered. So it is important to plan accordingly so that you can complete all activities needed before closing the Sample Company.

To increase the amount of time from one (1) hour to three (3) hours before the log out for inactivity occurs:

1. From Craig's Design and Landscaping Services QBO Sample Company, select the **Gear** icon

2. Under the Your Company section, select **Account and Settings**

3. Select **Advanced**

4. Select **Other preferences**

5. For the option Sign me out if inactive for, select **3 hours**

6. Select **Save**

7. Select **Done**

> ⚠️ **The Sample Company** will reset each time it is reopened. This allows you to explore and practice QBO without concern about carrying forward errors to later chapters. However, you will want to make certain to allow enough time to complete all chapter activities before closing the Sample Company. Otherwise, you will lose the work you have entered when you reopen the Sample Company.

Section 3.3

QBO LISTS

As a company conducts business operations, the company enters into transactions with customers, vendors, and employees. Before recording these transactions in QBO, we typically want to make sure our QBO Lists are up to date.

WHAT ARE QBO LISTS?

QBO Lists are a time saving feature so we don't have to continually re-enter the same information each time we enter a transaction. Lists permit us to collect information that we will reuse, so we do not have to repeatedly re-enter accounts, customers, vendors, and so on.

Some of the lists we might use when entering transactions include:

- Chart of Accounts
- Customers List
- Vendors List
- Employees List
- Products and Services List

To view QBO Lists, select the lists as follows.

1 From the Navigation Bar, select **Accounting > Chart of Accounts** to display the Chart of Accounts. (If necessary, select See your Chart of Accounts.)

Chart of Accounts is a list of all the accounts a company uses when recording transactions. Accounts, such as the Checking account, permit us to sort and track accounting information.

2 Select **Sales > Customers** to display the Customers List.

Customers List, also called the Clients List, collects information about customers, such as customer name, customer number, address, and contact information.

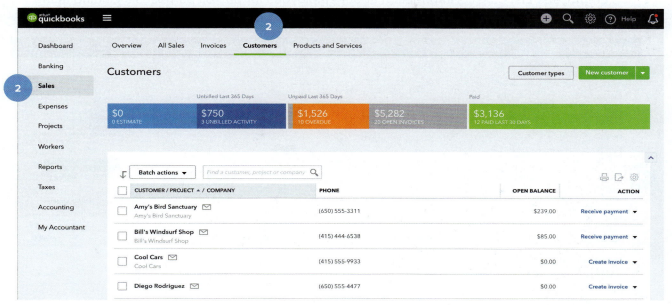

3 Select **Expenses > Vendors** to display the Vendors List.

Vendors List collects information about vendors, such as vendor name, vendor number, and contact information.

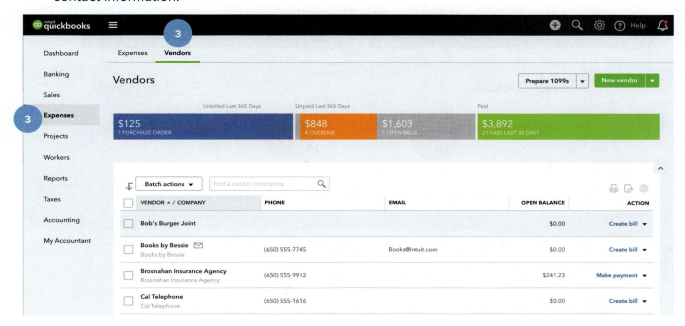

4   Select **Workers > Employees** to view the Employees List.

Employees List collects information about employees for payroll purposes including name, Social Security number, and address.

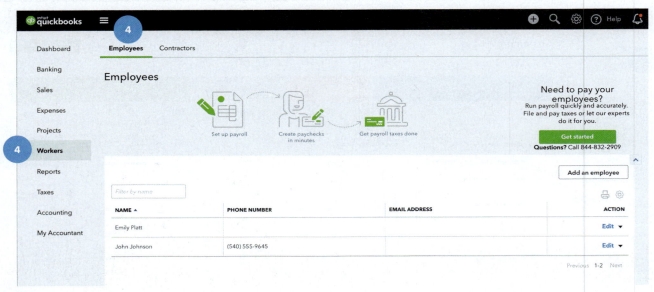

5   Select **Sales > Products and Services** to view the Products and Services List.

Products and Services List collects information about the products and services that a company buys from vendors and/or sells to customers.

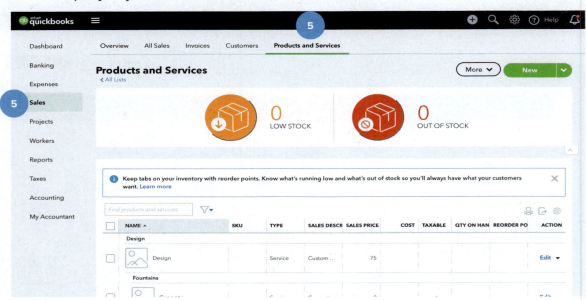

The Sample Company Products and Services List contains information about products and services that Craig's Design and Landscaping Service buys and/or sells.

> **Note:** If items in the Products and Services List appear in a different order than shown here, click the Name tab in the column header to resort the Products and Services List.

All lists, including the Products and Services List, are also found under the Gear icon as shown below.

1 Select **Gear** icon

2 Under the Lists section, select **All Lists**

3 Under the Lists section, select **Product and Services**

Craig's Design and Landscaping Services

Your Company	Lists	Tools	Profile
Account and Settings	All Lists	Import Data	User Profile
Manage Users	Products and Services	Export Data	Feedback
Custom Form Styles	Recurring Transactions	Reconcile	Privacy
Chart of Accounts	Attachments	Budgeting	
QuickBooks Labs		Audit Log	Sign Out
		Order Checks	
		SmartLook	

HOW DO WE UPDATE QBO LISTS?

There are basically two ways that we can update QBO Lists.
1. *Before* entering transactions
2. *While* entering transactions

1.   *Before* entering transactions, we can update lists from the QBO Navigation Bar as follows.

1   Select **Accounting > Chart of Accounts** to display and update the Chart of Accounts. (If necessary, select See your Chart of Accounts.)

2   Select **Sales > Customers** to display and update the Customers List. Select **Sales > Products and Services** to view and update the Product and Services List.

3   Select **Expenses > Vendors** to display and update the Vendors List

4   Select **Workers > Employees** to view and update the Employees List

2. *While* entering transactions, we can update lists on the fly from the screen where we enter the transaction. If a customer, for example, has not been entered in the Customers List, we can add the customer as follows from an onscreen Invoice form.

1 To view an onscreen Invoice form, select the **Create (+)** icon

2 Select **Invoice**

3 On the Invoice form, select **Choose a customer drop-down arrow**

4 To add a new customer, select **+ Add new**

5 In the New Customer window, we would enter the new customer information. In this case, in the Name field, enter **Your Name**.

6 Select **Save** to save the new customer information

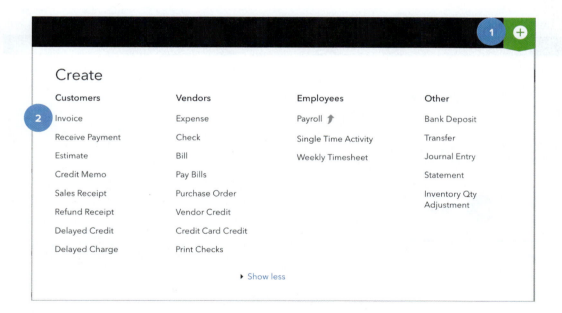

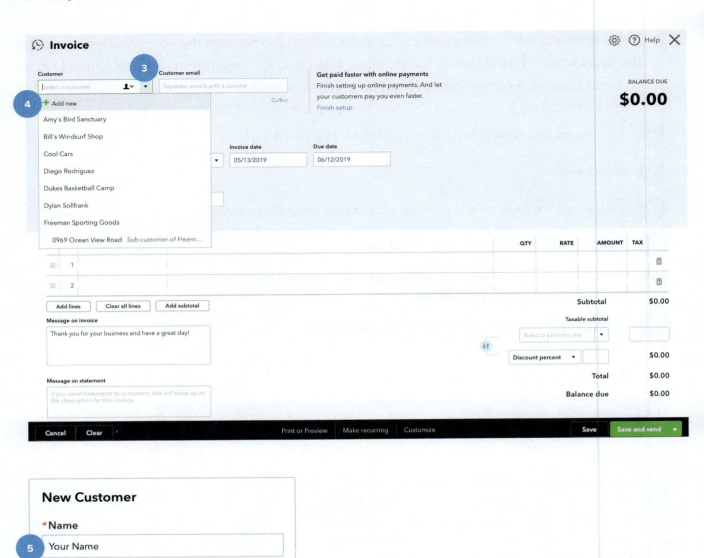

HOW DO WE CREATE A PRODUCTS AND SERVICES LIST?

The Products and Services List contains the listing of all products and services *purchased from vendors*. Also, it lists all the products and services *sold to customers*. Basically, there is one Products and Services List that contains all the items purchased from vendors and/or sold to customers.

To update the Products and Services List:

1 Select **Sales** on the Navigation Bar

2 Select **Product and Services** tab

3 To enter new products or services, select **New**

4 Select **Product/Service Type: Service**

5 Enter **Service Name: Butterfly Garden**

6 Enter SKU or other product/service identification number. In this case, leave **SKU blank**.

7 If available, attach a product/service photo. In this case, leave **Photo blank**.

8 Select **Product/Service Category: Design**

9 Select **I sell this product/service to my customers**

10 Enter **Description: Butterfly Garden Design Services**

11 Enter **Sales Price/Rate: 80.00**

12 Select **Income Account: Design income**. This selection connects the service item with the appropriate account in the Chart of Accounts. When this service is recorded on an invoice, then the amount will be recorded in the Design income account.

13 Select **Sales Tax Category: Nontaxable**

14 Under Purchasing information **uncheck I purchase this product/service from a vendor.**

15 Select **Save and close**

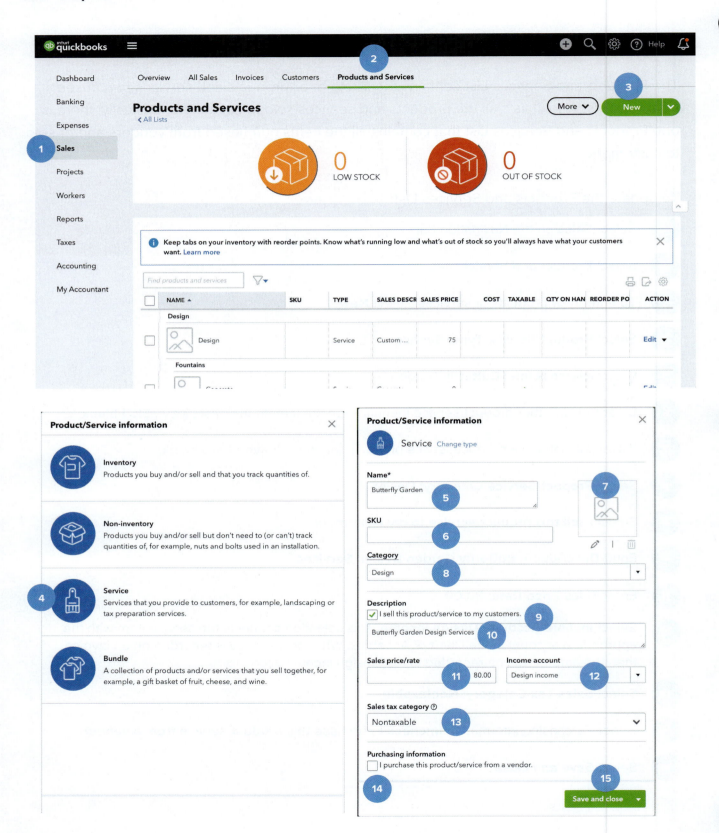

To export the Products and Services List:

1 From the Products and Services screen, select **More** to display the drop-down menu

2 Select **Run Report**

3 After the Product/Service List Report appears, select the **Export** icon to display the drop-down menu

4 Select **Export to PDF**

5 Select **Save as PDF**. The Products and Services List in PDF format should download automatically.

6 Select **Close**

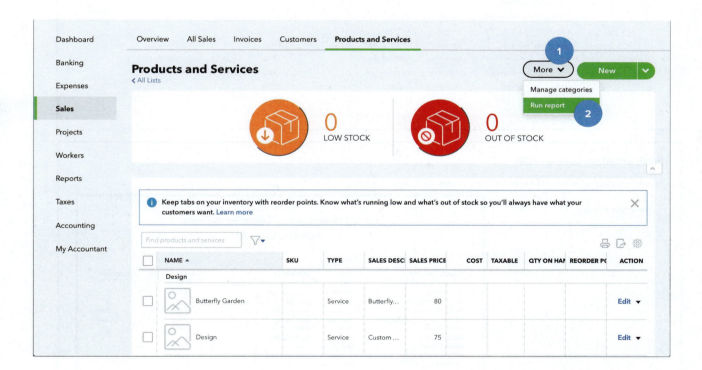

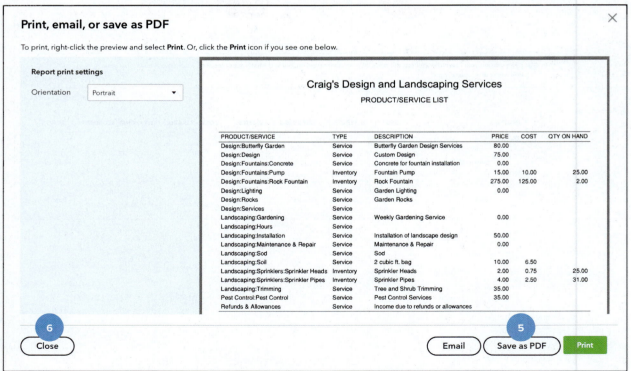

Section 3.4

HOW DO WE ENTER TRANSACTIONS IN QBO?

GIVE AND RECEIVE

Our QBO financial system needs to collect information about transactions.

Transactions are exchanges. A business enters into transactions or exchanges between the business and other parties, such as customers, vendors, and employers. The business gives and receives something in an exchange.

A business can exchange services, products, cash, or a promise to pay later (Accounts Payable). A transaction must have two parts to the exchange: something must be given and something must be received.

For example, when a business sells 1 hour of consulting services to a customer, the two parts to the transaction are:
1. The business gives the customer 1 hour of consulting services.
2. In exchange, the business receives cash (or a promise to pay later) from the customer.

When we record transactions in QBO, we need to record what is exchanged: what is given and what is received.

ONSCREEN FORM OR ONSCREEN JOURNAL

QBO offers two different ways to enter transaction information:
1. Onscreen Journal
2. Onscreen forms

Onscreen Journal. We can make debit and credit entries in an onscreen Journal to record transactions. To view the onscreen Journal:

1 Select **Create (+)** icon

2 Select **Journal Entry**

3 The onscreen Journal has columns for **Account**, **Debit** amount, and **Credit** amount

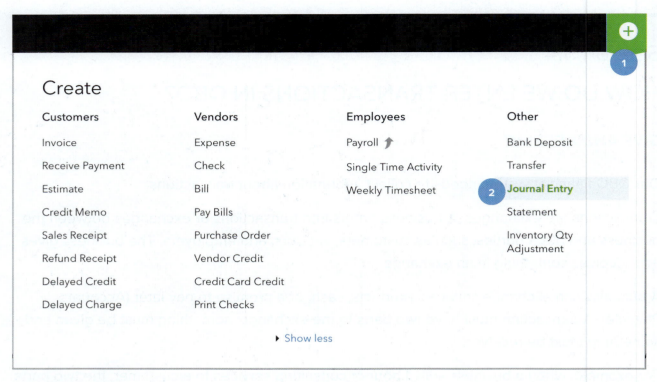

An onscreen Journal is often used to make adjusting entries at year end to bring accounts up to date before preparing financial statements.

Instead of using the onscreen Journal, we can use onscreen forms to enter transaction information in QBO.

Onscreen Forms. We can enter information about transactions using onscreen forms, such as the following Expense form. After using the business credit card to make a charge for a car wash, we would use the QBO onscreen form for recording the expense and the credit card charge.

When we enter information into an onscreen form, behind the screen QBO automatically converts that information into a journal entry with debits and credits. QBO maintains a list of journal entries for all the transactions entered—whether entered using the onscreen Journal or onscreen forms.

For example, to view the journal entry that QBO created behind the screen for the transaction entered and saved using an onscreen form, complete the following steps.

1. To view the onscreen Expense form, from the Navigation Bar, select **Expenses**

2. Select the **Expenses** tab

3. From the Expense Transactions screen, click on an **Expense transaction**, such as a Credit Card Expense like the one shown. Note that the date for the transaction in your Sample Company may differ from the date shown here.

4. The Expense window that appears is an example of an onscreen form. Information about the expense transaction is entered into this onscreen form. Select **More** at the bottom of the Expense window.

5. Select **Transaction journal**

6. Behind the screen, QBO automatically converted the information in the onscreen Expense form into a journal entry with debits and credits

7. Select **Cancel** to leave the Expense window

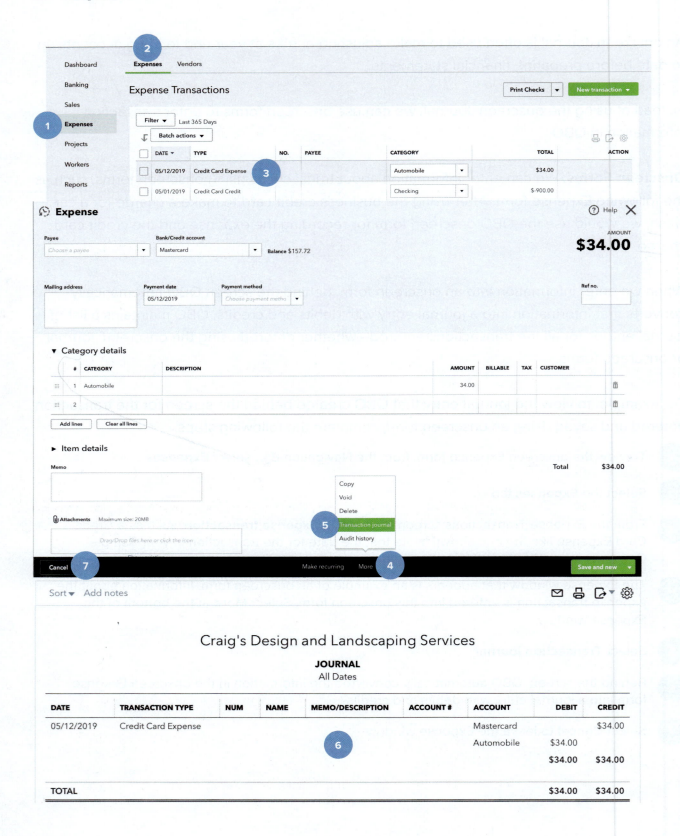

3 WAYS TO ENTER TRANSACTIONS IN QBO

QBO offers us three different options to navigate entering transactions by using the:

1 Navigation Bar

2 Create (+) icon

3 Gear icon > Recurring transactions

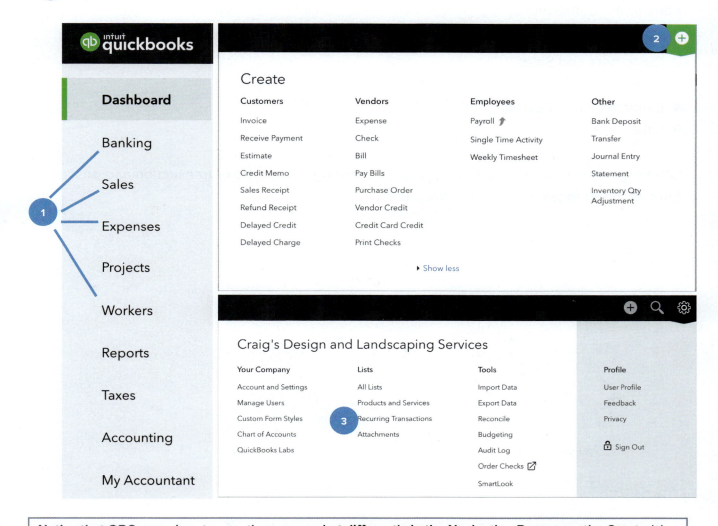

Notice that **QBO organizes transactions** somewhat differently in the Navigation Bar versus the Create (+) icon. In the Navigation Bar, Banking, Sales, and Expenses are the main transactions. In the Create (+) icon, banking transactions, such as bank deposit and transfer are shown under the heading Other. In addition, the Create (+) icon labels the transactions by parties to the transactions such as Customers, Vendors, and Employees.

Section 3.5

WHAT ARE THE DIFFERENT TYPES OF TRANSACTIONS?

A transaction is simply an exchange between our QBO business and another party, such as a customer, vendor, or employee. Although there are many different types of transactions, generally we can group transactions into the following different types based upon the other party to the transaction:

1. Banking and Credit Card
2. Customers and Sales
3. Vendors and Expenses
4. Employees and Payroll
5. Other

QBO organizes how we enter transactions according to the type of transaction and onscreen form we need to use to enter the transaction.

Section 3.6

BANKING AND CREDIT CARD TRANSACTIONS

Transactions that involve depositing or transferring funds with our bank can be entered using the Create (+) icon.

To access Banking transactions through the Create (+) icon:

1 Select **Create (+)** icon

2 Select **Bank Deposit** to record a bank deposit

3 Select **Transfer** to record a transfer between our company's bank accounts

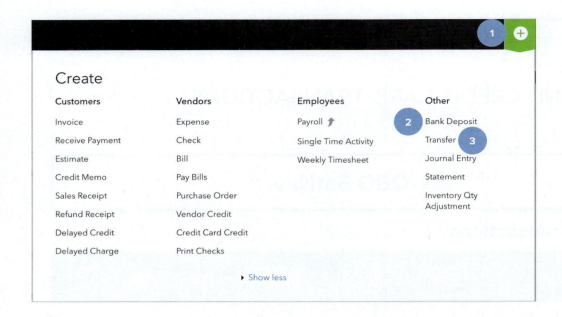

RECORD DEPOSIT

To record a bank deposit:

1   Select **Create (+)** icon

2   Under the Other column, select **Bank Deposit**

3   Select **Checking** account

4   Enter **Date** of deposit

5   The **Select The Payments Included in This Deposit** section lists payments received from customers but not deposited yet. These customer payments listed are undeposited funds that have been recorded as received but not yet deposited in the bank. Since these amounts will be deposited at a later time, leave these customer payments **unchecked**. Customer payments are covered in the next chapter.

6   In the **Add Funds to This Deposit** section, enter **Received From**

7   Select the appropriate **Account**

8   Enter a **Description** of the deposit. The Description field typically displays in reports, but not in the Bank Register.

9 Enter **Payment Method**

10 Enter **Amount**

11 Enter **Memo**. The Memo field typically displays in the Bank Register, making it easier to identify specific transactions in the Register. However, the Memo field does not usually appear in reports.

12 Select **Attachments** to add a file or photo of any accompanying document

13 Normally we would select Save and New or Save and Close, but in this case select **Cancel**

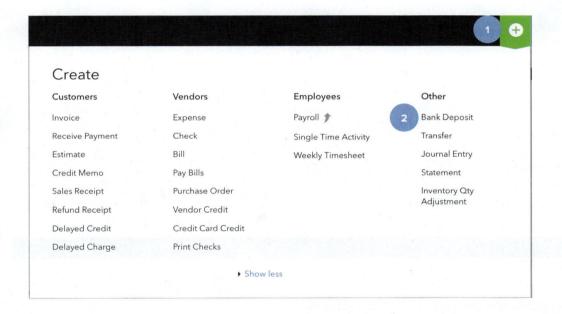

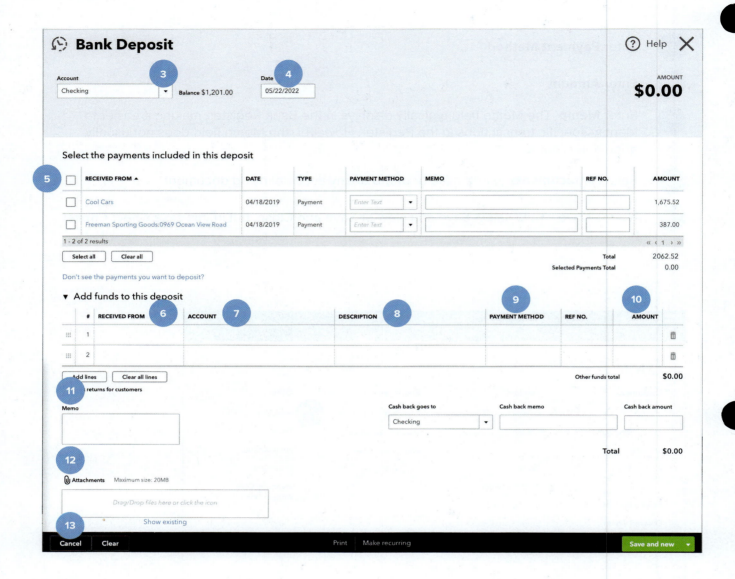

Additional banking activities are covered in Chapter 4.

Section 3.7

CUSTOMERS AND SALES TRANSACTIONS

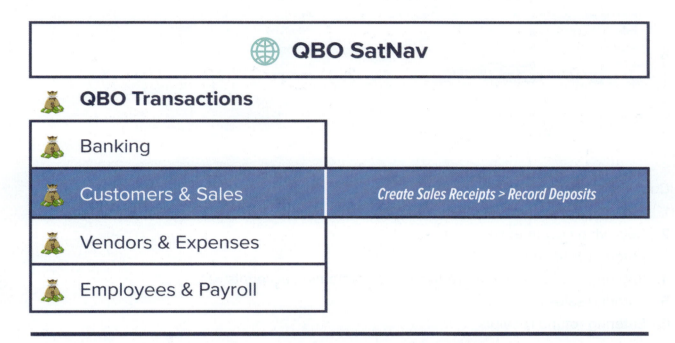

Customers transactions are exchanges between our company and our customers. Typically, these exchanges focus on sales transactions. Customers include parties to whom we sell products or services.

We can enter customers and sales transactions using either the Navigation Bar or the Create (+) icon.

To use the Create (+) icon to enter Customers transactions:

1 Select **Create (+)** icon

2 From the **Customers** column, select the appropriate task

Create

Customers	Vendors	Employees	Other
Invoice	Expense	Payroll	Bank Deposit
Receive Payment	Check	Single Time Activity	Transfer
Estimate	Bill	Weekly Timesheet	Journal Entry
Credit Memo	Pay Bills		Statement
Sales Receipt	Purchase Order		Inventory Qty Adjustment
Refund Receipt	Vendor Credit		
Delayed Credit	Credit Card Credit		
Delayed Charge	Print Checks		

▸ Show less

Customers transactions can include:

1. Entering invoices
2. Receiving customer payments
3. Entering estimates
4. Entering credit memos for reductions to customers accounts
5. Entering sales receipts
6. Entering refund receipts

CREATE INVOICE

An Invoice is one of the QBO forms that can be used to record a customer transaction. Typically, an Invoice is used to record sales when the customer will pay later. The Invoice form collects information about the transaction, such as date of the transaction, the item(s) sold, the sales price of the item(s), and the quantity of the item(s) sold.

To create an Invoice for a sale to a customer:

1. Select **Create (+)** icon

2. Select **Invoice**

3. Select **Customer** from the Customer List drop-down menu: **Cool Cars**

4. Enter **Terms: Net 30**

5   Select **Invoice Date: Current Date**

6   Verify **Due Date**

7   Select Product or Service from the Product/Service List drop-down menu or Add New Product/Service. In this case, select **Product/Service: Design**

8   The **Description** of sales transaction should appear automatically: **Custom Design**

9   Enter **Quantity (QTY): 3**

10   The **Rate** should appear automatically: **75**

11   The **Amount** should appear automatically: **225**

12   Select **Tax** if sale is taxable. In this case, since it is a service being provided, there is no sales tax.

13   Select appropriate **Sales Tax** if applicable

14   If desired, enter **Message on Statement** describing the sale

15   Add **Attachments**, such as source documents associated with the sale

16   If you wished to email the Invoice to the customer, you would select Save and send. In this case, select the **arrow** by Save and send and then select **Save and close**.

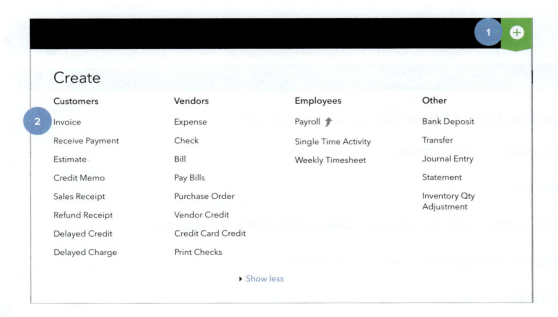

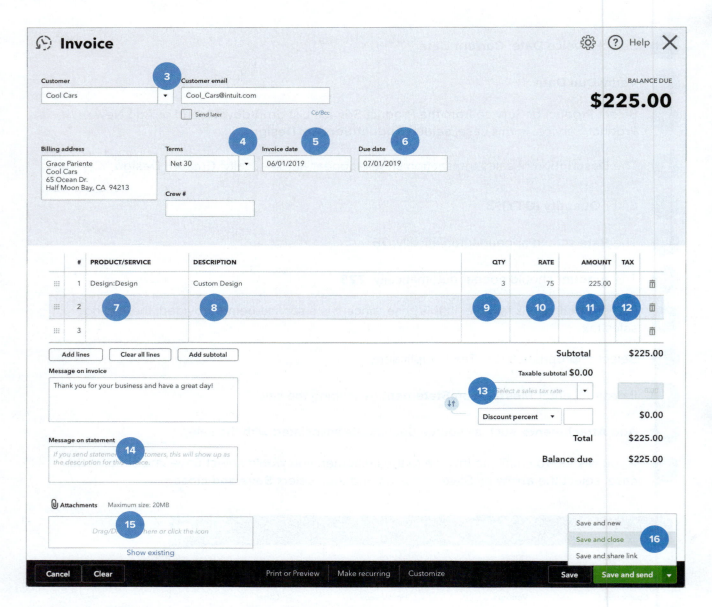

To view the Transaction Journal for the Invoice we just created:

1 From the Navigation Bar, select **Sales**

2 Select **Invoices** tab

3 From the Sales Transactions List, select the **Cool Cars Invoice** just entered

4 From the bottom of the Cool Cars Invoice, select **More**

5 Select **Transaction Journal**

6 In the journal entry recorded behind the screen for the Invoice, notice the **Debit** to Accounts Receivable for $225.00

7 In the journal entry recorded behind the screen for the Invoice, notice the **Credit** to Design Income for $225.00

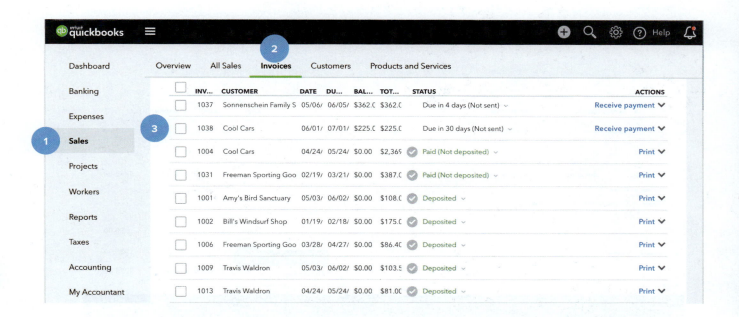

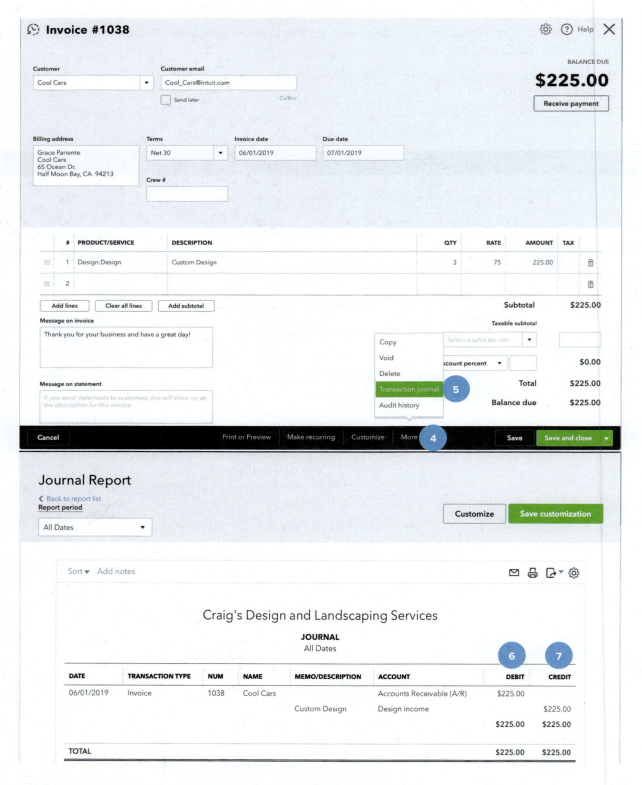

Additional customer transactions are covered in Chapter 5.

Section 3.8

VENDORS AND EXPENSES TRANSACTIONS

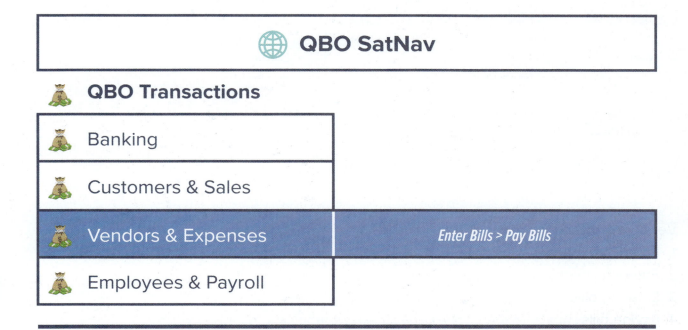

Vendors transactions are exchanges between our company and our vendors. Typically, these exchanges focus on expense transactions. Vendors include suppliers who sell products and professionals who provide services to our company.

We can enter vendors and expenses transactions using either the Navigation Bar or the Create (+) icon. To use the Create (+) icon to enter Vendors transactions:

1   Select **Create (+)** icon

2   From the **Vendors** column, select the appropriate task

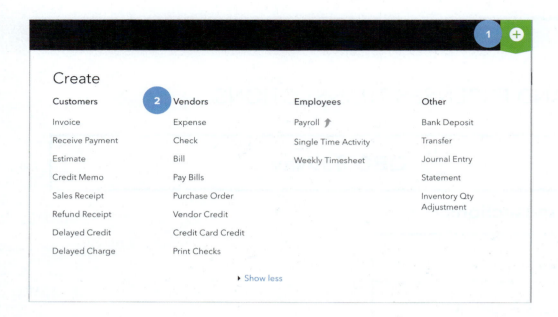

Vendors transactions can include:

1. Entering expenses
2. Entering checks
3. Entering bills
4. Paying bills
5. Entering purchase orders
6. Entering vendor credits
7. Entering credit card credits

CREATE EXPENSE

The Expense form is one of the QBO forms that can be used to record a vendor transaction. If our payment is *made at the same time* we make a purchase, then we can record the purchase using the Expense form. Our payment may consist of cash, check, or credit card. The Expense form collects detailed information about the vendor transaction.

To create an Expense to record a vendor transaction:

1 Select **Create (+)** icon

2 Select **Expense** to record the vendor transaction when we make payment at the same time the expense is incurred and we pay with cash, check, or credit card

3 From the Payee drop-down menu, select **Vendor: Lee Advertising**. If a message appears, asking if you want to autofill the form using prior information, select Yes.

4 Using the drop-down menu, select the **Payment Account: Mastercard**

5 Enter **Payment Date: Current Date**

6 From the Payment Method drop-down menu listing Cash, Check, or various Credit Cards, select **Payment Method: MasterCard**

7 If Payment Method is Check, enter the Check No. in **Reference No.**

8 In the Category Details section, select appropriate Category from the drop-down menu. The drop-down Category list contains accounts that can be used to record the expense. If it does not appear automatically, select **Category: Advertising**.

9 Enter **Description: Advertising Services**

10 Enter **Amount** of the expense: **100.00**

11 Select Billable if the expense is billable to a specific customer. In this case since Advertising does not relate to a specific customer, leave **Billable unchecked**.

12 Select Tax if purchase is taxable. Leave **Tax unchecked**.

13 If billable, select appropriate Customer associated with the expense. Leave **Customer field blank**.

14 An expense transaction can be entered using **Item details** instead of Account details, which is covered in Chapter 7

15 If additional detail is needed, enter **Memo** describing the transaction

16 Add **Attachments**, such as source documents associated with the transaction

17 Select **Save**. Leave the Expense window open.

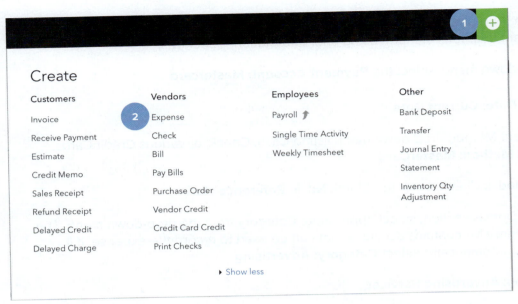

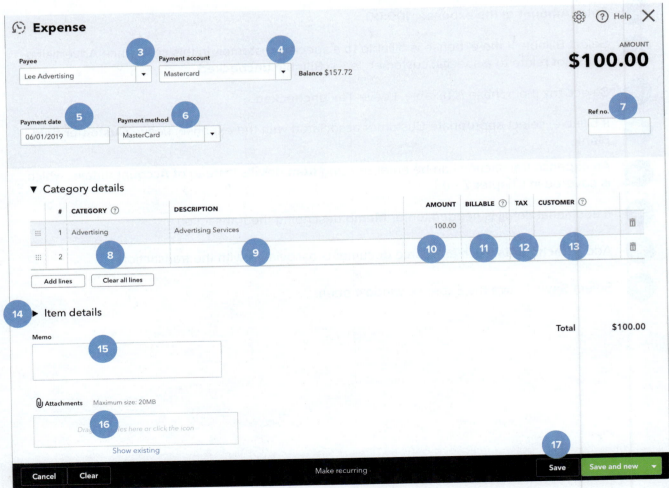

To view the Transaction Journal for the Expense we just created:

1 From the Expense window just saved, select **More**

2 Select **Transaction Journal**

3 In the journal entry recorded behind the screen for the Expense, notice the **Debit** to Advertising (Expense) for $100.00. Also notice that QBO does not always list the Debits before the Credits in a Journal Entry.

4 In the journal entry recorded behind the screen for the Expense, notice the **Credit** to the Mastercard (Liability) account for $100.00

DATE	TRANSACTION TYPE	NUM	NAME	MEMO/DESCRIPTION	ACCOUNT	DEBIT	CREDIT
06/01/2019	Expense		Lee Advertising		Mastercard		$100.00
				Advertising Services	Advertising	$100.00	
						$100.00	$100.00
TOTAL						**$100.00**	**$100.00**

> **The Transaction Journal for Expenses** can also be accessed by selecting Expenses on the Navigation Bar > Expenses tab. Then from the Expense Transactions List, select the specific expense transaction to view the Expense window. From the bottom of the Expense window, select More > Transaction Journal.

Additional vendor transactions are covered in Chapters 6 and 7.

Section 3.9

EMPLOYEES AND PAYROLL TRANSACTIONS

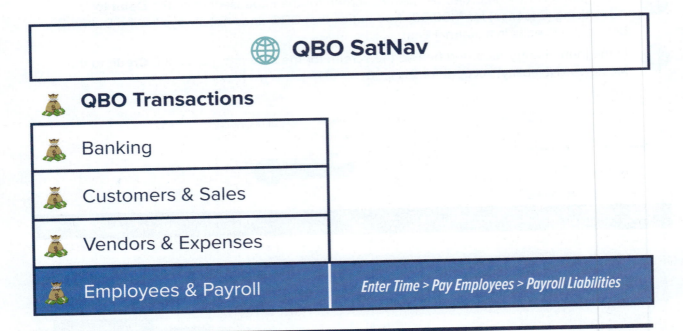

Employee transactions are exchanges between our company and our employees. Typically, these exchanges focus on payroll transactions, including tracking employee time and paying employees for their services to the company.

We can enter employees and payroll transactions using either the Navigation Bar or the Create (+) icon.

To use the Create (+) icon to access Employees transactions:

1 Select **Create (+)** icon

2 From the **Employees** column, select the appropriate task

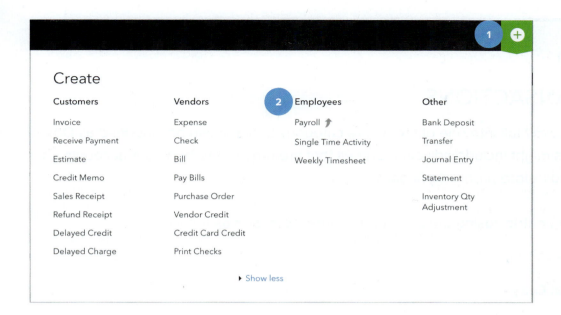

Notice that QBO can be used to track employee time using Single Time Activity or Weekly Timesheet.

Payroll and employees transactions are covered in Chapter 8.

Section 3.10

OTHER TRANSACTIONS

If a transaction doesn't fall into one of the above categories, then it can be classified as Other. Other transactions might include adjusting entries that are required to bring our accounts up to date at year end before preparing financial reports.

We make adjusting entries using the onscreen Journal accessed as follows.

1 Select **Create (+)** icon

2 Select **Journal Entry**

3 In the Journal, we would record the transaction by entering **Accounts**, **Debit** amounts, and **Credit** amounts

4 Select **Cancel** to close the Journal screen

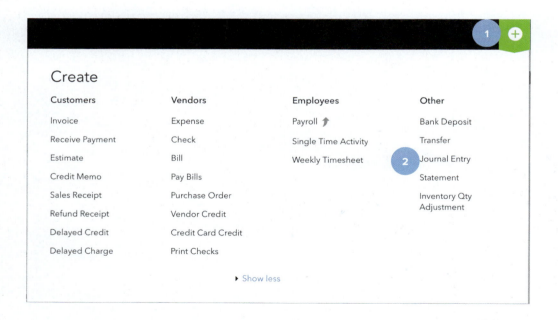

Create			
Customers	**Vendors**	**Employees**	**Other**
Invoice	Expense	Payroll ⚡	Bank Deposit
Receive Payment	Check	Single Time Activity	Transfer
Estimate	Bill	Weekly Timesheet	Journal Entry
Credit Memo	Pay Bills		Statement
Sales Receipt	Purchase Order		Inventory Qty Adjustment
Refund Receipt	Vendor Credit		
Delayed Credit	Credit Card Credit		
Delayed Charge	Print Checks		

▸ Show less

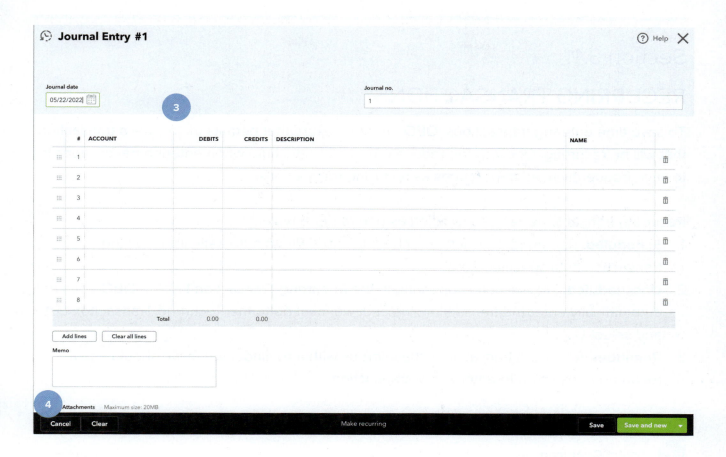

Section 3.11

RECURRING TRANSACTIONS

To save time entering transactions, QBO offers a feature that permits us to save a transaction that will be recurring. One way we reduce errors and save time when entering transactions is to save frequently used transactions as recurring transactions.

Recurring transactions can be classified as one of three types:

1. **Scheduled.** Recurring transactions scheduled for QBO to automatically enter the transaction on a specified date.
2. **Unscheduled.** Transactions appearing in the Recurring Transaction List but QBO does not automatically enter the transaction. Instead, we must go to the Recurring Transaction List and select Use.
3. **Reminder.** Recurring transactions that alert us with a reminder when we should use a recurring transaction to enter a new transaction.

To access the Recurring Transactions List, complete the following steps.

1 Select **Gear** icon

2 Select **Recurring Transactions**

3 If you need to add a new recurring transaction, you would select **New**

4 If you need to change a recurring transaction previously entered, select **Edit**

5 From the drop-down list for the Telephone Bill, select **Use** to use the recurring transaction to enter a new transaction

6 From the Bill window, update as needed. In this case, update the **Amount** to **$81.00**.

7 Select **Save and close**. (If necessary, select the **arrow** beside the Save and new button, then select Save and close.)

8 This completes the chapter activities. **Close** the QBO Sample Company web browser window to reset the Sample Company before proceeding to the exercises at the end of this chapter.

Craig's Design and Landscaping Services

Your Company	Lists	Tools	Profile
Account and Settings	All Lists	Import Data	User Profile
Manage Users	Products and Services	Export Data	Feedback
Custom Form Styles	Recurring Transactions	Reconcile	Privacy
Chart of Accounts	Attachments	Budgeting	
QuickBooks Labs		Audit Log	🔒 Sign Out
		Order Checks 🗗	
		SmartLook	

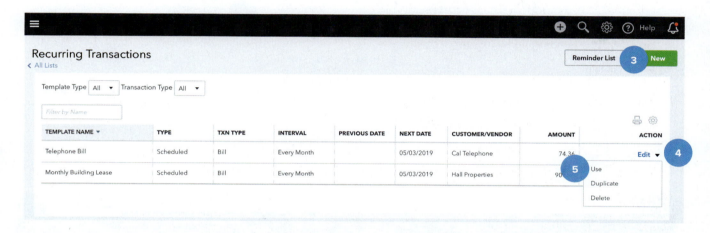

Recurring Transactions
‹ All Lists

Reminder List   New

Template Type [All ▼]   Transaction Type [All ▼]

Filter by Name

TEMPLATE NAME ▾	TYPE	TXN TYPE	INTERVAL	PREVIOUS DATE	NEXT DATE	CUSTOMER/VENDOR	AMOUNT	ACTION
Telephone Bill	Scheduled	Bill	Every Month		05/03/2019	Cal Telephone	74.36	Edit ▾
Monthly Building Lease	Scheduled	Bill	Every Month		05/03/2019	Hall Properties	90_	

Use
Duplicate
Delete

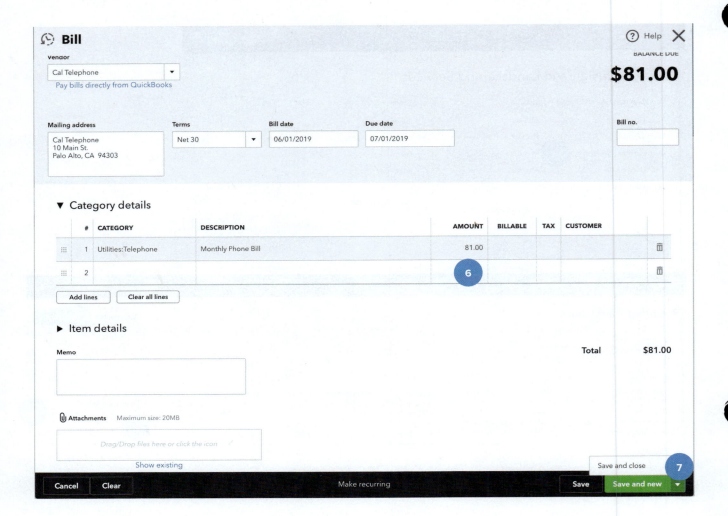

Section 3.12

ACCOUNTING ESSENTIALS
Double-Entry Accounting

Accounting Essentials summarize important foundational accounting knowledge you may find useful when using QBO

What is double-entry accounting?

- Double-entry accounting is used with a journal to record what is exchanged in a transaction:

  1. The amount received, such as equipment purchased, is recorded with a debit
  2. The amount given, such as cash or a promise to pay later, is recorded with a credit

- Each journal entry must balance: debits must equal credits. This is true whether it is a manual accounting system or a cloud-based accounting system, such as QBO.

In double-entry accounting, how do we know if a debit is an increase or a decrease to an account? How do we know if a credit is an increase or a decrease to an account?

- Whether a debit or credit increases or decreases an account depends upon the type of account.

Account Type	Debit	Credit
Assets	Increase	Decrease
Liabilities	Decrease	Increase
Equity	Decrease	Increase
Revenues (Income)	Decrease	Increase
Expenses	Increase	Decrease

What are the different types of accounts and the effect of debits and credits on the accounts?

- Five different types of accounts are listed below along with the normal balance of the account that increases the account balance.

Account Type	Debit/Credit	Effect on Balance
Asset	Debit	Increase
Liabilities	Credit	Increase
Equity	Credit	Increase
Revenues (Income)	Credit	Increase
Expenses	Debit	Increase

- For example, if the transaction is the owner invests $100,000 in the business, the journal entry with debits and credits would be as follows.

Account	Account Type	Debit/Credit	Effect on Balance	Amount
Checking	Asset	Debit	Increase	$100,000
Capital Stock	Equity	Credit	Increase	$100,000

Practice Quiz 3

Q3.1

In QuickBooks Online, information about transactions can be entered in onscreen forms, such as:

a. Check

b. Invoice

c. Purchase Order

d. All of the above

Q3.2

Which of the following two items are displayed in the QBO Navigation Bar:

a. Sales

b. Adjusting Entries

c. Banking

d. Products and Services

Q3.3

Which of the following two transactions are considered Customers and Sales transactions:

a. Invoice

b. Receive Payment

c. Pay Bills

d. Check

Q3.4

Which of the following two transactions are considered Vendors and Expenses transactions:

a. Invoice

b. Receive Payment

c. Pay Bills

d. Check

Q3.5

To enter transactions in QBO:

a. From the Navigation Bar, select Reports

b. From the Create (+) icon, select transaction to enter

c. From the Gear icon, select transaction to enter

d. From the Navigation Bar, select Home

Q3.6

QBO Lists include:

a. Chart of Accounts

b. Customers List

c. Vendors List

d. Employees List

e. All of the above are QBO Lists

Q3.7

The Products and Services List can be accessed from the:

a. Navigation Bar > Expenses

b. Gear icon

c. Create (+) icon

d. None of the above

Q3.8

Match the following transactions with the type of transaction.

Transaction Types

1. **Banking**
2. **Customers and Sales**
3. **Vendors and Expenses**
4. **Employees and Payroll**

a. Estimate

b. Deposit

c. Print Checks

d. Single-Time Activity

Q3.9

Two ways to update QBO Lists are:

a. Before entering transactions

b. While entering transactions

c. After entering transactions

Q3.10

Two different ways to enter transaction information into QBO are:

a. Onscreen forms

b. Chart of Accounts

c. Onscreen Journal

d. QBO Lists

Q3.11

Which of the following QBO features can be used to save a transaction that will be re-used in the future?

a. Saved transactions

b. Create (+) icon

c. Recurring transactions

d. None of the above

Q3.12

Access the Recurring Transactions List from the:

a. Navigation Bar

b. Gear icon

c. Create (+) icon

d. None of the above

Q3.13

Recurring transactions can be classified as which of the following types?

a. Scheduled

b. Unscheduled

c. Reminder

d. All of the above

Q3.14

Which of the following two are correct when double-entry accounting journal entries are used to record what is exchanged in a transaction?

a. The amount received is recorded with a credit

b. The amount received is recorded with a debit

c. The amount given is recorded with a debit

d. The amount given is recorded with a credit

Exercises 3

> We use the QBO Sample Company, Craig's Design and Landscaping Services, for practice throughout the exercises. The Sample Company will reset each time it is reopened. So make certain to allow enough time to complete exercise before closing the Sample Company. Otherwise, you will lose the work you have entered.

> ⚠️ Since the Sample Company resets each time it is reopened, be certain to close any web browser windows displaying the QBO Sample Company before starting these exercises. Closing the browser window and starting with a new browser window for the QBO Sample Company resets the data before starting the exercises.

To access the QBO Sample Company, complete the following steps.

1 After closing any open web browser windows displaying the QBO Sample Company, open a new web browser window. (Note: using a new web browser window to access the QBO Sample Company, resets the Sample Company to its original settings for the exercises.)

2 Go to https://qbo.intuit.com/redir/testdrive

3 Follow onscreen instructions for security verification

Craig's Design and Landscaping Services should appear on your screen.

E3.1 Transaction Types

What is the Transaction Type for the following transactions?

Transaction Types

- **Banking**
- **Customers and Sales**
- **Vendors and Expenses**
- **Employees and Payroll**

Transaction	Transaction Type
1. Transfers	
2. Weekly Timesheet	
3. Credit Card Credit	
4. Purchase Order	
5. Estimate	
6. Bill	
7. Invoice	
8. Pay Bills	
9. Receive Payment	
10. Deposit	
11. Sales Receipt	
12. Credit Memo	

E3.2 QBO Lists

Which QBO List would be used with the following transactions?

QBO Lists

- **Customers List**
- **Vendors List**
- **Employees List**
- **Recurring Transactions List**

Transaction	QBO List
1. Weekly Payroll	
2. Expense	
3. Credit Card Credit	
4. Invoice	
5. Estimate	
6. Bill	
7. Purchase Order	
8. Pay Bills	
9. Receive Payment	
10. Saved Deposit Transaction	
11. Sales Receipt	
12. Check	

E3.3 Invoice and Transaction Journal

Using the QBO Sample Company, Craig's Design and Landscaping Services, complete the following.

1. Complete an Invoice.
    a. Select **Create (+) icon > Invoice**
    b. Select **Customer: Bill's Windsurf Shop**
    c. Select **Product/Service: Design**
    d. Select **QTY: 2**
    e. Select **Rate: 75.00**
    f. The balance due for the invoice is $_____
    g. Select **Save and close**

2. View the Transaction Journal for the Invoice.
    a. From the Navigation Bar, select **Sales**
    b. From the Sales Transactions List, select the **Bill's Windsurf Shop Invoice** just entered
    c. From the bottom of the Bill's Windsurf Shop Invoice, select **More > Transaction Journal**
    d. What are the Account and Amount Debited?
    e. What are the Account and Amount Credited?

E3.4 Expense and Transaction Journal

Using the QBO Sample Company, Craig's Design and Landscaping Services, complete the following.

1. Complete an Expense.
    a. Select **Create (+) icon > Expense**
    b. Select **Payee: Books by Bessie**
    c. Select **Category: Office Expenses**
    d. Select **Payment Account: Visa**
    e. Select **Payment Method: Visa**
    f. Enter **Amount: 50.00**
    g. What is the Total Amount for the Expense?
    h. Select **Save and close**

2. View the Transaction Journal for the Expense.
    a. From the Navigation Bar, select **Expenses**
    b. From the Expense Transactions List, select the **Books by Bessie Expense** just entered
    c. From the bottom of the Books by Bessie Expense, select **More > Transaction Journal**
    d. What are the Account and Amount Debited?
    e. What are the Account and Amount Credited?

E3.5 Check and Transaction Journal

Using QBO Sample Company, Craig's Design and Landscaping Services, complete the following.

1. Complete a Check.
   a. Select **Create (+) icon > Check**
   b. Select **Payee: Ellis Equipment Rental**
   c. Select **Bank Account: Checking**
   d. Select **Category: Rent or Lease**
   e. Enter **Amount: 200.00**
   f. What is the Total for the Check?
   g. Select **Save and close**

2. View the Transaction Journal for the Check.
   a. From the Navigation Bar, select **Expenses**
   b. From the Expense Transactions List, select the **Ellis Equipment Rental Check** just entered
   c. From the bottom of the Ellis Equipment Rental Check, select **More > Transaction Journal**
   d. What are the Account and Amount Debited?
   e. What are the Account and Amount Credited?

E3.6 Recurring Transactions

Using QBO Sample Company, Craig's Design and Landscaping Services, complete the following.

1. Edit a Recurring Transaction.
   a. Select **Gear icon > Recurring Transactions**
   b. From the Recurring Transaction List, select **Telephone Bill > Edit**
   c. What is the amount for the Recurring Bill?
   d. Update the amount to **$81.00**
   e. Select **Save Template**

2. Use a Recurring Transaction.
   a. From the Recurring Transaction List, select **Monthly Building Lease Edit drop-down arrow > Use**
   b. Select **Save**
   c. From the bottom of the Hall Properties Building Lease Bill, select **More > Transaction Journal**
   d. What are the Account and Amount Debited?
   e. What are the Account and Amount Credited?

E3.7 Debits and Credits

Complete the following statements using:

- **Debits**
- **Credits**

1. Assets are increased by _____

2. Liabilities are increased by _____

3. Equity is increased by _____

4. Revenue (Income) is increased by _____

5. Expenses are increased by _____

6. Assets are decreased by _____

7. Liabilities are decreased by _____

8. Equity is decreased by _____

9. Revenue (Income) is decreased by _____

10. Expenses are decreased by _____

E3.8 Debits and Credits

The following accounts are from Craig's Design and Landscaping Services Chart of Accounts.

For each account indicate:
- If the account is increased by a:
  - **Debit**
  - **Credit**
- Type of account as:
  - **Asset**
  - **Liability**
  - **Equity**
  - **Revenue (Income)**
  - **Expense**

Account	Debit/Credit	Account Type
1. Design Income		
2. Savings		
3. Accounts Receivable (A/R)		
4. Rent or Lease		
5. Prepaid Expenses		
6. Notes Payable		
7. Inventory Asset		
8. Opening Balance Equity		
9. Utilities		
10. Undeposited Funds		
11. Accounts Payable (A/P)		
12. MasterCard		
13. Visa		
14. Loan Payable		
15. Sales of Product Income		
16. Legal and Professional Fees		
17. Advertising		
18. Meals and Entertainment		
19. Retained Earnings		
20. Checking		
21. Landscaping Services		
22. Pest Control Services		
23. Cost of Goods Sold		
24. Automobile: Fuel		
25. Bank Charges		
26. Interest Earned		

Project 3.1

Mookie the Beagle™ Concierge

> **Project 3.1 is a continuation of Project 2.1. You will use the QBO Company you created for Project 1.1 and updated in Project 2.1. Keep in mind the QBO Company for Project 3.1 does not reset and carries your data forward, including any errors. So it is important to check and crosscheck your work to verify it is correct before clicking the Save button.**

BACKSTORY

Mookie The Beagle™ Concierge provides convenient, high-quality pet care. Cy, the founder of Mookie The Beagle Concierge, asks you to assist in using QBO to save time recording transactions for the business.

Complete the following for Mookie The Beagle Concierge.

QBO SATNAV

Project 3.1 focuses on QBO Transactions, including Banking, Sales, and Expenses transactions, as shown in the following QBO SatNav.

 QBO SatNav

⚙ **QBO Settings**

⚙ Company Settings
⚙ Chart of Accounts

 QBO Transactions

 Banking	*Record Deposits	Write Checks*
Customers & Sales	*Create Sales Receipts > Record Deposits*
Vendors & Expenses	*Enter Bills > Pay Bills*
 Employees & Payroll	

📊 **QBO Reports**

📊 Reports

HOW TO LOG INTO QBO

To log into QBO, complete the following steps.

1 Using a web browser go to qbo.intuit.com

2 Enter **User ID** (the email address you used to set up your QBO Account)

3 Enter **Password** (the password you used to set up your QBO Account)

4 Select **Sign in**

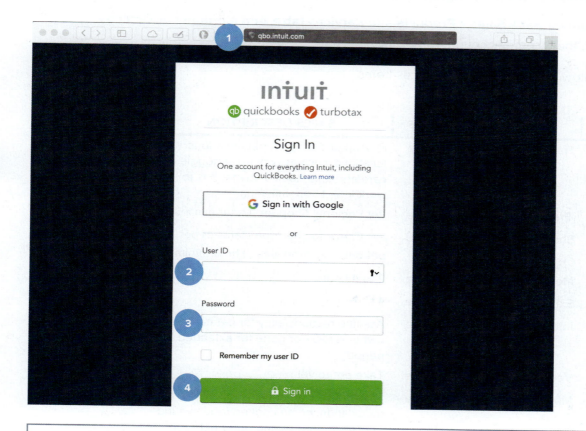

If you are <u>not</u> using a public or shared computer, to speed up login, you can save your login to your desktop and select Remember Me. If you are using a public computer or shared computer, do not save to the desktop and unselect Remember Me.

The new QBO Company we created in Project 1 will carry all work forward into future chapters. So it is important to check and crosscheck your work to verify it is correct before clicking the Save button. Any uncorrected errors will be carried forward in your QBO Company for text projects.

P3.1.1 QBO Lists

Since Mookie The Beagle Concierge doesn't have a complete list of customers and vendors to enter into a Customers List and Vendors List before we begin entering transactions, we will enter customer and vendor information as we enter transactions.

We can create a QBO Products and Services List with the following information Cy summarized about the services Mookie The Beagle Concierge will be providing customers. None of the services are subject to sales tax.

To enter the services into the Products and Services List:

1. Select **Navigation Bar > Sales > Products and Services tab > Add a product or service > Service**. Use the Income account: **4002 Sales**.

2. Enter the following Products and Services Items.

CATEGORY	NAME	TYPE	SALES DESCRIPTION	SALES PRICE
Pet Care	Transport	Service	Pick up and drop off pet at various locations, such as pick up at doggie day care and take home if owner has to work late, 1 hour minimum	$60
Pet Care	Errand	Service	Pet Personal Shopper, 1 hour minimum	$40
Pet Care	Short Visit	Service	Pet Check to check on status of pet, let pet out, and short walk, 1 hour minimum	$40
Pet Care	Medium Visit	Service	2 to 4 hours	$30
Pet Care	Extended Visit	Service	4 to 8 hours	$40
Pet Care	Intensive	Service	Assume responsibility for pet care while owner is OOT or gone for extended period	$50
Pet Wellness	Vet Visit	Service	Take pet to vet	$120
Pet Wellness	Medium Wellness	Service	1 to 4 hours with administration of medication, home cooked food, wound dressing changes and other pet healthcare services	$60
Pet Wellness	Extended Wellness	Service	4 to 8 hours providing pet healthcare services	$50
Pet Wellness	Intensive Wellness	Service	Assume responsibility for pet healthcare while owner is OOT or intensive healthcare responsibilities	$70

> **Note:** After we begin adding products and services to the Products and Services List, QBO may automatically add some additional accounts to our Chart of Accounts. Examples of such accounts include: Inventory Asset, Sales of Product Income, and Purchases. We can easily identify the added accounts since they do not display account numbers. If desired, account numbers can be entered for these added accounts. For more information about how to enter account numbers, see Chapter 2.

3. Export the Products and Services List to PDF. From the Products and Services screen, select **More > Run Report > Export icon > Export to PDF**.

P3.1.2 Deposit Transaction

1. Complete a Deposit.
   a. Select **Create (+) icon > Bank Deposit**
   b. Select **Account: Checking**
   c. Select **Payment Date: 01/01/2022**
   d. In the Add Funds to This Deposit section, select **Account: Owner's Investment**
   e. Select **Payment Method: Check**
   f. Enter **Ref No.: 5001**
   g. Enter **Amount: 10000.00**
   h. What type of account is Owner's Investment?
   i. Select **Save and close**

2. View the Transaction Journal for the Deposit.
   a. From the Navigation Bar, select **Accounting**
   b. From the Chart of Accounts, select **Checking > View Register > Deposit > Edit**
   c. From the bottom of the screen, select **More > Transaction Journal**
   d. What are the Account and Amount Debited?
   e. What are the Account and Amount Credited?

To launch Mookie The Beagle Concierge, Cy invests $10,000 of his personal savings. Record the transactions as follows.

P3.1.3 Expense Transaction Check

Mookie The Beagle Concierge hired Carole Design Media to promote Mookie The Beagle Concierge's launch using social media marketing. Mookie The Beagle Concierge paid the bill in full when received. The bill was for 20 hours of service at $100 per hour.

Enter the Expense Transaction as follows.

1. Create an Expense.
    a. Select **Create (+) icon > Expense**
    b. Add **Payee: +Add New > Carole Design Media > Vendor Type > Save**
    c. Select **Payment Date: 01/05/2022**
    d. Select **Payment Account: Checking**
    e. Select **Payment Method: Check**
    f. Enter **Category: Advertising & Marketing**
    g. Enter **Amount** for **20 hours @ $100.00 per hour**
    h. What is the Total Amount paid to Carole Design Media?
    i. Select **Save**. Leave the Expense window open.

2. View the Transaction Journal for the Expense.
    a. From the bottom of the Carole Design Media Expense window, select **More > Transaction Journal**
    b. What are the Account and Amount Debited?
    c. What are the Account and Amount Credited?

P3.1.4 Expense Transaction Credit Card

Mookie The Beagle Concierge obtained liability insurance from Cyrus Insurance at a cost of $600 for 3 months of insurance coverage. The liability insurance protects Mookie The Beagle Concierge from the risk of legal liability for injury or damages of its business operations in providing pet care and pet wellness services.

1. Create an Expense.
    a. Select **Create (+) icon > Expense**
    b. Add **Payee: Cyrus Insurance**
    c. Select **Payment Date: 01/07/2022**
    d. Select **Payment Account: VISA Credit Card**
    e. Select **Payment Method: Credit Card**
    f. Select **Category: Insurance: Liability Insurance Expense**
    g. Enter **Amount: 600.00**
    h. What is the Total Amount paid to Cyrus Insurance?
    i. Select **Save**. Leave the Expense window open.

2. View the Transaction Journal for the Expense.
    a. From the bottom of the Cyrus Insurance Expense, select **More > Transaction Journal**
    b. What are the Account and Amount Debited?
    c. What are the Account and Amount Credited?

P3.1.5 Invoice Transaction

Mookie The Beagle Concierge negotiated an agreement with a local university veterinary program for student interns to work as contractors to provide Mookie The Beagle Concierge services as needed.

Mookie The Beagle Concierge's first customer, Mimi, used the Mookie The Beagle Concierge app to schedule care for her pet French Bulldog puppy, Bebe, whose paw was injured at doggie day care. Mimi was unable to leave work so she was relieved to be able to use the Mookie The Beagle Concierge app to schedule pet wellness services.

- Pet Care: Transport 1 hour (pickup at doggie day care)
- Pet Wellness: Vet Visit 2 hours
- Pet Wellness: Intensive 6 hours
- Pet Care: Errand 1 hour to obtain pet supplies

In order to avoid confusion with customer names, the customer name will be the pet name followed by the pet parent name.

1. Complete an Invoice.
    a. Select **Create (+) icon > Invoice**
    b. Add New **Customer: Bebe Mimi**
    c. Select **Invoice Date: 01/02/2022**
    d. Select **Product/Service: Pet Care: Transport**
    e. Select **QTY: 1**
    f. **Rate** and **Amount** fields should autofill
    g. Select **Product/Service: Pet Wellness: Vet Visit**
    h. Select **QTY: 2**
    i. **Rate** and **Amount** fields should autofill
    j. Select **Product/Service: Pet Wellness: Intensive Wellness**
    k. Select **QTY: 6**
    l. **Rate** and **Amount** fields should autofill
    m. Select **Product/Service: Pet Care: Errand**
    n. Select **QTY: 1**
    o. **Rate** and **Amount** fields should autofill
    p. What is the Balance Due for the Invoice?
    q. Select **Save**. Leave the Invoice window open.

2. View the Transaction Journal for the Invoice.
    a. From the bottom of the Bebe Invoice, select **More > Transaction Journal**
    b. What are the Account and Amount Debited?
    c. What are the Accounts and Amounts Credited?

P3.1.6 Invoice Transaction

Using the Mookie The Beagle Concierge app, Graziella requests pet care services for Mario, her pet Italian Greyhound, during an unexpected 2-day out of town business trip.

Services provided by Mookie The Beagle Concierge were as follows.

- Pet Care: Intensive (48 hours total)

1. Complete an Invoice.
    a. Select **Create (+) icon > Invoice**
    b. Add New **Customer: Mario Graziella**
    c. Select **Invoice Date: 01/04/2022**
    d. Select **Product/Service: Pet Care: Intensive**
    e. Select **QTY: 48**
    f. **Rate** and **Amount** fields should autofill
    g. What is the Balance Due for the Invoice?
    h. Select **Save**. Leave the Invoice window open.

2. View the Transaction Journal for the Invoice.
    a. From the bottom of the Mario Invoice, select **More > Transaction Journal**
    b. What are the Account and Amount Debited?
    c. What are the Account and Amount Credited?

P3.1.7 Recurring Transactions

Mookie The Beagle Concierge will have recurring Contractor Expense to pay the vet program students who provide the pet care services. Cy asks us to save the Contractor Expense as a QBO Recurring Transaction for ease of future use.

Mary Dolan was the contractor who provided the pet care services for both Bebe and Mario. Mookie The Beagle Concierge will pay Mary Dolan $20 per hour for those services.

1. Create a Recurring Transaction.
    a. Select **Gear icon > Recurring Transactions > New**
    b. Select **Transaction Type: Expense > OK**
    c. Enter **Template Name: Contractors Expense**
    d. Select **Type: Unscheduled**
    e. Add **Payee: + Add New > Vendor Type.** Enter Name: **Mary Dolan**
    f. Select **Account: Checking**
    g. Select P**ayment Method: Check**
    h. Select **Category: Contractors Expense**
    i. Enter **Amount: based upon the number of hours Mary Dolan provided for Bebe and Mario**
    j. What is the Amount for the Recurring Expense?
    k. Select **Save Template**

2. Use a Recurring Transaction.
    a. From the Recurring Transaction List, select **Contractors Expense > Use**
    b. Select **Payment Date: 01/10/2022**
    c. Select **Payment Method: Check**
    d. Select **Save**
    e. From the bottom of the Contractors Expense window, select **More > Transaction Journal**
    f. What are the Account and Amount Debited?
    g. What are the Account and Amount Credited?

P3.1.8 COA Debits and Credits

The following accounts are from Mookie The Beagle Concierge Chart of Accounts. For each account indicate:

- If the account is increased by a:
    - **Debit**
    - **Credit**
- Type of account as:
    - **Asset**
    - **Liability**
    - **Equity**
    - **Revenue (Income)**
    - **Expense**

Account	Debit/Credit	Account Type
1. Checking		
2. Accounts Receivable (A/R)		
3. Inventory		
4. Prepaid Expenses		
5. Prepaid Expenses: Insurance		
6. Prepaid Expenses: Rent		
7. Prepaid Expenses: Supplies		
8. Undeposited Funds		
9. Accounts Payable (A/P)		
10. VISA Credit Card		
11. Unearned Revenue		
12. Owner Distributions		
13. Owner's Investment		
14. Retained Earnings		
15. Sales		
16. Advertising & Marketing		
17. Bank Charges & Fees		
18. Contractors		
19. Insurance: Liability Insurance Expense		
20. Interest Paid		
21. Legal & Professional Services		
22. Office Supplies & Software		
23. Rent & Lease		
24. Repairs & Maintenance		
25. Utilities		

Chapter 4

Banking

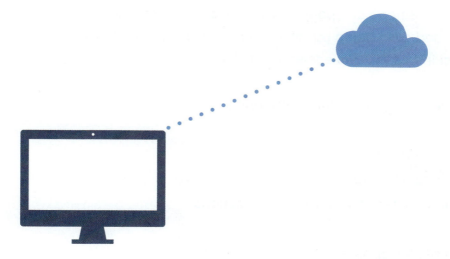

Cy Walker knows that one of the key factors in the long-term success of a business is the ability to pay bills on time. Several of his friends who started businesses had great ideas, fantastic social media marketing, and outstanding employee teams, but didn't survive because the businesses ran out of cash and couldn't pay their bills. So Cy knows that he needs to keep close track of cash flow for Mookie The Beagle Concierge to ensure they have adequate cash to pay bills when due. Cy needs a way to track cash going into and out of the business bank accounts, as well as track business credit card charges, payments, and balances. Your next step is to learn more about how to use QuickBooks Online for banking functions, including Checking accounts and credit cards.

Chapter 4

LEARNING OBJECTIVES

The QBO Banking function encompasses Checking accounts and credit cards. Adequate cash flows determine whether a company can pay its bills on time. So a business needs to track cash going into and cash going out of its bank accounts. QBO provides several banking features to make tracking cash flows easier for businesses.

In Chapter 4 you will learn about the following topics:

- Check Register
  - View Check Register
  - Check Register Drill-Down
  - Use Check Register To Add New Transactions
- Money In
  - Recording Bank Deposits
- Money Out
  - Recording Expenses
  - Recording Checks
- Connecting Bank and Credit Cards with QBO
  - Add Bank and Credit Card Accounts for Automatic QBO Downloads
  - Add Bank and Credit Card Transactions
  - Match Bank and Credit Card Transactions
- Accounting Essentials: Banking for Business

Section 4.1

 QBO SatNav

QBO SatNav is your satellite navigation for QuickBooks Online, assisting you in navigating QBO

Chapter 4 focuses on QBO Banking Transactions, shown in the following QBO SatNav.

 QBO SatNav

 QBO Settings

Company Settings
Chart of Accounts

QBO Transactions

 Banking	*Record Deposits	Write Checks*
Customers & Sales	
Vendors & Expenses	
Employees & Payroll	

QBO Reports

 Reports

Section 4.2

QBO SAMPLE COMPANY LOGIN

To log into the QBO Sample Company:

1 Open a web browser. (Note: Intuit recommends using Google Chrome.)

2 Go to https://qbo.intuit.com/redir/testdrive

3 Follow onscreen instructions for security verification

Craig's Design and Landscaping Services should appear on your screen.

To increase the amount of time from one (1) hour to three (3) hours before the log out for inactivity occurs:

1 From Craig's Design and Landscaping Services QBO Sample Company, select the **Gear** icon

2 Under Your Company section, select **Account and Settings**

3 Select **Advanced**

4 Select **Other preferences**

5 For the option Sign me out if inactive for, select **3 hours**

6 Select **Save**

7 Select **Done**

> ⚠️ **The Sample Company** will reset each time it is reopened. This allows you to explore and practice QBO without concern about carrying forward errors to later chapters. However, you will want to make certain to allow enough time to complete all chapter activities before closing the Sample Company. Otherwise, you will lose the work you have entered when you reopen the Sample Company.

To set QBO preferences to display account numbers in the Chart of Accounts:

1 Select the **Gear** icon to display options

2 Select **Account and Settings**

3 Select **Advanced**

4 For Chart of Accounts, select the **Edit Pencil**, then select **Enable account numbers**

5 Select **Show account numbers**

6 Select **Save**

7 Select **Done** to close Account and Settings

Section 4.3

CHECK REGISTER

The Check Register is a record of all transactions affecting the Checking account. Typically banking transactions involve money going into and out of our company's bank accounts. Some of the banking activities that we can use QBO to record include the following:

- Bank deposits (money into bank accounts)
- Bank transfers (money into and out of bank accounts)
- Bank checks (money out of bank accounts)
- Enter and pay credit card charges (money out of bank accounts)

VIEW CHECK REGISTER

The QBO Check Register looks similar to a checkbook register used to manually record deposits and checks.

To view the QBO Check Register:

1. From the Navigation Bar, select **Accounting**

2. If necessary, select the **Chart of Accounts** tab and **See your Chart of Accounts**

3. From the Chart of Accounts window, select **View Register** for the Checking account

4. **Date** column lists the date of the transaction

5. **Ref No. Type** column lists the reference number, such as check number, and type of transaction, such as Deposit

6. **Payee Account** column lists the payee and the account used to record the transaction

7. **Payment** column lists the amount of money out of the Checking account

8. **Deposit** column lists the amount of money into the Checking account

9. ✓ column indicates whether the bank transaction is C (Cleared), R (Reconciled), or blank (Uncleared, Unreconciled)

10. **Balance** column displays the running balance for the Checking account, updating the balance with each new transaction in the account

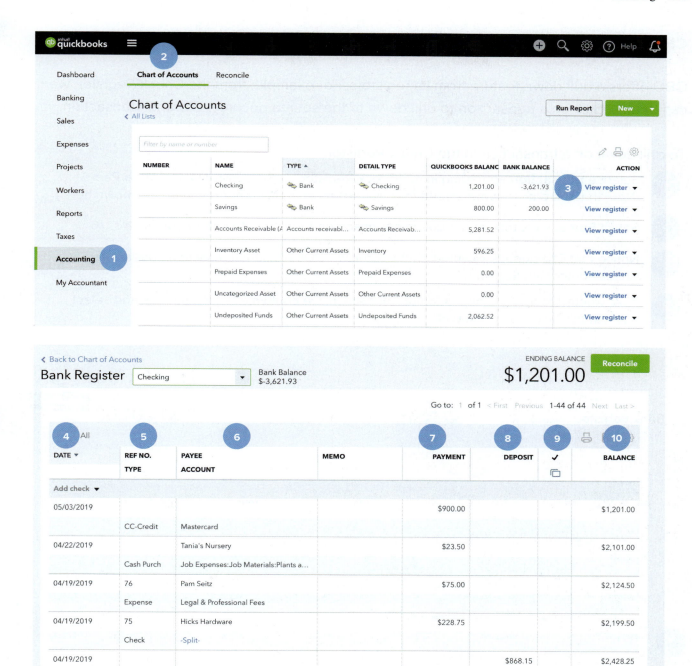

Small enterprises that have strictly cash-based operations sometimes simply use the Check Register to record all transactions. Such enterprises record payments and deposits directly into the Check Register. However, most business enterprises require more advanced features of QBO that are covered in the following chapters.

CHECK REGISTER DRILL DOWN

QBO offers a drill-down feature from its registers. For example, from the Check Register, we can double click on a transaction to drill down to the source document for that transaction.

To drill down on a transaction in the Check Register:

1 Select a **transaction** appearing in the Check Register, such as Expense No. 76 to Pam Seitz. (Note that the date on your screen for this transaction may differ from the date shown here.)

2 Select **Edit** to view the source document onscreen form used to enter Expense No. 76

3 Notice that Checking is selected on the form, which is why the transaction appears in the Checking account Register.

4 If we wanted to make changes to the transaction, we could make the changes and select Save. In this case select **Cancel**.

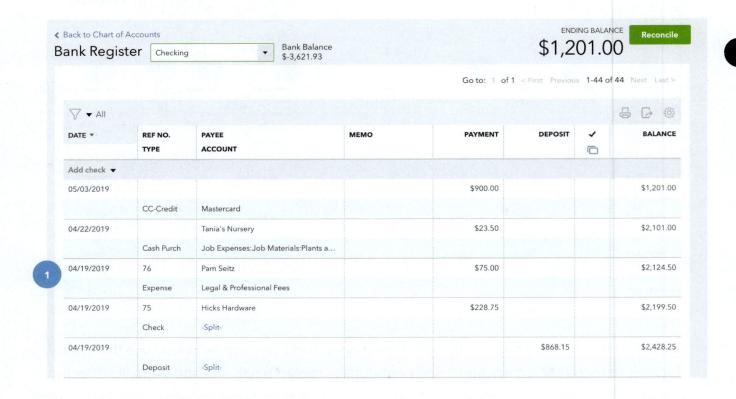

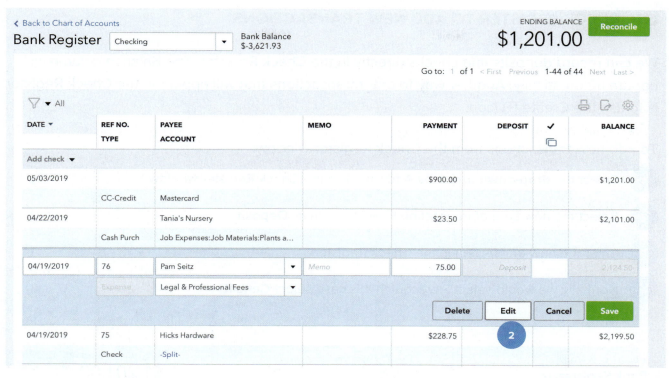

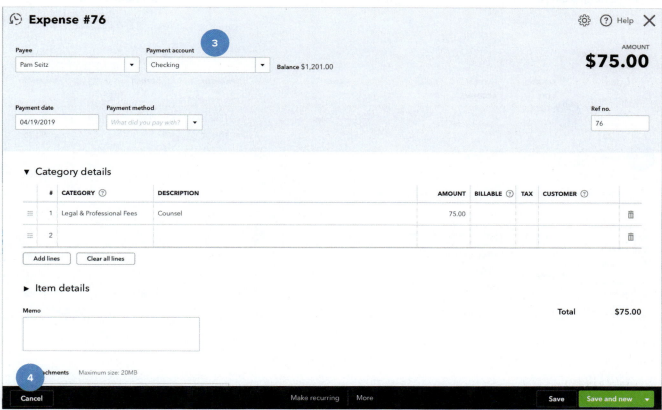

USE CHECK REGISTER TO ADD NEW TRANSACTIONS

We can record deposits and checks directly in the Check Register. The Balance column will update automatically. Another way to enter transactions that will appear in the Check Register is to use the Create (+) icon.

To add new transactions from the Check Register window:

1 Select the **drop-down arrow** by Add Check in the Check Register window

2 Select the new type of transaction to enter, such as **Deposit**

3 Enter the new transaction in the Check Register

4 Normally we would select Save, but in this case select **Cancel**

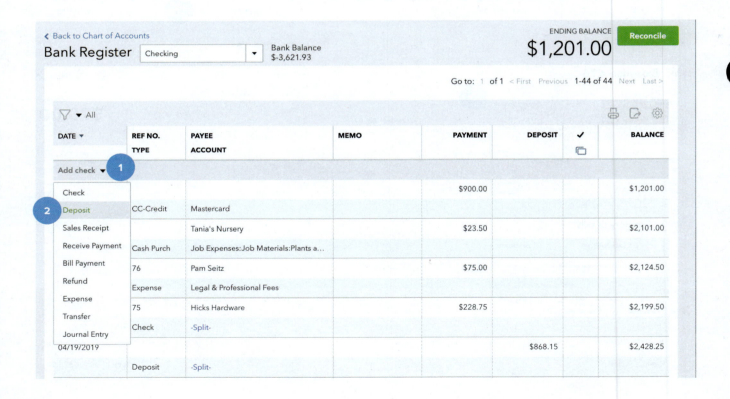

Section 4.4

MONEY IN

Money coming into the business must be recorded in QBO so there is a record and paper trail. Three main ways to use QBO to record money coming in are:

1. Customer Sales using Sales Receipts
2. Customer Sales using Invoices > Receive Payments
3. Bank Deposit

When using QBO, customer sales can be recorded using Sales Receipts (option 1) or Invoices (option 2). These customer sales tasks are covered in the next chapter. The current chapter focuses on bank deposits other than customer sales (option 3).

MONEY IN: BANK DEPOSITS NOT RELATED TO CUSTOMER SALES

If money coming in is not related to customer sales, then we can use a Bank Deposit form to record the money coming in. Examples of money coming in that is not a customer sale include:

- Investments from company owners
- Cash received from loans
- Interest earned
- Other income, such as rental income when our primary business is not a rental business

The above items can be recorded using the Bank Deposit form.

> **Customer sales** should be only recorded using Sales Receipts or Invoices. The Bank Deposit form that is discussed next only should be used for bank deposits not related to customer sales. Recording customer sales is covered in the next chapter.

MONEY IN: RECORDING BANK DEPOSITS

To record a bank deposit not related to a customer sale:

1 Select **Create (+)** icon

2 Under the Other column, select **Bank Deposit**

3 Select **Account: Checking** (or other appropriate Bank account)

4 Enter **Date** of deposit

5 The **Select The Payments Included in This Deposit** section lists payments received from customers but not deposited yet. These customer payments listed are undeposited funds that have been recorded as received but not yet deposited in the bank. Since these amounts will be deposited at a later time, leave these customer payments **unchecked**. Customer payments are covered in the next chapter.

6 In the **Add Funds to This Deposit** section, enter **Received From**

7 Select the appropriate **Account**

8 Enter a **Description** of the deposit

9 Enter **Payment Method**

10 Enter **Amount**

11 Enter **Memo**

12 Select **Attachments** to add a file or photo of any accompanying document

13 Normally we would select Save and new or Save and close but in this case, select **Cancel**

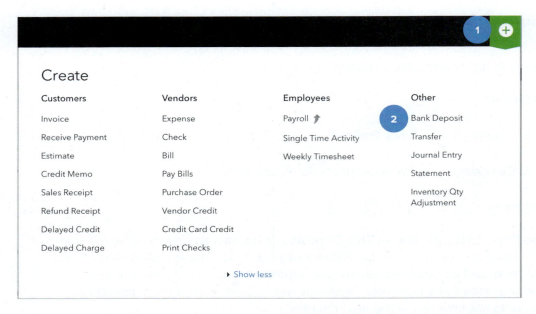

Create

Customers	Vendors	Employees	Other
Invoice	Expense	Payroll	Bank Deposit
Receive Payment	Check	Single Time Activity	Transfer
Estimate	Bill	Weekly Timesheet	Journal Entry
Credit Memo	Pay Bills		Statement
Sales Receipt	Purchase Order		Inventory Qty Adjustment
Refund Receipt	Vendor Credit		
Delayed Credit	Credit Card Credit		
Delayed Charge	Print Checks		

▸ Show less

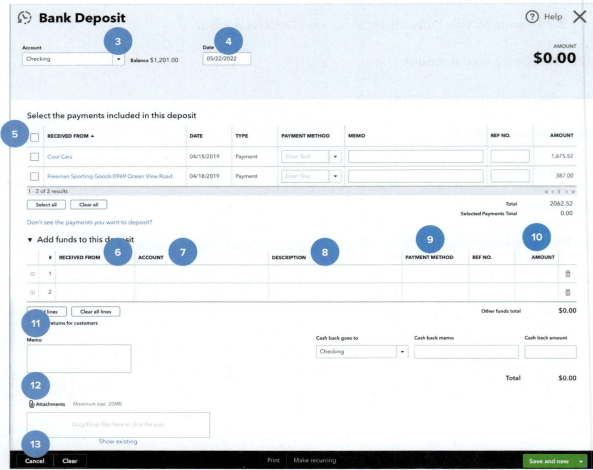

Section 4.5
MONEY OUT

A business needs to track all money out, including all cash paid out of the company's Checking account. Examples of payments include purchases of inventory, office supplies, employee salaries, rent payments, and insurance payments.

Supporting documents (source documents) for payments include canceled checks, receipts, and paid invoices. These source documents provide proof that the transaction occurred; therefore, source documents should be kept on file for tax purposes. QBO permits us to add source documents as attachments.

Four main ways to use QBO to record money out include:
1. Expense
2. Check
3. Bill > Pay Bills
4. Purchase Order > Bill > Pay Bills

The current chapter focuses on using an Expense (option 1) or Check (option 2) to record money out. Recording money out using Bill > Pay Bills (option 3) is covered in Chapter 6. Recording money out using Purchase Order > Bill > Pay Bills (option 4) is covered in Chapter 7.

MONEY OUT: CHECK OR EXPENSE FORM

If money going out is paid at the time the product or service is received (instead of later), it can be recorded using the Expense or Check onscreen form. Examples of money going out that could be recorded using the Expense or Check onscreen form include:

- Rent expense
- Utilities expense
- Insurance expense
- Office supplies expense
- Services expense, such as accounting or legal services

If we are paying a bill immediately using cash, check, or credit card, then we can use the Expense onscreen form.

If we are paying a bill immediately with a check, then we can use the Check onscreen form to record the check.

Examples of money going out that should not be recorded using a Check or Expense onscreen form include:

- Paychecks to employees for wages and salaries
- Payroll taxes and liabilities
- Sales taxes
- Bills already entered using the Bill onscreen form

MONEY OUT: RECORDING EXPENSES

To record a bill payment that is made immediately with cash, check, or credit card, use the Expense form as follows:

1 Select **Create (+)** icon

2 Under Vendors column, select **Expense**

3 Select **Payee: Computers by Jenni**

4 Using the drop-down menu, select **Payment Account: Visa**

5 Enter **Payment Date: Current Date**

6 Select **Payment Method: Visa**

7 In the Category Details section, select appropriate Category from the drop-down menu. The drop-down Category list contains accounts that can be used to record the expense. If it does not appear automatically, select **Category: Office Expenses**.

8 Enter a **Description**: **Purchase of computer cable**

9 Enter **Amount** of the expense: **13.00**

10 Select Billable if the expense is billable to a specific customer. In this case since Office Expenses does not relate to a specific customer, leave **Billable unchecked**.

11 Select Tax if purchase is taxable. Leave **Tax unchecked**.

12 If billable, select appropriate Customer associated with the expense. Leave **Customer** field **blank**.

13 Enter **Memo** describing the transaction: **Purchase of replacement computer cable**

14   Select **Save**. Leave the Expense form open.

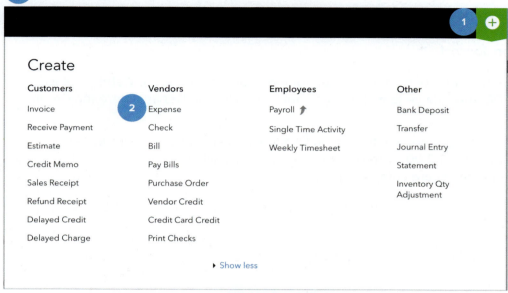

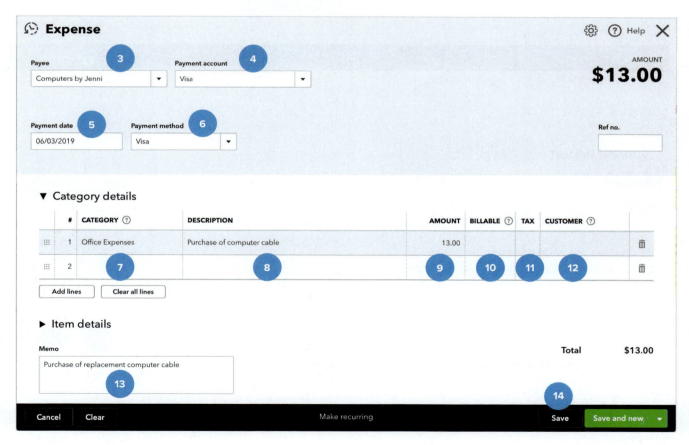

To view the Transaction Journal for the Expense we just created:

1 From the Expense window just saved, select **More**

2 Select **Transaction Journal**

3 In the journal entry recorded behind the screen for the Expense, notice the **Debit** to Office Expenses for $13.00. Also notice that QBO does not always list the Debits before the Credits in a Journal Entry.

4 In the journal entry recorded behind the screen for the Expense, notice the **Credit** to the Visa (Liability) account for $13.00. A credit card is a type of liability since Craig's now has an obligation to pay the credit card company $13.00.

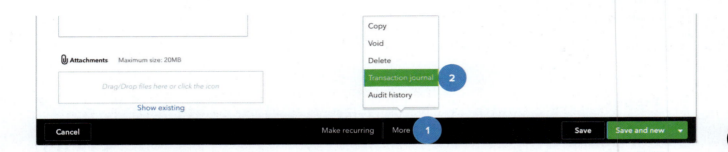

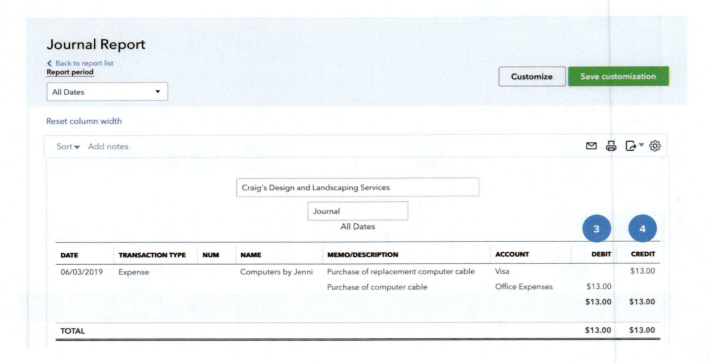

Journal Report

‹ Back to report list
Report period

All Dates ▾

Customize   Save customization

Reset column width

Sort ▾   Add notes

Craig's Design and Landscaping Services

Journal

All Dates

DATE	TRANSACTION TYPE	NUM	NAME	MEMO/DESCRIPTION	ACCOUNT	DEBIT	CREDIT
06/03/2019	Expense		Computers by Jenni	Purchase of replacement computer cable	Visa		$13.00
				Purchase of computer cable	Office Expenses	$13.00	
						$13.00	$13.00
TOTAL						**$13.00**	**$13.00**

MONEY OUT: RECORDING CHECKS

To record a bill payment that is made immediately with a check:

1 Select **Create (+)** icon

2 Under Vendors column, select **Check**

3 Select **Payee: Squeaky Kleen Car Wash**. After the Payee is selected, some of the information on the form will autofill, such as Mailing address. This information is pulled from the Vendors List.

4 Select **Bank Account: Checking**

5 Enter **Payment Date: Current Date**

6 Notice that the **Check No.** autofills

7 In the Category Details section, select appropriate Category from the drop-down menu. The drop-down Category list contains accounts that can be used to record the expense. Sometimes QBO will autofill this field using information from the last transaction entered for the specific Payee. In this case, if it does not autofill, enter **Category: Automobile (Expenses)**.

8 Enter **Description: Car Wash**

9 Enter **Amount: 15.99**

10 If the payment was billable to a specific customer, select Billable. In this case since the Automobile Expense does not relate to a specific customer, leave **Billable unchecked**.

11 Select Tax if applicable. In this case, leave **Tax unchecked**.

12 If the payment was billable to a specific customer, select that customer in the Customer column from the Customer drop-down list. In this case, leave **Customer** field **blank**.

13 Enter **Memo: Car Wash**

14 Select **Attachments** to add a file or photo of any accompanying source document, such as a bill

15 Select **Save and close**

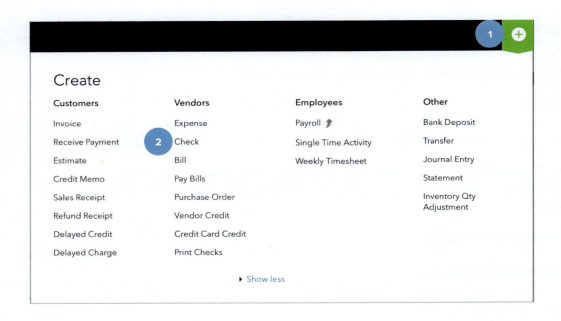

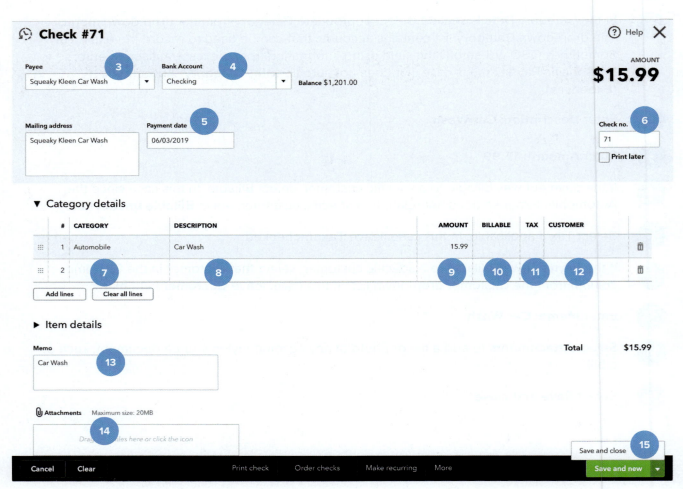

To view the Transaction Journal for the Check we just created:

1 From the Navigation Bar, select **Expenses**

2 Select the **Expenses** tab

3 From the Expense Transactions List, select: **View/Edit** for the Check to **Squeaky Kleen Car Wash** just entered

4 From the bottom of the Squeaky Kleen Car Wash Check, select **More**

5 Select **Transaction Journal**

6 In the journal entry recorded behind the screen for the Check, notice the **Debit** to Automobile (Expense) for $15.99

7 In the journal entry recorded behind the screen for the Check, notice the **Credit** to Checking for $15.99

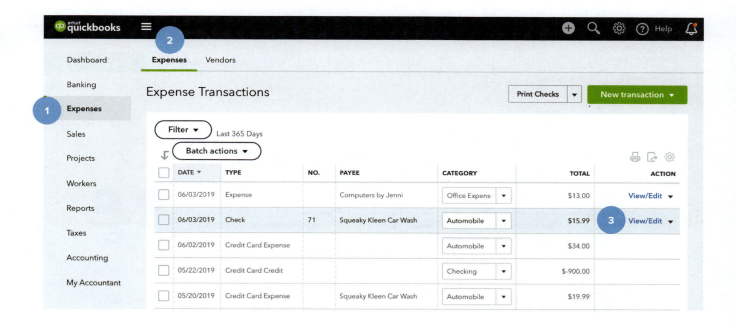

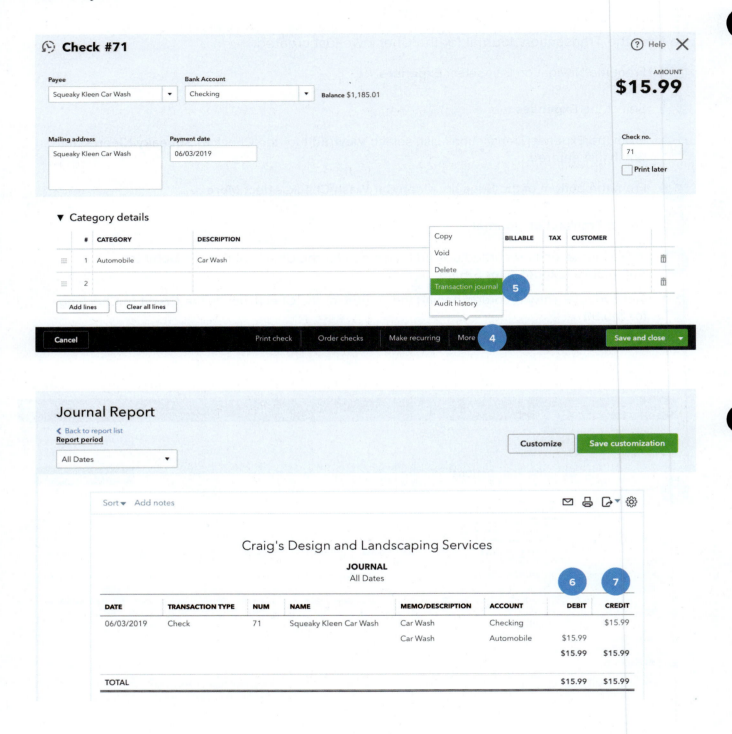

Section 4.6

CONNECTING BANK AND CREDIT CARDS WITH QBO

We can connect our bank accounts and our credit card accounts with QBO. This results in the expenses automatically being downloaded from the bank or credit card company into QBO. Then we can Add or Match the downloaded bank and credit card transactions with our QBO entries.

ADD BANK AND CREDIT CARD ACCOUNTS FOR AUTOMATIC DOWNLOADS

To connect a bank or credit card account to QBO for automatic downloads:

1. From the Navigation Bar, select **Accounting** to add the Checking or Credit Card account to the Chart of Accounts

2. After the appropriate Checking or Credit Card account has been added to the Chart of Accounts, select **Banking** from the Navigation Bar to display the Bank and Credit Cards window

3. If necessary, select the **Banking** tab

4. From the Bank and Credit Cards window, select **Add Account**. Follow the onscreen instructions to complete adding the account.

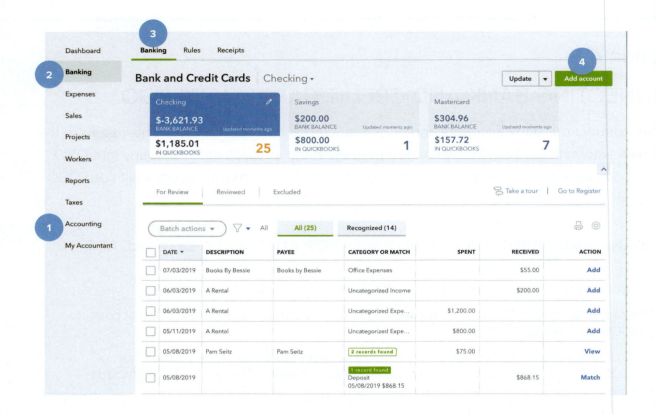

After bank and credit card accounts are connected to QBO, then the transactions download automatically as shown above in the Bank and Credit Cards window. Each connected account appears in a card at the top of the Bank and Credit Cards window, showing the bank balance and your QBO balance.

QBO automatically compares downloaded bank transactions with our QBO data to identify possible matches. The number of unmatched transactions appears on the card. For example, there are 7 unmatched transactions in the MasterCard account.

ADD BANK AND CREDIT CARD TRANSACTIONS

To add a bank or credit card downloaded transaction that we have not entered in QBO yet:

1. From the Bank and Credit Cards screen, select **Update** to update the downloaded transactions

2. Select the appropriate **bank** or **credit card account** to display the downloaded transactions: **Checking**

3   Select the **For Review** tab to view new downloaded transactions that have not been added or matched yet

4   Select a transaction to expand and review details for the transaction: **Books by Bessie**

5   Select **Category: Office Expenses**

6   Select **Add**

7   The transaction will disappear from the For Review tab and be moved to the **Reviewed** tab on the Bank and Credit Cards window

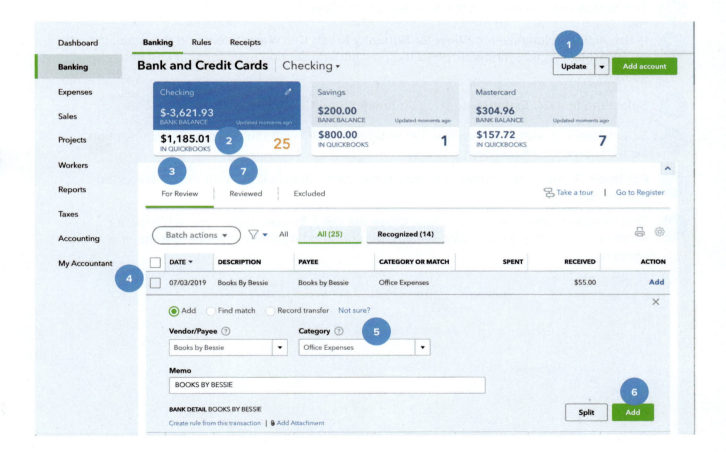

MATCH BANK AND CREDIT CARD TRANSACTIONS

To match a bank or credit card downloaded transaction to a transaction we have already entered in QBO:

1. From the Banks and Credit Cards screen, select **Update** to update the downloaded transactions

2. Select the appropriate bank or credit card account to display the downloaded transactions. In this case select: **Mastercard**

3. Select the **For Review** tab to view new downloaded transactions that have not been added or matched yet

4. The **Action** column may display **Add**, **Match**, or **View**

5. In the Action column, select **View** for **Squeaky Kleen Car Wash** to expand the transaction to review details. This window displays the possible transaction matches that QBO has identified.

6. Select the first **CC Expense** item for **Squeaky Kleen Car Wash**

7. Select **Match** to match the transaction entered in QBO with the downloaded transaction from the credit card company

8. For Bob's Burgers, select **Match** to match the transaction in QBO with the downloaded transaction

9. This completes the chapter activities. **Close** the QBO Sample Company web browser window to reset the Sample Company before proceeding to the exercises at the end of this chapter.

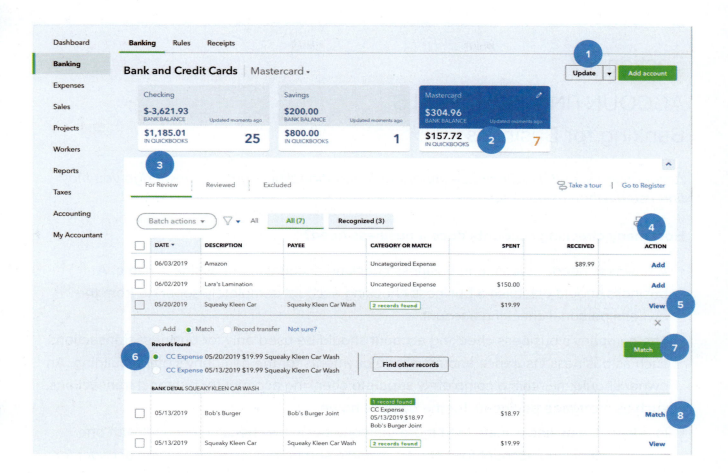

Note that transactions with an Action item: Match are bank and credit card transactions that were
entered into QBO *before* the transaction was downloaded from the bank or credit card company and
identified by QBO as a possible Match.

Section 4.7

ACCOUNTING ESSENTIALS
Banking for Business

Accounting Essentials summarize important foundational accounting knowledge you may find useful when using QBO

How many checking accounts does a business need?

- A business needs at least one business checking account in the business name. A business should establish a business checking account completely separate from the owner's personal checking account.
- The company's business checking account should be used only for business transactions, such as business insurance and mortgage payments for the company's office building. An owner should maintain a completely separate checking account for personal transactions, such as mortgage payments for the owner's home.
- In addition, a business may need more than one business checking account with one business checking account for operations and a separate business checking account for payroll, for example.

What is a bank reconciliation?

- Typically once a month, the bank sends you a Checking account bank statement. The bank statement lists each deposit, check, and withdrawal from the account during the month. A bank reconciliation is the process of comparing, or reconciling, the bank statement with your accounting records for the Checking account.

What are the objectives of a bank reconciliation?

- The bank reconciliation has two objectives: (1) to detect errors and (2) to update your accounting records for unrecorded items listed on the bank statement (such as service charges). Reconciling bank statements is part of good internal controls that involve comparing the actual asset (what the bank says you have) with your accounting records (QBO Checking account).

- Note that with QBO's ability to match downloaded bank transactions with QBO data on an ongoing basis, some QBO users find that they no longer use a monthly bank reconciliation. Basically, they are comparing the bank balance with their QBO balance on a real time basis instead of a monthly basis, which provides even better internal control since they become aware of discrepancies and potential issues sooner.

Why are there differences between the bank statement and my accounting records?

- Differences between the balance the bank reports on the bank statement and the balance the business shows in its accounting records usually arise for two reasons:
  1. **Errors**. Errors can be either the bank's error(s) or the company's error(s).
  2. **Timing differences**. This occurs when the company records an amount before the bank does or the bank records an amount before the company does. For example, the company may record a deposit in its accounting records, but the bank does not record the deposit before the company's bank statement is prepared.

  Timing differences include:
  - Items the bank has not recorded yet, such as:
    - ✓ **Deposits in transit.** Deposits the company has recorded but the bank has not.
    - ✓ **Outstanding checks.** Checks the company has written and recorded but the bank has not recorded yet.
  - Items the company has not recorded yet, such as:
    - ✓ **Unrecorded charges.** Charges that the bank has recorded on the bank statement but the company has not recorded in its accounting records yet. Unrecorded charges include service charges, loan payments, automatic withdrawals, and ATM withdrawals.
    - ✓ **Interest earned on the account.** Interest the bank has recorded as earned but the company has not recorded yet.

Practice Quiz 4

Q4.1

The Checking Register:

a. Tracks company purchase orders and vendors
b. Tracks company invoices and customers
c. Records all transactions affecting the Checking account
d. Lists all accounts and their account numbers

Q4.2

In the Check Register, the term "split" indicates the payment is split between two or more:

a. Purchase orders
b. Invoices
c. Checks
d. Accounts

Q4.3

Deposits other than customer payments are entered using:

a. Receive Payments
b. Pay Bills
c. Bank Deposit
d. All of the above

Q4.4

If we are paying a bill immediately when we receive products or services, we can use the Expenses onscreen form when we pay with:

a. Cash
b. Check
c. Credit Card
d. All of the above

Q4.5

Examples of money going out that can be recorded using the Expense or Check onscreen forms include all of the following except:

a.   Rent expense

b.   Payroll expense

c.   Insurance expense

d.   Legal Services expense

Q4.6

Examples of money going out that should *not* be recorded using a Check or Expense onscreen form include:

a.   Paychecks to employees

b.   Payroll taxes

c.   Sales taxes

d.   Bills already entered using the Bills onscreen form

e.   All of the above

Q4.7

Ways to record money out using QBO include:

a.   Enter Bill > Pay Bills

b.   Check

c.   Expense

d.   Purchase Order > Bill > Pay Bills

e.   All of the above

Q4.8

Ways to record money coming into QBO include:

a. Customer Sales using Sales Receipts

b. Customer Sales using Invoices and Receive Payments

c. Bank Deposit

d. All of the above

Q4.9

To record a bill payment that is made immediately with a credit card when the product or service is received, use the following onscreen form:

a. Bill
b. Check
c. Pay Bills
d. Expense

Q4.10

Identify the order in which the following steps should be completed in order to connect a bank or credit card account to QBO for automatic downloads.

a. Select Banking from the Navigation Bar
b. Select Add Account from the Bank and Credit Cards window
c. Select Accounting to add the bank or credit card account to the Chart of Accounts

Q4.11

A company should always use the same checking account for business transactions and for the owner's personal transactions to streamline recording transactions.

a. True
b. False

Q4.12

Differences between the balance the bank reports on the bank statement and the balance the business shows in its accounting records usually arise for which of the following two reasons:

a. Adjusting entries have been made twice
b. Errors (bank errors or company errors)
c. Timing differences between when the bank records and when the company records an item
d. Closing entries have been made

Q4.13

One of the objectives of reconciling bank statements is:

a. To update the bank's records
b. Update accounting records with unrecorded items

c. To record monthly adjusting entries

d. To update the Chart of Accounts

Q4.14

When reconciling a bank account, which of the following is not considered a timing difference (difference between the bank balance and the book balance)?

a. Interest earned

b. Deposits in transit

c. Errors

d. Unrecorded charges

Exercises 4

We use the **QBO Sample Company, Craig's Design and Landscaping Services,** for practice throughout the exercises. The Sample Company will reset each time it is reopened. So make certain to allow enough time to complete exercises before closing the Sample Company. Otherwise, you will lose the work you have entered when you reopen the Sample Company.

⚠ Since the **Sample Company** resets each time it is reopened, be certain to close any web browser windows displaying the **QBO Sample Company** before starting these exercises. Closing the browser window and starting with a new browser window for the **QBO Sample Company** resets the data before starting the exercises.

To access the QBO Sample Company, complete the following steps.

1   Open a web browser. (Note: Intuit recommends using Google Chrome.)

2   Go to https://qbo.intuit.com/redir/testdrive

3   Follow onscreen instructions for security verification

Craig's Design and Landscaping Services should appear on your screen.

E4.1 Check Register

Go to QBO Sample Company, Craig's Design and Landscaping Services. Match the following items identified in the Checking account Bank Register with the description of the items.

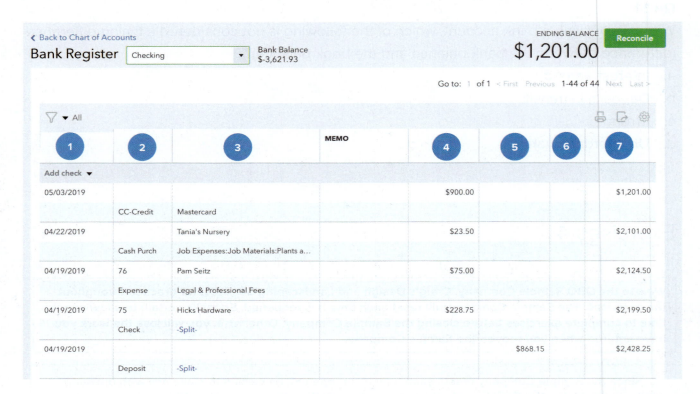

Check Register Item Descriptions

a. Deposit column listing the amount of money going into the Checking account

b. ✓ column indicating whether the bank transaction is Cleared, Reconciled, or blank (Uncleared and Unreconciled)

c. Date column listing the date of the transaction

d. Ref No. and Type lists the type of transaction

e. Balance column displaying the running balance for the Checking account

f. Payee Account column listing the payee and the account used to record the transaction

g. Payment column listing the amount of money going out of the Checking account

Check Register Item

1 _____

2 _____

3 _____

4 _____

5 _____

6 _____

7 _____

E4.2 Check

Using the QBO Sample Company, Craig's Design and Landscaping Services, complete the following.

1. Create a Check.
   a. Select **Create (+) icon > Check**
   b. Select **Payee: Kookies by Kathy**
   c. Select **Bank Account: Checking**
   d. Select **Category: Office Expenses**
   e. Enter **Description: Office party**
   f. Enter **Amount: 33.00**
   g. What is the Total for the Check?
   h. Select **Save and close**

2. View the Transaction Journal for the Check.
   a. From the Navigation Bar, select **Expenses**.
   b. From the Expense Transactions List, select the **Kookies by Kathy Check** just entered
   c. From the bottom of the Kookies by Kathy Check, select **More > Transaction Journal**.
      Note: with some browsers you may need to scroll down to view and select More in order to display the More menu.
   d. What are the Account and Amount Debited?
   e. What are the Account and Amount Credited?

E4.3 Check

Using the QBO Sample Company, Craig's Design and Landscaping Services, complete the following.

1. Create a Check.
    a. Select **Create (+) icon > Check**
    b. Select **Payee: Pye's Cakes**
    c. Select **Bank Account: Checking**
    d. Select **Category: Office Expense**
    e. Enter **Description: Office party**
    f. Enter **Amount: 42.00**
    g. What is the Total for the Check?
    h. Select **Save and close**

2. View the Transaction Journal for the Check.
    a. From the Navigation Bar, select **Expenses**
    b. From the Expense Transactions List, select the **Pye's Cakes Check** just entered
    c. From the bottom of the Pye's Cakes Check, select **More > Transaction Journal**
    d. What are the Account and Amount Debited?
    e. What are the Account and Amount Credited?

E4.4 Check

Using the QBO Sample Company, Craig's Design and Landscaping Services, complete the following.

1. Create a Check.
    a. Select **Create (+) icon > Check**
    b. Select **Payee: Computers by Jenni**
    c. Select **Bank Account: Checking**
    d. Select **Category: Supplies**
    e. Enter **Description: Computer cable replacement**
    f. Enter **Amount: 12.00**
    g. What is the Total for the Check?
    h. Select **Save and close**

2. View the Transaction Journal for the Check.

    a. From the Navigation Bar, select **Expenses**

    b. From the Expense Transactions List, select the **Computers by Jenni Check** just entered

    c. From the bottom of the Computers by Jenni Check, select **More > Transaction Journal**

    d. What are the Account and Amount Debited?

    e. What are the Account and Amount Credited?

E4.5 Expense

Using the QBO Sample Company, Craig's Design and Landscaping Services, complete the following.

1. Create an Expense.

    a. Select **Create (+) icon > Expense**

    b. Select **Payee: Cal Telephone**

    c. Select **Payment Account: Mastercard**

    d. Select **Category: Utilities: Telephone**

    e. Enter **Amount: 22.00**

    f. What is the Total for the Expense?

    g. Select **Save**

2. View the Transaction Journal for the Expense.

    a. From the bottom of the Cal Telephone Expense, select **More > Transaction Journal**

    b. What are the Account and Amount Debited?

    c. What are the Account and Amount Credited?

E4.6 Expense

Using the QBO Sample Company, Craig's Design and Landscaping Services, complete the following.

1. Create an Expense.

    a. Select **Create (+) icon > Expense**

    b. Select **Payee: Lee Advertising**

    c. Select **Payment Account: Visa**

    d. Select **Category: Advertising**

    e. Enter **Amount: 54.00**

    f. What is the Total for the Expense?

    g. Select **Save**

2. View the Transaction Journal for the Expense.

    a. From the bottom of the Lee Advertising Expense, select **More > Transaction Journal**

    b. What are the Account and Amount Debited?

    c. What are the Account and Amount Credited?

E4.7 Bank Transfer

Using the QBO Sample Company, Craig's Design and Landscaping Services, complete the following.

1. Record a Transfer.

    a. Select **Create (+) icon > Transfer**

    b. Select **Transfer Funds From**: **Savings**

    c. Select **Transfer Funds To: Checking**

    d. What is the Balance in the Savings Account?

    e. Enter **Transfer Amount: 100.00**

    f. Select **Save and close**

    g. What is the Balance in the Savings account after transfer?

2. View the Transaction Journal for the Savings Account transfer.

    a. From the Navigation Bar, select **Banking > Banking tab**

    b. At the top of the Bank and Credit Cards screen, select the **Savings card**

    c. Select **Go to Register**

    d. Select the entry in the Savings Account Register for the **$100 Transfer to Checking > Edit**

    e. From the bottom of the Transfer form, select **More > Transaction Journal**

    f. What are the Account and Amount Debited?

    g. What are the Account and Amount Credited?

E4.8 Banking Update Add

Using the QBO Sample Company, Craig's Design and Landscaping Services, complete the following.

1. Complete a Bank Add.
    a. From the Navigation Bar, select **Banking**
    b. Select the **Mastercard card** at the top of the Bank and Credit Cards screen
    c. Select **Lara's Lamination** to expand the transaction for details
    d. Change Uncategorized Expense to **Office Expenses**
    e. Select **Add**
    f. After selecting Add, how many unmatched items appear on the Mastercard card at the top of the screen?

E4.9 Banking Update Match

This assignment is a continuation of E4.8

Using the QBO Sample Company, Craig's Design and Landscaping Services, complete the following.

1. Complete a Bank Match.
    a. From the Navigation Bar, select **Banking**
    b. Select the **Checking card** at the top of the Bank and Credit Cards screen
    c. For **Hicks Hardware** for **$228.75** select **Match**
    d. After selecting Match, how many open items appear on the Checking card at the top of the screen?

2. Complete a Bank Match.
    a. From the Bank and Credit Cards screen, select the **Mastercard card** at the top of the screen
    b. For **Bob's Burger** for **$18.97** select **Match**
    c. After selecting Match, how many open items appear on the Mastercard card at the top of the screen?

3. Complete a Bank Match.
    a. From the Bank and Credit Cards screen select the **Savings** card at the top of the screen
    b. For the **$200** deposit select **Match**
    c. After selecting Match, what appears for open items on the Savings card at the top of the screen?

Project 4.1

Mookie the Beagle™ Concierge

Project 4.1 is a continuation of Project 3.1. You will use the QBO Company you created for Project 1.1 and updated in subsequent Projects 2.1 and 3.1. Keep in mind the QBO Company for Project 4.1 does not reset and carries your data forward, including any errors. So it is important to check and crosscheck your work to verify it is correct before clicking the Save button.

BACKSTORY

Mookie The Beagle™ Concierge provides convenient, high-quality pet care on demand. Cy, the founder, has asked for your assistance in identifying how QBO can be used for business banking transactions.

Complete the following for Mookie The Beagle Concierge.

🌐 QBO SATNAV

Project 4.1 focuses on QBO Transactions, specifically Banking Transactions as shown in the following QBO SatNav.

🌐 QBO SatNav

⚙️ QBO Settings

| ⚙️ Company Settings |
| ⚙️ Chart of Accounts |

💰 QBO Transactions

💰 Banking	**Record Deposits	Write Checks**
💰 Customers & Sales	
💰 Vendors & Expenses	
💰 Employees & Payroll	

📊 QBO Reports

| 📊 Reports |

HOW TO LOG INTO QBO

To log into QBO, complete the following steps.

1 Using a web browser go to qbo.intuit.com

2 Enter **User ID** (the email address you used to set up your QBO Account)

3 Enter **Password** (the password you used to set up your QBO Account)

4 Select **Sign in**

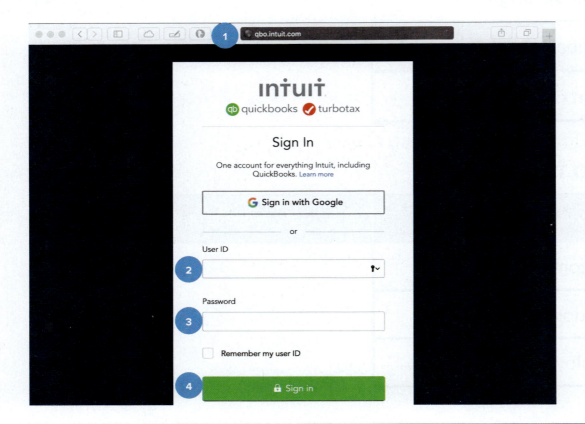

> If you are <u>not</u> using a public or shared computer, to speed up login, you can save your login to your desktop and select Remember Me. If you are using a public computer or shared computer, do not save to the desktop and unselect Remember Me.

> The new QBO Company we created in Project 1.1 will carry all work forward into future chapters. So it is important to check and crosscheck your work to verify it is correct before clicking the Save button. Any uncorrected errors will be carried forward in your QBO Company for text projects.

P4.1.1 Bank Deposit

Cy loans Mookie The Beagle Concierge $2,000 at 6% annual interest. Record the transaction as a loan payable as follows.

1. Complete a Deposit.
    a. Select **Create (+) icon > Bank Deposit**
    b. Select **Account: Checking**
    c. Select **Date: 01/12/2022**
    d. In Add Funds to This Deposit section, select **Account: + Add New > Loan Payable > Account Type: Other Current Liabilities > Detail Type: Loan Payable > Name: Loan Payable**
    e. Select **Payment Method: Check**
    f. Enter **Ref No.: 5002**
    g. Enter **Amount: 2000.00**
    h. Select **Save and close**
    i. What is the Amount of the Loan Payable?

2. View the Transaction Journal for the Deposit.
    a. From the Navigation Bar, select **Accounting**
    b. From the Chart of Accounts, select **Loan Payable > View Register**
    c. From the Register, select the transaction just recorded > **Edit**
    d. From the bottom of the Loan Payable transaction, select **More > Transaction Journal**
    e. What are the Account and Amount Debited?
    f. What are the Account and Amount Credited?

P4.1.2 Expense Credit Card

Complete the following to record Internet services that Mookie The Beagle Concierge incurred.

1. Create an Expense paid with Credit Card.
    a. Select **Create (+) icon > Expense**
    b. Add **Vendor Payee: Luminesse Link**
    c. Select **Payment Date: 01/13/2022**
    d. Select **Payment Account: VISA Credit Card**
    e. Select **Payment Method: Credit Card**
    f. Enter **Category: Utilities**
    g. Enter **Description: Internet Service**
    h. Enter **Amount: 200.00**
    i. What is the Total Amount paid to Luminesse Link?
    j. Select **Save** and leave the Expense screen displayed

2. View the Transaction Journal for the Expense.
    a. From the displayed Expense, select **More > Transaction Journal**
    b. What are the Account and Amount Debited?
    c. What are the Account and Amount Credited?

P4.1.3 Expense Credit Card

Complete the following to record telephone service that Mookie The Beagle Concierge incurred and paid by credit card.

1. Create an Expense paid with Credit Card.
    a. Select **Create (+) icon > Expense**
    b. Select **Payee: Luminesse Link**
    c. Select **Payment Date: 01/14/2022**
    d. Select **Payment Account: VISA Credit Card**
    e. Select **Payment Method: Credit Card**
    f. Enter **Category: Utilities**
    g. Enter **Description: Telephone Service**
    h. Enter **Amount: 144.00**
    i. What is the Total Amount paid to Luminesse Link?
    j. Select **Save**. Leave the Expense window displayed.

2. View the Transaction Journal for the Expense.
    a. From the displayed Expense, select **More > Transaction Journal**
    b. What are the Account and Amount Debited?
    c. What are the Account and Amount Credited?

P4.1.4 Check

Complete the following to record office expenses that Mookie The Beagle Concierge incurred and paid by check.

1. Create a Check.
   a. Select **Create (+) icon > Check**
   b. Add **Vendor Payee: Bichotte Supplies**
   c. Select **Payment Date: 01/13/2022**
   d. Select **Bank Account: Checking**
   e. Select **Category: Office Supplies & Software (Expenses)**
   f. Enter **Description: Office Supplies**
   g. Enter **Amount: 84.00**
   h. What is the Total for the Check?
   i. Select **Save and close**

2. View the Transaction Journal for the Check.
   a. From the Navigation Bar, select **Expenses**
   b. From the Expense Transactions List, select the **Bichotte Supplies Check** just entered
   c. From the bottom of the Bichotte Supplies Check, select **More > Transaction Journal**
   d. What are the Account and Amount Debited?
   e. What are the Account and Amount Credited?

P4.1.5 Check

Complete the following to record technology accessories that Mookie The Beagle Concierge paid by check to Sofia Raphael Associates, a firm that specializes in technology supplies and consulting services.

1. Create a Check.
   a. Select **Create (+) icon > Check**
   b. Add **Vendor Payee: Sofia Raphael Associates**
   c. Select **Payment Date: 01/16/2022**
   d. Select **Bank Account: Checking**
   e. Select **Category: Office Supplies & Software (Expenses)**
   f. Enter **Description: Technology Supplies**
   g. Enter **Amount: 116.00**
   h. What is the Total for the Check?
   i. Select **Save and close**

2. View the Transaction Journal for the Check.

   a. From the Navigation Bar, select **Expenses**

   b. From the Expense Transactions List, select the **Sofia Raphael Associates Check** just entered

   c. From the bottom of the Sofia Raphael Associates Check, select **More > Transaction Journal**

   d. What is the Account and Amount Debited?

   e. What is the Account and Amount Credited?

P4.1.6 Match Bank Transactions Checking

Mookie The Beagle Concierge has the following Checking account transactions in spreadsheet form. MTB needs to upload these bank transactions into QBO and then match them against QBO transactions previously entered.

CHECKING				
Type	**Trans Date**	**Post Date**	**Description**	**Amount**
Sale	01/15/2022	01/16/2022	SOFIA RAPHAEL ASSOCIATES	-116.00
Sale	01/13/2022	01/14/2022	BICHOTTE SUPPLIES	-84.00
Deposit	01/12/2022	01/13/2022	CY WALKER	2000.00
Sale	01/10/2022	01/11/2022	MARY DOLAN	-1160.00
Sale	01/05/2022	01/06/2022	CAROLE DESIGN MEDIA	-2000.00
Deposit	01/01/2022	01/02/2022	CY WALKER	10000.00

1. Upload Checking Account Transactions to QBO.
   a. From the Navigation Bar, select **Banking > Upload Transactions Add Manually**
   b. Select **Browse** to select the file to upload > select **File: QBO 2E P4.1.6 Checking.csv > Next**
   c. Select **QuickBooks Account: Checking**
   d. Select **Next**
   e. Select **Your Statement Fields Date: Column 2 Trans Date MM/dd/yyyy**
   f. Select **Your Statement Fields Description: Column 4 Description**
   g. Select **Your Statement Fields Amount: Column 5: Amount**
   h. Select **CSV file has amounts in: 1 column: both positive and negative numbers**
   i. Select **Next**
   j. Select **CSV transactions for import: Select All > Next**
   k. When asked, Do you want to import now?, select **Yes**
   l. How many transactions were imported?
   m. Select **Let's go!**

2. Complete a Checking Account Bank Match.
   a. From the Navigation Bar, select **Banking**
   b. How many open items appear on the Checking card at the top of the screen?
   c. Select **Match** for all Matching items
   d. Now how many open items appear on the Checking card at the top of the screen?

P4.1.7 Match Bank Transactions Credit Card

Mookie The Beagle Concierge has the following transactions for its VISA Credit Card in spreadsheet form. MTB needs to upload the credit card transactions into QBO and then match them to QBO transactions previously entered.

VISA CREDIT CARD				
Type	**Trans Date**	**Post Date**	**Description**	**Amount**
Sale	01/14/2022	01/14/2022	LUMINESSE LINK	-144.00
Sale	01/13/2022	01/13/2022	LUMINESSE LINK	-200.00
Deposit	01/07/2022	01/08/2022	CYRUS INSURANCE	-600.00

1. Upload Credit Card Account Transactions to QBO.
   a. From the Navigation Bar, select **Banking** > **File upload**
   b. Select **Browse** to select the file to upload > select **File: QBO 2E P4.1.7 Credit Card.csv** > **Next**
   c. Select **QuickBooks Account: VISA Credit Card**
   d. Select **Next**
   e. Select **Your Statement Fields Date: Column 2 Trans Date MM/dd/yyyy**
   f. Select **Your Statement Fields Description: Column 4 Description**
   g. Select **Your Statement Fields Amount: Column 5: Amount**
   h. Select **CSV file has amounts in: 1 column: both positive and negative numbers**
   i. Select **Next**
   j. Select **CSV transactions for import: Select All** > **Next**
   k. When asked, Do you want to import now?, select **Yes**
   l. How many transactions were imported?
   m. Select **Let's go!**

2. Complete a Credit Card Account Bank Match.
   a. From the Navigation Bar, select **Banking**
   b. How many open items appear on the VISA Credit Card at the top of the screen?
   c. Select **Match** for all Matching items
   d. Now how many open items appear on the VISA Credit Card at the top of the screen?

Chapter 5

Customers and Sales

As sales for Mookie the Beagle Concierge ramp up, Cy Walker wants to make certain that all sales to customers are captured and correctly recorded in the financial system. Cy also realizes the importance of collecting and recording customer payments. He knows that collecting customer payments on time is the only way MTB will have adequate cash to pay vendor bills when due. So your next step is to learn more about using QuickBooks Online to record customers and sales transactions, including sales to customers and collection of customers' payments.

Chapter 5

LEARNING OBJECTIVES

Chapter 5 focuses on customers and sales transactions for services, such as Craig's Design and Landscaping selling landscaping design services to customers. A later chapter will cover recording customers and sales transactions for products, such as Craig's Design and Landscaping selling a landscape fountain.

In this chapter, you will learn about the following topics:
- Navigating Sales Transactions
  - Navigation Bar
  - Create (+) Icon
- Customers List
  - Update Customers List Before Entering Transactions
  - Update Customers List While Entering Transactions
- Products and Services List
  - Inventory
  - Non-inventory
  - Service
  - Bundle
- Record Sales Transactions Using Sales Receipts
  - Create Sales Receipt
  - Create Bank Deposit for Undeposited Funds From Sales Receipt
- Record Sales Transactions Using Invoices
  - Create Invoice
  - Create Receive Payment
  - Create Bank Deposit For Undeposited Funds From Receive Payment
- Accounting Essentials: Customer Sales and Accounts Receivable

Section 5.1

 QBO SATNAV

QBO SatNav is your satellite navigation for QuickBooks Online, assisting you in navigating QBO

Chapter 5 focuses on QBO Customers and Sales Transactions, shown in the following QBO SatNav.

 **QBO Settings**

Company Settings
Chart of Accounts

 **QBO Transactions**

Banking
Customers & Sales
Vendors & Expenses
Employees & Payroll

 **QBO Reports**

Reports

Section 5.2

QBO SAMPLE COMPANY LOGIN

To log into the QBO Sample Company:

1. Open a web browser. (Note: Intuit recommends using Google Chrome.)

2. Go to https://qbo.intuit.com/redir/testdrive

3. Follow onscreen instructions for security verification

Craig's Design and Landscaping Services should appear on your screen.

To increase the amount of time from one (1) hour to three (3) hours before the log out for inactivity occurs:

1. From Craig's Design and Landscaping Services QBO Sample Company, select the **Gear** icon

2. Under Your Company section, select **Account and Settings**

3. Select **Advanced**

4. Select **Other preferences**

5. For the option Sign me out if inactive for, select **3 hours**

6. Select **Save**

7. Select **Done**

> ⚠️ **The Sample Company** will reset each time it is reopened. This allows you to explore and practice QBO without concern about carrying forward errors to later chapters. However, you will want to make certain to allow enough time to complete all chapter activities before closing the Sample Company. Otherwise, you will lose the work you have entered when you reopen the Sample Company.

To set QBO preferences to display account numbers in the Chart of Accounts:

1 Select the **Gear** icon

2 Select **Account and Settings**

3 Select **Advanced**

4 For Chart of Accounts, select the **Edit Pencil**, then select **Enable account numbers**

5 Select **Show account numbers**

6 Select **Save**

7 Select **Done** to close Account and Settings

Section 5.3

NAVIGATING SALES TRANSACTIONS

Two different ways to navigate sales transactions entry for QBO are:

1. Navigation Bar
2. Create (+) icon

NAVIGATION BAR

To use the Navigation Bar to enter sales transactions:

1 From the Navigation Bar, select **Sales**

2 Select **All Sales** tab

3 From the Sales Transactions window, select the drop-down arrow for **New transaction**

4 Select the type of **new transaction** to enter and complete the onscreen form for the new transaction

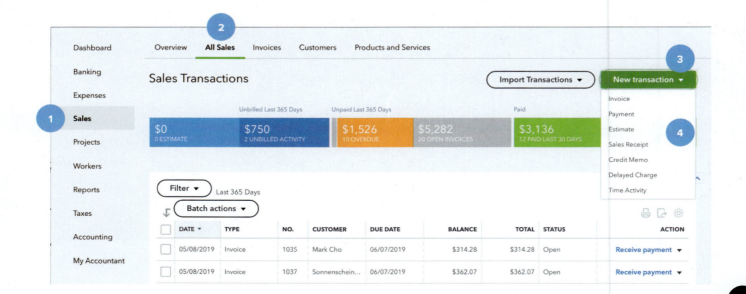

CREATE (+) ICON

To use the Create (+) icon to enter sales transactions:

1 Select **Create (+)** icon

2 Select the **new transaction** from the Customers transactions shown

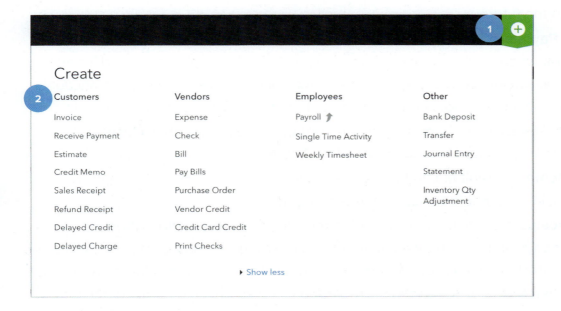

Section 5.4

TYPES OF SALES TRANSACTIONS

Types of sales transactions that we can enter using QBO include:

- **Invoice.** The Invoice form is used to record a sales transaction when the product or service is provided to the customer and the customer promises to pay later. These customer promises are called *accounts receivable* — amounts that we expect to *receive* in the future.

- **Receive Payment.** The Receive Payment form is used to record a related sales transaction when a customer pays its account with cash, check, credit card, or online payment. When a customer payment is received and recorded, customer's accounts receivable balance is reduced by the amount of the customer payment.

- **Estimate.** The Estimate form is used to record estimated costs of products and services to be provided to a customer in the future.

- **Credit Memo.** A Credit Memo form is used when we need to record a credit, or reduction, in the amount the customer is charged.

- **Sales Receipt.** A Sales Receipt is used to record a sales transaction when the customer pays at the same point in time that the product or service is provided to the customer. (Note that if a customer promises to pay later, after receiving a product or service, then the sales transaction is recorded using the Invoice form, not the Sales Receipt form.)

- **Refund Receipt.** The Refund Receipt form is used when we give the customer a refund.

- **Delayed Credit.** A Delayed Credit form is used to record a pending credit to a customer that will occur at a specified future date.

- **Delayed Charge.** A Delayed Charge form is used to record a pending charge to a customer that will occur at a specified future date.

When we enter the above customers and sales transactions, we need to use two QBO Lists:
1. Customers List
2. Products and Services List

Section 5.5

CUSTOMERS LIST

The QBO Customers List permits us to collect and store information about the customer, such as customer name, address, and mobile number. The Customers List is a time-saving feature. Each time we enter a new transaction for a customer, we can use information from the Customers List instead of continually re-entering the same customer information over and over for each sales transaction.

Two ways that we can update the Customers List are:
1. *Before* entering transactions
2. *While* entering transactions

UPDATE CUSTOMERS LIST BEFORE ENTERING TRANSACTIONS

Before entering transactions, we can update the Customers List from the QBO Navigation Bar as follows.

1 From the Navigation Bar, select **Sales**

2 Select **Customers**

3 To enter new customers, select **New customer**

4 Enter **Company Name: Ella's Knittery**

5 Enter **First Name: Marie**

6 Enter **Last Name: Brewer**

7 Select **Display Name as: Ella's Knittery**

8 Enter **Mobile: 415-555-3600**

9 Enter **Billing Address Street: 18 Spring Street**

10 Enter **Billing Address City: Bayshore**

11 Enter **Billing Address State: CA**

12 Enter **Billing Address ZIP: 94326**

13 Enter **Billing Address Country: USA**

14 Select **Shipping Address: Same as billing address**

15 Select **Tax info tab**

16 Check **This customer is taxable**

17 Select **Default Tax Code: California**

18 Select **Payment and billing tab**

19 Select **Preferred Payment Method: Visa**

20 Select **Terms: Due on receipt**

21 Select **Save**

22 To edit an existing customer, select the customer on the Customer List: **Amy's Bird Sanctuary**

23 From the customer window, select **Edit**

24 Enter **Mobile: 650-555-1111**. Notice that after pressing **tab**, QBO automatically reformats the mobile number to (650) 555-1111.

25 Select **Save**

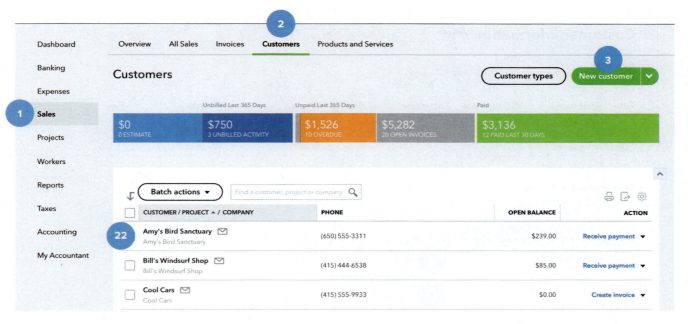

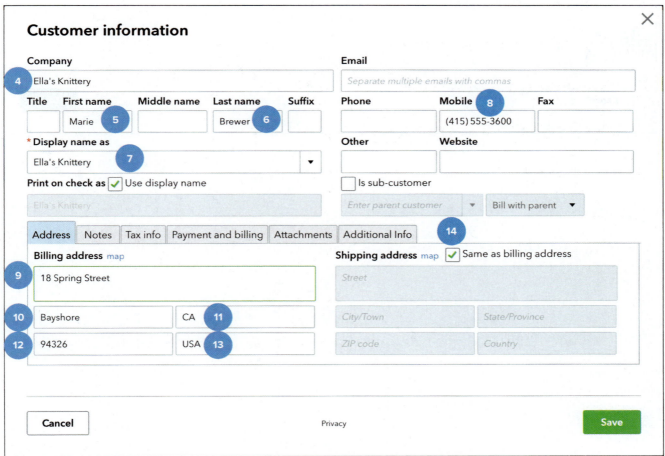

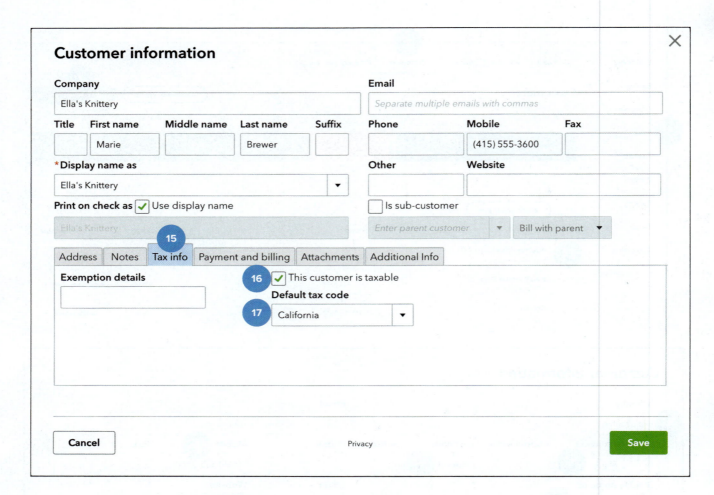

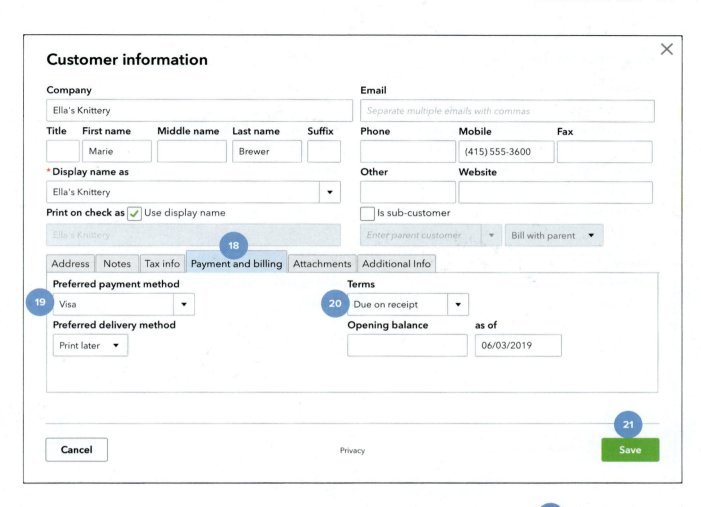

Customer information   ✕

Company					Email		

Ella's Knittery

Separate multiple emails with commas

Title	First name	Middle name	Last name	Suffix	Phone	Mobile	Fax
	Marie		Brewer			(415) 555-3600	

* Display name as   **Other**   **Website**

Ella's Knittery   ▼

Print on check as ✅ Use display name   □ Is sub-customer

Ella's Knittery   *Enter parent customer* ▼   Bill with parent ▼

Address	Notes	Tax info	**Payment and billing**	Attachments	Additional Info

18

Preferred payment method   **Terms**

19 Visa   ▼   **20** Due on receipt   ▼

Preferred delivery method   **Opening balance**   **as of**

Print later   ▼   06/03/2019

Cancel   Privacy   **21** **Save**

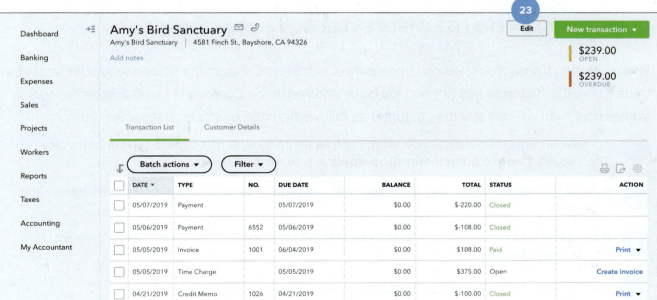

23 Edit   **New transaction** ▼

Dashboard	≡→ **Amy's Bird Sanctuary** ✉ ✑
	Amy's Bird Sanctuary | 4581 Finch St., Bayshore, CA 94326
Banking	
	Add notes
Expenses	
Sales	
Projects	
Workers	

$239.00 OPEN
$239.00 OVERDUE

Transaction List \| Customer Details

Batch actions ▼   Filter ▼

DATE ▼	TYPE	NO.	DUE DATE	BALANCE	TOTAL	STATUS	ACTION
05/07/2019	Payment		05/07/2019	$0.00	$-220.00	Closed	
05/06/2019	Payment	6552	05/06/2019	$0.00	$-108.00	Closed	
05/05/2019	Invoice	1001	06/04/2019	$0.00	$108.00	Paid	Print ▼
05/05/2019	Time Charge		05/05/2019	$0.00	$375.00	Open	Create invoice
04/21/2019	Credit Memo	1026	04/21/2019	$0.00	$-100.00	Closed	Print ▼

Reports
Taxes
Accounting
My Accountant

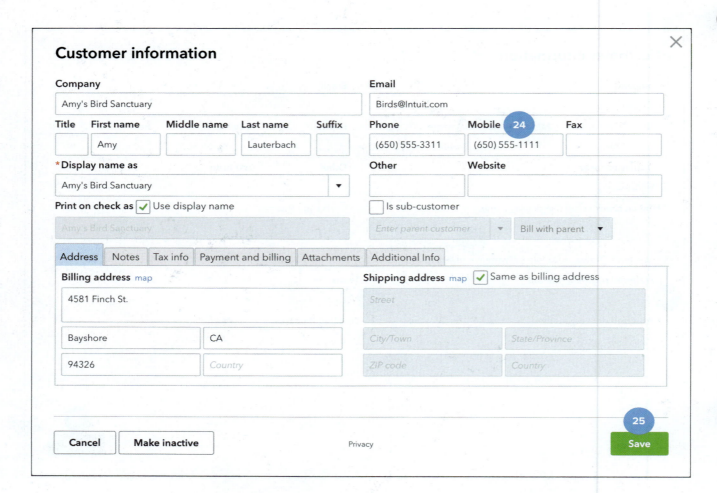

UPDATE CUSTOMERS LIST WHILE ENTERING TRANSACTIONS

While entering transactions, we can update the Customers List from the screen where we enter the transaction. If a customer has not already been entered in the Customers List before entering the transaction, then we can add the customer as follows from the onscreen transaction form.

1   To view an onscreen transaction form, such as an Invoice, select **Create (+) icon** > **Invoice**. Then select **Choose a customer drop-down arrow** > **+ Add new**.

2   If we only needed to add the customer name, we would enter the new customer's name, and then select Save

3   If we wanted to enter more customer detail in addition to the customer's name, then we would select **Details**

4   Next, in the Customer Information window, we would enter customer details

5 Normally, we would then select Save to save the new customer information. In this case, select **Cancel** to leave the Customer Information window.

6 Normally, we would complete and save the Invoice. In this case, select **Cancel** to leave the Invoice window.

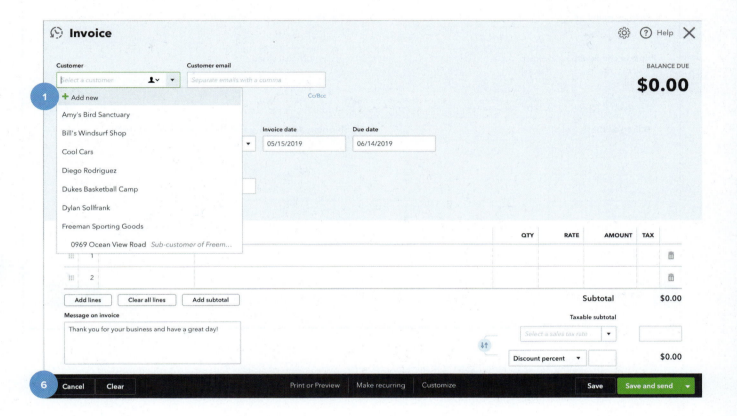

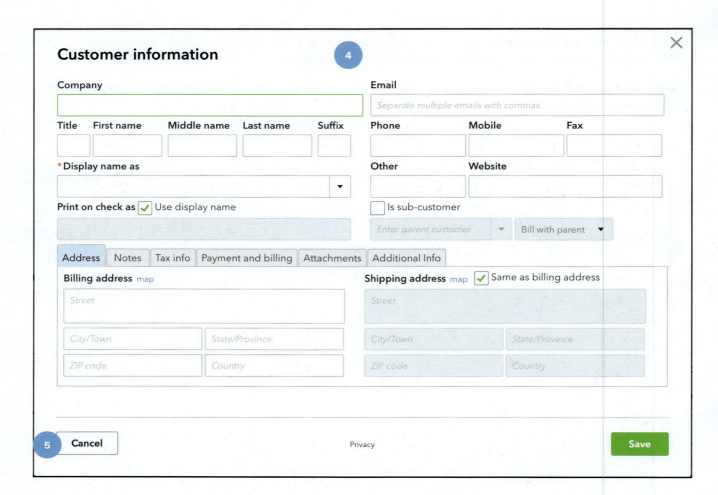

Section 5.6

PRODUCTS AND SERVICES LIST

The Products and Services List collects information about the products and services sold to customers. The Products and Services List is a time-saving feature so that we do not have to continually re-enter the same products and services information each time we enter a new sales transaction.

QBO uses four types of products and services:

1. **Inventory.** Products that we sell for which we track quantities, such as fountains that Craig's Design and Landscaping sells.
2. **Non-inventory.** Products that we sell but we don't need to track the quantity of the product. An example would be bolts that Craig's Design and Landscaping uses in fountain installations.
3. **Service.** Services that we provide to customers, such as Craig's Design and Landscaping providing design consulting services.
4. **Bundle.** A bundle is a collection of products and services that we sell together as a bundle. For example, installation of a fountain by Craig's Design and Landscaping might include a bundle of hoses (products) and installation hours (services).

In this chapter we will focus on services, and in Chapter 7 we will focus on products.

Two ways that we can update the Products and Services List are:
1. *Before* entering transactions
2. *While* entering transactions

UPDATE PRODUCTS AND SERVICES LIST BEFORE ENTERING TRANSACTIONS

Before entering transactions, we can update the Products and Services List as follows.

1 Select **Sales** on the Navigation Bar

2 Select **Product and Services** tab

3 To enter new products or services, select **New**

4 Select **Product/Service Type: Service**

5 Enter **Service Name: Sculpture Garden**

6 Enter SKU or other product/service identification number. In this case, leave **SKU blank**.

7 If available, attach a product/service photo. In this case leave **Photo blank**.

8 Select **Product/Service Category: Design**

9 Select: **I sell this product/service to my customers.**

10 Enter **Description: Sculpture Garden Design Services**

11 Enter **Sales Price/Rate: 90.00**

12 Select **Income Account: Design Income**. This selection connects the service item with the appropriate account in the Chart of Accounts. When this service is recorded on an Invoice, for example, then the amount will be recorded in the Design Income account.

13 Select **Sales Tax Category: Nontaxable**

14 Under Purchasing Information **uncheck I purchase this product/service from a vendor.**

15 Select **Save and close**

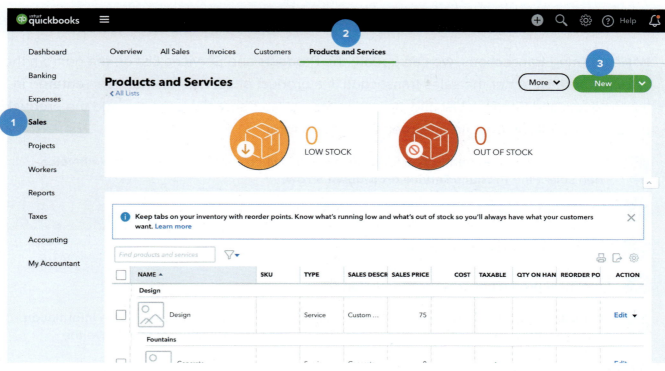

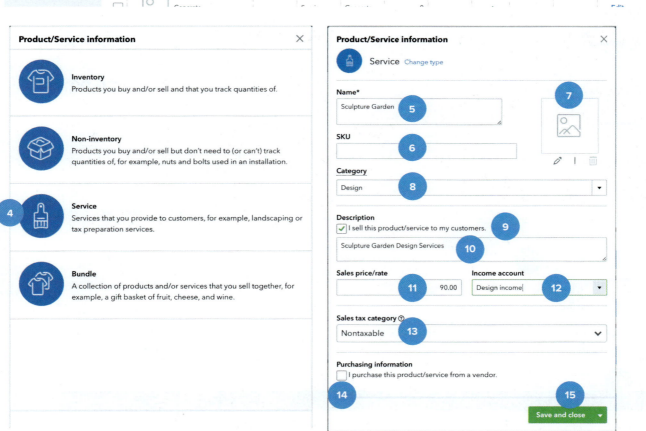

UPDATE PRODUCTS AND SERVICES LIST WHILE ENTERING TRANSACTIONS

While entering transactions, we can update the Products and Services List on the go from the screen where we enter the sales transaction. If a product or service has not been entered in the Products and Services List and is needed for a sales transaction, we can add the product or service as follows from an onscreen transaction form.

1 To view an onscreen transaction form, such as an Invoice, select **Create (+)** icon > **Invoice**. Then select the **Product/Service drop-down arrow**.

2 Select + **Add new**

3 Select **Product/Service Type: Service**

4 Enter **new product or service information**

5 Normally, we would then select Save and Close to save the new product/service information. Then we would complete and save the Invoice. In this case, select **Cancel** to leave the Invoice window.

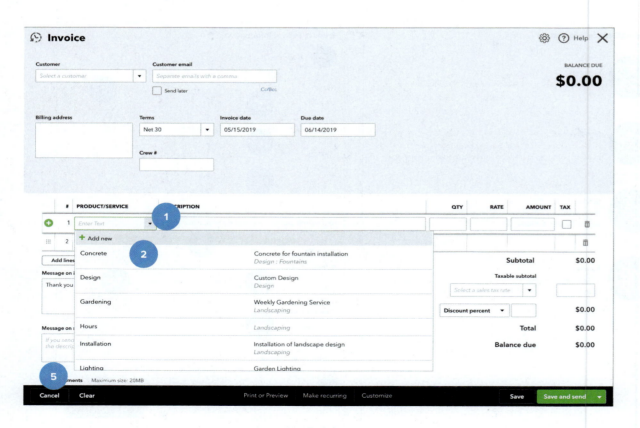

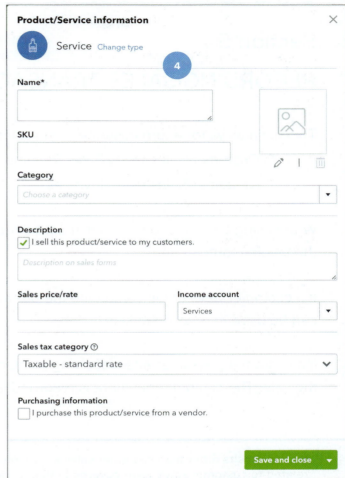

Section 5.7

RECORDING SALES TRANSACTIONS

Two main ways to record customers and sales transactions using QBO are:

- Customer Sales using Sales Receipts
- Customer Sales using Invoices

When using QBO, customer sales must be recorded using either the Sales Receipts form or the Invoice form.

If a customer pays at the same time the product or service is provided, then a Sales Receipt can be used to record the sale.

If a customer pays later after receiving products or services, then an Invoice is used to record the sale. The customer payment is recorded later using the Receive Payments form.

Bank deposits other than customer sales are recorded using the Bank Deposit form. **Bank deposits not related to customer sales were covered in the previous chapter.**

Section 5.8

CUSTOMER SALES RECEIPTS

If a customer's payment is *received at the same time* the product or service is provided, we record the customer sale using the Sales Receipt form. The customer payment may consist of cash, check, or credit card.

When using Sales Receipts to record customer sales:

1 Select **Create (+)** icon

2 Create **Sales Receipt** to record the customer sale for product given and customer payment received in the form of cash, check or credit card. If the customer payment is deposited to the Checking account on the Sales Receipt form, this is the last step. If Undeposited Funds is selected on the Sales Receipt, then complete the next step to transfer the customer payment from the Undeposited Funds account to the Checking account.

3 Create **Bank Deposit** to move customer payment from the Undeposited Funds account to the Checking account. This step is only required if Undeposited Funds is selected on the Sales Receipt. Otherwise, this step is not necessary.

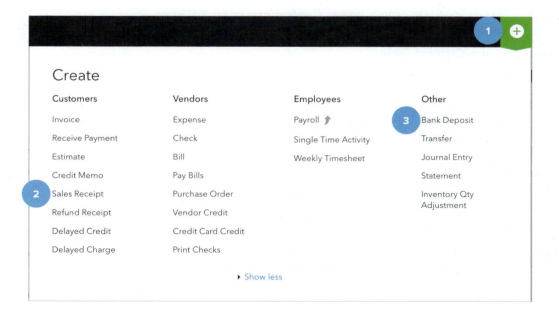

As shown in the following diagram, if Deposit to: Checking account is selected on the Sales Receipt form, then the customer payment is recorded directly in the Checking account. If Deposit to: Undeposited Funds account is selected on the Sales Receipt form, the funds are recorded in the Undeposited Funds account. Then the funds must be transferred from the Undeposited Funds account to the Checking account using the Bank Deposit form.

Deposit to: **Checking Account** Selected on Sales Receipt Form	**Sales Receipt**	➡	➡	➡	**Checking Account**
Deposit to: **Undeposited Funds Account** Selected on Sales Receipt Form	**Sales Receipt**	➡	**Undeposited Funds Account**	➡	**Checking Account**

CREATE SALES RECEIPT

To create a Sales Receipt for a customer sale:

1. Select **Create (+)** icon

2. Select **Sales Receipt**

3. From the Customer List drop-down menu, select **Customer: Dylan Solfrank**

4. Enter **Sales Receipt Date: Current Date**

5. Enter **Payment Method: Check**

6. If Payment Method is Check, enter the customer Check No. as Reference No. In this case, enter **Reference No.: 10265**.

7. Select Deposit to account from the drop-down list. If this deposit will be bundled with other deposits, then select Undeposited Funds, and after completing the Sales Receipt, enter a Bank Deposit to move the funds from Undeposited Funds to the Checking account. If this deposit is not bundled with other deposits, then select the appropriate Checking account from the drop-down list. The funds are deposited directly to the Checking account selected and we do not enter a separate Bank Deposit. In this case, since we want to bundle this deposit with other deposits, select **Deposit to: Undeposited Funds**.

8 From the Product/Service List drop-down menu, select **Product/Service**: **Custom Design**

9 If the Description does not autofill, enter **Description: Custom Design**

10 Enter **Quantity (QTY): 3**

11 Enter **Rate: 75.00**

12 **Amount** should calculate automatically

13 Select Tax if sale is taxable. In this case, since this is a service, not a product, leave **Tax unchecked**.

14 Select appropriate Sales Tax if applicable. In this case, leave **Sales Tax blank**.

15 Enter **Message displayed on statement**: **Custom design services**

16 Add **Attachments**, such as source documents associated with the sales receipt, if any

17 Select **Save** and leave the Sales Receipt form open

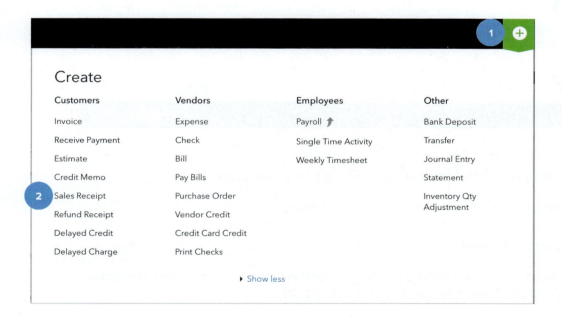

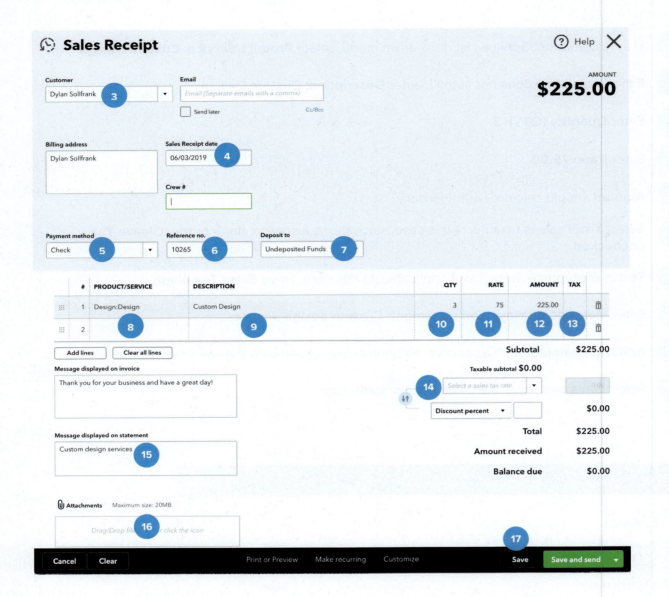

To view the Transaction Journal for the Sales Receipt we just created:

1 From the Sales Receipt window just saved, select **More**

2 Select **Transaction Journal**

3 In the journal entry recorded behind the screen for the Sales Receipt, notice the **Debit** to Undeposited Funds (Other Current Assets) for $225.00

4 In the journal entry notice the **Credit** to the Design Income account for $225.00

CREATE BANK DEPOSIT FOR UNDEPOSITED FUNDS FROM SALES RECEIPT

If the Undeposited Funds account was selected on the Sales Receipt, then we must create a Bank Deposit to transfer the funds from the Undeposited Funds account to the appropriate Checking account. Sometimes the Undeposited Funds account is used on the Sales Receipt if the customer payment will be bundled with other customer payments when deposited. Then our QBO deposit totals will correspond to the deposit total shown by the bank.

> If we selected Undeposited Funds on the Sales Receipt, we *must* create a bank deposit to transfer the funds from the Undeposited Funds account to the appropriate bank account. Otherwise, the funds will remain in the Undeposited Funds account and our QBO Checking account will not reflect the correct balance.

> If we selected a specific bank account, such as Checking account, on the Sales Receipt, we do *not* need to create a separate bank deposit. We have already recorded the deposit of the customer payment in the bank account.

To record a bank deposit related to a customer sale when Undeposited Funds was selected on the Sales Receipt:

1. Select **Create (+)** icon

2. Under Other column, select **Bank Deposit**

3. Select **Account: Checking**

4. Enter **Date: Current Date**

5. The Select the Payments Included in This Deposit section lists customer payments received but not deposited yet. The customer payments listed are undeposited funds that have been recorded as received but not yet deposited in the bank. **Select the Payments Included in this Deposit: Cool Cars** and **Dylan Solfrank**.

6. Enter **Payment Method: Check**

7. Verify **Amount** is correct

8. If there were additional funds to deposit that had not been recorded using the Sales Receipts form or the Invoice form, then those funds could be listed in the Add Funds to This Deposit section. In this case, leave the **Add Funds to This Deposit** section **blank**.

9. Select **Save and close**

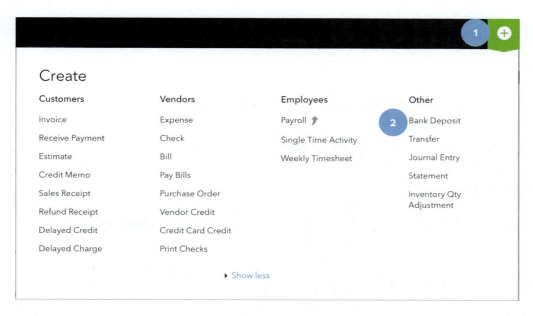

Create

Customers	Vendors	Employees	Other
Invoice	Expense	Payroll	Bank Deposit
Receive Payment	Check	Single Time Activity	Transfer
Estimate	Bill	Weekly Timesheet	Journal Entry
Credit Memo	Pay Bills		Statement
Sales Receipt	Purchase Order		Inventory Qty Adjustment
Refund Receipt	Vendor Credit		
Delayed Credit	Credit Card Credit		
Delayed Charge	Print Checks		

▸ Show less

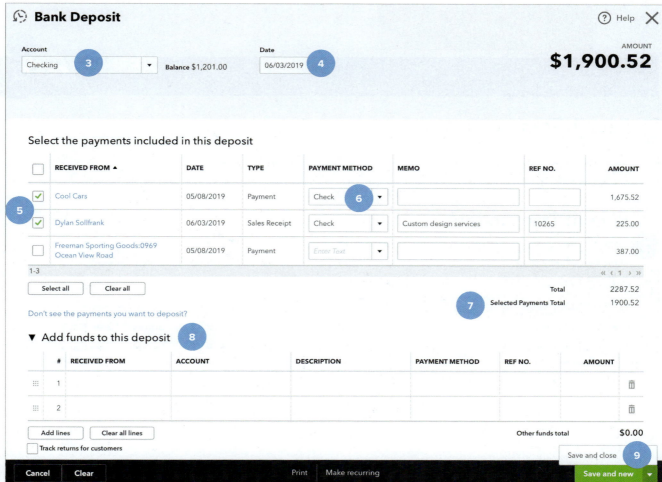

Bank Deposit   ⑦ Help ✕

Account   Date   AMOUNT
Checking   ▾   Balance $1,201.00   06/03/2019   **$1,900.52**

Select the payments included in this deposit

	RECEIVED FROM ▲	DATE	TYPE	PAYMENT METHOD	MEMO	REF NO.	AMOUNT
☑	Cool Cars	05/08/2019	Payment	Check ▾			1,675.52
☑	Dylan Sollfrank	06/03/2019	Sales Receipt	Check ▾	Custom design services	10265	225.00
☐	Freeman Sporting Goods:0969 Ocean View Road	05/08/2019	Payment	Enter Text ▾			387.00

1-3   « ‹ 1 › »

Select all   Clear all   Total   2287.52
                                                                       Selected Payments Total   1900.52

Don't see the payments you want to deposit?

▼ **Add funds to this deposit**

	#	RECEIVED FROM	ACCOUNT	DESCRIPTION	PAYMENT METHOD	REF NO.	AMOUNT	
⠿	1							🗑
⠿	2							🗑

Add lines   Clear all lines   Other funds total $0.00

☐ Track returns for customers

Save and close

Cancel   Clear   Print   Make recurring   **Save and new** ▾

To view the Transaction Journal for the Bank Deposit we just created:

1 From the Tool Bar, select the **Search icon**

2 Under Recent Transactions, select the **Deposit** that we just entered

3 From the bottom of the Bank Deposit form, select **More**

4 Select **Transaction Journal**

5 In the journal entry recorded behind the screen for the Deposit, notice the **Debit** to the Checking account for the total deposit amount of $1,900.52

6 In the journal entry recorded behind the screen for the Deposit, notice the **Credit** to Undeposited Funds for $1,675.52 and $225.00

Search Transactions

Txn no., mm/dd/yyyy, $no.

Advanced Search

Recent Transactions

2 Deposit	06/03/2019	$1,900.52	
Sales Receipt No.1038	06/03/2019	$225.00	Dylan Sollfrank
Credit Card Expense	06/02/2019	$34.00	
Credit Card Expense	05/14/2019	$42.40	Hicks Hardware
Credit Card Expense	05/20/2019	$19.99	Squeaky Kleen Car W…
Credit Card Expense	05/13/2019	$19.99	Squeaky Kleen Car W…

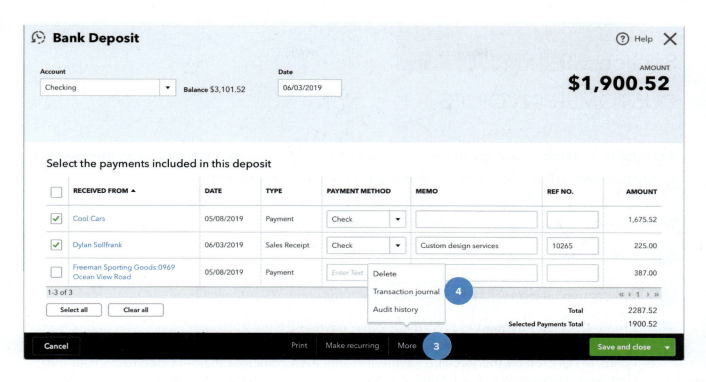

Section 5.9

CUSTOMER INVOICES

If products or services are given to the customer and the customer will pay later, then we use an Invoice instead of a Sales Receipt to record the sales transaction.

When using an Invoice to record customer sales:

1 Select **Create (+)** icon

2 Create **Invoice** to record the customer sale for product or service given to customer

3 Create **Receive Payment** to record customer payment. If the customer payment is deposited to the Checking account on the Receive Payment form, this is the last step. If Undeposited Funds is selected on the Receive Payments form, then complete the next step to transfer the customer payment from the Undeposited Funds account to the Checking account.

4 Create **Bank Deposit** to move the customer payment from the Undeposited Funds account to the appropriate Checking account. This step is only required if Undeposited Funds is selected on the Receive Payments form. Otherwise, this step is not necessary.

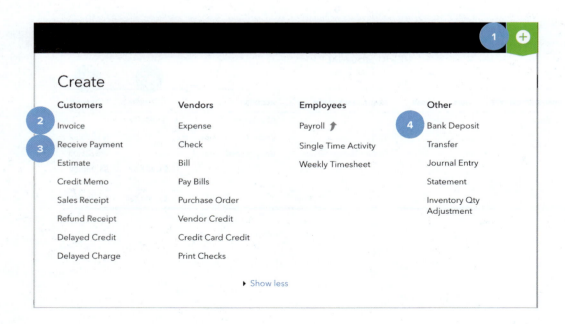

As shown in the following diagram, if Deposit to: Checking account is selected on the Receive Payments form, then the customer payment is recorded directly in the Checking account. If Deposit to: Undeposited Funds account is selected on the Receive Payments form, the funds are recorded in the Undeposited Funds account. Then the funds must be transferred from the Undeposited Funds account to the Checking account using the Bank Deposit form.

Deposit to: **Checking Account** Selected on Receive Payment Form	Invoice	Receive Payment	➡	➡	➡	Checking Account
Deposit to: **Undeposited Funds Account** Selected on Receive Payment Form	Invoice	Receive Payment	➡	Undeposited Funds Account	➡	Checking Account

CREATE INVOICE

An Invoice is used to record sales when the customer will pay later. An Invoice is a bill that contains detailed information about the products and services provided to a customer.

To create an Invoice:

1 Select **Create (+)** icon

2 Select **Invoice**

3 From the Customer List drop-down menu, select **Customer: Dukes Basketball Camp**

4 Select **Terms: Net 30**

5 Enter **Invoice Date: Current Date**

6 Verify **Due Date**

7 From the Product/Service List drop-down menu, select **Product/Service: Custom Design**

8 If the Description does not autofill, enter **Description: Custom Design**

9 Enter **Quantity (QTY): 2**

10 The **Rate** should autofill: **75.00**

11 Verify **Amount** is correct

12 Select Tax if sale is taxable. In this case, the design service is not taxable, so leave **Tax unchecked**.

13 Select appropriate Sales Tax if applicable. In this case, leave **Sales Tax blank**.

14 Select **Save** and leave the Invoice form open

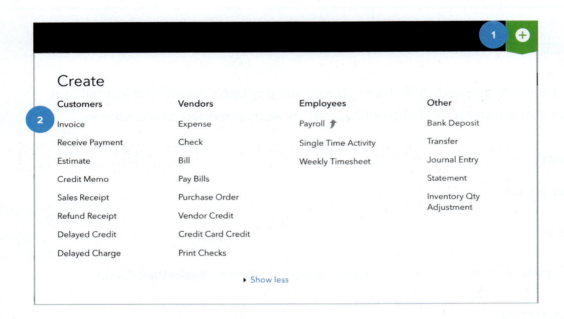

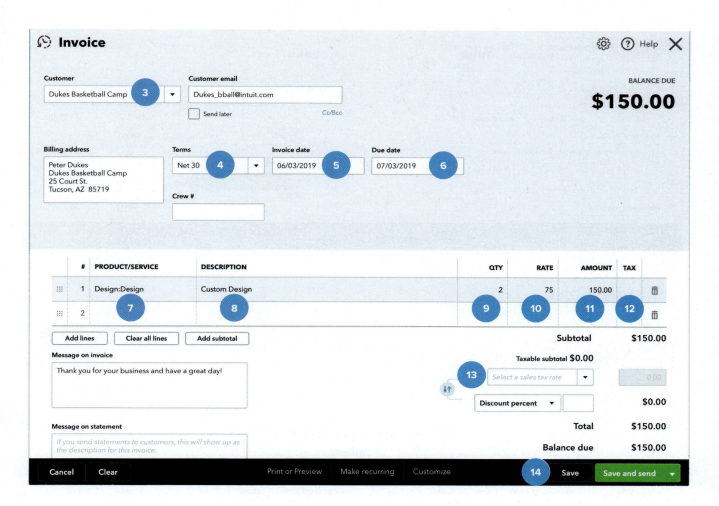

To view the Transaction Journal for the Invoice we just created:

1 From the Invoice window just saved, select **More**

2 Select **Transaction Journal**

3 In the journal entry recorded behind the screen for the Invoice, notice the **Debit** to the Accounts Receivable account for $150.00

4 In the journal entry notice the **Credit** to the Design Income account for $150.00

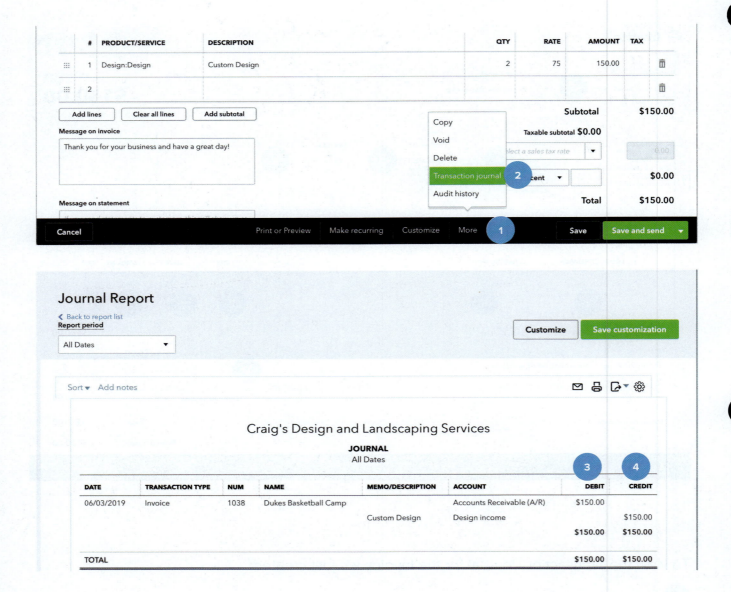

CREATE RECEIVE PAYMENT

Customers may pay in the following ways:

1. **Credit card**, such as Visa or MasterCard, over the phone, in person, or by mail. Using QuickBooks' Merchant Account Service, you can obtain online authorization and then download payments directly into QuickBooks.
2. **Online** by credit card or bank account transfer.
3. **Customer check** delivered either in person or by mail.

To record a customer's payment received to pay an outstanding Invoice:

1 Select **Create (+)** icon

2 Select **Receive Payment**

3 From the Customer List drop-down menu, select **Customer: Dukes Basketball Camp**

4 Enter **Payment Date: Current Date**

5 Enter **Payment Method: Visa**

6 Select Deposit to account from the drop-down list. If this deposit will be bundled with other deposits, then select Undeposited Funds and after completing the Invoice, enter a Bank Deposit to move the funds from Undeposited Funds to the Checking account. If this deposit is not bundled with other deposits, then select the appropriate Checking account from the drop-down list. The funds are deposited directly to the Checking account selected and we do not enter a separate Bank Deposit. In this case, select **Deposit to: Checking**.

7 In the Outstanding Transactions section, select the **Invoice** to which payment should be applied. In this case, select the Invoice we just created for Dukes Basketball Camp for **$150.00**.

8 The **Payment Amount** should autofill for **150.00**

9 Select **Save and close**

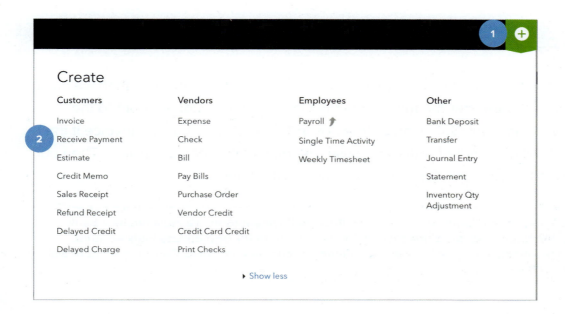

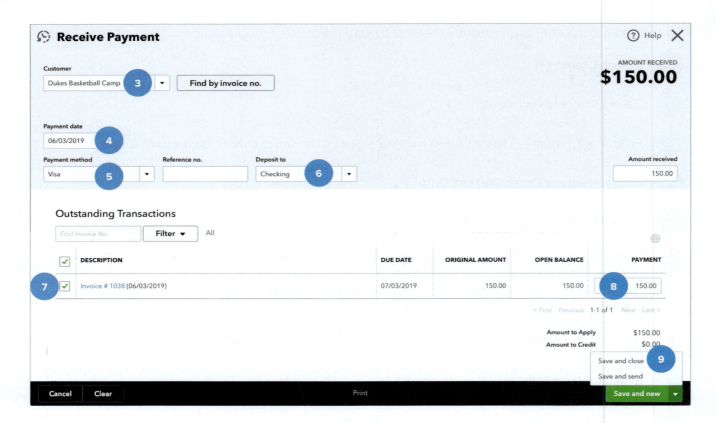

> **Another way to record receiving a customer payment toward an open Invoice** is from the Navigation Bar, select Sales > Invoices tab > Receive payment in the Action column for the open Invoice.

CREATE BANK DEPOSIT FOR UNDEPOSITED FUNDS FROM RECEIVE PAYMENT

If the Undeposited Funds account was selected on the Receive Payment form, then we must create a Bank Deposit to transfer the funds from the Undeposited Funds account to the appropriate Checking account. Sometimes Undeposited Funds is used on the Invoice if the customer payment will be bundled with other customer payments when deposited. Then our totals will correspond to the bank deposit total shown by the bank.

> **If we selected the Undeposited Funds account on the Receive Payment form,** we *must* create a bank deposit to transfer the funds from the Undeposited Funds account to the appropriate bank account. Otherwise, the funds will remain in the Undeposited Funds account and our QBO Checking account will not reflect the correct balance.

> If we selected a specific bank account, such as Checking account, on the Receive Payment form, we do *not* need to create a separate bank deposit. We have already recorded the deposit of the customer payment in the bank account.

To record a bank deposit related to a customer sale when the Undeposited Funds account was selected on the Receive Payment form:

1 Select **Create (+)** icon

2 Under Other column, select **Bank Deposit**

3 Select **Bank Account**

4 Enter **Date** of deposit

5 The Select the Payments Included in This Deposit section lists customer payments received but not deposited yet. The customer payments listed are undeposited funds that have been recorded as received but not yet deposited in the bank. Select the **existing customer payment** to deposit.

6 Enter appropriate **Payment Method**

7 If appropriate, enter **Memo** describing the deposit

8 Verify **Amount** is correct

9 Select **Attachments** to add a file or photo of any accompanying document

10 Typically, we would select Save and close. In this case, since we already recorded the Deposit to Checking from the Receive Payments form, select **Cancel**.

11 This completes the chapter activities. **Close** the QBO Sample Company web browser window to reset the Sample Company before proceeding to the exercises at the end of this chapter.

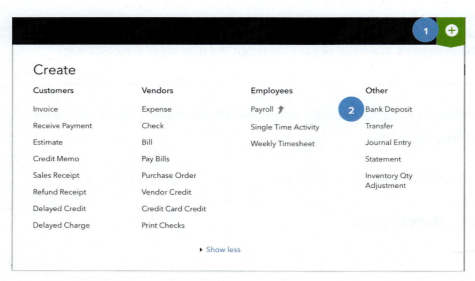

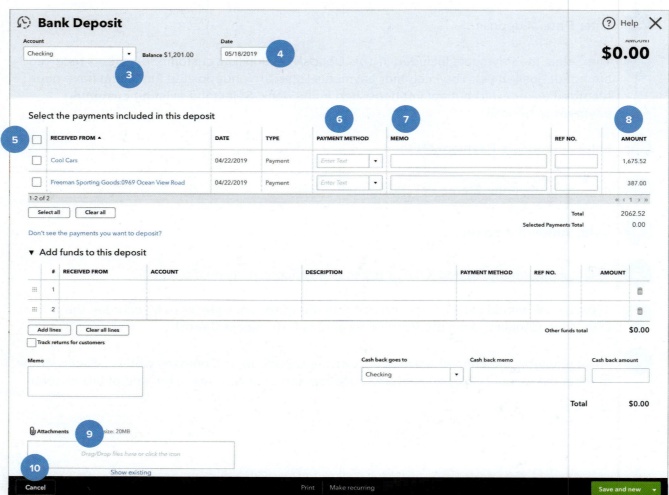

Section 5.10

ACCOUNTING ESSENTIALS
Customer Sales and Accounts Receivable

Accounting Essentials summarize important foundational accounting knowledge you may find useful when using QBO

What are Accounts Receivable?

- Accounts Receivable are amounts that a customer owes our business. When our business makes a credit sale, our business provides goods and services to a customer in exchange for the customer's promise to pay later.
- When a credit sale is recorded on an Invoice, QuickBooks Online increases (debits) Account Receivable—an amount to be received from the customer in the future. When the customer's payment is received, the Account Receivable account is reduced (credited).
- Sometimes the customer breaks the promise and does not pay. So a business should have a credit policy to ensure that credit is extended only to customers who are likely to keep their promise and pay their bills.
- After credit has been extended, a business needs to track accounts receivable to determine if accounts are being collected in a timely manner.

How can a business track accounts receivable to make certain customers are paying on time?

- Accounts Receivable Aging reports provide information about which customers owe our business money, how much the customer owes, and the age of the customer accounts receivable balances.
- In general, the older an account, the less likely the customer will pay the account. So it is important to monitor the age of accounts receivable and take action to collect old accounts.

What happens if a customer does not pay the accounts receivable balance?

- When a customer does not pay the accounts receivable balance, then it is called a bad debt or uncollectible account.
- At the time a credit sale occurs, it is recorded as an increase to sales and an increase to accounts receivable.
- Occasionally a company is unable to collect a customer payment and must write off the customer's account as a bad debt or uncollectible account. When an account is uncollectible, the account receivable is written off or removed from the accounting records.
- There are two different methods that can be used to account for bad debts:
  1. **Direct write-off method.** This method records bad debt expense when it becomes apparent that the customer is not going to pay the amount due. If the direct write-off method is used, the customer's uncollectible account receivable is removed and bad debt expense is recorded at the time a specific customer's account becomes uncollectible. The direct write-off method is used for tax purposes.
  2. **Allowance method.** The allowance method estimates bad debt expense and establishes an allowance or reserve for uncollectible accounts. When using the allowance method, uncollectible accounts expense is estimated in advance of the write-off. The estimate can be calculated as a percentage of sales or as a percentage of accounts receivable. (For example, 2% of credit sales might be estimated to be uncollectible.) This method should be used if uncollectible accounts have a material effect on the company's financial statements used by investors and creditors.
- To record a bad debt, make a journal entry to remove the customer's account receivable (credit Accounts Receivable) and debit either Bad Debt Expense (direct write-off method) or the Allowance for Uncollectible Accounts (allowance method).

Practice Quiz 5

Q5.1

When a sale is recorded on an Invoice, QBO records a:

a. Debit (increase) to cash
b. Credit (increase) to owner's contribution
c. Debit (increase) to accounts receivable
d. Credit (increase) to accounts payable

Q5.2

To enter a sales transaction with payment to be received later:

a. From the Navigation Bar, select Vendors
b. From the Navigation Bar, select Expenses
c. From the Create (+) icon, select Invoice
d. From the Gear icon, select Sales Transactions

Q5.3

When a customer pays cash at the time of sale, what do you record?

a. A sales receipt
b. An invoice
c. A purchase order
d. A thank you note

Q5.4

When a customer purchases products or services but does not pay at the point of sale, what do you record?

a. A sales receipt
b. An invoice
c. A purchase order
d. A reminder

Q5.5

We can update the Customers List at which of the following two points?

a.   Before entering transactions

b.   While entering transactions

c.   After entering transactions

Q5.6

Which of the following two are Customers and Sales transactions?

a.   Invoice

b.   Receive Payment

c.   Pay Bills

d.   Check

Q5.7

Types of products and services on the Products and Services List include which two of the following?

a.   Service

b.   Batch

c.   Inventory

d.   All of the above

Q5.8

Which of the following products and services types track quantities?

a.   Service items

b.   Inventory items

c.   Non-inventory items

d.   None of the above

Q5.9

When preparing a Sales Receipt, if we select Deposit to Undeposited Funds, then we must:

a.   Create a Bank Deposit to move the customer payment from Undeposited Funds to the Checking account

b.   No further action is required

c.   Create a second Sales Receipt depositing the amount to the Checking account

d.   Create a subsequent Invoice depositing the amount to the Checking account

Q5.10

When preparing a Sales Receipt, if we select Deposit to a Checking account, then we:

a. Create a Bank Deposit to move the customer payment from the Checking account to the Undeposited Funds account

b. No further action is required

c. Create a second Sales Receipt depositing the amount to the Checking account

d. Create a subsequent Invoice depositing the amount to the Checking account

Q5.11

Indicate the order in which the following onscreen customers and sales transaction forms typically should be prepared:

a. Invoice > Bank Deposit > Receive Payment

b. Invoice > Sales Receipt > Bank Deposit

c. Invoice > Receive Payment > Bank Deposit

d. None of the above

Q5.12

Which of the following reports provides information about which customers owe money to a business?

a. Profit & Loss

b. Balance Sheet

c. Statement of Cash Flows

d. Accounts Receivable Aging

Q5.13

Accounts Receivable (A/R) are:

a. Amounts totaling the net worth of a company

b. Amounts paid to owners

c. Amounts that customers owe your business

d. Amounts owed to others and are future obligations

Exercises 5

We use the **QBO Sample Company, Craig's Design and Landscaping Services,** for practice throughout the exercises. The Sample Company will reset each time it is reopened. So make certain to allow enough time to complete exercise before closing the Sample Company. Otherwise, you will lose the work you have entered when you reopen the Sample Company.

⚠️ **Since the Sample Company** resets each time it is reopened, be certain to close any web browser windows displaying the QBO Sample Company before starting these exercises. Closing the browser window and starting with a new browser window for the QBO Sample Company resets the data before starting the exercises.

To access the QBO Sample Company, complete the following steps.

1. Open a web browser

2. Go to the https://qbo.intuit.com/redir/testdrive

3. Follow onscreen instructions for security verification

Craig's Design and Landscaping Services should appear on your screen.

E5.1 Customers and Sales Transactions

Match the following customers and sales transactions with the description of the transaction.

Customers and Sales Transaction Descriptions

a. The onscreen form used when we need to record a credit, or reduction, in the amount the customer is charged.

b. An onscreen form used to record a sales transaction when the customer pays at the time of sale when the product or service is provided to the customer.

c. A sales transaction recorded when the product or service is provided to the customer, and the customer promises to pay later.

d. This onscreen form is used when we give the customer a refund.

e. This onscreen form is used to record the transaction when the customer pays its account with cash, check, credit card, or online payment.

f. A form used to record a pending credit to a customer that will occur at a specified future date.

g. This onscreen form is used to record projected costs of products and services to be provided to a customer in the future.

h. An onscreen form used to record a pending charge to a customer that will occur at a specified future date.

Customers and Sales Transaction

1. Invoice

2. Receive Payment

3. Estimate

4. Credit Memo

5. Sales Receipt

6. Refund Receipt

7. Delayed Credit

8. Delayed Charge

E5.2 Customers Transaction: Create Sales Receipt

Using the QBO Sample Company, Craig's Design and Landscaping Services, complete the following.

1. Create Sales Receipt.
    a. Select **Create (+) icon > Sales Receipt**
    b. Select **Customer: Sonnenschein Family Store**
    c. Select **Sales Receipt Date: Current Date**
    d. Select **Payment Method: Check**
    e. Enter **Reference No.: 2020**
    f. Select **Deposit to: Checking**
    g. Select **Product/Service: Landscaping: Gardening (Weekly Gardening Service)**
    h. Enter **QTY: 5**
    i. Enter **Rate: 27.00**
    j. What is the Total for the Sales Receipt?
    k. Select **Save** and leave the Sales Receipt form open

2. View the Transaction Journal for the Sales Receipt.
    a. From the bottom of the Sonnenschein Family Store Sales Receipt, select **More > Transaction Journal**
    b. What are the Account and Amount Debited?
    c. What are the Account and Amount Credited?

E5.3 Customers Transaction: Create Sales Receipt

Using the QBO Sample Company, Craig's Design and Landscaping Services, complete the following.

1. Create Sales Receipt.
    a. Select **Create (+) icon > Sales Receipt**
    b. Select **Customer: Dukes Basketball Camp**
    c. Select **Sales Receipt Date: Current Date**
    d. Select **Payment Method: Check**
    e. Enter **Reference No.: 432**
    f. Select **Deposit to: Undeposited Funds**
    g. Select **Product/Service: Landscaping: Maintenance & Repair**
    h. Enter **QTY: 9**
    i. Enter **Rate: 33.00**
    j. What is the Total for the Sales Receipt?
    k. Select **Save** and leave the Sales Receipt form open

2. View the Transaction Journal for the Sales Receipt.
    a. From the bottom of the Dukes Basketball Camp Sales Receipt, select **More >
        Transaction Journal**
    b. What are the Account and Amount Debited?
    c. What are the Account and Amount Credited?

E5.4 Customers Transaction: Create Bank Deposit

This assignment is a continuation of E5.3

Using the QBO Sample Company, Craig's Design and Landscaping Services, complete the
following.

1. Create Bank Deposit.
    a. Select **Create (+) icon > Bank Deposit**
    b. Select **Account: Checking**
    c. Select **Date: Current Date**
    d. Select **The Payments Included in This Deposit: Dukes Basketball Camp**
    e. What is the Selected Payments Total?
    f. Select **Save and close**

2. View the Transaction Journal for the Deposit.
    a. From the Navigation Bar, select **Accounting**
    b. From the Chart of Accounts, select **View Register** for the Checking account
    c. Select **Dukes Basketball Camp deposit > Edit**
    d. From the bottom of the Dukes Basketball Camp Deposit, select **More > Transaction
        Journal**
    e. What are the Account and Amount Debited?
    f. What are the Account and Amount Credited?

E5.5 Customers Transaction: Create Invoice

Using the QBO Sample Company, Craig's Design and Landscaping Services, complete the following.

1. Create Invoice.
   a. Select **Create (+) icon > Invoice**
   b. Select **Customer: Sushi by Katsuyuki**
   c. Select **Invoice Date: Current Date**
   d. Select **Product/Service: Design**
   e. Enter **QTY: 22**
   f. **Rate** should autofill
   g. What is the Total for the Invoice?
   h. Select **Save** and leave the Invoice displayed

2. View the Transaction Journal for the Invoice.
   a. From the bottom of the Sushi by Katsuyuki Invoice, select **More > Transaction Journal**
   b. What are the Account and Amount Debited?
   c. What are the Account and Amount Credited?

E5.6 Customers Transaction: Receive Payment

This assignment is a continuation of E5.5

Using the QBO Sample Company, Craig's Design and Landscaping Services, complete the following.

1. Create Receive Payment.
   a. Select **Create (+) icon > Receive Payment**
   b. Select **Customer: Sushi by Katsuyuki**
   c. Select **Payment Date: Current Date**
   d. Select **Payment Method: Check**
   e. Select **Deposit to: Undeposited Funds**
   f. Select **Invoice** just entered
   g. After selecting the Invoice, what is the Amount Received displayed?
   h. Select **Save and close**

2. View the Transaction Journal for Receive Payment.
   a. From the Navigation Bar, select **Sales > Invoices tab**
   b. From the Invoices List, select the **Sushi by Katsuyuki Receive Payment** just entered
   c. From the bottom of the Sushi by Katsuyuki Receive Payment, select **More > Transaction Journal**
   d. What are the Account and Amount Debited?
   e. What are the Account and Amount Credited?

E5.7 Customers Transaction: Create Bank Deposit

This assignment is a continuation of E5.5 and E5.6

Using the QBO Sample Company, Craig's Design and Landscaping Services, complete the following.

1. Create Bank Deposit.
    a. Select **Create (+) icon > Bank Deposit**
    b. Select **Account: Checking**
    c. Select **Date: Current Date**
    d. Select **The Payments Included in This Deposit: Sushi by Katsuyuki**
    e. What is the Total for Selected Payments?
    f. Select **Save and close**

2. View the Transaction Journal for the Deposit.
    a. From the Navigation Bar, select **Accounting**
    b. From the Chart of Accounts, select **View Register** for the Checking account
    c. Select **Sushi by Katsuyuki deposit > Edit**
    d. From the bottom of the Sushi by Katsuyuki Deposit, select **More > Transaction Journal**
    e. What are the Account and Amount Debited?
    f. What are the Account and Amount Credited?

E5.8 Customers Transaction: Create Invoice

Using the QBO Sample Company, Craig's Design and Landscaping Services, complete the following.

1. Create Invoice.
    a. Select **Create (+) icon > Invoice**
    b. Select **Customer: Gevelber Photography**
    c. Select **Invoice Date: Current Date**
    d. Select **Product/Service: Design**
    e. Enter **QTY: 13**
    f. **Rate** should autofill
    g. What is the Total for the Invoice?
    h. Select **Save** and leave the Invoice displayed

2. View the Transaction Journal for the Invoice.
    a. From the bottom of the Gevelber Photography Invoice, select **More > Transaction Journal**
    b. What are the Account and Amount Debited?
    c. What are the Account and Amount Credited?

E5.9 Customers Transaction: Credit Memo

This assignment is a continuation of E5.8

Using the QBO Sample Company, Craig's Design and Landscaping Services, complete the following to credit Gevelber Photography for overcharging design by 2 hours.

1. Create Credit Memo.
   a. Select **Create (+) icon > Credit Memo**
   b. Select **Customer: Gevelber Photography**
   c. Select **Credit Memo Date: Current Date**
   d. Select **Product/Service: Design**
   e. Enter **QTY: 3**
   f. **Rate** should autofill
   g. What is the Total for the Credit Memo?
   h. Select **Save and close**

2. View the Transaction Journal for Credit Memo.
   a. From the Navigation Bar, select **Sales > All Sales tab**
   b. From the Sales Transactions List, select the **Gevelber Photography Credit Memo** just entered
   c. From the bottom of the Gevelber Photography Credit Memo, select **More > Transaction Journal**
   d. What are the Account and Amount Debited?
   e. What are the Account and Amount Credited?

E5.10 Customers Transaction: Receive Payment

This assignment is a continuation of E5.8 and E5.9

Using the QBO Sample Company, Craig's Design and Landscaping Services, complete the following.

1. Create Receive Payment.
   a. Select **Create (+) icon > Receive Payment**
   b. Select **Customer: Gevelber Photography**
   c. Select **Payment Date: Current Date**
   d. Select **Payment Method: Visa**
   e. Select **Deposit to: Checking**
   f. Select **Invoice** entered
   g. What is the Original Amount of the Invoice?
   h. What is the Open Balance?
   i. After selecting the Invoice, what is the Amount Received displayed on the Invoice?
   j. Select **Save and close**

2. View the Transaction Journal for Receive Payment.
   a. From the Navigation Bar, select **Sales > All Sales tab**
   b. From the Sales Transactions List, select the **Gevelber Photography Receive Payment** just entered
   c. From the bottom of the Gevelber Photography Receive Payment, select **More > Transaction Journal**
   d. What are the Account and Amount Debited?
   e. What are the Account and Amount Credited?

Project 5.1

Mookie the Beagle™ Concierge

> **Project 5.1 is a continuation of Project 4.1. You will use the QBO Company you created for Project 1.1 and updated in subsequent Projects 2.1 through 4.1. Keep in mind the QBO Company for Project 5.1 does not reset and carries your data forward, including any errors. So it is important to check and crosscheck your work to verify it is correct before clicking the Save button.**

BACKSTORY

Mookie The Beagle™ Concierge provides convenient, high-quality pet care services to customers on demand. Cy will be using QBO to process customers and sales transactions and has asked for your assistance in seeing that all sales are recorded properly.

To improve business processes and streamline operations, Cy knows that having up-to-date customer contact information is crucial to MTB business success. So he has requested that you place an emphasis on using the QBO Customers List to maintain customer contact details.

Complete the following for Mookie The Beagle Concierge.

 # QBO SATNAV

Project 5.1 focuses on QBO Transactions, specifically Customers and Sales Transactions as shown in the following QBO SatNav.

 **QBO SatNav**

QBO Settings

Company Settings
Chart of Accounts

 **QBO Transactions**

Banking
Customers & Sales
Vendors & Expenses
Employees & Payroll

 **QBO Reports**

Reports

HOW TO LOG INTO QBO

To log into QBO, complete the following steps.

1 Using a web browser go to qbo.intuit.com

2 Enter **User ID** (the email address you used to set up your QBO Account)

3 Enter **Password** (the password you used to set up your QBO Account)

4 Select **Sign in**

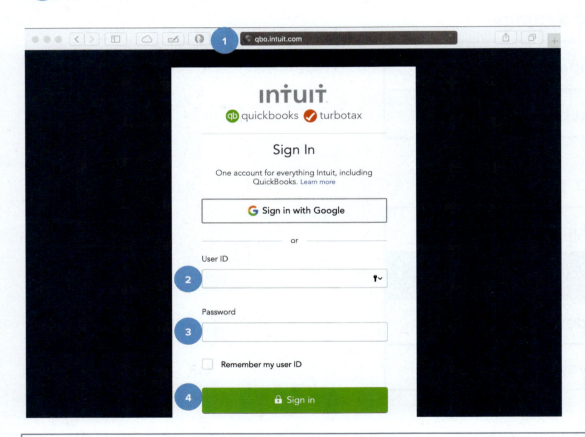

If you are <u>not</u> using a public or shared computer, to speed up login, you can save your login to your desktop and select Remember Me. If you are using a public computer or shared computer, do not save to the desktop and unselect Remember Me.

The new QBO Company we created in Project 1.1 will carry all work forward into future chapters. So it is important to check and crosscheck your work to verify it is correct before clicking the Save button. Any uncorrected errors will be carried forward in your QBO Company for text projects.

P5.1.1 Sales Receipt

Angel used the Mookie The Beagle Concierge app to schedule pet care for Kuno, her German Shepherd. Each Friday from 1 pm until 9 pm, Angel needs pet care for Kuno, starting on 01/14/2022. Kuno requires extra healthcare considerations, including medications, so the nine hours each week will be billed at the Pet Wellness: Extended Wellness rate. Angel paid in advance by check for 8 weeks of pet care services.

Complete the following for Mookie The Beagle Concierge to record a Sales Receipt for Angel.

1. Enter a New Customer in the Customers List.
    a. From the Navigation Bar, select **Sales > Customers tab**
    b. Select **New customer**
    c. Enter the following customer information.

Display Name As:	**Kuno Angel**
Email:	**kuno@www.com**
Mobile:	**415-555-0117**
Billing Address Street:	**86 University Avenue**
Billing Address City:	**Bayshore**
Billing Address State:	**CA**
Billing Address ZIP:	**94326**
Billing Address Country:	**USA**
Shipping Address:	**Same as billing address**

d. Select **Save**

2. Create Sales Receipt.
    a. Select **Create (+) icon > Sales Receipt**
    b. Select **Customer: Kuno Angel**
    c. Select **Sales Receipt Date: 01/14/2022**
    d. Select **Payment Method: Check**
    e. Enter **Reference No.: 3033**
    f. Select **Deposit to: Checking**
    g. Select **Product/Service: Pet Wellness: Extended Wellness**
    h. Enter **QTY: 64**
    i. Enter **Rate: 50.00**
    j. What is the Total for the Sales Receipt?
    k. Select **Save** and leave the Sales Receipt displayed

3. View the Transaction Journal for the Sales Receipt.
    a. From the bottom of the Kuno Angel Sales Receipt, select **More > Transaction Journal**
    b. What are the Account and Amount Debited?
    c. What are the Account and Amount Credited?

P5.1.2 Sales Receipt

Angel used the Mookie The Beagle Concierge app to schedule pet care for Kuno, her German Shepherd, for the last weekend in January (01/29/2022 2 pm until 01/30/2022 11 pm) while she is completing a charity run. Kuno requires extra healthcare considerations so the service will be billed at Pet Wellness: Intensive Wellness rates.

1. Create Sales Receipt.
    a. Select **Create (+) icon > Sales Receipt**
    b. Select **Customer: Kuno Angel**
    c. Select **Sales Receipt Date: 01/29/2022**
    d. Select **Payment Method: Check**
    e. Enter **Reference No.: 3042**
    f. Select **Deposit to: Checking**
    g. Select **Product/Service: Pet Wellness: Intensive Wellness**
    h. Enter **QTY: 33**
    i. Enter **Rate: 70.00**
    j. What is the Total for the Sales Receipt?
    k. Select **Save** and leave the Sales Receipt displayed

2. View the Transaction Journal for the Sales Receipt.
   a. From the bottom of the Kuno Angel Sales Receipt, select **More > Transaction Journal**
   b. What are the Account and Amount Debited?
   c. What are the Account and Amount Credited?

P5.1.3 Invoice

Asher has to work late to meet ridiculous deadlines on a major project, much later than the time that doggie day care closes for his pet Maltese puppy, Venus. So Asher uses the Mookie The Beagle Concierge app to schedule a pickup from doggie day care to take Venus home and pick up puppy food, which Asher hasn't had time to buy because of his demanding work schedule.

So when Asher is working late, he is pleased to have the Mookie The Beagle Concierge app to schedule the following pet care services.

* Pet Care: Transport 1 hour (pickup at doggie day care)
* Pet Care: Errand 1 hour (minimum) to obtain puppy food
* Pet Care: Medium Visit 4 hours

Complete the following to record the Invoice for services provided.

1. Enter a New Customer in the Customers List.
   a. From the Navigation Bar, select **Sales > Customers tab**
   b. Select **New customer**
   c. Enter the following customer information.

Display Name As:	**Venus Asher**
Email:	**asher@www.com**
Mobile:	**415-555-0144**
Billing Address Street:	**138 Astarte Avenue**
Billing Address City:	**Bayshore**
Billing Address State:	**CA**
Billing Address ZIP:	**94326**
Billing Address Country:	**USA**
Shipping Address:	**Same as billing address**

   d. Select **Save**

2. Create an Invoice.
   a. Select **Create (+) icon > Invoice**
   b. Select **Customer: Venus Asher**
   c. Select **Invoice Date: 01/18/2022**
   d. Select **Product/Service: Pet Care: Transport**
   e. Select **QTY: 1**
   f. **Rate** and **Amount** should autofill.
   g. Select **Product/Service: Pet Care: Errand**
   h. Select **QTY: 1**
   i. **Rate** and **Amount** should autofill.
   j. Select **Product/Service: Pet Care: Medium Visit**
   k. Select **QTY: 4**
   l. **Rate** and **Amount** should autofill
   m. What is the Balance Due for the invoice?
   n. Select **Save** and leave the Invoice displayed

3. View the Transaction Journal for the Invoice.
   a. From the bottom of the Venus Asher Invoice, select **More > Transaction Journal**
   b. What are the Account and Amount Debited?
   c. What are the Accounts and Amounts Credited?

P5.1.4 Invoice

Asher learns that he has to work late the next two nights, once again much later than the time that doggie day care closes for his pet Maltese, Venus. So Asher uses the Mookie The Beagle Concierge app to schedule a pickup from doggie day care to take Venus home and provide pet care services.

Asher uses the Mookie The Beagle Concierge app to schedule the following pet care services for the next two nights.

- Pet Care: Transport 1 hour (pickup at doggie day care)
- Pet Care: Medium Visit 4 hours
- Pet Care: Transport 1 hour (pickup at doggie day care)
- Pet Care: Extended Visit 5 hours

Complete the following to record the invoice for services provided.

1. Create an Invoice.
    a. Select **Create (+) icon > Invoice**
    b. Select **Customer: Venus Asher**
    c. Select **Invoice Date: 01/19/2022**
    d. Select **Product/Service: Pet Care: Transport**
    e. Select **QTY: 1**
    f. **Rate** and **Amount** should autofill.
    g. Select **Product/Service: Pet Care: Medium Visit**
    h. Select **QTY: 4**
    i. **Rate** and **Amount** should autofill.
    j. Select **Product/Service: Pet Care: Transport**
    k. Select **QTY: 1**
    l. **Rate** and **Amount** should autofill.
    m. Select **Product/Service: Pet Care: Extended Visit**
    n. Select **QTY: 5**
    o. **Rate** and **Amount** should autofill
    p. What is the Balance Due for the invoice?
    q. Select **Save** and leave the Invoice displayed

2. View the Transaction Journal for the Invoice.
    a. From the bottom of the Venus Asher Invoice, select **More > Transaction Journal**
    b. What are the Account and Amount Debited?
    c. What are the Accounts and Amounts Credited?

P5.1.5 Receive Payment

Record the payment that Mookie The Beagle Concierge receives from Mimi in payment for the prior invoice for services provided Bebe.

1. Edit a Customer in the Customers List.
    a. From the Navigation Bar, select **Sales > Customers tab**
    b. From the Customers List, select **Customer: Bebe Mimi**
    c. Update the following customer information.

Display Name As:	**Bebe Mimi**
Email:	**mimi@www.com**
Mobile:	**415-555-2160**
Billing Address Street:	**220 Alsace Avenue**
Billing Address City:	**Bayshore**
Billing Address State:	**CA**
Billing Address ZIP:	**94326**
Billing Address Country:	**USA**
Shipping Address:	**Same as billing address**

    d. Select **Save**

2. Create Receive Payment.
    a. Select **Create (+) icon > Receive Payment**
    b. Select **Customer: Bebe Mimi**
    c. Select **Payment Date: 01/13/2022**
    d. Select **Payment Method: Check**
    e. Select **Deposit to: Checking**
    f. Select **Invoice** previously entered
    g. After selecting the Invoice, what is the Amount Received displayed?
    h. Select **Save and close**

3. View the Transaction Journal for Receive Payment.
    a. From the Navigation Bar, select **Sales > All Sales tab**
    b. From the Sales Transactions List, select the **Bebe Mimi Payment** just entered
    c. From the bottom of the Bebe Mimi Receive Payment, select **More > Transaction Journal**
    d. What are the Account and Amount Debited?
    e. What are the Account and Amount Credited?

P5.1.6 Receive Payment

Record the payment that Mookie The Beagle Concierge receives from Graziella in payment for the prior invoice for services provided Mario.

1. Edit a Customer in the Customers List.
    a. From the Navigation Bar, select **Sales > Customers tab**
    b. From the Customers List, select **Customer: Mario Graziella**
    c. Update the following customer information.

Display Name As:	Mario Graziella
Email:	mario@www.com
Mobile:	415-555-7210
Billing Address Street:	13 Marco Drive
Billing Address City:	Bayshore
Billing Address State:	CA
Billing Address ZIP:	94326
Billing Address Country:	USA
Shipping Address:	Same as billing address

    d. Select **Save**

2. Create Receive Payment.
   a. Select **Create (+) icon > Receive Payment**
   b. Select **Customer: Mario Graziella**
   c. Select **Payment Date: 01/13/2022**
   d. Select **Payment Method: Check**
   e. Select **Deposit to: Checking**
   f. Select **Invoice** previously entered
   g. After selecting the Invoice, what is the Amount Received displayed?
   h. Select **Save and close**

3. View the Transaction Journal for Receive Payment.
   a. From the Navigation Bar, select **Sales > All Sales tab**
   b. From the Sales Transactions List, select the **Mario Graziella Payment** just entered
   c. From the bottom of the Mario Graziella Receive Payment, select **More > Transaction Journal**
   d. What are the Account and Amount Debited?
   e. What are the Account and Amount Credited?

P5.1.7 Receive payment

Record the payment that Mookie The Beagle Concierge receives from Asher in payment for the invoice dated 01/19/2022 for services provided Venus.

1. Create Receive Payment.
   a. Select **Create (+) icon > Receive Payment**
   b. Select **Customer: Venus Asher**
   c. Select **Payment Date: 01/20/2022**
   d. Select **Payment Method: Credit Card**
   e. Select **Deposit to: Undeposited Funds**
   f. Select **Invoice** dated **01/19/2022**
   g. After selecting the Invoice, what is the Amount Received displayed?
   h. Select **Save and close**

2. View the Transaction Journal for Receive Payment.
   a. From the Navigation Bar, select **Sales > All Sales tab**
   b. From the Sales Transactions List, select the **Venus Asher Payment** just entered
   c. From the bottom of the Venus Asher Receive Payment, select **More > Transaction Journal**
   d. What are the Account and Amount Debited?
   e. What are the Account and Amount Credited?

P5.1.8 Bank Deposit

Record the bank deposit for Mookie The Beagle Concierge related to the Asher payment for the first services provided Venus.

1. Create Bank Deposit.
   a. Select **Create (+) icon > Bank Deposit**
   b. Select **Account: Checking**
   c. Select **Date: 01/23/2022**
   d. **Select The Payments Included in This Deposit: Venus Asher**
   e. What is the Selected Payments Total?
   f. Select **Save and close**

2. View the Transaction Journal for the Deposit.
   a. From the Navigation Bar, select **Accounting**
   b. From the Chart of Accounts, select **View Register** for the Checking account
   c. Select **Venus Asher deposit > Edit**
   d. From the bottom of the Venus Asher Deposit, select **More > Transaction Journal**
   e. What are the Account and Amount Debited?
   f. What are the Account and Amount Credited?

P5.1.9 Customers List

Cy requested a copy of Mookie The Beagle Concierge's current Customers List.

To export the Customers List:

1. From the Navigation Bar, select **Reports** > **Standard tab** > **Sales and Customers** > **Customer Contact List** > **Run Report** > **Export icon** > **Export to PDF** > **Save as PDF**.

Chapter 6

Vendors and Expenses

In addition to tracking customers and sales transactions, Mookie the Beagle Concierge also needs to track vendors and expenses transactions. Cy Walker realizes the importance of all expenses being recorded accurately so MTB does not miss any tax deductions. Also, Cy needs an efficient way to track when vendor bills are due so the bills are paid on time. Paying bills on time is crucial to building a good credit rating for MTB. So your next step is to learn more about using QuickBooks Online for vendors and expenses transactions.

Chapter 6

LEARNING OBJECTIVES

Chapter 6 covers using QBO to record vendors and expenses transactions, such as purchasing from vendors, recording expenses, and paying bills. This chapter focuses on expenses and purchasing of services from vendors, such as Craig's Design and Landscaping Services purchasing legal services from its attorney. The next chapter will focus on purchasing products that are inventory for resale to customers, such as Craig's Design and Landscaping Services purchasing landscape fountains from vendors for resale to customers.

In this chapter, you will learn about the following topics:
- Navigating Vendors and Expenses Transactions
  - Navigation Bar
  - Create (+) Icon
- Vendors List
  - Update Vendors List Before Entering Transactions
  - Update Vendors List While Entering Transactions
- Record Vendors Transactions Using Expense Form
- Record Vendors Transactions Using Check Form
- Record Vendors Transactions Using Bill > Pay Bills
  - Create Bill
  - Create Pay Bills
- Accounting Essentials: Vendors Transactions, Accounts Payable, and 1099s

Section 6.1
 QBO SATNAV

QBO SatNav is our satellite navigation for QuickBooks Online, assisting us in navigating QBO

Chapter 6 focuses on QBO Vendors and Expenses transactions, shown in the following QBO SatNav.

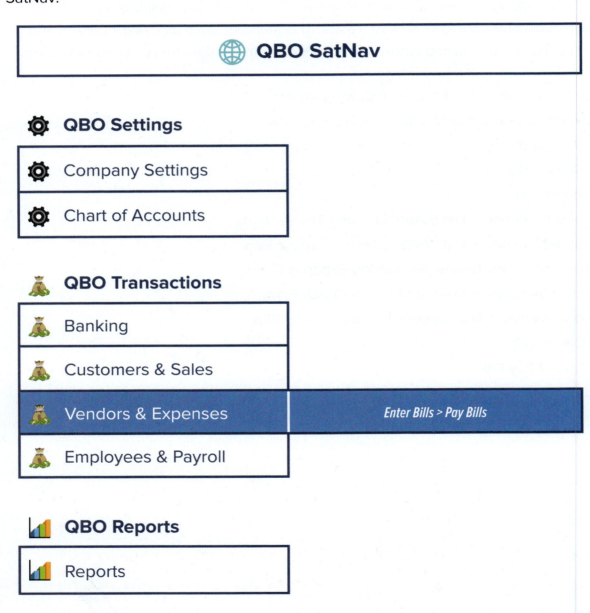

Section 6.2

QBO SAMPLE COMPANY LOGIN

To log into the QBO Sample Company:

1 Open a web browser. (Note: Intuit recommends using Google Chrome.)

2 Go to the https://qbo.intuit.com/redir/testdrive

3 Follow onscreen instructions for security verification

Craig's Design and Landscaping Services should appear on the screen.

To increase the amount of time from one (1) hour to three (3) hours before the log out for inactivity occurs:

1 From Craig's Design and Landscaping Services QBO Sample Company, select the **Gear** icon

2 Under the Your Company section, select **Account and Settings**

3 Select **Advanced**

4 Select **Other preferences**

5 For the option Sign me out if inactive for, select **3 hours**

6 Select **Save**

7 Select **Done**

> ⚠️ **The Sample Company** will reset each time it is reopened. This allows you to explore and practice QBO without concern about carrying forward errors to later chapters. However, you will want to make certain to allow enough time to complete all chapter activities before closing the Sample Company. Otherwise, you will lose the work you have entered if you close and reopen the Sample Company.

To set QBO preferences to display account numbers in the Chart of Accounts:

1 Select the **Gear** icon to display options

2 Select **Account and Settings**

3 Select **Advanced**

4 For Chart of Accounts, select the **Edit Pencil**, then select **Enable account numbers**

5 Select **Show account numbers**

6 Select **Save**

7 Select **Done** to close Account and Settings

Section 6.3

NAVIGATING VENDORS AND EXPENSES TRANSACTIONS

Two different ways to navigate entering vendors and expenses transactions into QBO are:

1. Navigation Bar
2. Create (+) icon

NAVIGATION BAR

To use the Navigation Bar to enter expenses transactions:

1 From the Navigation Bar, select **Expenses**

2 Select **Expenses** tab

3 From the Expense Transactions window, select the drop-down arrow for **New transaction**

4 Select the type of **new transaction** to enter and complete the onscreen form for the new transaction

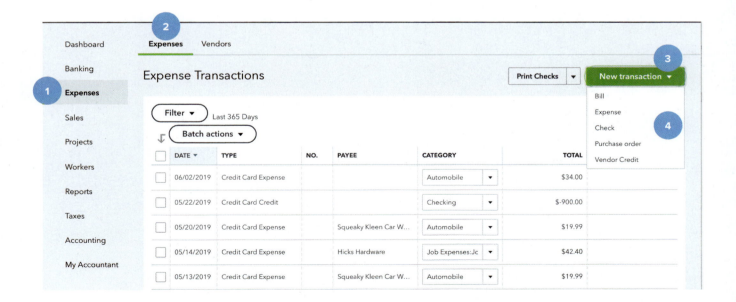

CREATE (+) ICON

To use the Create (+) icon to enter expense transactions:

1   Select **Create (+)** icon

2   Select the **new transaction** from the Vendors transactions shown

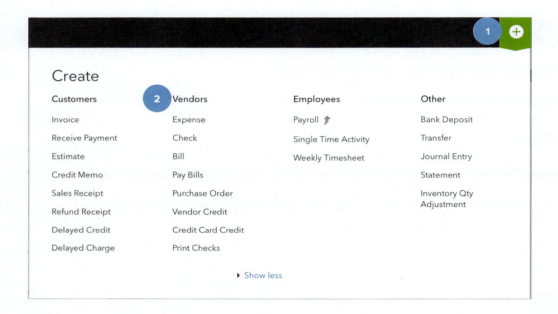

Section 6.4

TYPES OF VENDORS TRANSACTIONS

Types of vendor transactions that we can enter using QBO include:

- **Expense.** The Expense form can be used to record expenses that we pay for at the time we receive the product or service. We can pay using cash, credit card, or check.
- **Check.** The Check form is used when we write a check. Using the Check form was covered in Chapter 4, Banking.
- **Bill.** The Bill form is used to record services, such as utilities or accounting services. We use the Bill form to record a bill received (expense) and our obligation to pay the vendor later (accounts payable).
- **Pay Bills.** The Pay Bills form is used to select bills we want to pay.
- **Purchase Order.** A Purchase Order is used to track products ordered from vendors.
- **Vendor Credit.** The Vendor Credit form is used when a vendor gives us a refund, or reduction in the amount we owe the vendor, to our bill.
- **Credit Card Credit.** A Credit Card Credit form is used to record a credit, or reduction in charges by the vendor, to our credit card.

Section 6.5

VENDORS LIST

The QBO Vendors List permits us to collect and store information about a vendor, such as vendor name, address, and phone number. Then we can reuse the stored vendor information without re-entering it. After vendor information is entered in the Vendors List, when the specific vendor is selected on a vendor transaction form, such as a Check form, QBO automatically transfers the vendor information to the appropriate fields on the transaction form. This feature enables us to enter vendor information one time into QBO instead of re-entering the same vendor information each time a transaction form is created. Not only does this save time, but it also reduces errors.

QBO considers a vendor to be any individual or organization that provides products or services to our company. QBO considers all of the following to be vendors:

- Suppliers from whom we buy inventory or supplies
- Service companies that provide services to our company, such as cleaning services or landscaping services
- Financial institutions, such as banks, that provide financial services including checking accounts and loans
- Tax agencies, such as the IRS. The IRS is considered a vendor because we pay taxes to the IRS.
- Utility and telephone companies

Two ways that we can update the Vendors List are:
1. *Before* entering transactions
2. *While* entering transactions

UPDATE VENDORS LIST BEFORE ENTERING TRANSACTIONS

Before entering transactions, we can update the Vendors List from the QBO Navigation Bar as follows.

 From the Navigation Bar, select **Expenses**

2 Select **Vendors** tab

3 To enter a new vendor, select **New vendor**

4 In the Vendor Information form, enter **Company Name: Sofia Raphael Associates**

5 Enter **First Name: Sofia**

6 Enter **Last Name: Raphael**

7 Select **Display Name as: Sofia Raphael Associates**

8 Enter **Phone: 415-555-6543**

9 Enter **Address Street: 32 North Avenue**

10 Enter **Address City: Bayshore**

11 Enter **Address State: CA**

12 Enter **Address ZIP: 94326**

13 Enter **Address Country: USA**

14 Select **Terms: Net 15**

15 Enter **Account No.: 63728190**

16 Select **Save**

17 To edit an existing vendor, select the vendor on the Vendors List: **Books by Bessie**

18 From the vendor window, select **Edit**

19 Enter **Mobile: 650-555-9999**. Notice that after pressing **tab**, QBO automatically reformats the mobile number to (650) 555-9999.

20 Select **Save**

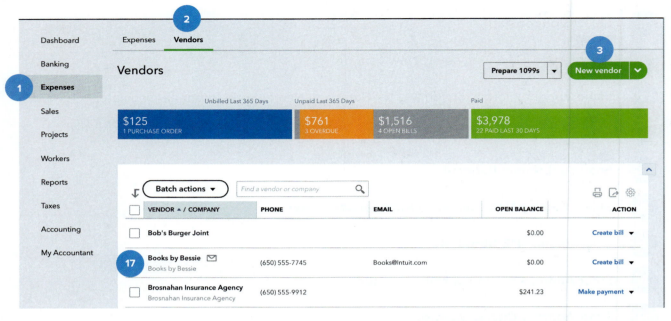

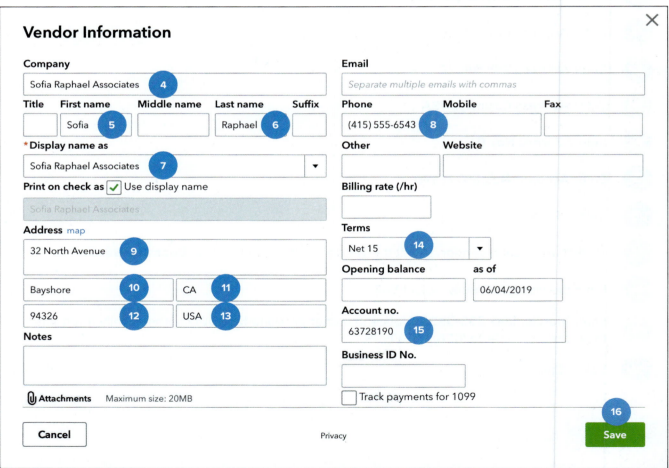

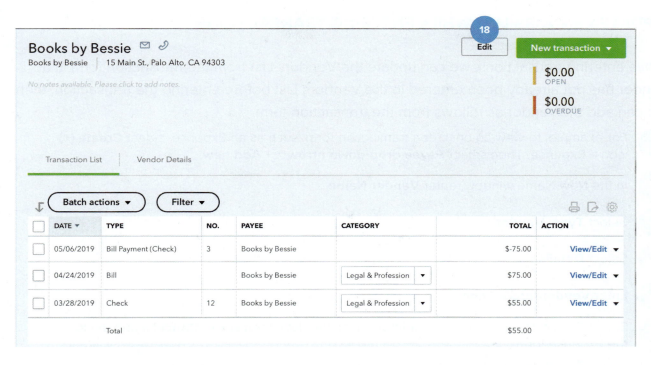

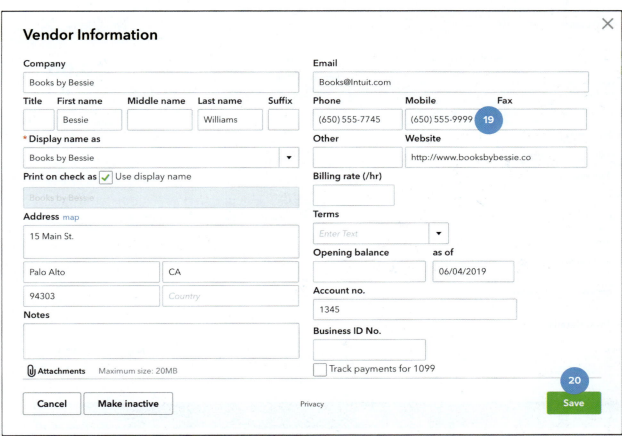

UPDATE VENDORS LIST WHILE ENTERING TRANSACTIONS

While entering transactions, we can update the Vendors List from the transaction form. If a vendor has not already been entered in the Vendors List before entering the transaction, then we can add the vendor as follows from the transaction form.

1. For example, to view an onscreen transaction form, such as an Expense, select **Create (+)** icon > **Expense**. Then select **Payee drop-down arrow** > + **Add new**.

2. In the New Name window, enter **Vendor Name**

3. Select **Type: Vendor**

4. Select **Details**

5. Enter **Vendor Information**

6. Select **Cancel** to close the Vendor Information window, then select **Cancel** again to close the Expense form

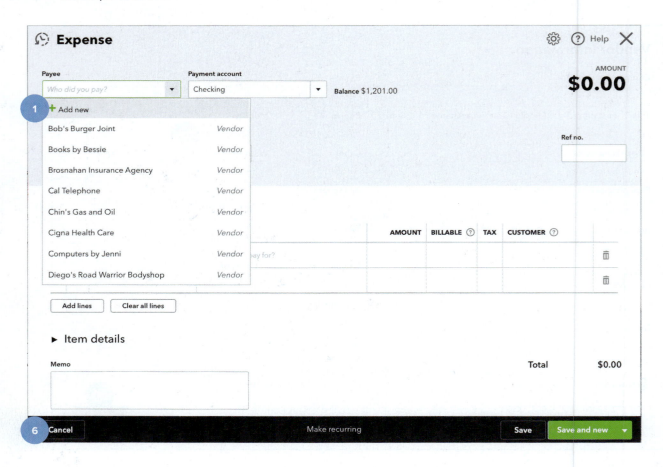

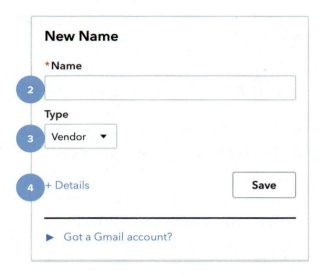

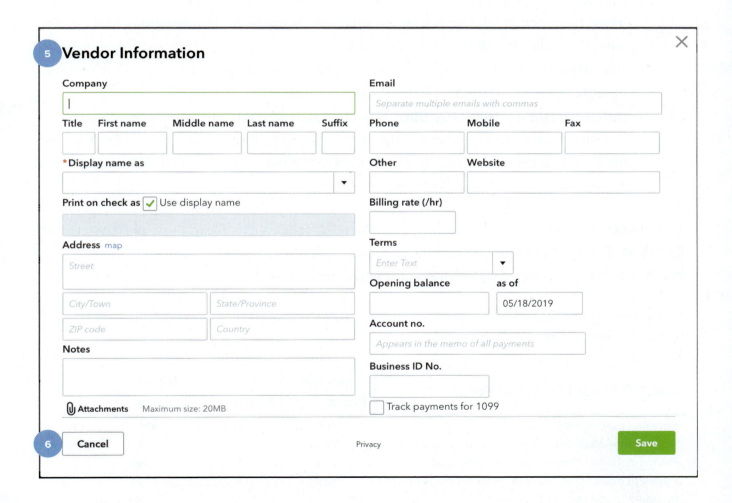

Section 6.6

RECORDING VENDORS TRANSACTIONS

After creating a Vendors List, we are ready to enter vendors and expenses transactions. Ways to record vendors and expenses transactions using QBO include using the following QBO onscreen forms in the following sequences:

- **Expense.** An Expense form can be used to record services purchased when the payment is made at the same time as the purchase. The payment can be by cash, credit card, or check. If the payment is to be made later, then Bill > Pay Bills should be used instead.
- **Check.** A Check form can be used to record services purchased when the payment is made by check at the same time the purchase is made. If the payment is to be made later, then Bill > Pay Bills should be used.
- **Bill > Pay Bills.** This approach is used to record services purchased, such as utilities or legal services. After the bill is entered, it is paid when due.
- **Purchase Order > Bill > Pay Bills.** This approach is used to record the purchase of inventory items. The purchase order provides a record of the items ordered. After the bill for the items is received, the bill is entered. When the bill is paid, the pay bills form is used to record the bill payment.

This chapter focuses on entering vendor transactions for services using Expense, Check, and Bill forms. The next chapter covers how to record the purchase of inventory items using Purchase Orders, followed by entering bills and paying bills.

The following summary shows whether an Expense, Check, or Bill form should be used for recording various vendors transactions.

QBO Transaction Form For...	Expense Form	Check Form	Bill Form
Services purchased?	Yes	Yes	Yes
Payment made at time of purchase by check?	Yes	Yes	No
Payment made at time of purchase by cash?	Yes	No	No
Payment made at time of purchase by credit card?	Yes	No	No
Payment made later after purchase?	No	No	Yes

Section 6.7

EXPENSE

If our payment is *made at the same time* we make a purchase, then we can record the purchase using the Expense form. When using the Expense form, our payment may consist of cash, check, or credit card.

> If our purchase is paid by check at the same time as the purchase, **then we can use the Expense form or the Check form to record the transaction.**

When using the Expense form to record a vendor transaction:

1   Select **Create (+)** icon

2   Create **Expense** to record the vendor transaction when we make payment at the same time the expense is incurred and we use cash, check, or credit card.

3   From the Payee drop-down menu, select **Vendor: Ellis Equipment Rental**. If a message appears, asking if you want to autofill the form using prior information, select **Yes**.

4   Using the drop-down menu, select the **Payment Account: Mastercard**

5   Enter **Payment Date: Current Date**

6   From the Payment Method drop-down menu listing Cash, Check, or various Credit Cards, select **Payment Method: MasterCard**

7   In the Category Details section, select appropriate Category from the drop-down menu. The drop-down Category list contains accounts that can be used to record the expense. If it does not appear automatically, select **Category: Equipment Rental**.

8   Enter **Description** of the transaction: **Equipment rental for 10 days**

9   Enter **Amount** of the expense: **200.00**

10   Select Billable if the expense is billable to a specific customer. In this case select **Billable**.

11   Select Tax if purchase is taxable. Leave **Tax unchecked**.

12   Since the expense is billable to a specific customer, select **Customer: Dukes Basketball Camp**

13 An expense transaction can be entered using **Item details** instead of Account details, which is covered in Chapter 7

14 Select **Save and close**

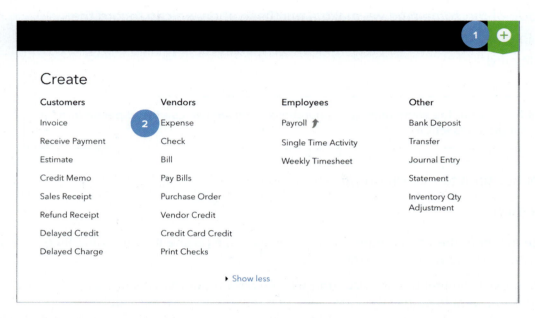

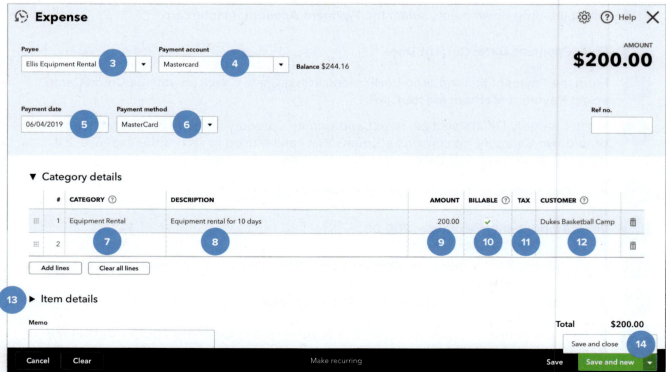

Section 6.8

CHECK

If our payment is *made by check at the same time* we make a purchase, then we can record the purchase using the Check form.

To use a Check form to record the vendor transaction:

1 Select **Create (+)** icon

2 Select **Check**

3 Select **Payee: Computers by Jenni**. After the Payee is selected, some of the information on the form will autofill, such as Mailing address. This information is pulled from the Vendors List.

4 Select **Bank Account: Checking**

5 **Mailing Address** should autofill when the vendor is selected

6 Enter **Payment Date: Current Date**

7 Notice that **Check No.** autofills

8 The drop-down Category List contains accounts that can be used to record the expense. Sometimes QBO will autofill this field using information from the last transaction entered for the specific Payee. In this case, if it does not autofill, enter **Category: Computers Repairs (Expenses)**.

9 Enter **Description: Computer repair and maintenance**

10 Enter **Amount: 99.00**

11 If the payment was billable to a specific customer, select Billable. In this case since the Computer Repairs (Expenses) does not relate to a specific customer, leave **Billable unchecked**.

12 Select Tax if applicable. In this case, leave **Tax unchecked**.

13 If the payment was billable to a specific customer, select that customer in the Customer column from the Customer drop-down list. In this case, leave **Customer** field **blank**.

14 A vendor transaction can be entered using **Item details** instead of Account details, which is covered in Chapter 7

15 If a printed check is required, select **Print Later** and complete the onscreen instructions. In this case, leave **Print Later unchecked**.

16 Select **Save and close**

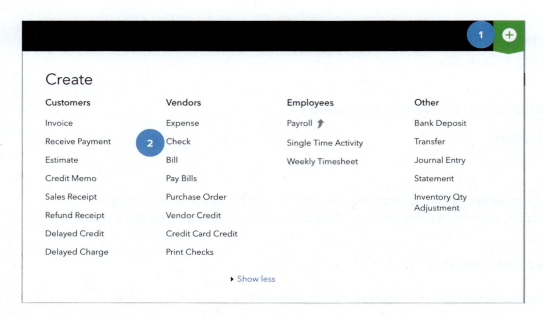

Create

Customers	Vendors	Employees	Other
Invoice	Expense	Payroll ⬆	Bank Deposit
Receive Payment	Check	Single Time Activity	Transfer
Estimate	Bill	Weekly Timesheet	Journal Entry
Credit Memo	Pay Bills		Statement
Sales Receipt	Purchase Order		Inventory Qty Adjustment
Refund Receipt	Vendor Credit		
Delayed Credit	Credit Card Credit		
Delayed Charge	Print Checks		

▸ Show less

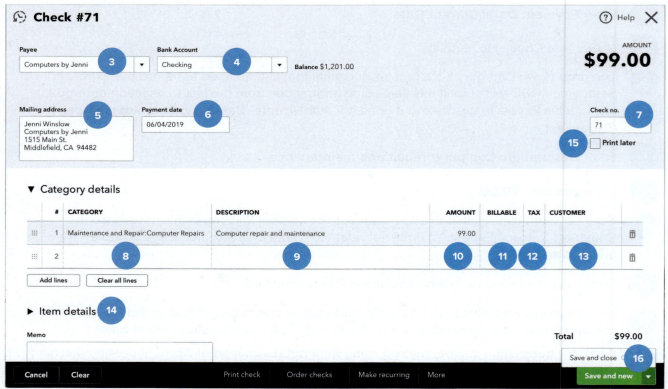

Check #71

⑦ Help ✕

Payee: Computers by Jenni

Bank Account: Checking   Balance $1,201.00

AMOUNT
$99.00

Mailing address:
Jenni Winslow
Computers by Jenni
1515 Main St.
Middlefield, CA 94482

Payment date: 06/04/2019

Check no.: 71

☐ Print later

▼ Category details

#	CATEGORY	DESCRIPTION	AMOUNT	BILLABLE	TAX	CUSTOMER	
1	Maintenance and Repair:Computer Repairs	Computer repair and maintenance	99.00				🗑
2							🗑

[Add lines] [Clear all lines]

▸ Item details

Memo

Total $99.00

Save and close

Cancel   Clear   Print check   Order checks   Make recurring   More   **Save and new** ▾

Section 6.9

BILL > PAY BILLS

If we receive a bill and plan to pay the bill later, then we use the Bill form to enter the bill and use the Pay Bills form when paying the bill at a later time.

When using the Bill and Pay Bills forms to record the vendors transactions:

1 Select **Create (+)** icon

2 Select **Bill** to enter a bill when received

3 Select **Pay Bills** to select bills when we are ready to pay

CREATE BILL

When we receive a bill from a vendor, we use the Bill form to create the bill in QBO. The Bill form is used to record vendor transactions that we will pay later. Examples of bills include rent, utilities expense, insurance expense, and accounting and professional services. QBO will record an obligation (accounts payable liability) to pay the bill later.

> **If we are paying the bill at the time we receive the product or service,** then we can use the Expense form to record the transaction.

To record a bill received that we will pay later:

1. Select **Create (+)** icon

2. Select **Bill**

3. From the Vendor drop-down menu, select **Vendor: Robertson & Associates**. If a message appears, asking if you want to autofill the form using prior information, select **Yes**.

4. **Mailing Address** should auto-fill when vendor is selected

5. If **Terms** does not auto-fill, select: **Net 30**

6. Select **Bill Date: Current Date**

7. Verify **Due Date** is correct

8. Leave **Bill No. blank**

9. Select **Category: Legal & Professional Fees: Accounting**

10. Enter **Description: Accounting services**

11. Enter **Amount: 186.00**

12. Select Billable if the expense is billable to a specific customer. In this case since Accounting does not relate to a specific customer, leave **Billable unchecked**.

13. Select Tax if purchase is taxable. Leave **Tax unchecked**.

14. If billable, select appropriate Customer associated with the expense. Leave **Customer** field **blank**.

15. A vendor transaction can be entered using **Item details** instead of Account details, which is covered in Chapter 7

16. If additional detail is needed, enter a **Memo** describing the transaction

17. Add **Attachments,** such as a copy of the vendor bill received, a source document associated with the transaction

18. Select **Save** and leave the Bill form open

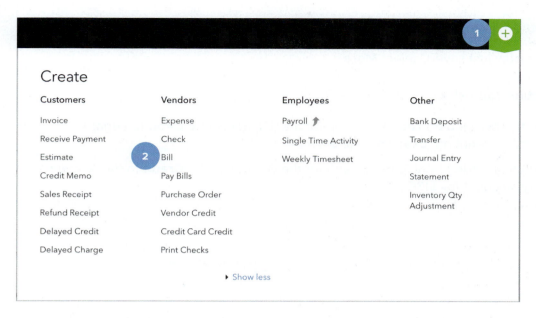

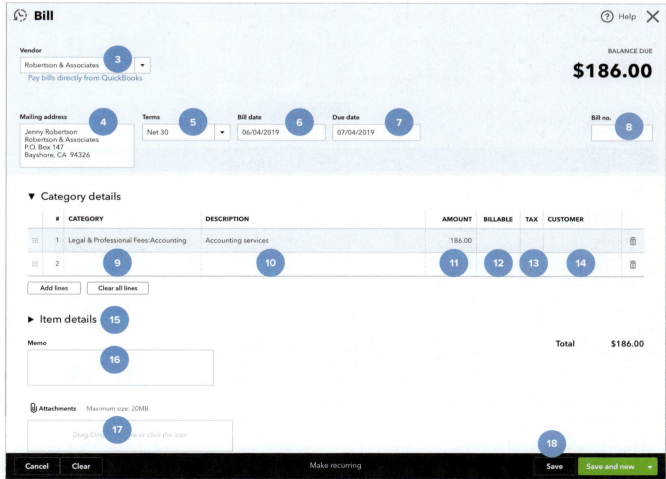

To view the Transaction Journal for the Bill we just created:

1 From the Bill window just saved, select **More**

2 Select **Transaction Journal**

3 In the journal entry recorded behind the screen for the Bill, notice the **Debit** to Legal & Professional Fees: Accounting (Expenses) for $186.00

4 In the journal entry recorded behind the screen for the Bill, notice the **Credit** to the Accounts Payable (Liability) account for $186.00

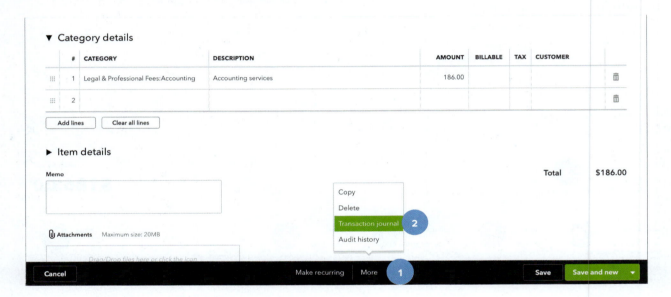

CREATE PAY BILLS

Use the Pay Bills form to select the bills that are due and we are ready to pay. If the bill has been entered using the Bill form, then the bill will automatically appear in the Pay Bills List.

> **Use Pay Bills only** for bills that have been entered using the Bill forms.

> **If the Expense form or the Check form** was used to enter the vendor transaction, we do *not* use the Pay Bills form for that item, since it has already been paid at the time the Expense or Check was entered into QBO.

To use Pay Bills to select bills to pay:

1 Select **Create (+)** icon

2 Select **Pay Bills**

3 Select **Payment Account: Checking**

4 Enter **Payment Date: Current Date**

5 Select **Bills to Pay: Robertson & Associates for $186.00**

6 The **Payment Amount** should autofill

7 Select **Save and close**

8 This completes the chapter activities. **Close** the QBO Sample Company web browser window to reset the Sample Company before proceeding to the exercises at the end of this chapter.

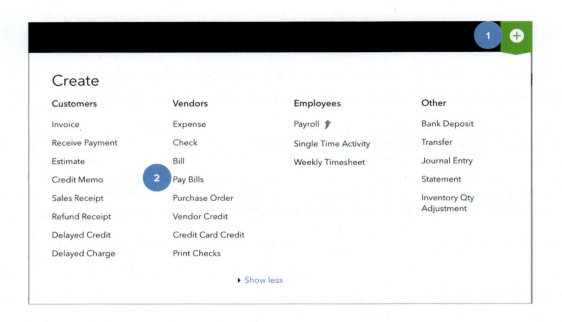

Create

Customers	Vendors	Employees	Other
Invoice	Expense	Payroll ⚡	Bank Deposit
Receive Payment	Check	Single Time Activity	Transfer
Estimate	Bill	Weekly Timesheet	Journal Entry
Credit Memo	Pay Bills		Statement
Sales Receipt	Purchase Order		Inventory Qty Adjustment
Refund Receipt	Vendor Credit		
Delayed Credit	Credit Card Credit		
Delayed Charge	Print Checks		

▸ Show less

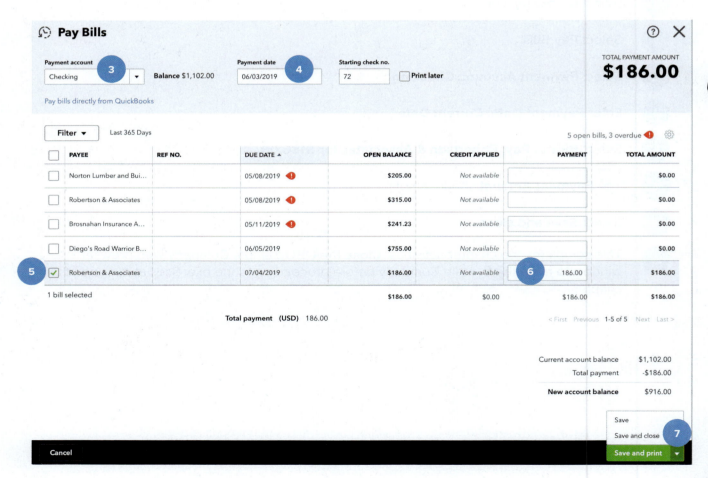

Section 6.10

ACCOUNTING ESSENTIALS
Vendors Transactions, Accounts Payable, and 1099s

Accounting Essentials summarize important foundational accounting knowledge you may find useful when using QBO

What are Accounts Payable?

- Accounts payable consists of amounts that our business is obligated to pay in the future. When our business makes purchases on credit, our business is promising to pay that amount in the future.
- When a purchase is made and recorded as a bill, accounts payable is increased by a credit. When the bill is paid, the accounts payable is decreased by a debit.

How can a business track Accounts Payable to ensure Accounts Payable are paid on time?

- Accounts Payable reports provide information for tracking amounts we owe vendors. An Accounts Payable Aging report summarizes accounts payable balances by the age of the account. This report helps us to track how much we owe vendors and when amounts are due, including the age of past due bills.

What is a 1099 and when does a company need to prepare 1099s?

- IRS Form 1099 must be completed for sole proprietorships and partnerships to which we paid $600 or more for services in a year. The vendor's Tax ID No. is required to complete the 1099. QBO can assist in tracking amounts and preparing 1099s for appropriate vendors. To learn more about preparing 1099s, see the Internal Revenue Service website at www.irs.gov.

Practice Quiz 6

Q6.1

To enter Vendors and Expenses transactions:

a. From the Navigation Bar, select Customers

b. From the Navigation Bar, select Expenses > New Transaction

c. From the Gear icon, select Vendors

d. From the Gear icon, select Expense Transactions

Q6.2

To enter an Expense transaction:

a. From the Navigation Bar, select Customers

b. From the Navigation Bar, select Sales

c. From the Create (+) icon, select Expense

d. From the Gear icon, select Vendor Transactions

Q6.3

QuickBooks considers all of the following to be vendors except:

a. Utility companies

b. Suppliers of inventory and supplies

c. Tax agencies such as the IRS

d. Customers purchasing products

Q6.4

Which of the following is not a vendor transaction?

a. Order products

b. Pay bills

c. Make deposits

d. Receive bills

Q6.5

We can update the Vendors List at which of the following two points:

a. Before entering transactions

b. While entering transactions

c. After entering transactions

Q6.6

Which of the following two are Vendors and Expenses transactions?

a.   Invoice

b.   Receive Payment

c.   Pay Bills

d.   Check

Q6.7

The Bill form is used to record which one of the following transactions?

a.   Owners investment

b.   Services received but not yet paid

c.   Products sold to customers

d.   Cash purchases of supplies

Q6.8

Which of the following activities, and the QBO form used to record it, is incorrect?

a.   Receive products, Customers List

b.   Order products, Purchase Order

c.   Record inventory information, Products and Services List

d.   Sell products and bill customers, Invoice

Q6.9

Indicate the order in which the following onscreen Vendors and Expenses transaction forms
typically should be prepared:

a.   Expense > Pay Bills

b.   Check > Pay Bills

c.   Bill > Pay Bills

d.   Invoice > Pay Bills

Q6.10

Which of the following reports tracks past due bills and bills that are due shortly?

a.   Profit & Loss

b.   Statement of Cash Flows

c.   Accounts Payable Aging

d.   Accounts Receivable Aging

Q6.11

Accounts Payable (A/P) are:

a. Amounts totaling the net worth of a company

b. Amounts paid to owners

c. Amounts that customers owe your business

d. Amounts owed to others that are obligations

Q6.12

When a purchase is recorded as a bill, QBO records a:

a. Debit (increase) to cash

b. Credit (increase) to owner's contribution

c. Debit (increase) to accounts receivable

d. Credit (increase) to accounts payable

Exercises 6

We use the QBO Sample Company, Craig's Design and Landscaping Services, for practice throughout the exercises. The Sample Company will reset each time it is reopened. So make certain to allow enough time to complete the exercises before closing the Sample Company. Otherwise, you will lose the work you have entered when you close and reopen the Sample Company.

⚠ Since the Sample Company resets each time it is reopened, be certain to close any web browser windows displaying the QBO Sample Company before starting these exercises. Closing the browser window and starting with a new browser window for the QBO Sample Company resets the data before starting the exercises.

To access the QBO Sample Company, complete the following steps.

1 Open a web browser. (Note: Intuit recommends using Google Chrome.)

2 Go to the https://qbo.intuit.com/redir/testdrive

3 Follow onscreen instructions for security verification

Craig's Design and Landscaping Services should appear on your screen.

E6.1 Vendors and Expenses Transactions

Match the following vendors and expenses transactions with the description of the transaction.

Vendors and Expenses Transaction Descriptions

a. The form used to select bills we want to pay.

b. The form used to order and track products from vendors.

c. The onscreen form used to record products and services that we pay for at the time we receive the product or service with cash, credit card, or check.

d. The form used when a vendor gives us a refund or reduction in our bill in what we owe the vendor.

e. This form can be used when we pay for products and services at the time of purchase, but cannot be used when we pay with cash or credit card.

f. A form used to record a reduction in charges by the vendor to our credit card.

g. The onscreen form used to record bills we received and the obligation to pay the vendor later (accounts payable).

Vendors and Expenses Transaction

1. Expense

2. Check

3. Bill

4. Pay Bills

5. Purchase Order

6. Vendor Credit

7. Credit Card Credit

E6.2 Vendors Transaction: Expense Credit Card

Using the QBO Sample Company, Craig's Design and Landscaping Services, complete the following.

1. Create Expense Paid with Credit Card.
   a. Select **Create (+) icon > Expense**
   b. Select **Payee: Squeaky Kleen Car Wash**
   c. Select **Payment Account: Mastercard**
   d. Select **Payment Date: Current Date**
   e. Select **Payment Method: MasterCard**
   f. Select **Category: Automobile**
   g. Enter **Amount: 21.99**
   h. What is the Total for the Expense?
   i. Select **Save** and leave the Expense displayed on your screen

2. View the Transaction Journal for the Expense.
   a. From the bottom of the Squeaky Kleen Car Wash Expense, select **More > Transaction Journal**
   b. What are the Account and Amount Debited?
   c. What are the Account and Amount Credited?

E6.3 Vendors Transaction: Expense Credit Card

Using the QBO Sample Company, Craig's Design and Landscaping Services, complete the following.

1. Create Expense Paid with Credit Card.
   a. Select **Create (+) icon > Expense**
   b. Select **Payee: Chin's Gas and Oil**
   c. Select **Payment Account: Visa**
   d. Select **Payment Date: Current Date**
   e. Select **Payment Method: Visa**
   f. Select **Category: Automobile: Fuel**
   g. Enter **Amount: 86.00**
   h. What is the Total for the Expense?
   i. Select **Save** and leave the Expense displayed on the screen

2. View the Transaction Journal for the Expense.
    a. From the bottom of the Chin's Gas and Oil Expense, select **More > Transaction Journal**
    b. What are the Account and Amount Debited?
    c. What are the Account and Amount Credited?

E6.4 Vendors Transaction: Credit Card Credit

This assignment is a continuation of E6.3

Go to the QBO Sample Company, Craig's Design and Landscaping Services. Craig's was overcharged by Chin's Gas and Oil. Complete the following to record the Credit Card Credit when Chin's reversed the overcharge.

1. Create Credit Card Credit.
    a. Select **Create (+) icon > Credit Card Credit**
    b. Select **Payee: Chin's Gas and Oil**
    c. Select **Bank/Credit Account: Visa**
    d. Select **Payment Date: Current Date**
    e. Select **Category: Automobile: Fuel**
    f. Enter **Amount: 26.00**
    g. What is the Total for the Credit Card Credit?
    h. Select **Save and close**

2. View the Transaction Journal for the Credit Card Credit.
    a. From the Navigation Bar, select **Expenses**
    b. From the Expense Transactions List, select **Chin's Gas and Oil Credit Card Credit**
    c. From the bottom of the Chin's Gas and Oil Credit Card Credit, select **More > Transaction Journal**
    d. What are the Account and Amount Debited?
    e. What are the Account and Amount Credited?

E6.5 Vendors Transaction: Expense Checking

Using the QBO Sample Company, Craig's Design and Landscaping Services, complete the following to record an Expense paid from the Checking account.

1. Create Expense Paid from the Checking account.
    a. Select **Create (+) icon > Expense**
    b. Select **Payee: Tania's Nursery**

c. Select **Payment Account: Checking**

d. Select **Payment Date: Current Date**

e. Select **Payment Method: Check**

f. Enter **Reference No.: 77**

g. Select Line 1: **Category: Job Expenses**

h. Enter **Amount: 54.00**

i. Select Line 2: **Category: Supplies**

j. Enter **Amount: 63.00**

k. What is the Total for the Expense?

l. Select **Save** and leave the Expense displayed

2. View the Transaction Journal for the Expense.

   a. From the bottom of the Tania's Nursery Expense, select **More > Transaction Journal**

   b. What are the Account and Amount Debited?

   c. What are the Account and Amount Debited?

   d. What are the Account and Amount Credited?

E6.6 Vendors Transaction: Checking and Debit Card

Using the QBO Sample Company, Craig's Design and Landscaping Services, complete the following to record a payment using Craig's Checking account Debit Card.

1. Create Check with Debit Card.

   a. Select **Create (+) icon > Check**

   b. Select **Payee: Bob's Burger Joint**

   c. Select **Bank Account: Checking**

   d. Select **Payment Date: Current Date**

   e. Enter **Reference No.: Debit**

   f. Select **Category: Meals and Entertainment**

   g. Enter **Amount: 20.00**

   h. What is the Total for the Check?

   i. Select **Save and close**

2. View the Transaction Journal for the Check.
   a. From the Navigation Bar, select **Accounting**
   b. From the Chart of Accounts, select **View Register** for the Checking account
   c. Select **Bob's Burger Joint Check > Edit**
   d. From the bottom of the Bob's Burger Joint Check, select **More > Transaction Journal**
   e. What are the Account and Amount Debited?
   f. What are the Account and Amount Credited?

E6.7 Vendors Transaction: Check

Using the QBO Sample Company, Craig's Design and Landscaping Services, complete the following.

1. Create Check.
   a. Select **Create (+) icon > Check**
   b. Select **Payee: Mahoney Mugs**
   c. Select **Bank Account: Checking**
   d. Select **Payment Date: Current Date**
   e. Enter **Reference No.: 78**
   f. Select **Category: Office Expenses**
   g. Enter **Description: Office Supplies**
   h. Enter **Amount: 27.00**
   i. What is the Total for the Check?
   j. Select **Save and close**

2. View the Transaction Journal for the Check.
   a. From the Navigation Bar, select **Accounting**
   b. From the Chart of Accounts, select **View Register** for the Checking account
   c. Select **Mahoney's Mugs Check > Edit**
   d. From the bottom of the Mahoney's Mugs Check, select **More > Transaction Journal**
   e. What are the Account and Amount Debited?
   f. What are the Account and Amount Credited?

E6.8 Vendors Transaction: Bill

Using the QBO Sample Company, Craig's Design and Landscaping Services, complete the following to enter a bill for legal fees.

1. Create Bill.
   a. Select **Create (+) icon > Bill**
   b. Select **Vendor: Tony Rondonuwu**

    c. Select **Bill Date: Current Date**

    d. Select **Category: Legal & Professional Fees: Lawyer**

    e. Enter **Amount: 360.00**

    f. What is the Total for the Bill?

    g. Select **Save** and leave the Bill displayed

2. View the Transaction Journal for the Bill.

    a. From the bottom of the Tony Rondonuwu Bill, select **More > Transaction Journal**

    b. What are the Account and Amount Debited?

    c. What are the Account and Amount Credited?

E6.9 Vendors Transaction: Bill

Using the QBO Sample Company, Craig's Design and Landscaping Services, complete the following.

1. Create Bill.

    a. Select **Create (+) icon > Bill**

    b. Select **Vendor: Pam Seitz**

    c. Select **Bill Date: Current Date**

    d. Select **Category: Legal & Professional Fees: Accounting**

    e. Enter **Amount: 180.00**

    f. What is the Total for the Bill?

    g. Select **Save** and leave the Bill displayed

2. View the Transaction Journal for the Bill.

    a. From the bottom of the Pam Seitz Bill, select **More > Transaction Journal**

    b. What are the Account and Amount Debited?

    c. What are the Account and Amount Credited?

E6.10 Vendors Transaction: Pay Bills

This assignment is a continuation of E6.8 and E6.9

Using the QBO Sample Company, Craig's Design and Landscaping Services, complete the following.

1. Pay Bills.

    a. Select **Create (+) icon > Pay Bills**

    b. Select **Payment Account: Checking**

    c. Select **Payment Date: Current Date**

    d. Select **Starting Check No.: 79**

    e. Select **Payee: Pam Seitz**

    f. Select **Payee: Tony Rondonuwu**

    g. What is the Total Payment Amount?

    h. Select **Save and close**

2. View the Transaction Journal for Paid Bills.

    a. From the Navigation Bar, select **Accounting**

    b. From the Chart of Accounts, select **View Register** for the Checking account

    c. Select **Bill Payment No. 79 > Edit**

    d. From the bottom of Bill Payment No. 79, select **More > Transaction Journal**

    e. What are the Account and Amount Debited?

    f. What are the Account and Amount Credited?

    g. From the Chart of Accounts, select **View Register** for the Checking account

    h. Select **Bill Payment No. 80 > Edit**

    i. From the bottom of Bill Payment No. 80, select **More > Transaction Journal**

    j. What are the Account and Amount Debited?

    k. What are the Account and Amount Credited?

E6.11 Vendors Transactions: Expense, Check, or Bill

Complete the following table to summarize which QBO form can be used to record vendors transactions.

QBO Transaction Form For...	Expense Form	Check Form	Bill Form
Services purchased?			
Payment made at time of purchase by check?			
Payment made at time of purchase by cash?			
Payment made at time of purchase by credit card?			
Payment made later after purchase?			

Project 6.1

Mookie the Beagle™ Concierge

> **Project 6.1 is a continuation of Project 5.1. You will use the QBO Company you created for Project 1.1 and updated in subsequent Projects 2.1 through 5.1. Keep in mind the QBO Company for Project 6.1 does not reset and carries your data forward, including any errors. So it is important to check and crosscheck your work to verify it is correct before clicking the Save button.**

BACKSTORY

Mookie The Beagle™ Concierge, a provider of convenient, high-quality pet care on demand, needs your assistance in processing vendors and expenses transactions using QBO.

Complete the following for Mookie The Beagle Concierge.

 QBO SATNAV

Project 6.1 focuses on QBO Transactions, specifically QBO Vendors & Expenses Transactions as shown in the following QBO SatNav.

QBO SatNav

 **QBO Settings**

 Company Settings

 Chart of Accounts

 **QBO Transactions**

Banking

Customers & Sales

| Vendors & Expenses | *Enter Bills > Pay Bills* |

Employees & Payroll

 **QBO Reports**

 Reports

HOW TO LOG INTO QBO

To log into QBO, complete the following steps.

1 Using a web browser go to qbo.intuit.com

2 Enter **User ID** (the email address you used to set up your QBO Account)

3 Enter **Password** (the password you used to set up your QBO Account)

4 Select **Sign in**

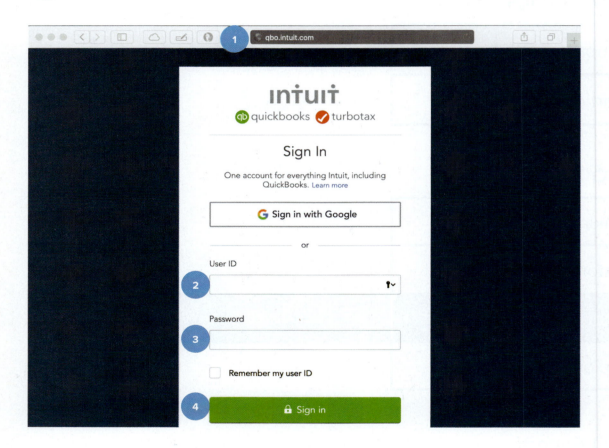

> **If you are not using a public or shared computer,** to speed up login, you can save your login to your desktop and select Remember Me. If you are using a public computer or shared computer, do not save to the desktop and unselect Remember Me.

> **The new QBO Company** we created in Project 1.1 will carry all work forward into future chapters. So it is important to check and crosscheck your work to verify it is correct before clicking the Save button. Any uncorrected errors will be carried forward in your QBO Company for text projects.

P6.1.1 Expense Credit Card

Complete the following to record supplies purchased by Mookie The Beagle Concierge from Bichotte Supplies with a credit card.

1. Edit a Vendor in the Vendors List.
    a. From the Navigation Bar, select **Expenses** > **Vendors tab**
    b. From the Vendors List, select **Vendor: Bichotte Supplies**
    c. Update the following vendor information.

Company:	**Bichotte Supplies**
Phone:	**415-555-4567**
Billing Address Street:	**810 Francais Drive**
Billing Address City:	**Bayshore**
Billing Address State:	**CA**
Billing Address ZIP:	**94326**
Billing Address Country:	**USA**

    d. Select **Save**

2. Create Expense paid with Credit Card.
    a. Select **Create (+) icon** > **Expense**
    b. Select **Payee: Bichotte Supplies**
    c. Select **Payment Account: VISA Credit Card**
    d. Select **Payment Date: 01/23/2022**
    e. Select **Payment Method: Credit Card**
    f. Select **Category: Office Supplies & Software (Expenses)**
    g. Enter **Amount: 240.00**
    h. What is the Total for the Expense?
    i. Select **Save** and leave the Expense displayed

3. View the Transaction Journal for the Expense.
    a. From the bottom of the Bichotte Supplies Expense, select **More** > **Transaction Journal**
    b. What are the Account and Amount Debited?
    c. What are the Account and Amount Credited?

P6.1.2 Vendors Transaction: Credit Card Credit

Bichotte Supplies mistakenly overcharged Mookie The Beagle Concierge by $40.00 on the supplies purchases made on 01/23/2022. Complete the following to record the Credit Card Credit when Bichotte Supplies reversed the overcharge.

1. Create Credit Card Credit.
   a. Select **Create (+) icon > Credit Card Credit**
   b. Select **Payee: Bichotte Supplies**
   c. Select **Bank/Credit Account: VISA Credit Card**
   d. Select **Payment Date: 01/24/2022**
   e. Select **Category: Office Supplies & Software (Expenses)**
   f. Enter **Amount: 40.00**
   g. What is the Total for the Credit Card Credit?
   h. Select **Save and close**

2. View the Transaction Journal for the Credit Card Credit.
   a. From the Navigation Bar, select **Expenses**
   b. From the Expense Transactions List, select **Bichotte Supplies Credit Card Credit**
   c. From the bottom of the Bichotte Supplies Credit Card Credit, select **More > Transaction Journal**
   d. What are the Account and Amount Debited?
   e. What are the Account and Amount Credited?

P6.1.3 Vendors Transaction: Expense Checking

Complete the following to record supplies purchased by Mookie The Beagle Concierge from Sofia Raphael Associates with a credit card.

1. Edit a Vendor in the Vendors List.
   a. From the Navigation Bar, select **Expenses > Vendors tab**
   b. From the Vendors List, select **Vendor: Sofia Raphael Associates**
   c. Update the following vendor information.

Company:	Sofia Raphael Associates
Phone:	415-555-5432
Mobile:	415-555-6543
Billing Address Street:	32 North Avenue
Billing Address City:	Bayshore
Billing Address State:	CA
Billing Address ZIP:	94326
Billing Address Country:	USA

    d. Select **Save**

2. Create Expense Paid with Credit Card.
    a. Select **Create (+) icon > Expense**
    b. Select **Payee: Sofia Raphael Associates**
    c. Select **Payment Account: VISA Credit Card**
    d. Select **Payment Date: 01/24/2022**
    e. Select **Payment Method: Credit Card**
    f. Select **Category: Office Supplies & Software (Expenses)**
    g. Enter **Amount: 432.00**
    h. What is the Total for the Expense?
    i. Select **Save** and leave the Expense displayed on your screen

3. View the Transaction Journal for the Expense.
    a. From the bottom of the Sofia Raphael Associates Expense, select **More > Transaction Journal**
    b. What are the Account and Amount Debited?
    c. What are the Account and Amount Credited?

P6.1.4 Vendors Transaction: Checking Debit Card

Complete the following to record a payment using Mookie The Beagle Concierge's Checking account Debit Card.

1. Create Check with Debit Card.
    a. Select **Create (+) icon > Check**
    b. Select **Payee: Bichotte Supplies**
    c. Select **Bank Account: Checking**

    d. Enter **Check No.: Debit**

    e. Select **Payment Date: 01/25/2022**

    f. Select **Category: Office Supplies & Software (Expenses)**

    g. Enter **Amount: 20.00**

    h. What is the Total for the Check?

    i. Select **Save and close**

2. View the Transaction Journal for the Check.

    a. From the Navigation Bar, select **Accounting**

    b. From the Chart of Accounts, select **View Register** for the Checking account

    c. Select **Bichotte Supplies Debit Check > Edit**

    d. From the bottom of the Bichotte Supplies Check, select **More > Transaction Journal**

    e. What are the Account and Amount Debited?

    f. What are the Account and Amount Credited?

P6.1.5 Vendors Transaction: Recurring Transaction Expense

Use a Recurring Transaction to record paying Mary Dolan as a contractor who provided the pet care services for Kuno over the charity run weekend. Mookie The Beagle Concierge pays Mary Dolan $20 per hour for those services.

1. Edit a Vendor in the Vendors List.

    a. From the Navigation Bar, select **Expenses > Vendors tab**

    b. From the Vendors List, select **Vendor: Mary Dolan**

    c. Update the following vendor information.

First Name:	**Mary**
Last Name:	**Dolan**
Mobile:	**415-555-1111**
Billing Address Street:	**99 Gale Street**
Billing Address City:	**Bayshore**
Billing Address State:	**CA**
Billing Address ZIP:	**94326**
Billing Address Country:	**USA**

    d. Select **Save**

2. Use a Recurring Transaction.

   a. From the Recurring Transaction List, select **Contractors Expense > Use**

   b. Update **Payment Date: 01/30/2022**

   c. Select **Payee: Mary Dolan**

   d. Verify **Payment Account: Checking**

   e. Verify **Category: Contractors (Expenses)**

   f. Enter Amount **based upon 33 hours Mary provided service to Kuno over the charity run weekend**

   g. What is the Amount for the Expense?

   h. Select **Save** and leave the Expense displayed

3. View the Transaction Journal for the Expense.

   a. From the bottom of the Contractor Expense, select **More > Transaction Journal**

   b. What are the Account and Amount Debited?

   c. What are the Account and Amount Credited?

P6.1.6 Vendors Transaction: Bill

Andre LaFortune, a vet student, provided pet care services as a contractor for Venus for a total of 17 hours summarized as follows:

- 6 hours on 01/18/2022
- 5 hours on 01/19/2022
- 6 hours on 01/20/2022

Mookie The Beagle Concierge pays Andre the same rate as Mary Dolan, $20 per hour. Complete the following to enter the bill on 01/30/2022. Mookie The Beagle Concierge will pay the contractor bill on 01/31/2022 (see P6.1.7).

1. Add a New Vendor to the Vendors List.

   a. From the Navigation Bar, select **Expenses > Vendors tab**

   b. Select **New vendor**

   c. Enter the following vendor information.

First Name	**Andre**
Last Name	**LaFortune**
Phone:	**415-555-1988**
Mobile:	**415-555-1955**
Billing Address Street:	**28 Beach Street**
Billing Address City:	**Bayshore**
Billing Address State:	**CA**
Billing Address ZIP:	**94326**
Billing Address Country:	**USA**

    d. Select **Save**

2. Create Bill.
   a. Select **Create (+) icon > Bill**
   b. Select **Vendor: Andre LaFortune**
   c. Select **Bill Date: 01/30/2022**
   d. Select **Category: Contractors (Expenses)**
   e. Enter **Amount based on the 17 hours Andre provided pet care services for Venus**
   f. What is the Total for the Bill?
   g. Select **Save** and leave the Bill displayed

3. View the Transaction Journal for the Bill.
   a. From the bottom of the Andre LaFortune Bill, select **More > Transaction Journal**
   b. What are the Account and Amount Debited?
   c. What are the Account and Amount Credited?

P6.1.7 Vendors Transaction: Pay Bills

Complete the following to pay the contractor bill for Andre LaFortune.

1. Pay Bills.
   a. Select **Create (+) icon > Pay Bills**
   b. Select **Payment Account: Checking**
   c. Select **Starting Check No.: 3**
   d. Select **Payment Date: 01/31/2022**
   e. Select **Payee: Andre LaFortune**
   f. Select **Bill** dated **01/30/2022**
   g. What is the Total Payment Amount?
   h. Select **Save and close**

2. View the Transaction Journal for Paid Bills.
   a. From the Navigation Bar, select **Accounting**
   b. From the Chart of Accounts, select **View Register** for the Checking account
   c. Select **Bill Payment 3 for Andre LaFortune > Edit**
   d. From the bottom of the Bill Payment, select **More > Transaction Journal**
   e. What are the Account and Amount Debited?
   f. What are the Account and Amount Credited?

P6.1.8 Vendors List

Cy requested a copy of Mookie The Beagle Concierge's current Vendors List.

To export the Vendors List:

1. From the Navigation Bar, select **Reports > Standard tab > Expenses and Vendors > Vendor Contact List > Run Report > Export icon > Export to PDF > Save as PDF**.

Chapter 7

Inventory

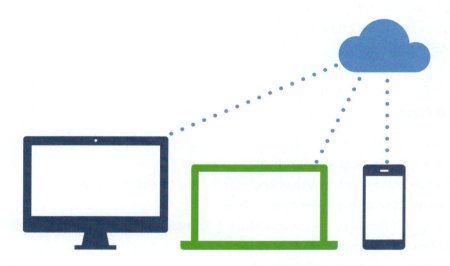

As Mookie the Beagle Concierge increases sales to customers for pet care services, Cy sees an opportunity for MTB to expand and sell MTB branded products to customers. With this expansion, Cy realizes that now the accounting system will need to be able to track inventory that is bought from vendors and sold to customers. So your next step is to learn more about using QuickBooks Online for tracking purchases and sales of inventory.

Chapter 7

LEARNING OBJECTIVES

Chapter 7 focuses on using QBO to record the purchase and sale of product inventory. For example, Craig's Design and Landscaping Services purchases landscape fountains from vendors for resale to customers. QBO has the ability to track both the purchase of the fountains and the subsequent resale to customers.

In this chapter, you will learn about the following topics:

- Navigating Inventory
- Products and Services List
  - Inventory
  - Non-inventory
  - Service
  - Bundle
- Vendors Transaction: Create Purchase Order
- Vendors Transaction: Enter Bill
- Vendors Transaction: Pay Bills
- Customers Transaction: Create Invoice
- Customers Transaction: Receive Payment
- Customers Transaction: Bank Deposit for Undeposited Funds
- Accounting Essentials: Inventory and Internal Control

Section 7.1

 # QBO SATNAV

QBO SatNav is our satellite navigation for QuickBooks Online, assisting us in navigating QBO

Chapter 7 focuses on QBO Customers & Sales Transactions and Vendors and Expenses Transactions related to product inventory, as shown in the following QBO SatNav.

⚙ **QBO Settings**

⚙ Company Settings
⚙ Chart of Accounts

🏞 **QBO Transactions**

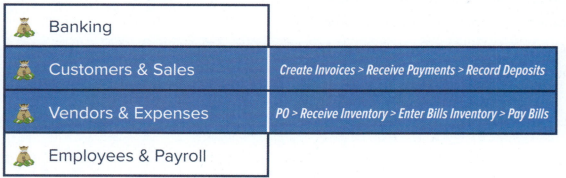

🏞 Banking	
🏞 Customers & Sales	*Create Invoices > Receive Payments > Record Deposits*
🏞 Vendors & Expenses	*PO > Receive Inventory > Enter Bills Inventory > Pay Bills*
🏞 Employees & Payroll	

📊 **QBO Reports**

📊 Reports

Section 7.2

QBO SAMPLE COMPANY LOGIN

To log into the QBO Sample Company:

1 Open a web browser. (Note: Intuit recommends using Google Chrome.)

2 Go to the https://qbo.intuit.com/redir/testdrive

3 Follow onscreen instructions for security verification

Craig's Design and Landscaping Services should appear on your screen.

To increase the amount of time from one (1) hour to three (3) hours before the log out for inactivity occurs:

1 From Craig's Design and Landscaping Services QBO Sample Company, select the **Gear** icon

2 Under Your Company section, select **Account and Settings**

3 Select **Advanced**

4 Select **Other preferences**

5 For the option Sign me out if inactive for, select **3 hours**

6 Select **Save**

7 Select **Done**

> ⚠️ **The Sample Company** will reset each time it is reopened. This allows you to explore and practice QBO without concern about carrying forward errors to later chapters. However, you will want to make certain to allow enough time to complete all chapter activities before closing the Sample Company. Otherwise, you will lose the work you have entered when you reopen the Sample Company.

To set QBO preferences to display account numbers in the Chart of Accounts:

1 Select the **Gear** icon to display options

2 Select **Account and Settings**

3 Select **Advanced**

4 For Chart of Accounts, select the **Edit Pencil**, then select **Enable account numbers**

5 Select **Show account numbers**

6 Select **Save**

7 Select **Done** to close Account and Settings

Section 7.3

NAVIGATING INVENTORY

If we buy and resell products, then we must maintain inventory records to account for the products we purchase from vendors and resell to customers.

VENDORS	→ Purchase Products from Vendors	OUR COMPANY	→ Sell Products to Customers	CUSTOMERS

We can use QBO for inventory to record:
1. **Vendor transactions**, including placing product orders, receiving products, and paying bills
2. **Customer transactions**, including recording sale of product on invoices and receiving customer payments

We can view the order of the QBO tasks we need to complete for inventory from the Create (+) screen:

1. **VENDORS: Purchase Order** to record our order of products from vendors. The purchase order is a record of the products and quantities we ordered.

2. **VENDORS: Bill** to record our obligation to pay the vendor for the products (Accounts Payable). Match vendor's bill with our purchase order to verify quantities and amounts are correct.

3. **VENDORS: Pay Bills** to pay vendor bills for products received.

4. **CUSTOMERS: Invoice** to record resale of product to customer and the customer's promise to pay later (Accounts Receivable).

5. **CUSTOMERS: Receive Payment** to record collection of the customer's payment.

6. **CUSTOMERS: Bank Deposit** to record customer's payment in the bank account. (Bank Deposit is used only if Undeposited Funds is selected on the Receive Payment form.)

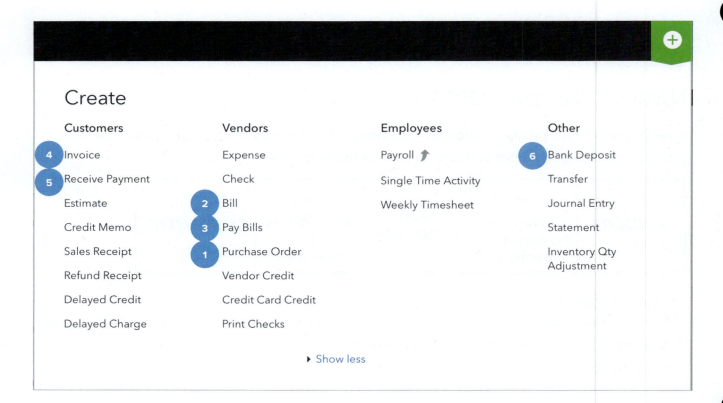

Section 7.4

PRODUCTS AND SERVICES LIST

When we enter inventory transactions, we need to use the following QBO Lists:
1. Vendors List
2. Customers List
3. Products and Services List

The Products and Services List collects information about the products purchased from vendors and/or sold to customers. Notice that the Products and Services List is used for products *both* purchased and sold. The Products and Services List is a time-saving feature so we can enter product information one time and eliminate re-entering the same product information each time we enter a new inventory transaction. In addition, we can enter one set of product information that can be used for both purchasing and sales of the product.

QBO uses four types of products and services:
1. **Inventory.** Products that we buy for which we track quantities, such as fountains that Craig's Design and Landscaping buys to resell. Inventory items are products that a business purchases, holds as inventory, and then resells to customers. QBO tracks the quantity and cost of inventory items in stock. For consistency, the same inventory item is used when recording sales and purchases. QBO has the capability to track both the cost and the sales price for inventory items. When the product is recorded on a sales invoice, QBO automatically updates our inventory records by reducing the quantity on hand. If we purchased the product, then we would record the product on the purchase order using the same inventory item number that we use on an invoice, except the purchase order uses the product's *cost* while the invoice uses the product's *selling price*.
2. **Non-inventory.** Products that we buy but we don't need to track the quantity of the product, such as pens used for office supplies.
3. **Service.** Services that we buy from vendors, such as legal services.
4. **Bundle.** A bundle is a collection of products and services that we sell together as a bundle. For example, installation of a fountain by Craig's Design and Landscaping Services might include hoses (products) and installation hours (services). Notice that we may buy the products separately, but then bundle the items for resale to customers.

Two ways that we can update the Products and Services List are:

1. *Before* entering transactions
2. *While* entering transactions

UPDATE PRODUCTS AND SERVICES LIST BEFORE ENTERING TRANSACTIONS

Before entering transactions, we can update the Products and Services List as follows.

1 From the Navigation Bar, select **Sales**

2 Select **Product and Services**

3 To enter a new products or services select **New**

4 Select **Product/Service Type: Inventory**

5 Enter **Name: Quartz Garden Sculpture**

6 Enter SKU or other product identification number. In this case, leave **SKU blank**.

7 Attach a Product/Service photo. In this case, leave **photo blank**.

8 Select an appropriate product/service **Category: Design**

9 Enter **Initial Quantity on Hand: 0**

10 Enter **As of Date: Current Date**

11 Enter **Reorder Point** when a new order should be placed to replenish product stock: **1**

12 Select **Inventory Asset Account: Inventory Asset**

13 Enter **Sales Information Description: Quartz Garden Sculpture**

14 Enter **Sales Price/Rate: 100.00**

15 Select **Income Account: Sales of Product Income**

16 Check **Is taxable**

17 Enter **Purchasing Information Description: Quartz Garden Sculpture**

18 Enter **Cost: 40.00**

19 Select **Expense Account: Cost of Goods Sold**

20 Select **Save and close**

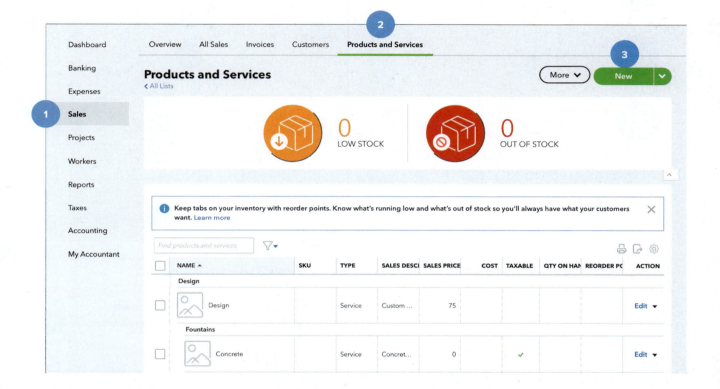

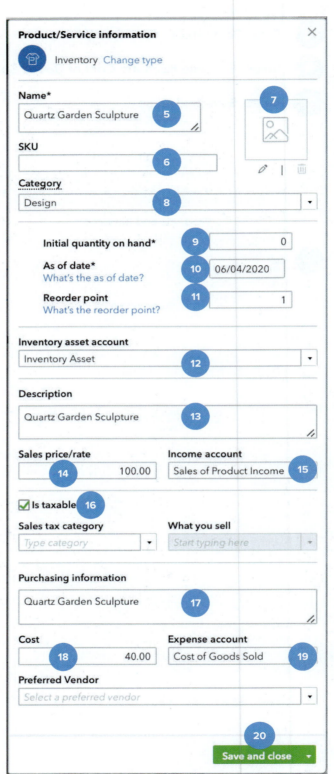

> Notice that the **Products and Services List links the product item to accounts in the Chart of Accounts for Inventory (Asset account), Sales of Product Income (Income account), and Cost of Goods Sold (Expense account). When we select this product on a QBO transaction form, then the linked accounts are automatically updated also.**

UPDATE PRODUCTS AND SERVICES LIST WHILE ENTERING TRANSACTIONS

While entering transactions, we can update the Products and Services List from the transaction form. If a product or service has not been entered in the Products and Services List, then we can add the product or service as follows from the onscreen transaction form.

1 To view a transaction form, such as an Invoice, select **Create (+)** icon > **Invoice**. Then select the **drop-down arrow** in the Product/Service field to display the menu.

2 Select + **Add new**

3 Select **Product/Service Type**

4 Enter **new product or service information**

5 Select **Save and close**

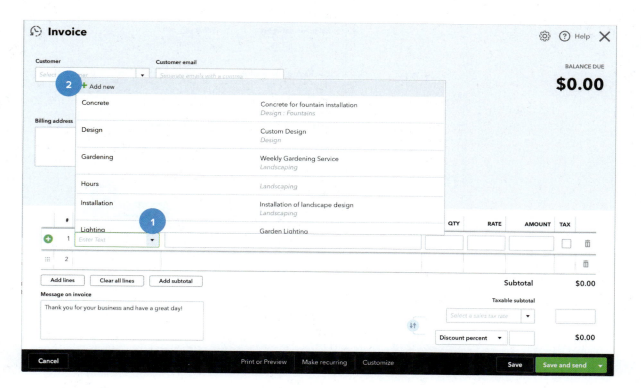

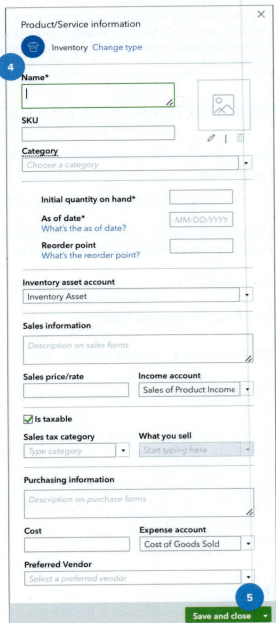

Section 7.5

PURCHASE ORDER

A Purchase Order is a record of an order to purchase products from a vendor. The Purchase Order lists the details of the purchase, such as date, vendor, specific items ordered, and quantity of each item ordered.

To create a Purchase Order:

1   Select **Create (+)** icon

2   Select **Purchase Order**

3   From the Vendor drop-down menu, select **Vendor: Norton Lumber and Building Materials**

4   **Mailing Address** and **Email** should auto-fill when the vendor is selected

5   Enter Ship to customer address if the product is to be shipped directly to a customer. In this case, leave the **Ship to** field **blank**.

6   Enter **Purchase Order Date: Current Date**

7   **Shipping Address** should autofill with **Craig's Design and Landscaping Services address**. Leave the **Ship via** field **blank**.

8   The Item Details section lists items to order. The product or service selected is linked to an account in the Chart of Accounts, so when we select the product, the linked account is automatically updated. If there are prior POs with the specific vendor, then the prior items ordered may autofill. In this case, select the product to order from the **Product/Service** drop-down list: **Quartz Garden Sculpture. Delete any autofilled items.**

9   If needed, enter **Description: Quartz Garden Sculpture**

10   Enter **QTY** to order: **2**

11   The **Rate** should autofill: **40.00**

12   Verify **Amount** is calculated correctly

13 If associated with a specific customer, select appropriate Customer. In this case, leave the **Customer** field **blank**.

14 To add lines for additional products, select Add lines. To delete extra items, select the Trash Can.

15 Enter **Your Message to Vendor** with additional instructions. In this case, leave the field **blank**.

16 Enter **Memo: Quartz Crystal Garden Sculpture**

17 Add **Attachments**, such as source documents associated with the transaction. For example, attach written authorization for the purchase order.

18 Select **Save and close**

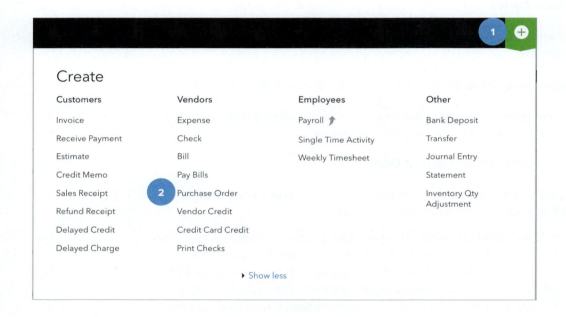

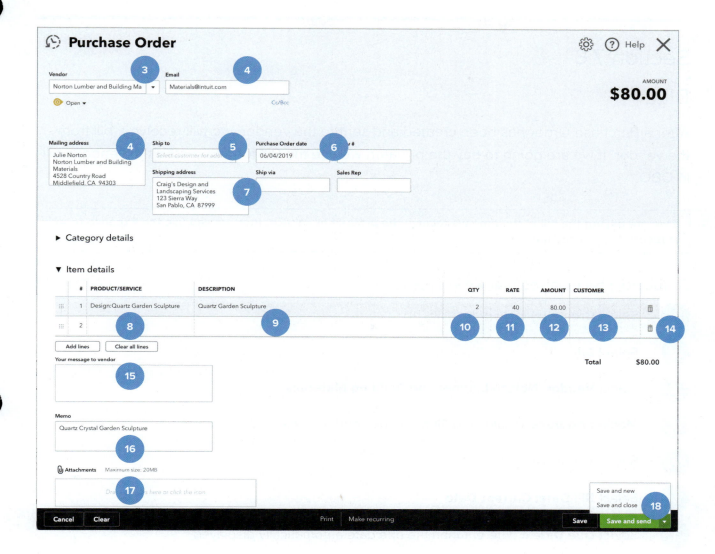

Section 7.6

BILL

After a Purchase Order has been created and sent to the vendor, we will receive a bill from the vendor. If we are going to pay the bill later, we use the Bill form to record the vendor's bill in QBO.

> **If we are paying the bill at the time we receive the product or service,** then we can use the Expense form to record the transaction.

To record a bill received that we will pay later:

1 Select **Create (+)** icon

2 Select **Bill**

3 Select **Vendor: Norton Lumber and Building Materials**

4 **Mailing Address** should auto-fill when the vendor is selected

5 Select **Terms: Net 30**

6 Select **Bill Date: Current Date**

7 Select **Due Date** if different than the due date automatically displayed

8 If the Item Details autofills, **delete** the autofilled items by selecting the Trash Can for the line item

9 When a vendor is selected, if there are open Purchase Orders, an Add to Bill drawer appears on the right side of the screen. Select **Add** to add the related open Purchase Order to the bill. If we were paying the bill at the same time, we could use the Expense form instead of the Bill form and attach the PO to the Expense in the same manner.

10 The information on the Purchase Order is added to a **Product/Service** line in the Item Detail section of the Bill form. The bill received from the vendor should be compared to the Purchase Order for any items received. Then any discrepancies should be noted and addressed.

11 Enter or update **Description**

12   Enter or verify automatically entered **QTY**

13   Enter or verify automatically entered **Rate**

14   Enter or verify automatically entered **Amount**

15   Select Billable if the item is billable to a specific customer. In this case, leave **Billable unchecked**.

16   Select Tax if taxable. In this case, leave **Tax unchecked**.

17   If billable, select appropriate Customer associated with the item. Leave the **Customer** field **blank**.

18   Enter **Memo** describing the transaction: **Purchase of 2 Quartz Garden Sculptures**

19   Select **Save and close**

> Notice that the vendor transaction is entered using Item Details **instead of Account Details, which was covered in Chapter 6. When we use Item Details for Products/Services, we have already linked these products/services to accounts in the Chart of Accounts when we entered the product/service in the Products and Services List.**

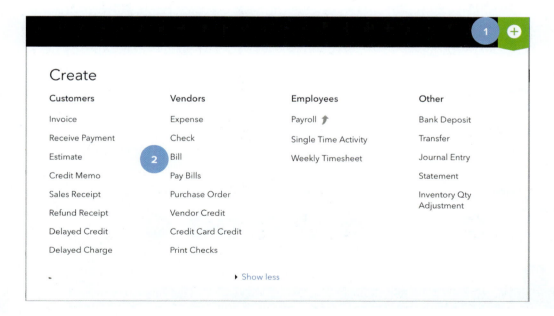

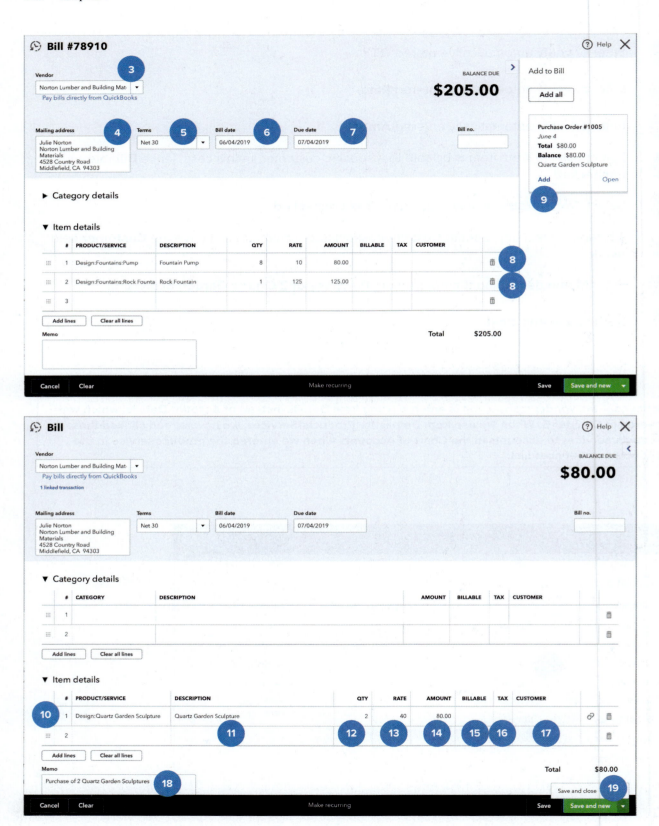

Section 7.7

PAY BILLS

Use Pay Bills to select the bills that are due and we are ready to pay. If the bill has been entered using the Bill form, then the bill will automatically appear in the Pay Bills List.

> **Use Pay Bills only** for bills that have been entered using the Bill form.

> **If the Expense form or the Check form** was used to enter the vendor transaction, we do *not* use the Pay Bills form for that item, since it has already been paid at the time the Expense or Check was entered into QBO.

To use Pay Bills to select bills to pay:

1 Select **Create (+)** icon

2 Select **Pay Bills**

3 Select **Payment Account**: **Visa**

4 Enter **Payment Date: Current Date**

5 Select **Bills to Pay: Norton Lumber and Building Materials with an Open Balance of $80.00**

6 If the Payment field autofills, verify the **Payment Amount**

7 Select **Save and close**

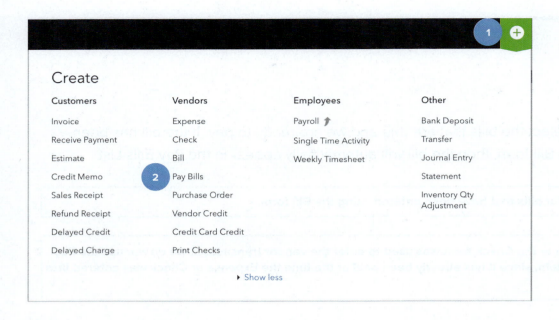

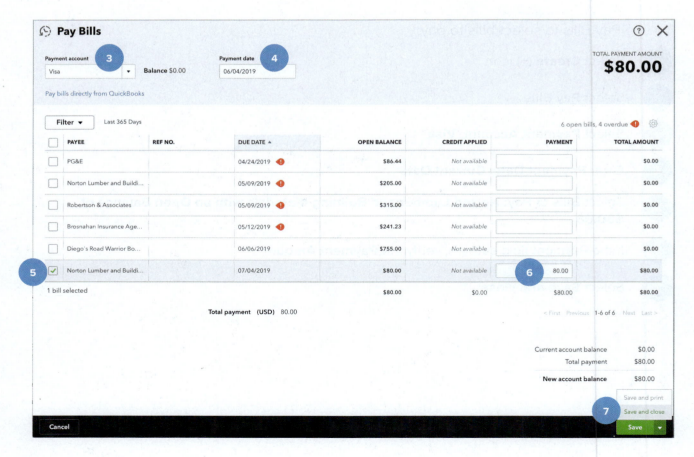

Section 7.8

INVOICE

An Invoice is used to record sales when the customer will pay later. An Invoice contains detailed information about the products and services provided to a customer.

To create an Invoice:

1. Select **Create (+)** icon

2. Select **Invoice**

3. Select **Customer: Amy's Bird Santuary**

4. Enter **Terms: Net 30**

5. Enter **Invoice Date: Current Date**

6. Verify **Due Date**

7. Select **Product/Service: Quartz Garden Sculpture**

8. If the Description field does not autofill, enter **Description: Quartz Garden Sculpture**

9. Enter **Quantity (QTY): 1**

10. If inventory tracking is turned on for an item, hover the cursor over QTY to see quantity of the inventory item on hand

11. Verify **Rate**

12. Verify **Amount**

13. Select **Tax**

14. **Sales Tax** should autofill: **California 8%**

15. Select **Save and send**

16. A screen appears showing the Invoice the customer will receive via email with a short message

17 Select **Save and close**. A message will appear indicating that emails cannot be sent from a Sample Company. If this were not a Sample Company, the email would be sent to the customer with the Invoice attached.

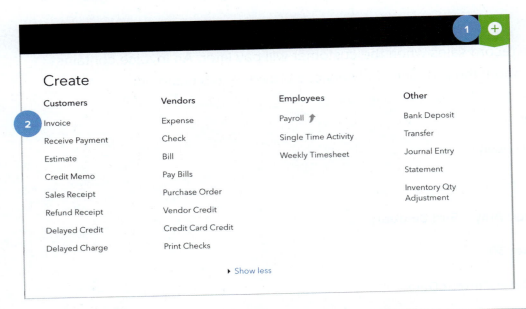

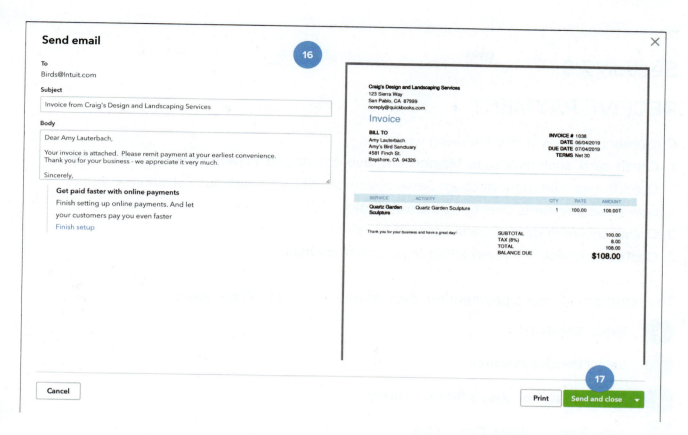

Section 7.9

RECEIVE PAYMENT

Customers may pay in the following ways:

1. **Credit card**, such as Visa or MasterCard, over the phone, in person, or by mail. Using QuickBooks' Merchant Account Service, you can obtain online authorization and then download payments directly into QuickBooks.
2. **Online** by credit card or bank account transfer.
3. **Customer check** delivered either in person or by mail.

To record a customer's payment received to pay an outstanding Invoice:

1. Select **Create (+)** icon

2. Select **Receive Payment**

3. Select **Customer**: **Amy's Bird Sanctuary**

4. Enter **Payment Date: Current Date**

5. Enter **Payment Method: MasterCard**

6. If this deposit will be bundled with other deposits, then select Undeposited Funds and after completing the Invoice, enter a Bank Deposit to move the funds from Undeposited Funds to the Checking account. If this deposit is not bundled with other deposits, then select the appropriate Checking account from the drop-down list. The funds are deposited directly to the Checking account selected and we do not enter a separate Bank Deposit. In this case, select **Deposit to: Checking**.

7. In the Outstanding Transactions section, select the Invoice to which payment should be applied. Select the Invoice you just entered with an **Open Balance of 108.00**.

8. Verify the **Payment Amount**

9. Select **Save and send**

10. A screen appears showing the Receipt the customer will receive via email with a short message

11. Select **Save and close**. A message will appear indicating that emails cannot be sent from a Sample Company. If this were not a Sample Company, the email would be sent to the customer with the Receipt attached.

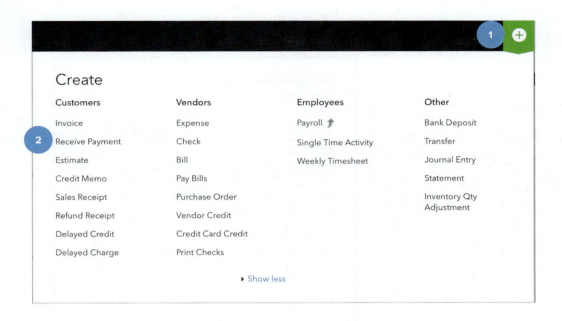

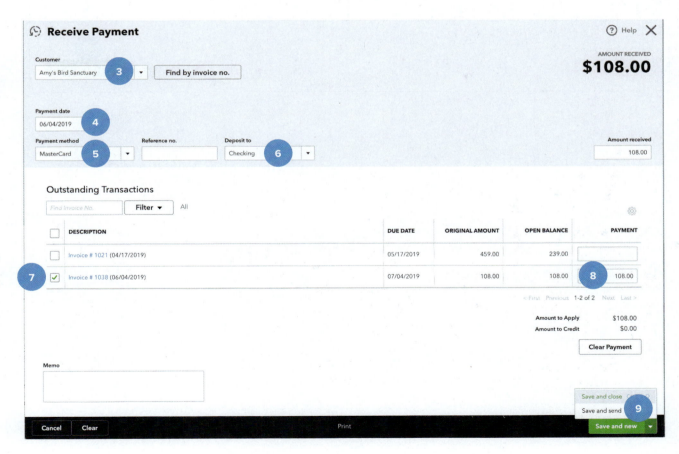

Section 7.10

BANK DEPOSIT FOR UNDEPOSITED FUNDS

If Undeposited Funds was selected on the Receive Payment form, then we must create a Bank Deposit to transfer the funds from the Undeposited Funds account to the appropriate Checking account. Sometimes Undeposited Funds is used on the Receive Payment form if the customer payment will be bundled with other customer payments when deposited. Then our totals will correspond to the bank deposit total shown by the bank.

> **If we selected Undeposited Funds on the Receive Payment form, we *must* create a bank deposit to transfer the funds from the Undeposited Funds account to the appropriate bank account. Otherwise, the funds will remain in the Undeposited Funds account and our Checking account balance will be incorrect.**

> **If we selected a specific bank account, such as Checking account, on the Receive Payment form, then we do *not* need to create a bank deposit. We have already recorded the deposit of the customer payment in the bank account.**

To record a bank deposit related to a customer sale when Undeposited Funds was selected on the Receive Payment form:

1 Select **Create (+)** icon

2 Under Other column, select **Bank Deposit**

3 Select **Bank** account

4 Enter **Date** of deposit

5 The Select Existing Payments section lists customer payments received but not deposited yet. When we received Amy's Bird Sanctuary customer payment, we already recorded it as a deposit to the Checking account. So Amy's Bird Sanctuary payment of $108.00 should not appear on the Existing Payments List for Undeposited Funds.

6 Enter appropriate **Payment Method**

7 If appropriate, enter **Memo** describing the deposit

8 Verify **Amount** is correct

9 Select **Attachments** to add a file or photo of any accompanying document

10 Since we already recorded the Amy's Bird Sanctuary customer payment in the Checking account, select **Cancel**

11 This completes the chapter activities. **Close** the QBO Sample Company web browser window to reset the Sample Company before proceeding to the exercises at the end of this chapter.

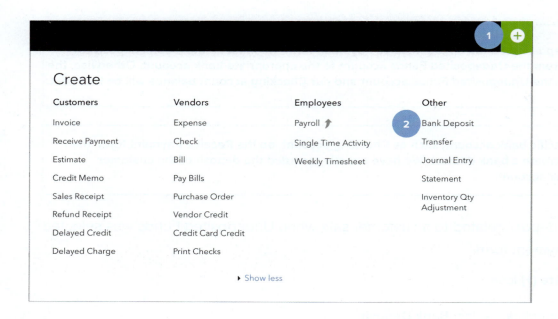

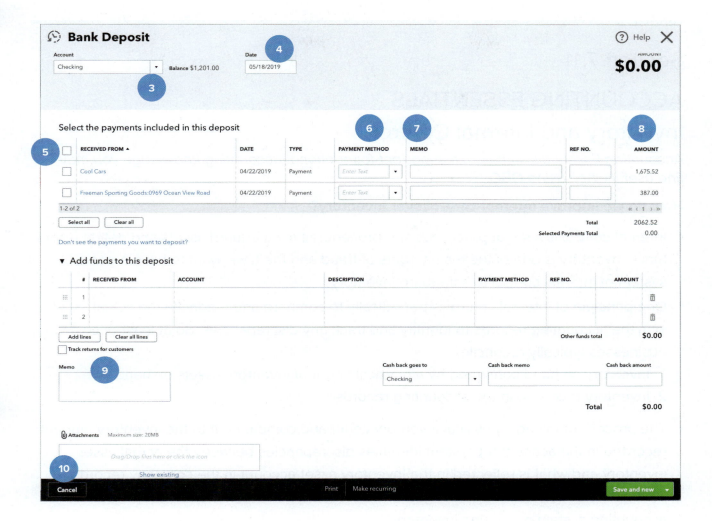

Section 7.11

ACCOUNTING ESSENTIALS
Inventory and Internal Control

Accounting Essentials summarize important foundational accounting knowledge you may find useful when using QBO

How do we improve internal control over inventory?

- Internal control is a set of processes and procedures to safeguard assets and detect errors. Since inventory is one of the main targets of fraud and theft, we want to have a good system of internal control to safeguard inventory.

- One principle of internal control is periodically to compare and reconcile the actual asset with the accounting records to identify and track any discrepancies. So at least once a year, businesses typically reconcile:
  1. Inventory on hand confirmed by a physical count of inventory assets on hand with
  2. Inventory recorded in the accounting records

- The process of taking a physical inventory count and comparing it to the inventory amounts recorded in the accounting system identifies discrepancies between the actual asset Inventory and what is reflected in the Inventory asset account in the company records. Discrepancies can then be investigated to determine whether it is an error in the accounting system or missing inventory.

What is a 3-way match?

- Another principle of internal control is to use a 3-way match when ordering, receiving, and paying for inventory.

- 3-way match compares:
  1. What was *ordered*?
  2. What was *received*?
  3. What was *billed*?

- Basically, we want to compare what we *ordered* with what we *received*, and what we were *billed*. These three amounts should agree so that we are not paying for more than what we ordered or received.

Practice Quiz 7

Q7.1

To enter Customers and Sales transactions:

a. From the Navigation Bar, select Transactions > Customers

b. From the Navigation Bar, select Transactions > Expenses > New Transaction

c. From the Create (+) icon, select the appropriate customer transaction

d. From the Gear icon, select Expense Transactions

Q7.2

To enter Vendors and Expenses transactions:

a. From the Navigation Bar, select Transactions > Customers

b. From the Navigation Bar, select Transactions > Sales

c. From the Create (+) icon, select the appropriate vendor transaction

d. From the Gear icon, select Vendor transactions

Q7.3

QuickBooks considers all of the following to be vendors except:

a. Utility companies

b. Suppliers of inventory and supplies

c. Tax agencies such as the IRS

d. Customers purchasing products

Q7.4

Which of the following is a vendors transaction?

a. Purchase Order

b. Invoice

c. Make deposit

d. Receive Payment

Q7.5

We can update the Products and Services List at which of the following two points:

a. Before entering transactions

b. While entering transactions

c. After entering transactions

Q7.6

Which of the following is a Customers transaction?

a. Invoice

b. Purchase Order

c. Pay Bills

d. Bill

Q7.7

Types of products and services on the Products and Services List include:

a. Service

b. Non-inventory

c. Inventory

d. All of the above

Q7.8

Which of the following products and services types track quantities?

a. Service items

b. Inventory items

c. Non-inventory items

d. None of the above

Q7.9

The Purchase Order form is used to record which one of the following transactions?

a. Owner's investment

b. Services received but not yet paid

c. Products sold to customers

d. Products ordered from vendors

Q7.10

Which of the following activities, and the QBO form used to record it, is incorrect?

a. Receive customer payment, Pay Bills

b. Order products, Purchase Order

c. Receive bill to be paid later, Bill

d. Sell products and bill customers, Invoice

Q7.11

Indicate two of the following that show the order in which the following onscreen vendor transaction forms typically should be prepared.

a.   Expense > Pay Bills

b.   Purchase Order > Bill > Pay Bills

c.   Bill > Pay Bills

d.   Invoice > Pay Bills

Q7.12

Recording a purchase of products using QBO involves all of the following steps except:

a.   Create invoice to bill vendors for purchases

b.   Create purchase order to order items from vendors

c.   Receive bill and record obligation to pay vendor later

d.   Pay bill entered previously

Q7.13

To record a bill received that we will pay later, we use which of the following QBO forms?

a.   Purchase Order

b.   Pay Bills

c.   Expense

d.   Bill

Q7.14

Use the Pay Bills form only for:

a.   Bills that have been entered using the Bill form

b.   Bills that have been entered using the Expense form

c.   Bill that have been entered using the Check form

d.   Bills that have never been entered in QBO

Exercises 7

> **We use the QBO Sample Company, Craig's Design and Landscaping Services, for practice throughout the exercises. The Sample Company will reset each time it is reopened. So make certain to allow enough time to complete exercise before closing the Sample Company. Otherwise, you will lose the work you have entered when you reopen the Sample Company.**

> ⚠️ **Since the Sample Company resets each time it is reopened, be certain to close any web browser windows displaying the QBO Sample Company before starting these exercises. Closing the browser window and starting with a new browser window for the QBO Sample Company resets the data before starting the exercises.**

To access the QBO Sample Company, complete the following steps.

1 Open a web browser. (Note: Intuit recommends using Google Chrome.)

2 Go to the https://qbo.intuit.com/redir/testdrive

3 Follow onscreen instructions for security verification

Craig's Design and Landscaping Services should appear on your screen.

E7.1 Vendors and Expenses Transactions

Match the following vendors and expenses transactions with the description of the transaction.

Vendors and Expenses Transaction Descriptions

a. The form used to select bills we want to pay.

b. The form used to order and track products from vendors.

c. The onscreen form used to record products and services that we pay for at the time we receive the product or service with cash, credit card, or check.

d. The form used when a vendor gives us a refund or reduction in our bill.

e. This form can be used when we pay for products and services at the time of purchase, but cannot be used when we pay with cash or credit card.

f. A form used to record a reduction in charges by the vendor to our credit card.

g. The form used to record bills we receive and our obligation to pay the vendor later (accounts payable).

Vendors and Expenses Transaction

1. Expense

2. Check

3. Bill

4. Pay Bills

5. Purchase Order

6. Vendor Credit

7. Credit Card Credit

E7.2 Inventory Flow

Match the following items with the appropriate diagram number.

a. Sell Products to Customers

b. Purchase Products from Vendors

c. Customers

d. Vendors

e. Our Company

Item

1 _____

2 _____

3 _____

4 _____

5 _____

E7.3 Inventory and Transactions

Match the following transaction descriptions with the order in which the transactions typically would be recorded.

Transaction Descriptions

a. Records our obligation to pay the vendor for the products (Accounts Payable).

b. Records our order of products from vendors.

c. Records resale of product to customer and the customer's promise to pay later (Accounts Receivable).

d. Records customer's payment in the bank account, used only if Undeposited Funds is selected on the Receive Payment form.

e. Records collection of the customer's payment.

f. Pays vendors for products received.

Transaction Order

1. _____

2. _____

3. _____

4. _____

5. _____

6. _____

E7.4 Vendors Transaction: Purchase Order

Using the QBO Sample Company, Craig's Design and Landscaping Services, complete the following.

1. Create Purchase Order.
   a. Select **Create (+) icon > Purchase Order**
   b. Select **Vendor: Hicks Hardware**
   c. Select **Purchase Order Date: Current Date**
   d. Select Item Details Line 1: **Product/Service: Design: Fountains: Rock Fountain**
   e. Enter **QTY: 3**
   f. Enter **Rate: 125**
   g. **Amount** should autofill
   h. Select **Customer: Red Rock Diner**
   i. Select Item Details Line 2: **Product/Service: Design: Fountains: Pump**
   j. Enter **QTY: 6**

    k. Enter **Rate: 10**

    l. **Amount** should autofill

    m. Select **Customer: Red Rock Diner**

    n. What is the Total for the Purchase Order?

    o. Select **Save and new**

2. Create Purchase Order.

    a. If necessary, select **Create (+) icon > Purchase Order**

    b. Select **Vendor: Hicks Hardware**

    c. Select **Purchase Order Date: Current Date**

    d. Select Item Details Line 1: **Product/Service: Design: Fountains: Rock Fountain**

    e. Enter **QTY: 2**

    f. Enter **Rate: 125**

    g. **Amount** should autofill

    h. Select **Customer: Cool Cars**

    i. Select Item Details Line 2: **Product/Service: Design: Fountains: Pump**

    j. Enter **QTY: 5**

    k. Enter **Rate: 10**

    l. **Amount** should autofill

    m. Select **Customer: Cool Cars**

    n. What is the Total for the Purchase Order?

    o. Select **Save and close**

E7.5 Vendors Transaction: Bill

This assignment is a continuation of E7.4

Using the QBO Sample Company, Craig's Design and Landscaping Services, complete the following to record a bill received for products ordered.

1. Create Bill.

    a. Select **Create (+) icon > Bill**

    b. Select **Vendor: Hick's Hardware**

    c. The two Purchase Orders entered in the previous exercise should appear in the drawer on the right side of the screen. Select **Add All** to add both POs to the bill. Item Details should now show the items from the POs.

    d. What is the Total for the Bill?

    e. Select **Save**

2. View the Transaction Journal for the Bill.
   a. From the bottom of the Hick's Hardware Bill, select **More > Transaction Journal**
   b. What are the Accounts and Amounts Debited?
   c. What are the Account and Amount Credited?

E7.6 Vendors Transaction: Pay Bills
This assignment is a continuation of E7.4 and E7.5

Using the QBO Sample Company, Craig's Design and Landscaping Services, complete the following.

1. Pay Bills.
   a. Select **Create (+) icon > Pay Bills**
   b. Select **Payment Account: Checking**
   c. Select **Payment Date: Current Date**
   d. Select **Payee: Hicks Hardware**
   e. What is the Total Payment Amount?
   f. Select **Save and close**

2. View the Transaction Journal for Pay Bills.
   a. From the Navigation Bar, select **Expenses**
   b. From the Expense Transactions List, select **Bill Payment to Hick's Hardware**
   c. From the bottom of Hick's Hardware Bill Payment, select **More > Transaction Journal**
   d. What are the Account and Amount Debited?
   e. What are the Account and Amount Credited?

E7.7 Customers Transaction: Invoice
This assignment is a continuation of E7.4 - E7.6

Using the QBO Sample Company, Craig's Design and Landscaping Services, complete the following.

1. Create Invoice.
   a. Select **Create (+) icon > Invoice**
   b. Select **Customer: Red Rock Diner**
   c. Select **Invoice Date: Current Date**

d. Select Item Details Line 1: **Product/Service: Design: Fountains: Rock Fountain**

e. Enter **QTY: 5**

f. Enter **Rate: 275**

g. **Amount** should autofill

h. Check **Tax**

i. Select Item Details Line 2: **Product/Service: Design: Fountains: Pump**

j. Enter **QTY: 11**

k. Enter **Rate: 15**

l. **Amount** should autofill

m. Check **Tax**

n. Select **Sales Tax Rate: California (8%)**

o. What is the Subtotal for the Invoice?

p. What is the Total for the Invoice?

q. Select **Save** and leave the Invoice displayed

2. View the Transaction Journal for the Invoice.

   a. From the bottom of the Red Rock Diner Invoice, select **More > Transaction Journal**

   b. What are the Accounts and Amounts Debited?

   c. What are the Accounts and Amounts Credited?

E7.8 Customers Transaction: Receive Payment

This assignment is a continuation of E7.4 - E7.7

Using the QBO Sample Company, Craig's Design and Landscaping Services, complete the following.

1. Create Receive Payment.

   a. Select **Create (+) icon > Receive Payment**

   b. Select **Customer: Red Rock Diner**

   c. Select **Payment Date: Current Date**

   d. Select **Payment Method: Visa**

   e. Select **Deposit to: Checking**

   f. Select the **Red Rock Diner Invoice** just entered

   g. What is the Amount Received?

   h. Select **Save and close**

2. View the Transaction Journal for Receive Payments.
   a. From the Navigation Bar, select **Sales > All Sales tab**
   b. From the Sales Transactions List, select **Red Rock Diner Payment** just entered
   c. From the bottom of Red Rock Diner Receive Payment, select **More > Transaction Journal**
   d. What are the Account and Amount Debited?
   e. What are the Account and Amount Credited?

E7.9 Customers Transaction: Invoice

This assignment is a continuation of E7.4 and E7.5

Using the QBO Sample Company, Craig's Design and Landscaping Services, complete the following.

1. a. Select **Create (+) icon > Invoice**
   b. Select **Customer: Cool Cars**
   c. Select **Invoice Date: Current Date**
   d. Select Item Details Line 1: **Product/Service: Design: Fountains: Rock Fountain**
   e. Enter **QTY: 1**
   f. Enter **Rate: 275**
   g. **Amount** should autofill
   h. Check **Tax**
   i. Select Item Details Line 2: **Product/Service: Design: Fountains: Pump**
   j. Enter **QTY: 3**
   k. Enter **Rate: 15**
   l. **Amount** should autofill
   m. Check **Tax**
   n. Select **Sales Tax Rate: California (8%)**
   o. What is the Subtotal for the Invoice?
   p. What is the Total for the Invoice?
   q. Select **Save** and leave the Invoice displayed

2. View the Transaction Journal for the Invoice.
   a. From the bottom of the Cool Cars Invoice, select **More > Transaction Journal**
   b. What are the Accounts and Amounts Debited?
   c. What are the Accounts and Amounts Credited?

E7.10 Customers Transaction: Receive Payment

This assignment is a continuation of E7.4, E7.5, and E7.10

Using the QBO Sample Company, Craig's Design and Landscaping Services, complete the following.

1. Create Receive Payment.
    a. Select **Create (+) icon > Receive Payment**
    b. Select **Customer: Cool Cars**
    c. Select **Payment Date: Current Date**
    d. Select **Payment Method: MasterCard**
    e. Select **Deposit to: Checking**
    f. Select the **Cool Cars Invoice** just entered
    g. What is the Amount Received?
    h. Select **Save and close**

2. View the Transaction Journal for Receive Payments.
    a. From the Navigation Bar, select **Sales > All Sales tab**
    b. From the Sales Transactions List, select **Cool Cars Payment** just entered
    c. From the bottom of Cool Cars Receive Payment, select **More > Transaction Journal**
    d. What are the Account and Amount Debited?
    e. What are the Account and Amount Credited?

Project 7.1

Mookie the Beagle™ Concierge

> **Project 7.1 is a continuation of Project 6.1. You will use the QBO Company you created for Project 1.1 and updated in subsequent Projects 2.1 through 6.1. Keep in mind the QBO Company for Project 7.1 does not reset and carries your data forward, including any errors. So it is important to check and crosscheck your work to verify it is correct before clicking the Save button.**

BACKSTORY

Mookie The Beagle™ Concierge discovers that the young professionals using its pet care services, often don't have time to go shopping for pet care items. So MTB starts stocking high demand items, such as doggy hammocks, dog cones, activated charcoal for suspected poisoning, gauze wrap with adhesive tape for wound dressing, gauze nonstick bandages, sterile towels, and oral syringes for administering medications.

All the products are branded as Mookie The Beagle Concierge products and can be ordered through the MTB app. Delivery can be scheduled coinciding with a Mookie The Beagle Concierge pet care visit or immediately via Mookie The Beagle Concierge delivery service. MTB has asked for your assistance using QBO to account for inventory of its new product line.

🌐 QBO SATNAV

Project 7.1 focuses on QBO Transactions, specifically on Customers & Sales Transactions and Vendors & Expenses Transactions as shown in the following QBO SatNav.

🌐 **QBO SatNav**

⚙️ **QBO Settings**

⚙️ Company Settings

⚙️ Chart of Accounts

💰 **QBO Transactions**

💰 Banking

💰 Customers & Sales	*Create Invoices > Receive Payments > Record Deposits*
💰 Vendors & Expenses	*PO > Receive Inventory > Enter Bills Inventory > Pay Bills*

💰 Employees & Payroll

📊 **QBO Reports**

📊 Reports

HOW TO LOG INTO QBO

To log into QBO, complete the following steps.

1 Using a web browser go to qbo.intuit.com

2 Enter **User ID** (the email address you used to set up your QBO Account)

3 Enter **Password** (the password you used to set up your QBO Account)

4 Select **Sign in**

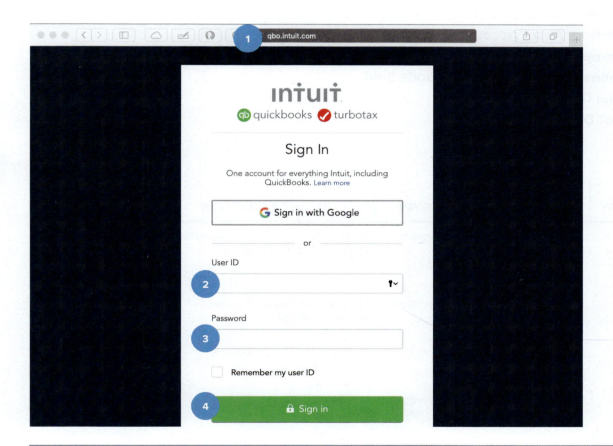

> **If you are _not_ using a public or shared computer,** to speed up login, you can save your login to your desktop and select Remember Me. If you are using a public computer or shared computer, do not save to the desktop and unselect Remember Me.

> **The new QBO Company** we created in Project 1.1 will carry all work forward into future chapters. So it is important to check and crosscheck your work to verify it is correct before clicking the Save button. Any uncorrected errors will be carried forward in your QBO Company for text projects.

P7.1.1 Products and Services List

> **Before starting P7.1.1, verify** that QBO Inventory Tracking is turned on. Go to Gear icon > **Account and Settings** > **Sales** > **Products and Services** > **Track quantity and price/rate On** > **Track inventory quantity on hand** > **On.**

To enter products into the Products and Services List:

1. From the Navigation Bar, select **Sales** > **Products and Services** > **New** > **Inventory**

2. Enter the following information about Mookie The Beagle Concierge branded products.

   Use the following when entering inventory:
   - **Inventory Asset Account: Inventory Asset**
   - **Income Account: Sales of Product Income**
   - **Expense Account: Cost of Goods Sold**
   - **Initial Quantity on Hand: -0-**
   - **As of Date: 01/01/2022**

CATEGORY	NAME	TYPE	SALES DESCRIPTION	SALES PRICE	COST
Pet Food Supplies	Mookie The Beagle Bon Appetite Organic Doggie Food	Inventory	Mookie The Beagle Bon Appetite Organic Doggie Food	$ 60	$ 26
Doggie Hammocks	Mookie The Beagle Hammock Small	Inventory	Mookie The Beagle Doggie Hammock Small	$ 200	$ 80
Doggie Hammocks	Mookie The Beagle Hammock Medium	Inventory	Mookie The Beagle Doggie Hammock Medium	$ 300	$ 120
Doggie Hammocks	Mookie The Beagle Hammock Large	Inventory	Mookie The Beagle Doggie Hammock Large	$ 400	$ 160
Pet Wellness Supplies	E-Collar Cone	Inventory	E-Collar Cone Adjustable (Fits Various Size Doggie Necks for Wound Healing)	$ 40	$ 16
Pet Wellness Supplies	Activated Charcoal	Inventory	Activated Charcoal for Suspected Poisoning	$ 36	$ 10

CATEGORY	NAME	TYPE	SALES DESCRIPTION	SALES PRICE	COST
Pet Wellness Supplies	Gauze Bandages	Inventory	Gauze Bandages for Wound Dressing	$ 24	$ 6
Pet Wellness Supplies	Sterile Towels	Inventory	Sterile Towels for Wound Cleaning	$ 30	$ 8
Pet Wellness Supplies	Oral Syringes	Inventory	Oral Syringes for Medication Administration (10 pack)	$ 20	$ 4
Pet Wellness Supplies	Sterile Latex Gloves	Inventory	Sterile Latex Gloves (50 pack)	$ 72	$ 24

3. Export the Products and Services List to PDF.
   a. From the Products and Services List screen, select **More > Run Report**
   b. Select **Export drop-down arrow > Export to PDF > Save as PDF**

4. Update Mookie The Beagle Concierge Shipping Address.
   a. Select **Gear icon > Account and Settings > Company > Address > Company Address**
   b. Enter **Address: 432 Denmark Way**
   c. Enter **City: Mountain View**
   d. Enter **State: CA**
   e. Enter **Zip: 94043**
   f. Select **Customer-facing Address: Same as company address**
   g. Select **Legal Address: Same as company address**
   h. Select **Save > Done**

P7.1.2 Vendors Transaction: Purchase Order

Complete the following Mookie The Beagle Concierge Purchase Order to order Mookie The Beagle doggie hammocks.

1. Add a new Vendor to the Vendors List.
   a. From the Navigation Bar, select **Expenses > Vendors tab**
   b. Select **New vendor**

c. Enter the following vendor information.

Company:	**Maddy's Marvels**
First Name:	**Maddy**
Display Name As:	**Maddy's Marvels**
Phone:	**415-555-2727**
Billing Address Street:	**27 Aquarian Rue**
Billing Address City:	**Bayshore**
Billing Address State:	**CA**
Billing Address ZIP:	**94326**
Billing Address Country:	**USA**

d. Select **Save**

2. Create Purchase Order.
    a. Select **Create (+) icon > Purchase Order**
    b. Select **Vendor: Maddy's Marvels**
    c. Select **Purchase Order Date: 01/18/2022**
    d. Verify **Shipping Address: Mookie The Beagle Concierge, 432 Denmark Way, Mountain View, CA 94043**
    e. Select Item Details Line 1: **Product/Service: Doggie Hammocks: Mookie The Beagle Hammock Small**
    f. Enter **QTY: 2**
    g. **Rate** and **Amount** fields should autofill
    h. What is the Rate that autofills?
    i. What is the Total Amount for Line 1?

3. Enter PO Line 2.
   a. Select Item Details Line 2: **Product/Service: Doggie Hammocks: Mookie The Beagle Hammock Medium**
   b. Enter **QTY: 3**
   c. **Rate** and **Amount** fields should autofill
   d. What is the Rate that autofills?
   e. What is the Total Amount for Line 2?

4. Enter PO Line 3.
   a. Select Item Details Line 3: **Product/Service: Doggie Hammocks: Mookie The Beagle Hammock Large**
   b. Enter **QTY: 1**
   c. **Rate** and **Amount** fields should autofill
   d. What is the Rate that autofills?
   e. What is the Total Amount for Line 3?

5. Total PO.
   a. What is the Total Amount for the Purchase Order?
   b. Select **Save and close**

P7.1.3 Vendors Transaction: Purchase Order

Complete the following Mookie The Beagle Concierge Purchase Order to order Mookie The Beagle Concierge pet wellness inventory.

1. Add a new Vendor to the Vendors List.
   a. From the Navigation Bar, select **Expenses > Vendors tab**
   b. Select **New vendor**
   c. Enter the following vendor information.

Company:	**Meta Pet Supply**
Phone:	**415-555-8866**
Billing Address Street:	**86 Tron Boulevard**
Billing Address City:	**Bayshore**
Billing Address State:	**CA**
Billing Address ZIP:	**94326**
Billing Address Country:	**USA**

   d. Select **Save**

2. Create Purchase Order.
   a. Select **Create (+) icon** > **Purchase Order**
   b. Select **Vendor: Meta Pet Supply**
   c. Select **Purchase Order Date: 01/18/2022**
   d. Select Item Details Line 1: **Product/Service: Pet Wellness Supplies: E-Collar Cone**
   e. Enter **QTY: 1**
   f. **Rate** and **Amount** fields should autofill
   g. What is the Rate that autofills?
   h. What is the Total Amount for Line 1?

3. Enter PO Line 2.
   a. Select Item Details Line 2: **Product/Service: Pet Wellness Supplies: Activated Charcoal**
   b. Enter **QTY: 5**
   c. **Rate** and **Amount** fields should autofill
   d. What is the Rate that autofills?
   e. What is the Total Amount for Line 2?

4. Enter PO Line 3.
   a. Select Item Details Line 3: **Product/Service: Pet Wellness Supplies: Gauze Bandages**
   b. Enter **QTY: 4**
   c. **Rate** and **Amount** fields should autofill
   d. What is the Rate that autofills?
   e. What is the Total Amount for Line 3?

5. Enter PO Line 4.
   a. Select Item Details Line 4: **Product/Service: Pet Wellness Supplies: Sterile Towels**
   b. Enter **QTY: 6**
   c. **Rate** and **Amount** fields should autofill
   d. What is the Rate that autofills?
   e. What is the Total Amount for Line 4?

6. Enter PO Line 5.
   a. Select Item Details Line 4: **Product/Service: Pet Wellness Supplies: Oral Syringes**
   b. Enter **QTY: 2**
   c. **Rate** and **Amount** fields should autofill
   d. What is the Rate that autofills?
   e. What is the Total Amount for Line 5?

7. Enter PO Line 6.

   a. Select Item Details Line 4: **Product/Service: Pet Wellness Supplies: Sterile Latex Gloves**

   b. Enter **QTY: 6**

   c. **Rate** and **Amount** fields should autofill

   d. What is the Rate that autofills?

   e. What is the Total Amount for Line 6?

8. Total PO.

   a. What is the Total Amount for the Purchase Order?

   b. Select **Save and new**

P7.1.4 Vendors Transaction: Purchase Order

Complete the following Purchase Order to order Mookie The Beagle Bon Appetite Organic Doggie Food.

1. Add a new Vendor to the Vendors List.

   a. From the Navigation Bar, select **Expenses > Vendors tab**

   b. Select **New vendor**

   c. Enter the following vendor information.

Company:	**Only The Best Pet Food**
Phone:	**415-555-6354**
Billing Address Street:	**91 Elsker Avenue**
Billing Address City:	**Bayshore**
Billing Address State:	**CA**
Billing Address ZIP:	**94326**
Billing Address Country:	**USA**

   d. Select **Save**

2. Create Purchase Order.
   a. Select **Create (+) icon > Purchase Order**
   b. Select **Vendor: Only The Best Pet Food**
   c. Select **Purchase Order Date: 01/18/2022**
   d. Select Item Details Line 1: **Product/Service: Pet Food Supplies: Mookie The Beagle Bon Appetite Organic Doggie Food**
   e. Enter **QTY: 10**
   f. **Rate** and **Amount** fields should autofill
   g. What is the Rate that autofills?
   h. What is the Total Amount for Line 1?

3. Total PO.
   a. What is the Total Amount for the Purchase Order?
   b. Select **Save and close**

P7.1.5 Vendors Transaction: Bill

Complete the following to record a bill received for the Mookie The Beagle Doggie Hammocks ordered.

1. Create Bill.
   a. Select **Create (+) icon > Bill**
   b. Select **Vendor: Maddy's Marvels**
   c. Select **Bill Date: 01/21/2022**
   d. The Purchase Order entered previously should appear in the Add to Bill drawer on the right side of the screen. Select **Add** to add the PO to the bill. Item Details should now show the items from the PO.
   e. What is the Total for the Bill?
   f. Select **Save**

2. View the Transaction Journal for the Bill.
   a. From the bottom of the Maddy's Marvels Bill, select **More > Transaction Journal**
   b. What are the Accounts and Amounts Debited?
   c. What are the Account and Amount Credited?

P7.1.6 Vendors Transaction: Bill

Complete the following to record a bill received for the Mookie The Beagle Concierge pet wellness supplies ordered.

1. Create Bill.
    a. Select **Create (+) icon > Bill**
    b. Select **Vendor: Meta Pet Supply**
    c. Select **Bill Date: 01/23/2022**
    d. The Purchase Order entered previously should appear in the Add to Bill drawer. Select **Add** to add the PO to the bill. Item Details should now show the items from the PO.
    e. What is the Total for the Bill?
    f. Select **Save**

2. View the Transaction Journal for the Bill.
    a. From the bottom of the Meta Pet Supply Bill, select **More > Transaction Journal**
    b. What are the Accounts and Amounts Debited?
    c. What are the Account and Amount Credited?

P7.1.7 Vendors Transaction: Bill

Complete the following to record a bill received for the Mookie The Beagle Organic Doggie Food ordered.

1. Create Bill.
    a. Select **Create (+) icon > Bill**
    b. Select **Vendor: Only the Best Pet Food**
    c. Select **Bill Date: 01/23/2022**
    d. The Purchase Order entered previously should appear in the Add to Bill drawer. Select **Add** to add the PO to the bill. Item Details should now show the items from the PO.
    e. What is the Total for the Bill?
    f. Select **Save**

2. View the Transaction Journal for the Bill.
    a. From the bottom of the Only the Best Pet Food Bill, select **More > Transaction Journal**
    b. What are the Account and Amount Debited?
    c. What are the Account and Amount Credited?

P7.1.8 Vendors Transaction: Pay Bills

Complete the following to pay Mookie The Beagle Concierge bills.

1. Pay Bills.
   a. Select **Create (+) icon > Pay Bills**
   b. Select **Payment Account: Checking**
   c. Select **Payment Date: 01/24/2022**
   d. Select **Payee: Maddy's Marvels**
   e. Select **Payee: Only the Best Pet Food**
   f. What is the Total Payment Amount?
   g. Select **Save and close**

2. View the Transaction Journal for Pay Bills.
   a. From the Navigation Bar, select **Expenses**
   b. From the Expense Transactions List, select **Bill Payment to Maddy's Marvels**
   c. From the bottom of Maddy's Marvels Bill Payment, select **More > Transaction Journal**
   d. What are the Account and Amount Debited?
   e. What are the Account and Amount Credited?

3. View the Transaction Journal for Pay Bills.
   a. From the Navigation Bar, select **Expenses**
   b. From the Expense Transactions List, select **Bill Payment to Only the Best Pet Food**
   c. From the bottom of Only the Best Pet Food Bill Payment, select **More > Transaction Journal**
   d. What are the Account and Amount Debited?
   e. What are the Account and Amount Credited?

P7.1.9 Customers Transaction: Invoice

Complete the following to record the sale of a Mookie The Beagle Doggie Hammock to Graziella for Mario, her pet Italian Greyhound.

1. Set up Sales Tax.
   a. From the Navigation Bar, select **Taxes > Get started (or Set Up Sales Tax)**
   b. Verify **Business Address** for **Mookie The Beagle Concierge** > select **Next**
   c. Do you need to collect sales tax outside of California? Select **No > Next**
   d. **Close** the Automatic Sales Tax is All Set Up window
   e. Select **Filing Frequency: Quarterly > Save**

2. Create Invoice.
   a. Select **Create (+) icon > Invoice**
   b. Select **Customer: Mario Graziella**
   c. Select **Invoice Date: 01/25/2022**
   d. Select Item Details Line 1: **Product/Service: Doggie Hammocks: Mookie The Beagle Hammocks Medium**
   e. Enter **QTY: 1**
   f. **Rate** and **Amount** fields should autofill
   g. What is the Amount?
   h. Check **Tax**
   i. Select **Sales Tax**. Let's calculate your tax rate should display a Total tax standard rate of **9%**. If it displays a different amount, select Override this amount and change to 9%. Select **Close**.
   j. What is the Total for the Invoice?
   k. Select **Save** and leave the Invoice displayed

3. View the Transaction Journal for the Invoice.
   a. From the bottom of the Mario Graziella Invoice, select **More > Transaction Journal**
   b. What are the Accounts and Amounts Debited?
   c. What are the Accounts and Amounts Credited?

P7.1.10 Customers Transaction: Invoice

While Mimi's pet French Bulldog, Bebe, is recovering from her paw injury at Doggie Day Care, Bebe needs in home care. So Mimi ordered the following products and services using the Mookie The Beagle Concierge app.

- 1 Mookie The Beagle Doggie Hammock Small
- 1 Mookie The Beagle E-Collar Cone
- 3 Gauze Bandages
- 2 Sterile Towels
- 1 Oral Syringes (10 pack)
- 1 Sterile Latex Gloves (50 pack)
- 1 Pet Care Errand Service (to deliver the Mookie The Beagle Concierge supplies ordered)
- 2 Pet Wellness Medium Wellness Service (to administer medication and change wound dressings)

1.   Create Invoice.
     a. Select **Create (+) icon > Invoice**
     b. Select **Customer: Bebe Mimi**
     c. Select **Invoice Date: 01/27/2022**
     d. Select Item Details Line 1: **Product/Service: Doggie Hammocks: Mookie The Beagle Hammock Small**
     e. Enter **QTY: 1**
     f. **Rate** and **Amount** fields should autofill
     g. What is the Amount on Line 1?
     h. Check **Tax**

2.   Enter Invoice Line 2.
     a. Select Item Details Line 2: **Product/Service: Pet Wellness Supplies: E-Collar Cone**
     b. Enter **QTY: 1**
     c. **Rate** and **Amount** fields should autofill
     d. What is the Amount on Line 2?
     e. Check **Tax**

3.   Enter Invoice Line 3.
     a. Select Item Details Line 3: **Product/Service: Pet Wellness Supplies: Gauze Bandages**
     b. Enter **QTY: 3**
     c. **Rate** and **Amount** fields should autofill
     d. What is the Amount on Line 3?
     e. Check **Tax**

4.   Enter Invoice Line 4.
     a. Select Item Details Line 4: **Product/Service: Pet Wellness Supplies: Sterile Towels**
     b. Enter **QTY: 2**
     c. **Rate** and **Amount** fields should autofill
     d. What is the Amount on Line 4?
     e. Check **Tax**

5.   Enter Invoice Line 5.
     a. Select Item Details Line 5: **Product/Service: Pet Wellness Supplies: Oral Syringes**
     b. Enter **QTY: 1**
     c. **Rate** and **Amount** fields should autofill
     d. What is the Amount on Line 5?
     e. Check **Tax**

6. Enter Invoice Line 6.

    a. Select Item Details Line 6: **Product/Service: Pet Wellness Supplies: Sterile Latex Gloves**

    b. Enter **QTY: 1**

    c. **Rate** and **Amount** fields should autofill

    d. What is the Amount on Line 6?

    e. Check **Tax**

7. Enter Invoice Line 7.

    a. Select Item Details Line 7: **Product/Service: Pet Care: Errand**

    b. Enter **QTY: 1**

    c. **Rate** and **Amount** fields should autofill

    d. What is the Amount on Line 7?

    e. Uncheck **Tax**

8. Enter Invoice Line 8.

    a. Select Item Details Line 8: **Product/Service: Pet Wellness: Medium Wellness**

    b. Enter **QTY: 2**

    c. **Rate** and **Amount** fields should autofill

    d. What is the Amount on Line 8?

    e. Uncheck **Tax**

9. Select Tax Rate.

    a. What is the Subtotal for the Invoice?

    b. What is the Amount of Sales Tax?

    c. What is the Total for the Invoice?

    d. Select **Save** and leave the Invoice displayed

10. View the Transaction Journal for the Invoice.

    a. From the bottom of the Bebe Mimi Invoice, select **More > Transaction Journal**

    b. What are the Accounts and Amounts Debited?

    c. What are the Accounts and Amounts Credited?

P7.1.11 Customers Transaction: Invoice

Tracey Kari, a successful interior designer, used the Mookie The Beagle Concierge app to purchase the following products and services for her pet Labrador, Odin, when Tracey was detained for hours longer than planned on an interior design job gone awry.

- 1 Mookie The Beagle Doggie Hammock Medium
- 2 bags of Mookie The Beagle Bon Appetite Organic Doggie Food
- 1 Pet Care Errand Service (to deliver the Mookie The Beagle Concierge supplies ordered)
- 2 Pet Care Short Visit Service (to feed Odin and take him on a couple of short walks)

Complete the following for Mookie The Beagle Concierge to record an Invoice for Tracey Kari.

1. Enter a New Customer in the Customers List.
   a. From the Navigation Bar, select **Sales > Customers tab**
   b. Select **New customer**
   c. Enter the following customer information.

Display Name As:	**Odin Tracey Kari**
Email:	**odin@www.com**
Mobile:	**415-555-9999**
Billing Address Street:	**99 Reyke Drive**
Billing Address City:	**Bayshore**
Billing Address State:	**CA**
Billing Address ZIP:	**94326**
Billing Address Country:	**USA**
Shipping Address:	**Same as billing address**

   d. Select **Save**

2. Create Invoice and Enter Products Purchased.
   a. Select **Create (+) icon > Invoice**
   b. Select **Customer: Odin Tracey Kari**
   c. Select **Invoice Date: 01/28/2022**
   d. Select Item Details Line 1: **Product/Service: Doggie Hammocks: Mookie The Beagle Hammock Medium**
   e. Enter **QTY: 1**
   f. **Rate** and **Amount** fields should autofill
   g. What is the Amount for Line 1?
   h. Check **Tax**
   i. Select Item Details Line 2: **Product/Service: Pet Food Supplies: Mookie Bon Appetite Organic Doggie Food**
   j. Enter **QTY: 2**
   k. **Rate** and **Amount** fields should autofill
   l. What is the Amount for Line 2?
   m. Check **Tax**
   n. Select **Save** and leave the Invoice displayed

3. Enter Services Purchased on Invoice.
   a. Select Item Details Line 3: **Product/Service: Pet Care: Errand**
   b. Enter **QTY: 1**
   c. **Rate** and **Amount** fields should autofill
   d. What is the Amount for Line 3?
   e. Uncheck **Tax**
   f. Select Item Details Line 4: **Product/Service: Pet Care: Short Visit**
   g. Enter **QTY: 2**
   h. **Rate** and **Amount** fields should autofill
   i. What is the Amount for Line 4?
   j. Uncheck **Tax**
   k. Confirm **California Sales Tax Rate: 9%**
   l. What is the Subtotal for the Invoice?
   m. What is the Taxable Subtotal for the Invoice?
   n. What is the Amount of Sales Tax on the Invoice?
   o. What is the Total for the Invoice?
   p. Select **Save** and leave the Invoice displayed

4. View the Transaction Journal for the Invoice.
    a. From the bottom of the Odin Tracey Kari Invoice, select **More > Transaction Journal**
    b. What are the Accounts and Amounts Debited?
    c. What are the Accounts and Amounts Credited?

P7.1.12 Customers Transaction: Receive Payment

Complete the following to record a customer payment from Tracey Kari.

1. Create Receive Payment.
    a. Select **Create (+) icon > Receive Payment**
    b. Select **Customer: Odin Tracey Kari**
    c. Select **Payment Date: 01/30/2022**
    d. Select **Payment Method: Credit Card**
    e. Select **Deposit to: Checking**
    f. Select the **Odin Tracey Kari Invoice** just entered
    g. What is the Amount Received?
    h. Select **Save and close**

2. View the Transaction Journal for Receive Payments.
    a. From the Navigation Bar, select **Sales > All Sales tab**
    b. From the Sales Transactions List, select **Odin Tracey Kari Payment** just entered
    c. From the bottom of Odin Tracey Kari Receive Payment, select **More > Transaction Journal**
    d. What are the Account and Amount Debited?
    e. What are the Account and Amount Credited?

Chapter 8

Employees and Payroll

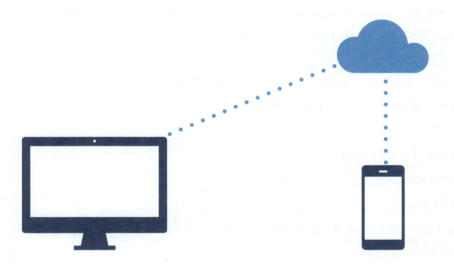

Mookie the Beagle Concierge needs to track time providing pet care for customers. Cy plans to use the tracked time to pay vendors he hires to provide the pet services. Also, he can use the tracked time to invoice customers for services provided. So your next task is to learn more about using QuickBooks Online for tracking time.

Chapter 8

LEARNING OBJECTIVES

Chapter 8 focuses on recording employees and payroll transactions. Payroll involves preparing employee paychecks, withholding the appropriate amount in taxes, and paying the company's share of payroll taxes. To assist in processing payroll, QBO offers a time-tracking feature that permits us to track the amount of time worked.

In Chapter 8, you will learn about the following topics:

- Navigating Employees Transactions
  - Payroll Setup
  - Payroll Processing
- Employees List
- Time Tracking
  - Turn on Time Tracking Preferences
  - Enter Time Tracking
  - Single Time Activity
  - Weekly Timesheet
- Set Up Payroll
- Pay Employees
- Pay Payroll Liabilities
- File Payroll Forms
- Accounting Essentials: Payroll Liabilities and Payroll Taxes

Section 8.1
 QBO SATNAV

QBO SatNav is our satellite navigation for QuickBooks Online, assisting us in navigating QBO

Chapter 8 focuses on QBO Employees & Payroll Transactions as shown in the following QBO SatNav.

 **QBO SatNav**

 **QBO Settings**

|  Company Settings |
| Chart of Accounts |

 **QBO Transactions**

| Banking |
| Customers & Sales |
| Vendors & Expenses |
| Employees & Payroll |  *Enter Time > Pay Employees > Payroll Liabilities* |

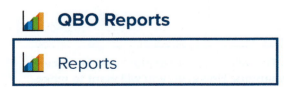 **QBO Reports**

| Reports |

Section 8.2

QBO SAMPLE COMPANY LOGIN

To log into the QBO Sample Company:

1 Open a web browser. (Note: Intuit recommends using Google Chrome.)

2 Go to https://qbo.intuit.com/redir/testdrive

3 Follow onscreen instructions for security verification

The QBO Sample Company Craig's Design and Landscaping Services should appear on the screen.

> Note: Although the Sample Company link should work, if for some reason the previous link for the Sample Company doesn't work with your browser, **using Google search type in "qbo.intuit.com Sample Company". Select the entry to Test Drive Sample Company.**

To increase the amount of time from one (1) hour to three (3) hours before the log out for inactivity occurs:

1 From Craig's Design and Landscaping Services QBO Sample Company, select the **Gear** icon

2 Under Your Company section, select **Account and Settings**

3 Select **Advanced**

4 Select **Other preferences**

5 For the option Sign me out if inactive for, select **3 hours**

6 Select **Save**

7 Select **Done**

> ⚠ **The Sample Company** will reset each time it is reopened. This allows you to explore and practice QBO without concern about carrying forward errors to later chapters. However, you will want to make certain to allow enough time to complete all chapter activities before closing the Sample Company. Otherwise, you will lose the work you have entered when you close and reopen the Sample Company.

To set QBO preferences to display account numbers in the Chart of Accounts:

1 Select the **Gear** icon to display options

2 Select **Account and Settings**

3 Select **Advanced**

4 For Chart of Accounts, select the **Edit Pencil**, then select **Enable account numbers**

5 Select **Show account numbers**

6 Select **Save**

7 Select **Done** to close Account and Settings

Section 8.3

NAVIGATING EMPLOYEES TRANSACTIONS

There are two main aspects to using QBO for Employees and Payroll Transaction purposes:

- Setting up payroll
- Processing payroll

PAYROLL SETUP

Payroll setup requires:

1. Set up **Employees List**
2. Turn on **Time Tracking** preference
3. Turn on **QBO Payroll**

PAYROLL PROCESSING

Payroll processing consists of the following four main types of tasks:

1. **Enter Time.** QBO permits us to track employee time worked to use in processing payroll and billing customers.
2. **Pay Employees.** Select employees to pay and create their paychecks.
3. **Pay Payroll Liabilities.** Pay payroll tax liabilities due governmental agencies, such as the IRS. Payroll tax liabilities include federal income taxes withheld, state income taxes withheld, FICA (Social Security and Medicare), and unemployment taxes.
4. **Process Payroll Forms.** Process payroll forms including Forms 940, 941, W-2, and W-3 that must be submitted to governmental agencies.

Section 8.4

EMPLOYEES LIST

The Employees List contains employee information such as address, telephone, salary or wage rate, and Social Security number.

To use the Employees List:

1   To view the Employees List, select **Workers** from the Navigation Bar

2   Select **Employee** tab

3   To edit an Employee, select **Edit** for the employee

4   To inactivate an Employee from the Employees List, select **Make inactive** from the drop-down menu

5   To view Employee information, double click on the **Employee's Name: Emily Platt**

6   View the Employee Information screen containing detailed employee information including address, email, phone, social security number, Employee ID, and date of birth. Enter **Mobile: 628-555-1111**.

7   Select **Save** to return to the Employees List

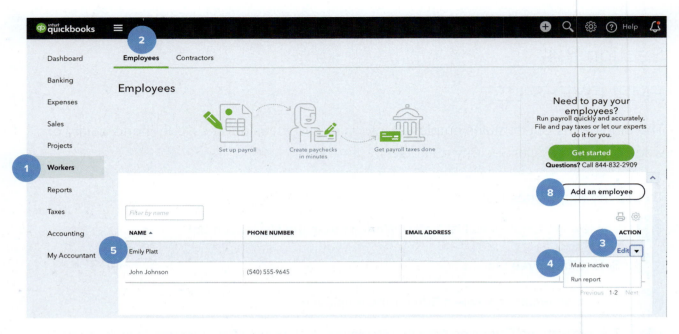

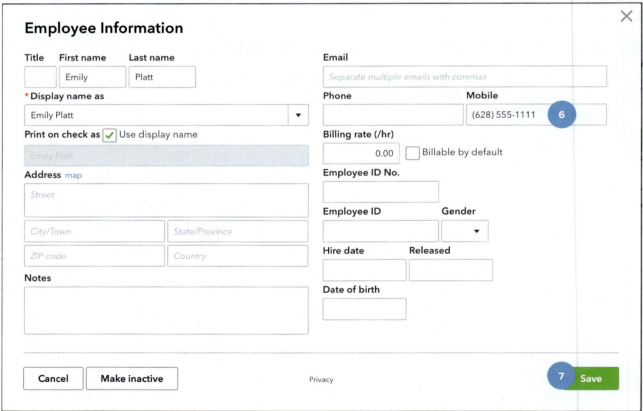

Section 8.5

TIME TRACKING

QBO time tracking permits us to track the amount of time worked. QBO uses time tracked to:

1. Calculate employee paychecks
2. Calculate contractor payments
3. Transfer time to sales invoices to bill customers for work performed

Work can be performed by employees, contractors, or owners. The time-tracking feature can be used to track time worked by any of the three. How we record the payment, however, depends upon who performs the work: employee, contractor, or business owner.

It is important that we determine the status of the individual performing the work. The status determines whether we record payments to the individual as an employee paycheck, vendor payment, or owner distribution.

Status	QBO Payment	Tax Form
Employee	Employee Paycheck	Form W-2
Contractor	Vendor Payment	Form 1099-MISC
Owner	Owner Distribution	Owner's Tax Return

TURN ON TIME-TRACKING PREFERENCES

To turn on QBO time-tracking preferences:

1. Select **Gear** icon

2. Under Your Company column, select **Account and Settings**

3. From the Account and Settings screen, select **Advanced**

4. Scroll down to the Time tracking section, and select the **Edit Pencil**

5 Check **Add Service field to timesheets** to display **On**

6 Check **Make Single-Time Activity Billable to Customer** to display **On**

7 Select First day of work week: **Monday**

8 Select **Save**

9 Select **Done**

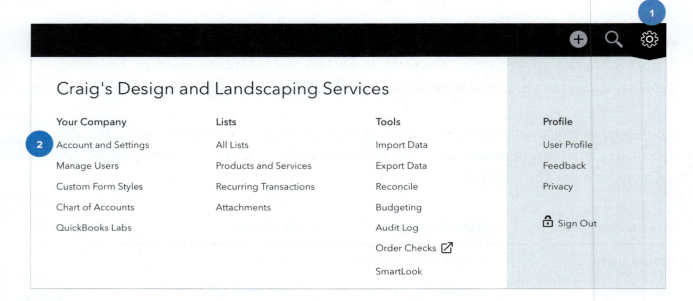

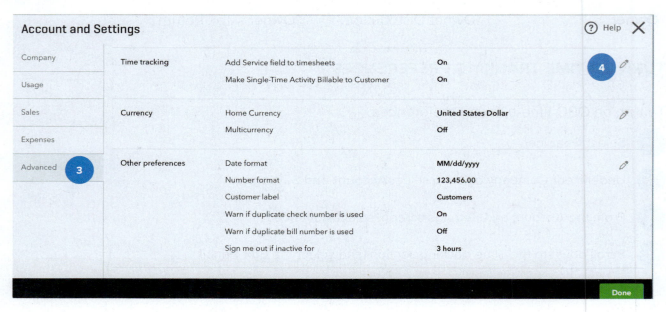

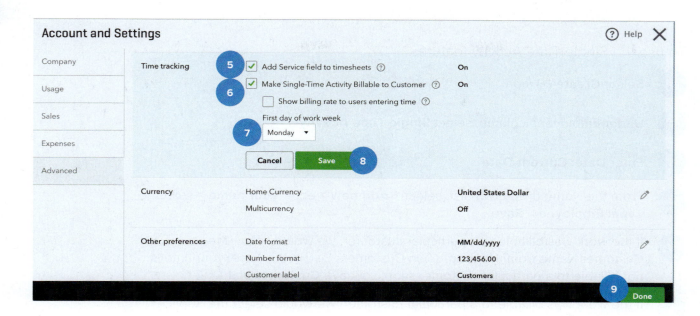

After turning on time-tracking preferences, we are ready to enter time.

ENTER TIME TRACKING

When employees or contractors use time tracking, the employee or contractor records total time worked and any time that is billable to a specific customer. Time data is then used to:

1. Prepare employee paychecks
2. Prepare contractor payments
3. Invoice customers for billable time

QBO provides two different ways to track time.

1. **Single Time Activity.** Use Single Time Activity time tracking to time one activity and enter the time data. QBO automatically records the time on the employee's weekly timesheet.
2. **Weekly Timesheet.** Use the weekly timesheet to enter time worked by each employee during the week, including time that is billable to specific customers.

SINGLE TIME ACTIVITY

The Single Time Activity for tracking time tracks the time for one activity. We will use the QBO Single Time Activity feature to time how long it takes to complete payroll activities in this chapter.

To use the Single Time Activity feature:

1. Select **Create (+)** icon

2. Under Employees column, select **Single Time Activity**

3. Enter **Date: Current Date**

4. From the Name drop-down list, select + **Add new** > enter **your name** > select **Type: Employee** > **Save**

5. If the work was billable to a particular customer, we would select the Customer Name from the drop-down Customers List. In this case, your time is not billable to a particular customer's job, so leave **Customer blank**.

6. If the work was billable to a particular customer, we would select the Service from the drop-down Services List. In this case, your time is not billable to a particular customer's job, so leave **Service blank**.

7. If the work was billable to a particular customer, we would check Billable. In this case, your time is not billable to a particular customer's job, so **uncheck Billable**.

8. Select **Enter Start and End Times**

9. Select **Start Time**, and enter the time you are starting this chapter

10. Select **End Time**, and enter the time that you estimate you will complete the Chapter 8 payroll activities

11. Enter any estimated **Break** that you plan to take when completing the QBO payroll chapter

12. Enter **Description** of your payroll activities for this chapter

13. Select **Save and close**

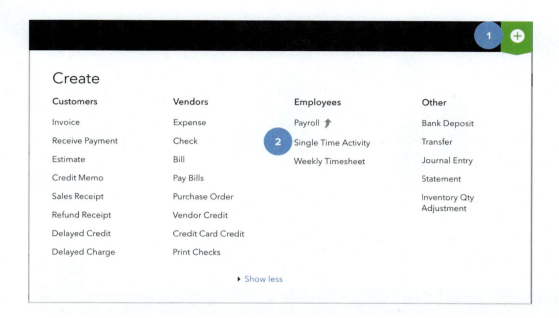

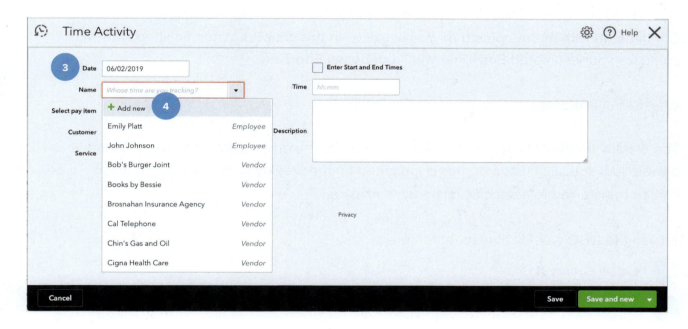

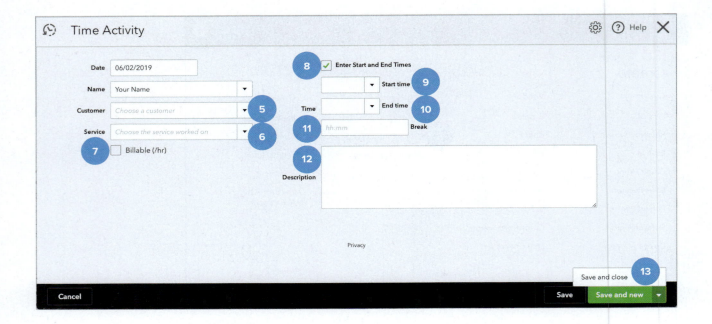

Continue on with the remaining payroll activities in this chapter. When finished, you will compare your estimated End Time with your actual End Time.

WEEKLY TIMESHEET

The weekly timesheet can be used to enter the hours worked during the week. If time is billable to a specific customer, this is indicated on the weekly timesheet. Later, billable time can be transferred to a specific customer's invoice.

To use the QBO weekly timesheet feature:

1 Select **Create (+)** icon

2 Under Employees column, select **Weekly Timesheet**

3 From the Weekly Timesheet screen, select **Employee Name: Emily Platt**

4 Use current **Dates** that autofills for weekly timesheet

5 Since Emily's work is billable to a specific customer, from the drop-down Customers List, select **Customer Name: Rondonuwu Fruit and Vegi**. If the work was not billable, leave the Customer field blank.

6 From the drop-down Services List, select **Service: Lighting (Design: Lighting)**

7 Since the work is billable to a specific customer, **check Billable**.

8 Enter **Billable Rate: 15.00**

9 Since the services provided are not taxed, **Uncheck Taxable**

10 Enter **Time** worked on specific days corresponding to the specific customer and service. In this case, enter **5** (hours) on Tuesday and **5** (hours) on Wednesday. Note that each time the specific customer or specific service changes, then we will move to the next line of the timesheet.

11 Verify the **Total for the Timesheet Line** that QBO calculates is correct

12 Verify the **Total for the Timesheet** that QBO calculates is correct

13 If the weekly timesheets are similar from week to week, select **Copy last timesheet**

14 If we need to delete a line on the timesheet, select the **Trash Can** for that line

15 Select **Save and close**

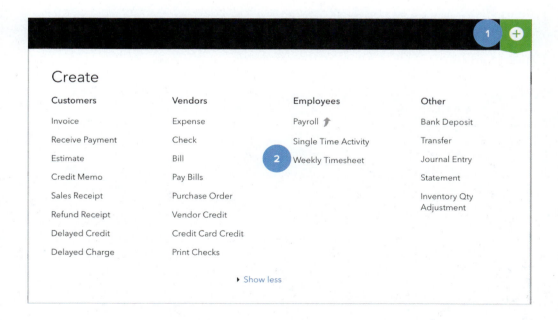

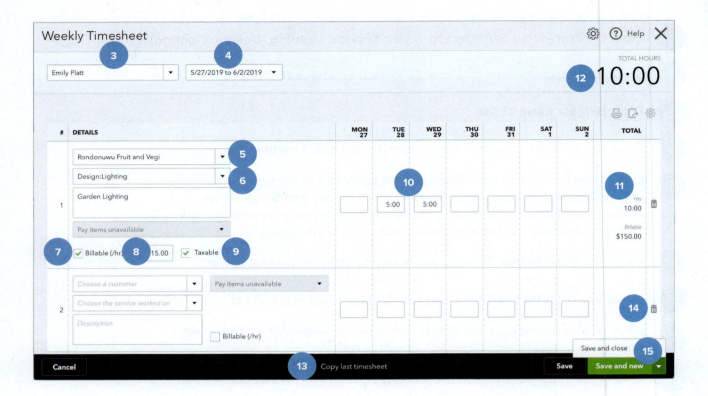

Section 8.6

SET UP PAYROLL

To use QBO payroll requires a subscription to QBO payroll service. The QBO payroll service is active for the QBO Sample Company so we can test drive the QBO payroll service.

To view QBO payroll:

1 From the Navigation Bar, select **Workers**

2 Select **Employees** tab

3 On the Employees screen, select **Get started**

4 If a message appears stating new updates are available, select **Reload**

5 The My Payroll screen should now appear, displaying the Employees List for payroll. Leave the My Payroll screen open.

> Note that the Sample Company used for Payroll Services may differ from Craig's Design and Landscaping Services Sample Company.

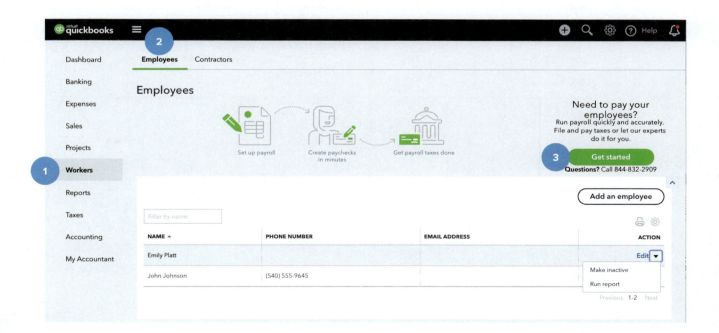

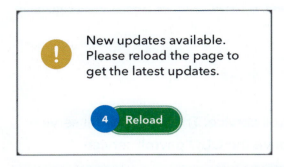

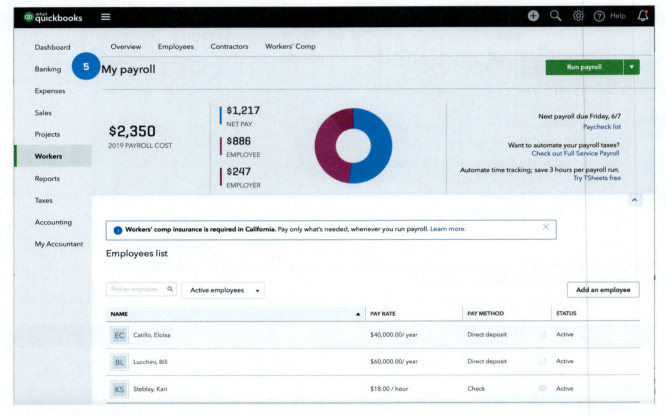

Section 8.7

PAY EMPLOYEES

PAY EMPLOYEES USING DIRECT DEPOSIT OR PRINT CHECKS

After entering time worked and setting up payroll, we would pay employees on a scheduled payroll payday. QBO Payroll will send you email reminders when payroll should be run.

After QBO Payroll Service is set up, then we would complete the following steps to run payroll and pay employees:

1 From the My Payroll screen, select **Run payroll**

2 From the Run Payroll screen, select **Bank Account: Checking**

3 Use the **Pay Period** that autofills

4 Use the **Pay Date** that autofills

5 Select to pay **Employee: Catillo, Eloisa**

6 Select **Preview payroll**

7 The Review and Submit screen summarizes payroll information for review, including Total Pay, Employee Taxes and Deductions, and Net Pay

8 Select **Submit payroll**

9 Select **Print paystubs**

10 The paystub should open in a new browser window. **Close** the browser window with the paystub.

11 After selecting the browser window for QBO, you can view associated payroll reports by selecting **View payroll reports** at the bottom of the screen

12 Select **Finish payroll**

13 If a Tax Payments Due message appears, select **I'll do it later**

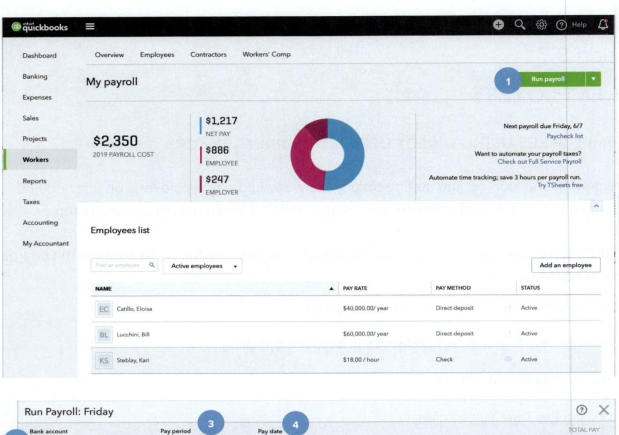

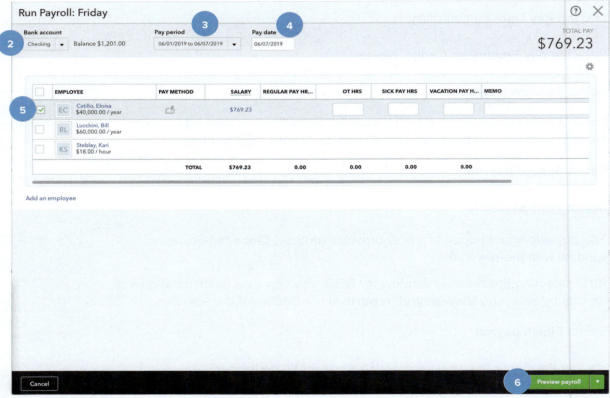

Employees and Payroll   435

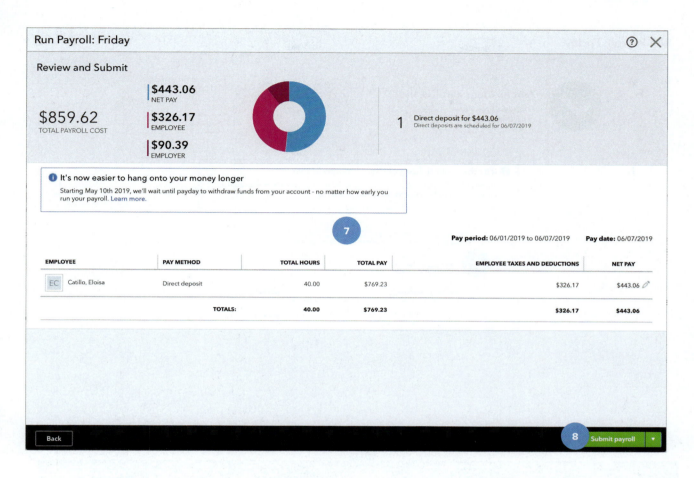

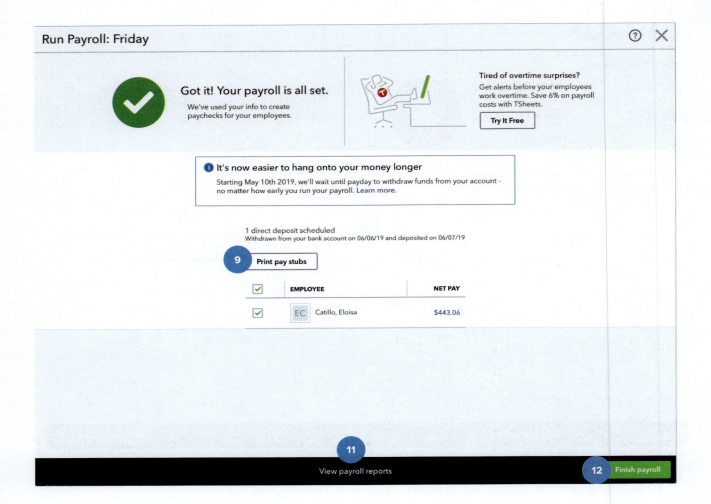

Collins Paint and Wallpaper Services
123 Main St.
Palo Alto CA 94306

(1)

Pay Stub Detail
PAY DATE:06/07/2019
NET PAY:$443.06

Eloisa Catillo
550 Front Boulevard
Menlo Park CA 94025

EMPLOYER
Collins Paint and Wallpaper Services
123 Main St.
Palo Alto CA 94306

PAY PERIOD	
Period Beginning	06/01/2019
Period Ending:	06/07/2019
Pay Date:	06/07/2019

EMPLOYEE
Eloisa Catillo
550 Front Boulevard
Menlo Park CA 94025

SS#: ...1111

BENEFITS	Used	Available
Sick	0.00	0.00
Vacation	0.00	41.54

NET PAY:	$443.06
Acct#....0000:	$200.00
Acct#....0000:	$243.06

MEMO:

PAY	Hours	Rate	Current	YTD
Salary	-	-	769.23	1,538.46

DEDUCTIONS	Current	YTD
401K	15.38	30.76
Bright Smile Insurance	40.00	80.00
Good Health Insurance	200.00	400.00

TAXES	Current	YTD
Federal Income Tax	0.00	0.00
Social Security	47.69	95.38
Medicare	11.16	22.31
CA Income Tax	4.25	8.50
CA State Disability Ins	7.69	15.38

SUMMARY	Current	YTD
Total Pay	$769.23	$1,538.46
Taxes	$70.79	$141.57
Deductions	$255.38	$510.76
Net Pay	**$443.06**	

Tax payments due

To avoid late fees and penalties, review and pay your taxes on time.

☐ Don't show this reminder again.

(13) I'll do it later   Review and pay

QBO Payroll offers the options of printing checks or using direct deposit to employees' bank accounts.

QBO MOBILE PAYROLL APP

The QBO Mobile Payroll app for Apple iPhone/iPad and Android offers employers the convenience of running payroll from their mobile devices. Then the payroll information is synced with QuickBooks Online.

Section 8.8

PAY PAYROLL LIABILITIES

Payroll liabilities include amounts for:

- Federal income taxes withheld from employee paychecks
- State income taxes withheld from employee paychecks
- FICA (Social Security and Medicare, including both the employee and the employer portions)
- Unemployment taxes

Federal income taxes, state income taxes, and the employee portion of FICA are withheld from the employee, and the company has an obligation (liability) to remit these amounts to the appropriate tax agency. The employer share of FICA and unemployment taxes are payroll taxes the employer owes.

QBO Payroll Service offers companies the ability to e-pay payroll liabilities. The company sets up e-pay by selecting which company bank accounts from which to pay the payroll liabilities. The appropriate federal and state agencies are selected to receive the payments. QBO Payroll even sends email reminders when it is time to e-pay the payroll liabilities.

To view payroll taxes due:

1. From the Navigation Bar, select **Taxes**

2. Select **Payroll Tax** tab

3. The Payroll Tax Center displays Taxes on the left side and Payroll Tax Forms on the right side. Select **Pay Taxes**.

4. The Pay Taxes screen lists Tax Payments due. When using the QBO Payroll Service, tax payments can be made by simply selecting **Create payment** for the appropriate tax payment due.

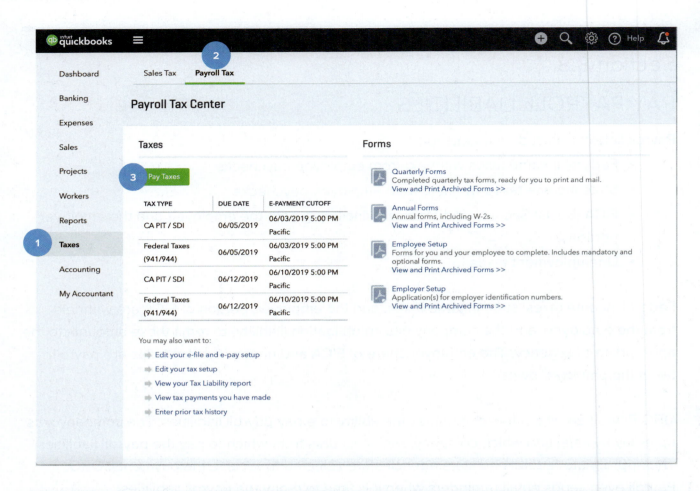

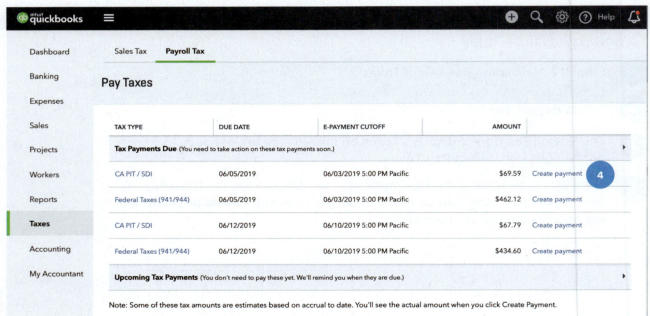

Section 8.9

FILE PAYROLL FORMS

Payroll tax forms summarize the amount of payroll withholdings that have been collected and remitted.

Payroll tax forms include:

- **Federal Form 940: Employer's Annual Federal Unemployment (FUTA) Tax Return.** This form summarizes the amount of unemployment tax paid and due by the employer.
- **Federal Form 941: Employer's Quarterly Federal Tax Return.** Filed with the IRS, this form summarizes the amount of federal income tax, Social Security, and Medicare withheld from employee paychecks for the quarter.
- **Federal Form 944: Employer's Annual Federal Tax Return.** Filed with the IRS, this form summarizes the amount of federal income tax, Social Security, and Medicare withheld from employee paychecks for the year. Form 944 is used by very small employers instead of filing Form 941 each quarter.
- **Form W-2: Wage and Tax Statement.** Before the end of January, an employer must provide W-2s to employees that summarize amounts paid for salaries, wages, and withholdings for the year.
- **Form W-3: Transmittal of Wage and Tax Statements.** Filed with the Social Security Administration, this form is a summary of the employer's W-2 forms.

QBO Payroll Service offers companies the ability to e-file payroll tax forms. The company must set up this feature for e-filing, but once setup is completed with all the appropriate agencies, it simply requires a click of a button to e-file. QBO Payroll Service sends email reminders when it is time to e-file the various payroll forms and sends confirmations once the e-filing has been completed.

To view payroll tax forms in QBO:

1 From the Navigation Bar, select **Taxes**

2 Select **Payroll Tax** tab

3 The Payroll Tax Center displays Taxes on the left side and Payroll Tax Forms on the right side

4 Select **Quarterly Forms** > **941**

5 Select **Preview** to view the Employer's Quarterly Tax Return

6 Form 941 Employer's Quarterly Federal Tax Return should open in a new browser window. **Close** the browser window for Form 941.

7 This completes the chapter activities. **Close** the QBO Sample Company web browser window to reset the Sample Company before proceeding to the exercises at the end of this chapter.

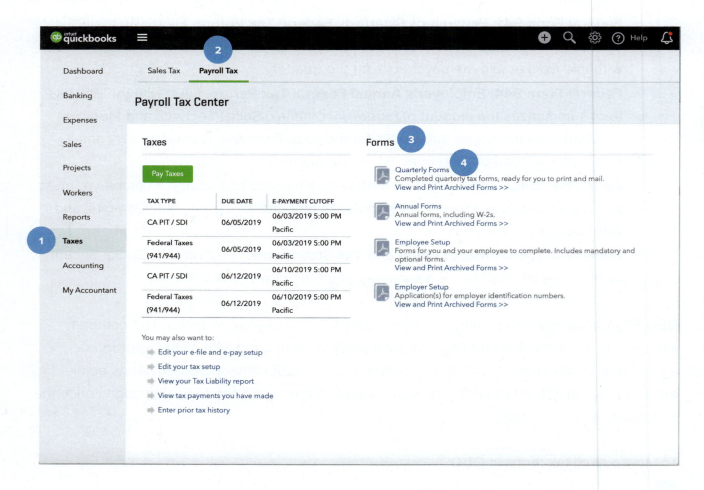

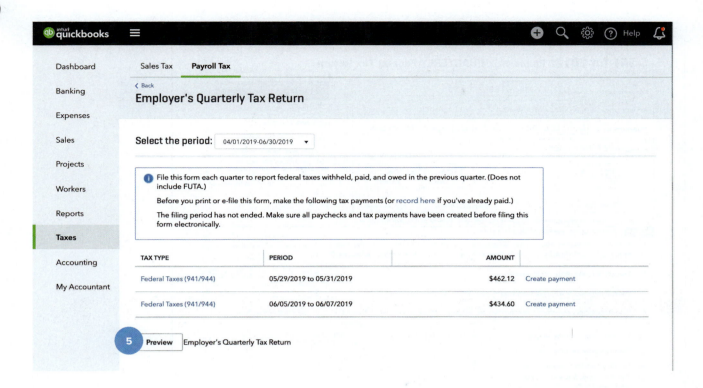

6

Form **941 for 2019:** **Employer's QUARTERLY Federal Tax Return**

(Rev. January 2019)   Department of the Treasury — Internal Revenue Service

950117

OMB No. 1545-0029

Employer identification number (EIN) 12-3456788

Name *(not your trade name)* Collins Paint & Wallpaper Services

Trade name *(if any)* Collins Paint and Wallpaper Services

Address 123 Main St.

Number   Street   Suite or room number

Palo Alto   CA   94306

City   State   ZIP code

Foreign country name   Foreign province/county   Foreign postal code

Report for this Quarter of 2019
(Check one.)

☐ **1:** January, February, March

☒ **2:** April, May, June

☐ **3:** July, August, September

☐ **4:** October, November, December

Go to *www.irs.gov/Form941* for
instructions and the latest information.

REV 04/26/19 OSP

Read the separate instructions before you complete Form 941. Type or print within the boxes.

Part 1:   Answer these questions for this quarter.

1	Number of employees who received wages, tips, or other compensation for the pay period including: *Mar. 12* (Quarter 1), *June 12* (Quarter 2), *Sept. 12* (Quarter 3), or *Dec. 12* (Quarter 4)	1	0
2	Wages, tips, and other compensation	2	3,824.86
3	Federal income tax withheld from wages, tips, and other compensation	3	280.72
4	If no wages, tips, and other compensation are subject to social security or Medicare tax	☐ Check and go to line 6.	

		Column 1		Column 2
5a	Taxable social security wages . .	4,026.16	× 0.124 =	499.24
5b	Taxable social security tips . . .		× 0.124 =	
5c	Taxable Medicare wages & tips. .	4,026.16	× 0.029 =	116.76
5d	Taxable wages & tips subject to Additional Medicare Tax withholding		× 0.009 =	

5e	Add Column 2 from lines 5a, 5b, 5c, and 5d	5e	616.00
5f	Section 3121(q) Notice and Demand—Tax due on unreported tips (see instructions) . .	5f	
6	Total taxes before adjustments. Add lines 3, 5e, and 5f	6	896.72
7	Current quarter's adjustment for fractions of cents	7	
8	Current quarter's adjustment for sick pay	8	
9	Current quarter's adjustments for tips and group-term life insurance	9	
10	Total taxes after adjustments. Combine lines 6 through 9	10	896.72
11	Qualified small business payroll tax credit for increasing research activities. Attach Form 8974	11	
12	Total taxes after adjustments and credits. Subtract line 11 from line 10	12	896.72
13	Total deposits for this quarter, including overpayment applied from a prior quarter and overpayments applied from Form 941-X, 941-X (PR), 944-X, or 944-X (SP) filed in the current quarter	13	
14	Balance due. If line 12 is more than line 13, enter the difference and see instructions . . .	14	896.72
15	Overpayment. If line 13 is more than line 12, enter the difference	Check one: ☐ Apply to next return. ☐ Send a refund.	

► You MUST complete both pages of Form 941 and SIGN it.   Next ►

For Privacy Act and Paperwork Reduction Act Notice, see the back of the Payment Voucher.   BAA   Form **941** (Rev. 1-2019)

⏱ **How long did it take you to complete the Chapter 8 payroll activities? Was you estimated time to complete the payroll activities close to your actual time to complete the activities?**

Section 8.10

ACCOUNTING ESSENTIALS
Payroll Liabilities and Payroll Taxes

Accounting Essentials summarize important foundational accounting knowledge you may find useful when using QBO

What are payroll liabilities?

- Payroll liabilities include two types of amounts:
  1. Amounts withheld from employee paychecks that must be paid to third parties
  2. Payroll tax expenses owed by the business

- Payroll liabilities include:
  - Federal income taxes withheld from employee paychecks
  - State income taxes withheld from employee paychecks
  - FICA (Social Security and Medicare, including both the employee and the employer portions)
  - Unemployment taxes

- Federal income taxes, state income taxes, and the employee portion of FICA are withheld from the employee, and the company has an obligation (liability) to remit these amounts to the appropriate tax agency. The employer share of FICA and unemployment taxes are payroll taxes the employer owes.

Payroll Liabilities (Federal)	Withheld from Employee Pay	Payroll Tax Expense Owed by Business
Federal Income Taxes	✓	
FICA (Social Security + Medicare)	✓	✓
Federal Unemployment Tax		✓

What are payroll tax forms?

- Basically, payroll tax forms summarize the amount of payroll withholdings that have been collected and remitted.
- Payroll tax forms include:
  - ▸ Federal **Form 940:** Employer's Annual Federal Unemployment (FUTA) Tax Return. This form summarizes the amount of unemployment tax paid and due by the employer.
  - ▸ **Federal Form 941:** Employer's Quarterly Federal Tax Return. Filed with the IRS, this form summarizes the amount of federal income tax, Social Security, and Medicare withheld from employee paychecks for the quarter.
  - ▸ **Federal Form 944:** Employer's Annual Federal Tax Return. Filed with the IRS, this form summarizes the amount of federal income tax, Social Security, and Medicare withheld from employee paychecks for the year. Form 944 is used by very small employers instead of filing Form 941 each quarter.
  - ▸ **Form W-2:** Wage and Tax Statement. Before the end of January, an employer must provide W-2s to employees that summarize amounts paid for salaries, wages, and withholdings for the year.
  - ▸ **Form W-3:** Transmittal of Wage and Tax Statements. Filed with the Social Security Administration, this form is a summary of the employer's W-2 forms.

Payroll Liabilities (Federal)	Federal Payroll Tax Form	
	Quarterly	Annual
Federal Income Taxes	941	944
FICA (Social Security + Medicare)	941	944
Federal Unemployment Tax		940

Practice Quiz 8

Q8.1

A company is not required to withhold payroll taxes for:

a.   Employees paid by the hour

b.   Salaried employees

c.   Out-of-state employees

d.   Independent contractors

Q8.2

A payment to a stockholder is recorded as a(n):

a.   Employee paycheck

b.   Vendor payment

c.   Distribution

d.   None of the above

Q8.3

In the Weekly Timesheet window you can record:

a.   Time billable to a specific vendor

b.   Time billable to a specific customer

c.   How many shipments of inventory items were received

d.   Number of purchase orders from each supplier

Q8.4

A company completes Form _____ to summarize for the IRS the amount of federal income tax, Social Security, and Medicare withheld from employee paychecks for the year.

a.   W-3

b.   940

c.   944

d.   None of the above

Q8.5

Which one of the following is not a payroll liability?

a.   Property taxes

b.   Unemployment taxes

c.   State income taxes withheld

d.   Federal income taxes withheld from employee paychecks

Q8.6

QuickBooks permits you to track employee time using which of the following two:

a.   Weekly Timesheet

b.   Paycheck

c.   Single Time Activity

d.   Monthly Timesheet

Q8.7

The employer must match which one of the following taxes paid by an employee?

a.   State Income

b.   Medicare

c.   Federal Income

d.   Federal Unemployment

Q8.8

All of the following are payroll liabilities owed to outside agencies except:

a.   Net Pay

b.   Federal Income taxes

c.   State Income taxes

d.   Unemployment taxes

Q8.9

The following taxes are reported on Form 941 except:

a.   FICA-Medicare (employer and employee)

b.   State income taxes withheld from the employee paychecks

c.   Federal income taxes withheld from the employee paychecks

d.   FICA-Social Security (employer and employee)

Q8.10

Net Pay is equal to:

a. Gross pay minus deductions for federal and state income taxes and unemployment taxes

b. Gross pay minus federal and state income taxes, but not FICA taxes

c. Gross pay plus deductions for FICA taxes and federal and state income taxes

d. Gross pay minus deductions for FICA taxes and federal and state income taxes

Q8.11

QBO Payroll Service can:

a. E-file payroll tax forms

b. E-pay payroll taxes from your company checking account

c. Direct deposit employee paychecks

d. All of the above

Q8.12

Payroll liabilities include the following two types of amounts:

a. Amounts withheld from employees paychecks that must be paid to third parties, such as federal income tax withheld

b. Payroll tax expenses owed by the business, such as unemployment tax

c. Net paycheck amount paid to employees

d. Contractor payments

Q8.13

To turn on QBO payroll:

a. From the Gear icon, select Employees > Turn on Payroll

b. From the Navigation Bar, select Transactions > Expenses > Turn on Payroll

c. From the Gear icon, select Transactions > Payroll

d. From the Navigation Bar, select Workers > Employees tab > Get Started

Q8.14

After turning on QBO payroll, to run QBO payroll:

a. From the Navigation Bar, select Workers > Employees tab > Run Payroll

b. From the Gear icon, select Employees > Run Payroll

c. From the Navigation Bar, select Transactions > Expenses

d. From the Gear icon, select Transactions > Run Payroll

Exercises 8

We use the **QBO Sample Company, Craig's Design and Landscaping Services,** for practice throughout the exercises. The Sample Company will reset each time it is reopened. So make certain to allow enough time to complete exercise before closing the Sample Company. Otherwise, you will lose the work you have entered when you reopen the Sample Company.

⚠ Since the **Sample Company** resets each time it is reopened, be certain to close any web browser windows displaying the QBO Sample Company before starting these exercises. Closing the browser window and starting with a new browser window for the QBO Sample Company resets the data before starting the exercises.

To access the QBO Sample Company, complete the following steps.

1 Open a web browser. (Note: Intuit recommends using Google Chrome.)

2 Go to the https://qbo.intuit.com/redir/testdrive

3 Follow onscreen instructions for security verification

Craig's Design and Landscaping Services should appear on your screen.

E8.1 Employees and Payroll Activities

Match the following activities with the following framework for navigating QBO payroll.

Employees and Payroll Activities

a. Enter Time to track employee time worked to use in processing payroll and billing customers

b. Process Payroll Forms including Forms 940, 941, W-2, and W-3 that must be submitted to governmental agencies

c. Turn on QBO Payroll

d. Pay Employees by selecting employees to pay and creating their paychecks

e. Turn on Time Tracking preference

f. Set up Employees List

g. Pay Payroll Liabilities, such as federal income taxes withheld, state income taxes withheld, FICA (Social Security and Medicare), and unemployment taxes due to governmental agencies.

Navigating Employee and Payroll Activities

PAYROLL SETUP

1. _____

2. _____

3. _____

PAYROLL PROCESSING

1. _____

2. _____

3. _____

4. _____

E8.2 Time Tracking and Status

Match the following items with the appropriate status of the individual performing work using time tracking.

Items

- Distributions

- Form W-2

- Paycheck

- Form 1099-MISC

- Owner's Tax Return

- Vendor Payment

Status	QBO Payment	Tax Form
Employee		
Contractor		
Owner		

E8.3 Payroll Liabilities

Place a ✓ in the following appropriate boxes to indicate whether the federal payroll item is paid by the employee or the employer.

Payroll Liabilities (Federal)	Withheld from Employee Pay	Payroll Tax Expense Owed by Business	
Federal Income Taxes			
FICA (Social Security + Medicare)			
Federal Unemployment Tax			

E8.4 Time Tracking Preferences

Answer the following questions about the Time Tracking preferences if a company plans to use QBO for time tracking.

1. If a company wants to turn on Time Tracking preferences, go to _____ icon > _____ >

   _____

2. What should be the setting for Add Service field to timesheets?

3. What should be the setting for Make Single-Time Activity Billable to Customer?

E8.5 Single Time Activity

Using the QBO Sample Company, Craig's Design and Landscaping Services, complete the following to track time by entering a Single Time Activity.

1. Create Single Time Activity.
   a. Select **Create (+) icon** > **Single Time Activity**
   b. Add New **Name: + Add new** > enter **Your Name** > **Employee Type** > **Save**
   c. Select **Customer: Cool Cars**

    d. Select **Service: Landscaping: Installation**

    e. Check **Billable(/hr): $50.00**

    f. Check **Enter Start and End Times**

    g. Select **Start Time: 8:00 AM**

    h. Select **End Time: 12:45 PM**

    i. What is the Summary of time worked in hours and minutes?

    j. What is the Total Cost of the time worked?

    k. Select **Save and new**

E8.6 Single Time Activity

Using the QBO Sample Company, Craig's Design and Landscaping Services, complete the following to track time by entering a Single Time Activity.

1.   Create Single Time Activity.

    a. If necessary, select **Create (+) icon > Single Time Activity**

    b. Select **Name: Your Name**

    c. Select **Customer: Cool Cars**

    d. Select **Service: Landscaping: Installation**

    e. Check **Billable (/hr): $50.00**

    f. Check **Enter Start and End Times**

    g. Select **Start Time: 1:15 PM**

    h. Select **End Time: 4:30 PM**

    i. What is the Summary of time worked in hours and minutes?

    j. What is the Total Cost of the time worked?

    k. Select **Save and new**

E8.7 Single Time Activity

Using the QBO Sample Company, Craig's Design and Landscaping Services, complete the following to track time by entering a Single Time Activity.

1.   Create Single Time Activity.

    a. If necessary, select **Create (+) icon > Single Time Activity**

    b. Select **Name: Your Name**

    c. Select **Customer: Red Rock Diner**

    d. Select **Service: Landscaping: Installation**

    e. Check **Billable (/hr): $50.00**

    f. Check **Enter Start and End Times**

    g. Select **Start Time: 5:30 PM**

    h. Select **End Time: 7:00 PM**

    i. What is the Summary of time worked in hours and minutes?

    j. What is the Total Cost of the time worked?

    k. Select **Save and close**

E8.8 Invoice and Time Tracking

This assignment is a continuation of E8.5 - E8.7

Using the QBO Sample Company, Craig's Design and Landscaping Services, complete the following.

1.   Create Invoice with Tracked Time.

    a. Select **Create (+) icon > Invoice**

    b. Select **Customer: Cool Cars**

    c. From the Add to Invoice drawer on the right side of the screen, select: **Don't group time > Add all**

    d. What is the Balance Due on the Invoice?

    e. Select **Save** and leave the Invoice displayed

2.   View the Transaction Journal for the Invoice.

    a. From the bottom of the Cool Cars Invoice, select **More > Transaction Journal**

    b. What are the Account and Amount Debited?

    c. What are the Accounts and Amounts Credited?

E8.9 Weekly Timesheet

This assignment is a continuation of E8.5 - E8.7

Using the QBO Sample Company, Craig's Design and Landscaping Services, complete the following to track time using the QBO Weekly Timesheet.

1. Create Weekly Timesheet.
   a. Select **Create (+) icon > Weekly Timesheet**
   b. Select **Your Name**
   c. Total Hours should be: **9:30**
   d. If needed, select **Add Lines**
   e. On the next open line, select **Customer Name: Red Rock Diner**
   f. Select **Service Item: Landscaping: Installation**
   g. Check **Billable (/hr): $50.00**
   h. Enter **8 hours for the 2 next days**
   i. What are the Total Hours for the Weekly Timesheet?
   j. Select **Save and close**

E8.10 Time Activity

This assignment is a continuation of E8.5, E8.6, E8.7, and E8.9

Using the QBO Sample Company, Craig's Design and Landscaping Services, complete the following.

1. View Time Activity for Cool Cars.
   a. From the Navigation Bar, select **Workers > Employees tab**
   b. From the Employees List, select the **Edit drop-down arrow** for **Your Name > Run report**
   c. Select **Time Activity Date to include all dates for which you entered time on the weekly timesheet**, then select **Run Report**
   d. What is the Total Amount for Billable Time for Cool Cars?
   e. What is the Total Duration for Cool Cars?

2. View Time Activity for Red Rock Diner.
   a. From the Time Activity Report from requirement 1, what is the Total Amount for Billable Time for Red Rock Diner?
   b. What is the Total Duration for Red Rock Diner?

Project 8.1

Mookie the Beagle™ Concierge

> **Project 8.1 is a continuation of Project 7.1. You will use the QBO Company you created for Project 1.1 and updated in subsequent Projects 2.1 through 7.1. Keep in mind the QBO Company for Project 8.1 does not reset and carries your data forward, including any errors. So it is important to check and crosscheck your work to verify it is correct before clicking the Save button.**

BACKSTORY

Mookie The Beagle Concierge, a business offering high-quality pet care on demand, has only one employee, Cy Walker. Cy is also the founder and owner of MTB. The others providing pet care services for MTB are hired as independent contractors, meeting all IRS requirements to be classified as such. Mookie The Beagle Concierge would like your assistance in using the QBO time tracking feature to track time for specific contractors providing pet care to customer pets.

 **QBO SatNav**

Project 8.1 focuses on QBO Transactions, specifically QBO Employees & Payroll Transactions as shown in the following QBO SatNav.

 **QBO Settings**

 Company Settings
Chart of Accounts

 **QBO Transactions**

Banking
Customers & Sales
Vendors & Expenses
Employees & Payroll · · · · · *Enter Time > Pay Employees > Payroll Liabilities*

 **QBO Reports**

Reports

HOW TO LOG INTO QBO

To log into QBO, complete the following steps.

1. Using a web browser go to qbo.intuit.com

2. Enter **User ID** (the email address you used to set up your QBO Account)

3. Enter **Password** (the password you used to set up your QBO Account)

4. Select **Sign in**

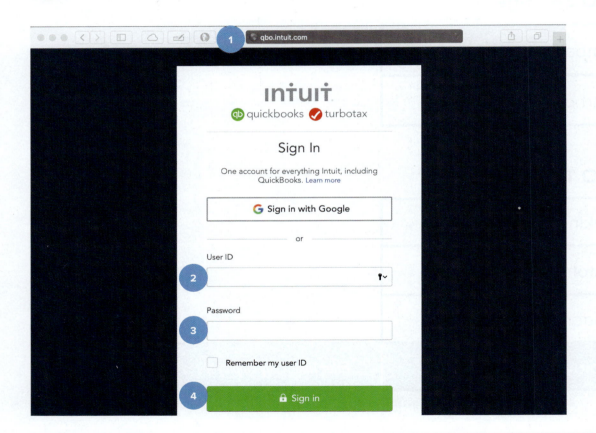

> If you are **not** using a public or shared computer, to speed up login, you can save your login to your desktop and select Remember Me. If you are using a public computer or shared computer, do not save to the desktop and unselect Remember Me.

> The new QBO Company we created in Project 1.1 will carry all work forward into future chapters. So it is important to check and crosscheck your work to verify it is correct before clicking the Save button. Any uncorrected errors will be carried forward in your QBO Company for text projects.

P8.1.1 Single Time Activity

Cy is still working as a full-time professional while launching Mookie The Beagle Concierge and would like a better idea of how many hours he is investing in his new startup. So he uses QBO to track his time coding the Mookie The Beagle Concierge app. Complete the following to enter Single Time Activity for Cy.

1. Turn on Service Field on Timesheet.
   a. Select **Gear icon > Account and Settings > Advanced**
   b. Select **Time Tracking Edit pencil**
   c. **Check Add Service field to time sheets** to change the setting to **On**
   d. **Check Make Single Time Activity Billable to Customer** to change the setting to **On**
   e. Select **Save > Done**

2. Create Single Time Activity.
   a. Select **Create (+) icon > Single Time Activity**
   b. Add **Name: + Add new** > enter **Cy Walker > Employee Type > Save**
   c. Select **Date: 01/18/2022**
   d. Add **Service: + Add new** > select **Service**
   e. Enter **Product/Service Information Name: MTB App Development**
   f. Select **Category: + Add New**
   g. Enter **New Category Name: Time Tracking**
   h. Select **Save**
   i. Select: **I purchase this product/service from a vendor**
   j. Enter **Cost: 0.00**
   k. Enter New **Expense Account: + Add New**
   l. Select **Account Type: Other Expense**
   m. Select **Detail Type: Other Miscellaneous Expense**
   n. Enter **Account Name: Time Tracking**
   o. Select **Save and Close** to close the Account form
   p. Select **Save and close** to close the Product/Service form
   q. Uncheck **Billable (/hr): $0.00**
   r. Check **Enter Start and End Times**
   s. Select **Start Time: 7:00 PM**
   t. Select **End Time: 9:00 PM**
   u. What is the Summary of time worked?
   v. Select **Save and new**

3. Create Single Time Activity.
    a. Select **Name: Cy Walker**
    b. Select **Date: 01/19/2022**
    c. Select **Service: MTB App Development**
    d. Uncheck **Billable (/hr) $0.00**
    e. Check **Enter Start and End Times**
    f. Select **Start Time: 7:00 PM**
    g. Select **End Time: 9:30 PM**
    h. What is the Summary of time worked?
    i. Select **Save and close**

4. Create Time Activities by Employee Detail Report.
    To view and verify time entered:
    a. Select **Reports > Standard tab > Employees > Time Activities by Employee Detail**
    b. Select **Time Activity Date: 01/18/2022 to 01/19/2022**
    c. Select **Group by: Employee**
    d. Select **Run Report**
    e. What is the Duration Total for Cy Walker?

P8.1.2 Single Time Activity and Time Activities Report

In addition to using QBO time tracking for tracking his time on MTB app development, Cy decides to use the time tracking feature to track time he spends on administrative tasks for MTB. This information might prove useful in assessing whether to hire additional administrative support staff in the future.

1. Create Single Time Activity.
    a. Select **Create (+) icon > Single Time Activity**
    b. Select **Name: Cy Walker**
    c. Select **Date: 01/20/2022**
    d. Add **Service: + Add new** > select **Service**
    e. Enter **Product/Service Information Name: MTB Administrative Services**
    f. Select **Category: Time Tracking**
    g. Select: **I purchase this product/service from a vendor**
    h. Enter **Cost: 0.00**

i. Select **Expense Account: Time Tracking**

j. Select **Save and close** to close the Product/Service form

k. Uncheck **Billable (/hr) $0.00**

l. Check **Enter Start and End Times**

m. Select **Start Time: 9:00 PM**

n. Select **End Time: 11:00 PM**

o. What is the Summary of time worked?

p. Select **Save and new**

2. Create Single Time Activity.

a. Select **Name: Cy Walker**

b. Select **Date: 01/21/2022**

c. Select **Service: MTB Administrative Services**

d. Uncheck **Billable (/hr) $0.00**

e. Check **Enter Start and End Times**

f. Select **Start Time: 8:00 PM**

g. Select **End Time: 10:00 PM**

h. What is the Summary of time worked?

i. Select **Save and new**

3. Create Single Time Activity.

a. Select **Name: Cy Walker**

b. Select **Date: 01/23/2022**

c. Select **Service: MTB Administrative Services**

d. Uncheck **Billable (/hr) $0.00**

e. Check **Enter Start and End Times**

f. Select **Start Time: 7:00 PM**

g. Select **End Time: 10:00 PM**

h. What is the Summary of time worked?

i. Select **Save and new**

4. Create Single Time Activity.
    a. Select **Name: Cy Walker**
    b. Select **Date: 01/24/2022**
    c. Select **Service: MTB App Development**
    d. Uncheck **Billable (/hr) $0.00**
    e. Check **Enter Start and End Times**
    f. Select **Start Time: 12:00 PM**
    g. Select **End Time: 8:00 PM**
    h. What is the Summary of time worked?
    i. Select **Save and close**

5. Create Time Activities by Employee Detail Report.
    To view and verify time entered:
    a. Select **Reports > Standard tab > Employees > Time Activities by Employee Detail**
    b. Select **Time Activity Date: 01/18/2022 to 01/24/2022**
    c. Select **Group by: Employee**
    d. Select **Run Report**
    e. What is the Duration Total for Cy Walker?
    f. Select **Group by: Product/Service**
    g. Select **Run Report**
    h. What is the Duration Total for MTB Administrative Services?
    i. What is the Duration Total for MTB App Development?
    j. What is the Duration Total for Time Tracking?

P8.1.3 Single Time Activity

To streamline billing customers and paying contractors, Cy would like to use the QBO time tracking feature for tracking contractor time. Jean Paulny, a vet student and Mookie The Beagle Concierge contractor, volunteers to participate in testing the time tracking feature. Jean Paulny will be providing pet care services for Tracey Kari's Labrador, Odin. Tracey is tied up in the evenings with an intensive interior design job, so Jean Paulny will be stopping by Odin's home each evening to feed and walk him.

Complete the following Single Time Activity for Jean Paulny.

1. Create Single Time Activity.
   a. Select **Create (+) icon > Single Time Activity**
   b. Add **Name: + Add new** > enter **Jean Paulny > Vendor Type > Save**
   c. Enter **Date: 01/23/2022**
   d. Select **Customer: Odin Tracey Kari**
   e. Select **Service: Pet Care: Short Visit**
   f. Check **Billable (/hr) $40.00**
   g. Check **Enter Start and End Times**
   h. Select **Start Time: 5:00 PM**
   i. Select **End Time: 6:00 PM**
   j. What is the Summary of time worked in hours and minutes?
   k. What is the Total Cost of the time worked?
   l. Select **Save and new**

P8.1.4 Single Time Activity

Complete the following Single Time Activity for Jean Paulny when he provides services to Tracey Kari's Labrador, Odin.

1. Create Single Time Activity.
   a. Select **Create (+) icon > Single Time Activity**
   b. Select **Name: Jean Paulny**
   c. Select **Date: 01/24/2022**
   d. Select **Customer: Odin Tracey Kari**
   e. Select **Service: Pet Care: Short Visit**
   f. Check **Billable (/hr) $40.00**
   g. Check **Enter Start and End Times**
   h. Select **Start Time: 5:15 PM**
   i. Select **End Time: 6:15 PM**
   j. What is the Summary of time worked in hours and minutes?
   k. What is the Total Cost of the time worked?
   l. Select **Save and new**

P8.1.5 Single Time Activity

Complete the following Single Time Activity for Jean Paulny when he provides services to Tracey Kari's Labrador, Odin.

1. Create Single Time Activity.
   a. Select **Create (+) icon > Single Time Activity**
   b. Select **Name: Jean Paulny**
   c. Select **Date: 01/25/2022**
   d. Select **Customer: Odin Tracey Kari**
   e. Select **Service: Pet Care: Short Visit**
   f. Check **Billable (/hr) $40.00**
   g. Check **Enter Start and End Times**
   h. Select **Start Time: 5:30 PM**
   i. Select **End Time: 6:30 PM**
   j. What is the Summary of time worked in hours and minutes?
   k. What is the Total Cost of the time worked?
   l. Select **Save and close**

P8.1.6 Single Time Activity and Time Activities Report

Complete the following to add services Jean Paulny provided to Tracey Kari's Labrador, Odin, and to create a Time Activities by Employee Detail report.

1. Create Single Time Activity.
   a. Select **Create (+) icon > Single Time Activity**
   b. Select **Name: Jean Paulny**
   c. Select **Date: 01/26/2022**
   d. Select **Customer: Odin Tracey Kari**
   e. Select **Service: Pet Care: Short Visit**
   f. Check **Billable (/hr) $40.00**
   g. Check **Enter Start and End Times**
   h. Select **Start Time: 6:00 PM**
   i. Select **End Time: 7:00 PM**
   j. What is the Summary of time worked in hours and minutes?
   k. What is the Total Cost of time worked?
   l. Select **Save and close**

2. Create Time Activities by Employee Detail Report.

    To view and verify time entered:

    a. Select **Reports > Standard tab > Employees > Time Activities by Employee Detail**
    b. Select **Time Activity Date: 01/18/2022 to 01/26/2022**
    c. Select **Group by: Employee**
    d. Select **Run Report**
    e. What is the Duration Total for Jean Paulny?
    f. What is the Amount Total for Jean Paulny?
    g. Select **Group by: Product/Service**
    h. Select **Run Report**
    i. What is the Total for Pet Care Amount?

P8.1.7 Invoice and Time Tracking

Using tracked time, complete the following to create an Invoice for services provided to Odin, Tracey Kari's pet Labrador.

1. Create Invoice with Tracked Time.

    a. Select **Create (+) icon > Invoice**
    b. Select **Customer: Odin Tracey Kari**
    c. Select **Date: 01/29/2022**
    d. From the Add to Invoice drawer on the right side of the screen, select: **Don't group time > Add all**
    e. What is the Balance Due on the Invoice?
    f. Select **Save** and leave the Invoice displayed

2. View the Transaction Journal for the Invoice.

    a. From the bottom of the Odin Tracey Kari Invoice just prepared, select **More > Transaction Journal**
    b. What are the Account and Amount Debited?
    c. What are the Accounts and Amounts Credited?

Chapter 9

QBO Adjustments

Cy Walker realizes that although QuickBooks Online can streamline and perform many accounting tasks automatically, QBO cannot automatically perform some tasks, such as adjusting entries. Cy knows adjusting entries are important because they bring accounts up to date so the correct account balances appear on financial reports.

Cy would like you to learn more about adjusting entries needed to bring Mookie the Beagle Concierge accounts up to date at the end of the accounting period. Also, you would like to learn how to streamline entering adjusting entries into QBO using the recurring transactions feature.

Chapter 9

LEARNING OBJECTIVES

Chapter 9 covers adjustments that are required to bring accounts up to date and show the correct account balances on financial reports. Adjustments are typically made at the end of the accounting period so accounts are up to date before year-end reports are prepared.

In Chapter 9, you will learn about the following topics:

- Accounting Cycle
- Make Adjusting Entries using QBO
  - Use the Onscreen Journal to Record Adjusting Entries
  - Use Recurring Transactions for Adjusting Entries
- Types of Adjusting Entries
  - Prepaid Items: Related Expense/Asset Accounts
  - Unearned Items: Related Revenue/Liability Accounts
  - Accrued Expenses: Related Expense/Liability Accounts
  - Accrued Revenues: Related Revenue/Asset Accounts
- Accounting Essentials: Adjustments and Corrections

Section 9.1
 QBO SATNAV

QBO SatNav is our satellite navigation for QuickBooks Online, assisting us in navigating QBO Chapter 9 covers adjustments, which are required to ensure we have reliable QBO Reports.

 **QBO SatNav**

 **QBO Settings**

 Company Settings
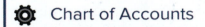 Chart of Accounts

 **QBO Transactions**

Banking
Customers & Sales
Vendors & Expenses
Employees & Payroll

 **QBO Reports**

Reports

Section 9.2

QBO SAMPLE COMPANY LOGIN

To log into the QBO Sample Company:

1. Open a web browser. (Note: Intuit recommends using Google Chrome.)

2. Go to the https://qbo.intuit.com/redir/testdrive

3. Follow onscreen instructions for security verification

Craig's Design and Landscaping Services should appear on your screen.

> **Note: Although the Sample Company link should work, if for some reason the previous link for the Sample Company doesn't work with your browser, using Google search type in "qbo.intuit.com Sample Company". Select the entry to Test Drive Sample Company.**

To increase the amount of time from one (1) hour to three (3) hours before the log out for inactivity occurs:

1. From Craig's Design and Landscaping Services QBO Sample Company, select the **Gear** icon

2. Under Your Company section, select **Account and Settings**

3. Select **Advanced**

4. Select **Other preferences**

5. For the option Sign me out if inactive for, select **3 hours**

6. Select **Save**

7. Select **Done**

> ⚠️ **The Sample Company** will reset each time it is reopened. This allows you to explore and practice QBO without concern about carrying forward errors to later chapters. However, you will want to make certain to allow enough time to complete all chapter activities before closing the Sample Company. Otherwise, you will lose the work you have entered when you close and reopen the Sample Company.

To set QBO preferences to display account numbers in the Chart of Accounts:

1. Select the **Gear** icon to display options

2. Select **Account and Settings**

3. Select **Advanced**

4. For Chart of Accounts, select the **Edit Pencil**, then select **Enable account numbers**

5. Select **Show account numbers**

6. Select **Save**

7. Select **Done** to close Account and Settings

Section 9.3

ACCOUNTING CYCLE

The accounting cycle is a series of accounting activities that a business performs each accounting period.

> **An accounting period can be one month, one quarter, or one year.**

The accounting cycle usually consists of the following steps.

- **Chart of Accounts.** The Chart of Accounts is a list of all accounts used to accumulate information about assets, liabilities, owners' equity, revenues, and expenses. Create a Chart of Accounts when the business is established and modify the Chart of Accounts as needed over time.
- **Transactions.** During the accounting period, record transactions with customers, vendors, employees, and owners.
- **Trial Balance.** A Trial Balance is also referred to as an unadjusted Trial Balance because it is prepared before adjustments. A Trial Balance lists each account and the account balance at the end of the accounting period. Prepare a Trial Balance to verify that the accounting system is in balance—total debits should equal total credits.
- **Adjustments.** At the end of the accounting period before preparing financial statements, make any adjustments necessary to bring the accounts up to date. Adjustments are entered in the Journal using debits and credits.
- **Adjusted Trial Balance.** Prepare an Adjusted Trial Balance (a Trial Balance after adjustments) to verify that the accounting system still balances. If additional account detail is required, print the general ledger (the collection of all the accounts listing the transactions that affected the accounts).
- **Financial Statements.** Prepare financial statements for external users (Profit and Loss, Balance Sheet, and Statement of Cash Flows). Prepare income tax summary reports and management reports.

Section 9.4

ADJUSTING ENTRIES

WHY DO WE MAKE ADJUSTING ENTRIES?

Adjusting entries record adjustments necessary to bring the accounts up to date at the end of an accounting period. We want to make adjusting entries before preparing financial reports so the accounts reflected on the reports are up to date.

HOW DO WE MAKE ADJUSTING ENTRIES?

Adjustments are also called adjusting entries because the way we enter adjustments is by making entries in the Journal. Adjusting entries are entered in the onscreen QBO Journal using debits and credits.

> **The onscreen Journal** using debits and credits to enter transactions is accessed from the Create (+) icon > Other > Journal Entry.

Some companies use QBO to maintain their financial system throughout the year and then have an accountant prepare the adjusting entries at year end to enter into QBO.

WHEN DO WE MAKE ADJUSTING ENTRIES?

Adjusting entries are dated the last day of the accounting period. Typically, we prepare adjusting entries after we prepare a Trial Balance to verify that our accounts are in balance. The Trial Balance lists all accounts with their debit and credit balances. This permits us to see that our total debits equal our total credits. The Trial Balance is discussed in more detail in the next chapter, Chapter 10.

Section 9.5

MAKE ADJUSTING ENTRIES USING QBO

USE THE ONSCREEN JOURNAL TO RECORD ADJUSTING ENTRIES

We can use the QBO onscreen Journal to enter adjusting entries. For example, we might want to record depreciation expense as an adjusting entry to allocate the cost of an asset over its useful life.

To make adjusting entries using QBO:

1 Select **Create (+)** icon

2 Select **Journal Entry** to access the onscreen Journal

3 Enter **Journal Date: December 31 of the current year**

4 Enter **Journal No.: ADJ 0**. QBO will automatically number Journal entries consecutively unless we modify the Journal No. Often we label adjusting entries as ADJ 1, ADJ 2, and so on. Then we can clearly see which Journal entries are adjusting entries.

5 On Line 1, from the drop-down list of accounts to debit, select **Account: Depreciation (Other Expense)**

6 Enter **Debit Amount: 300.00**

7 If applicable, enter **Description**

8 On Line 2, from the drop-down list of accounts to credit, select **Account: Truck: Depreciation (Accumulated Depreciation)**

9 Enter **Credit Amount: 300.00**

10 If applicable, enter **Description**

11 Enter **Memo: Adjusting entry to record annual depreciation expense.** If we had to make any calculations to determine the adjusting entry amounts, then we could include those calculations in the Memo field.

12 Add **Attachments** that are source documents related to the adjusting entry. For example, for the depreciation adjusting entry, we might attach the depreciation schedule.

13 Select **Save** and leave the Journal Entry window open

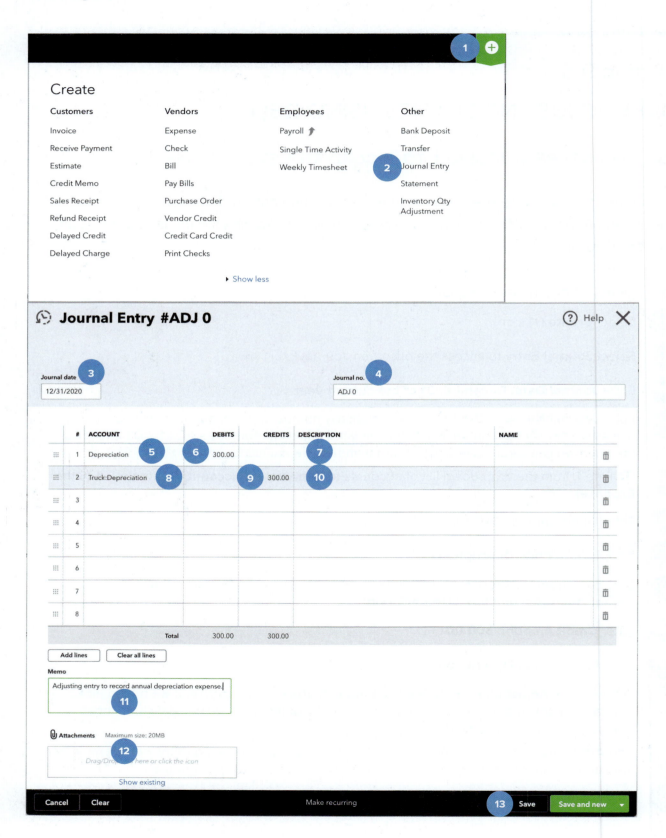

Create

Customers	Vendors	Employees	Other
Invoice	Expense	Payroll	Bank Deposit
Receive Payment	Check	Single Time Activity	Transfer
Estimate	Bill	Weekly Timesheet	Journal Entry
Credit Memo	Pay Bills		Statement
Sales Receipt	Purchase Order		Inventory Qty Adjustment
Refund Receipt	Vendor Credit		
Delayed Credit	Credit Card Credit		
Delayed Charge	Print Checks		

▸ Show less

Journal Entry #ADJ 0

Help

Journal date
12/31/2020

Journal no.
ADJ 0

#	ACCOUNT	DEBITS	CREDITS	DESCRIPTION	NAME	
1	Depreciation	300.00				
2	Truck:Depreciation		300.00			
3						
4						
5						
6						
7						
8						
	Total	300.00	300.00			

Add lines   Clear all lines

Memo
Adjusting entry to record annual depreciation expense.

Attachments   Maximum size: 20MB

Drag/Drop files here or click the icon

Show existing

Cancel   Clear   Make recurring   Save   Save and new ▾

> When making journal entries, including adjusting entries, accountants generally list Debits before Credits. **Note that QBO may not always list Debits before Credits in journal entries.**

USE RECURRING TRANSACTIONS FOR ADJUSTING ENTRIES

To save time, we can save our adjusting entries as recurring transactions.

There are two ways to save adjusting entries as recurring transactions:
1. From the journal screen
2. From the recurring transactions screen

To save the adjusting entry just created as a recurring transaction:

1 With the previous adjusting entry saved and still open on your screen, select **Make recurring** to save the adjusting entry as a recurring transaction

2 Enter **Template Name: Adjusting Entry Depreciation**. Since Recurring Transactions are listed alphabetically, we want to name the Templates so they automatically sort in an order that makes it easy for us to find the specific Template we need.

3 Select **Type: Reminder** so we will be reminded to use the Recurring Transaction Template to make the adjusting entry

4 Enter **Remind Days Before The Transaction Date: 3**

5 Enter **Interval: Yearly**

6 Select **Month: December**

7 Select **Date: Last**

8 Since you have already saved the adjusting entry for depreciation for the current year, for the recurring transaction enter **Start Date: 1 year after the date of your adjusting entry**

9 Enter **End: None**. (Note that if we knew we had 5 more years of depreciation to record for this specific asset, we could enter End: After 5 occurrences.)

10 Select **Save Template**

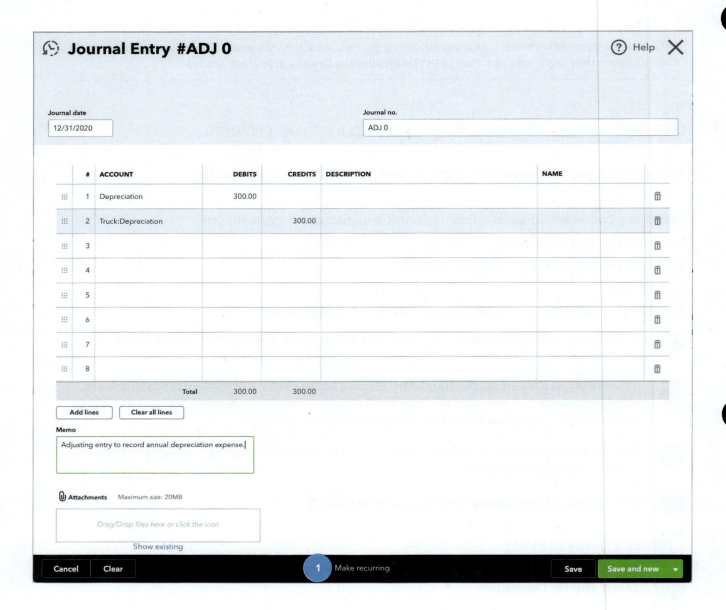

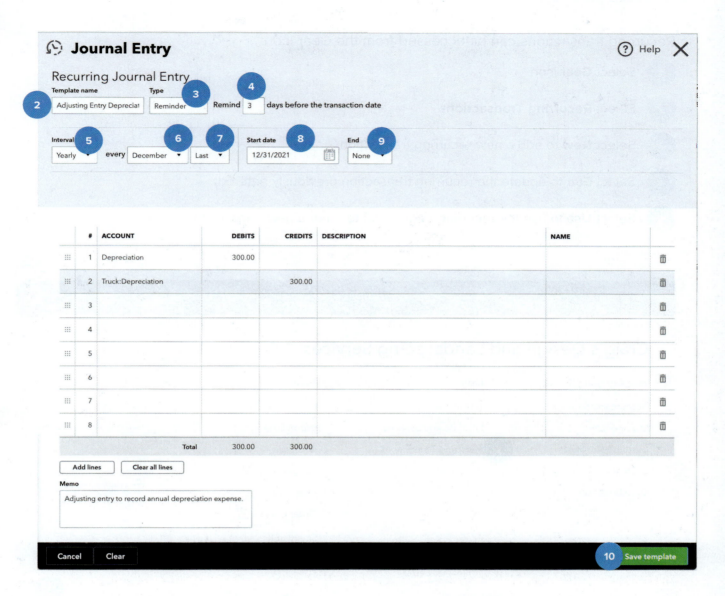

Recurring transactions can be accessed from the Gear icon:

1. Select **Gear** icon

2. Select **Recurring Transactions**

3. Select **New** to add a new recurring transaction

4. Select **Edit** to update the recurring transaction previously entered

5. Select **Use** to use the recurring transaction to enter a new transaction

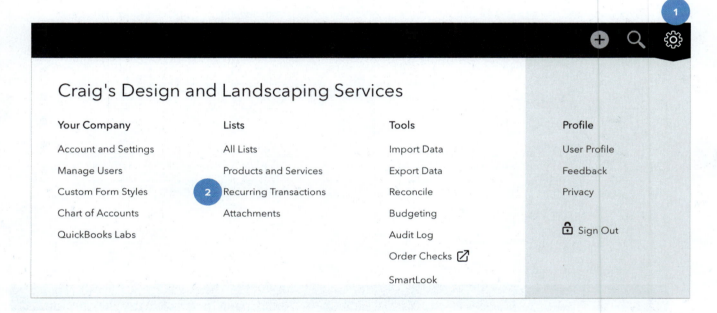

Recurring transactions can be classified as one of three types:

1. Scheduled
2. Unscheduled
3. Reminder

1. **Scheduled Recurring Transactions.** Notice in the Type column in the Recurring Transactions List shown previously has two recurring transactions that are **Scheduled**. This indicates that the recurring transaction is scheduled for QBO to automatically enter the transaction on a date we specified. Since we need to update adjusting entry amounts each year, Scheduled is typically not a good option to use for adjusting entry Recurring Transactions.

2. **Unscheduled Recurring Transactions.** Unscheduled transactions will appear in the Recurring Transaction List but QBO will not automatically enter the transaction. Instead, we must go to the Recurring Transaction List and select Use. Although we could use Unscheduled for an adjusting entry Recurring Transaction, this option will not remind us to make the adjusting entry.

3. **Reminder Recurring Transactions.** Recurring Transactions with Reminder option will alert us with a reminder when we should use a recurring transaction to enter a new transaction. Since we need to update the amounts for adjusting entries each year, select Reminder for adjusting entry Recurring Transactions.

Section 9.6

TYPES OF ADJUSTING ENTRIES

QBO can use the cash or the accrual basis for QBO reports. If we use the accrual basis of accounting to calculate profits, the following four types of adjusting entries may be necessary.

1. **Prepaid items.** Items that are prepaid, such as prepaid insurance or prepaid rent.
2. **Unearned items.** Items that a customer has paid us for, but we have not provided the product or service.
3. **Accrued expenses.** Expenses that are incurred but not yet paid or recorded.
4. **Accrued revenues.** Revenues that have been earned but not yet collected or recorded.

The accrual basis of accounting attempts to match expenses with the revenue (income) they generate. The cash basis records revenues (income) when cash is received and records expenses when cash is paid. The accrual basis attempts to record revenue (income) in the accounting period when it is earned (the product or service is provided) regardless of when the cash is received. The accrual basis attempts to record expenses in the accounting period it is incurred regardless of when the cash is paid.

Depreciation is a special type of prepaid item involving fixed assets, such as equipment. Depreciation is the allocation of an asset's cost over its useful life. Depreciation can be calculated in a number of different ways. For more information about calculating depreciation for tax purposes, go to www.irs.gov.

Section 9.7

PREPAID ITEMS: RELATED EXPENSE/ASSET ACCOUNTS

Prepaid items are items that are paid in advance, such as prepaid insurance or prepaid rent. An adjustment may be needed to record the amount of the prepaid item that has not expired at the end of the accounting period. For example, an adjustment may be needed to record the amount of insurance that has not expired as Prepaid Insurance (an asset with future benefit) and the amount of insurance that has expired as Insurance Expense.

Adjusting entries for prepaid items typically affect an Expense account and an Asset account. Examples of related Expense and Asset accounts used for prepaid item adjusting entries are as follows.

Prepaid Items	Expense Account	Asset Account
Prepaid Insurance	Insurance Expense	Prepaid Insurance
Prepaid Rent	Rent Expense	Prepaid Rent
Office Supplies	Office Supplies Expense	Office Supplies

Basically we want to make certain that the amounts in the related Expense (such as Insurance Expense) and Asset account (Prepaid Insurance) are appropriate.

The adjusting entry is a Journal entry recording the amount that needs to be transferred between the two accounts, an Expense account and an Asset account, to show the appropriate balance in each account.

Whether a debit or credit increases or decreases an account depends upon the type of account.

Account Type	Debit	Credit
Assets	Increase	Decrease
Liabilities	Decrease	Increase
Equity	Decrease	Increase
Revenues (Income)	Decrease	Increase
Expenses	Increase	Decrease

For example, if we need to make an adjusting entry to increase Insurance Expense and decrease Prepaid Insurance for $1,000, we would determine whether to debit or credit the accounts as follows:

Account	Account Type	Increase or Decrease?	Debit or Credit?	Amount
Insurance Expense	Expense	Increase	Debit	$1,000
Prepaid Insurance	Asset	Decrease	Credit	$1,000

To enter an adjusting entry for a prepaid item using the QBO Journal:

1 Select **Create (+)** icon

2 Select **Journal Entry** to access the onscreen Journal

3 Enter **Journal Date: December 31 of the current year**

4 Enter **Journal No.: ADJ 1**

5 On Line 1, from the drop-down list of accounts to debit, select **Account: Insurance (Expense)**

6 Enter **Debit Amount: 1,000.00**

7 On Line 2, from the drop-down list of accounts to credit, select **Account: Prepaid Expenses (Other Current Assets)**

8 Enter **Credit Amount: 1,000.00**

9 Enter **Memo: Adjusting entry for prepaid insurance**

10 Select **Save and new**

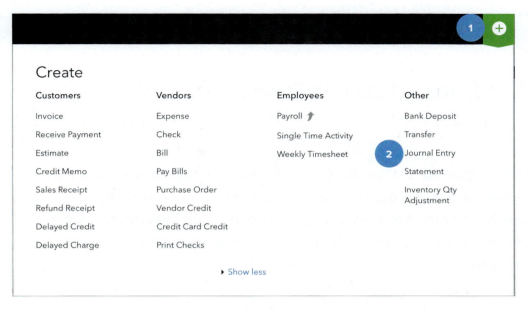

Create

Customers	Vendors	Employees	Other
Invoice	Expense	Payroll	Bank Deposit
Receive Payment	Check	Single Time Activity	Transfer
Estimate	Bill	Weekly Timesheet	Journal Entry
Credit Memo	Pay Bills		Statement
Sales Receipt	Purchase Order		Inventory Qty Adjustment
Refund Receipt	Vendor Credit		
Delayed Credit	Credit Card Credit		
Delayed Charge	Print Checks		

▸ Show less

Journal Entry #ADJ 1

Journal date
12/31/2020

Journal no.
ADJ 1

#	ACCOUNT	DEBITS	CREDITS	DESCRIPTION	NAME	
1	Insurance	1,000.00				🗑
2	Prepaid Expenses		1,000.00			🗑
3						🗑
4						🗑
5						🗑
6						🗑
7						🗑
8						🗑
	Total	1,000.00	1,000.00			

Add lines   Clear all lines

Memo
Adjusting entry for prepaid insurance

Cancel   Clear   Make recurring   Save   Save and new

Section 9.8

UNEARNED ITEMS: RELATED REVENUE/LIABILITY ACCOUNTS

Unearned items consist of revenue that we have not earned. If a customer pays in advance of receiving a service, such as when a customer pays a retainer, our business has an obligation (liability) to either provide the service in the future or return the customer's money. An adjustment may be necessary to bring the revenue account and unearned revenue (liability) account up to date.

Unearned Items	Revenue Account	Liability Account
Unearned Rent Revenue	Rent Revenue	Unearned Revenue
App Subscription	App Subscription Revenue	Unearned App Subscription Revenue

The adjusting entry is a Journal entry recording the amount that needs to be transferred between the two accounts, a Revenue account and a Liability account, to show the appropriate balance in each account.

If we need to make an adjusting entry to increase Rent Revenue and decrease Unearned Revenue for $2,000, we would determine whether to debit or credit the accounts as follows:

Account	Account Type	Increase or Decrease?	Debit or Credit?	Amount
Rent Revenue	Revenue	Increase	Credit	$2,000
Unearned Revenue	Liablity	Decrease	Debit	$2,000

To enter an adjusting entry for unearned revenue using the QBO Journal:

1 Enter **Journal Date: December 31 of the current year**

2 Enter **Journal No.: ADJ 2**

3 On Line 1, from the drop-down list of accounts to debit: select **Account: + Add New >
Unearned Revenue (Other Current Liabilities)**

4 Enter **Debit Amount: 2,000.00**

5 On Line 2, select credit **Account: + Add New > Rent Revenue (Other Income > Other
Miscellaneous Income)**

6 Enter **Credit Amount: 2,000.00**

7 Enter **Memo: Adjusting entry for unearned revenue**

8 Select **Save and new**

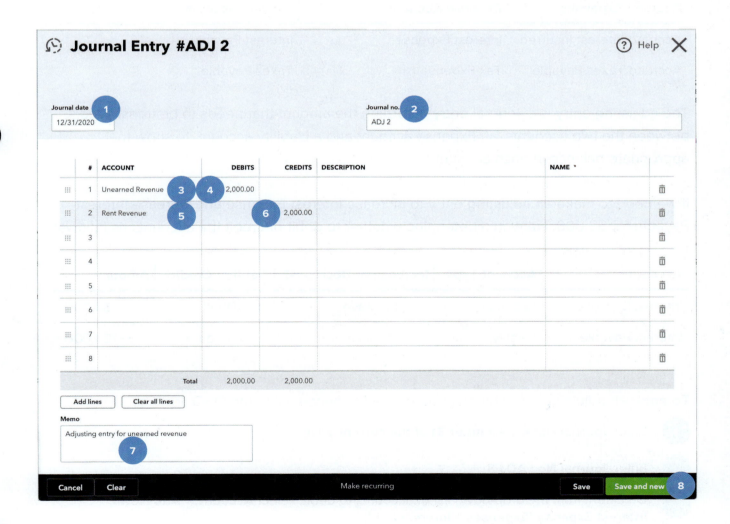

Section 9.9

ACCRUED EXPENSES: RELATED EXPENSE/LIABILITY ACCOUNTS

Accrued expenses are expenses that are incurred but not yet paid or recorded. Examples of accrued expenses include accrued interest expense (interest expense that has been incurred but not yet paid).

Accrued Expenses	Expense Account	Liability Account
Accrued Interest Incurred	Interest Expense	Interest Payable
Accrued Taxes Payable	Tax Expense	Taxes Payable

The adjusting entry is a Journal entry recording the amount that needs to be transferred between the two accounts, an Expense account and a Liability account, to show the appropriate balance in each account.

If we need to make an adjusting entry to increase Interest Expense and increase Interest Payable for $3,000, we would determine whether to debit or credit the accounts as follows:

Account	Account Type	Increase or Decrease?	Debit or Credit?	Amount
Interest Expense	Expense	Increase	Debit	$3,000
Interest Payable	Liablity	Increase	Credit	$3,000

To enter an adjusting entry for accrued interest expense using the QBO Journal:

1 Enter **Journal Date: December 31 of the current year**

2 Enter **Journal No.: ADJ 3**

3 On Line 1, from the drop-down list of accounts to debit, select **Account: + Add New >
Interest Expense (Expenses > Interest Paid)**

④ Enter **Debit Amount: 3,000.00**

⑤ On Line 2, select credit **Account: + Add New > Interest Payable (Other Current Liabilities)**

⑥ Enter **Credit Amount: 3,000.00**

⑦ Enter **Memo: Adjusting entry for accrued interest expense**

⑧ Select **Save and new**

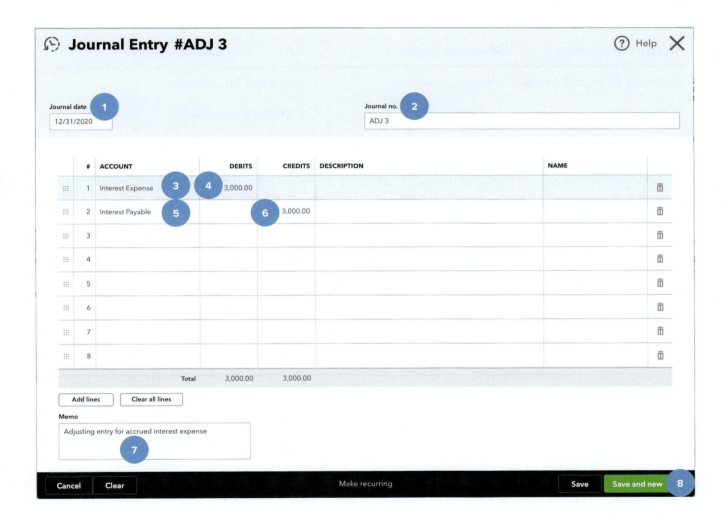

Section 9.10

ACCRUED REVENUES: RELATED REVENUE/ASSET ACCOUNTS

Accrued revenues are revenues that have been earned but not yet collected or recorded. Examples of accrued revenues include interest revenue that has been earned but not yet collected or recorded.

Accrued Revenues	Revenue Account	Asset Account
Accrued Interest Earned	Interest Revenue	Interest Receivable
Accrued Rent Revenue	Rent Revenue	Rent Receivable

The adjusting entry is a Journal entry recording the amount that needs to be transferred between the two accounts, a Revenue account and an Asset account, to show the appropriate balance in each account.

If we need to make an adjusting entry to increase Interest Revenue and increase Interest Receivable for $4,000, we would determine whether to debit or credit the accounts as follows:

Account	Account Type	Increase or Decrease?	Debit or Credit?	Amount
Interest Revenue	Revenue	Increase	Credit	$4,000
Interest Receivable	Asset	Increase	Debit	$4,000

To enter an adjusting entry for accrued interest revenue using the QBO Journal:

1. Enter **Journal Date: December 31 of the current year**

2. Enter **Journal No.: ADJ 4**

3 On Line 1, from the drop-down list of accounts to debit, select **Account: + Add New >
   Interest Receivable (Other Current Assets)**

4 Enter **Debit Amount: 4,000.00**

5 On Line 2, select credit **Account: + Add New > Interest Revenue (Other Income > Interest
   Earned)**

6 Enter **Credit Amount: 4,000.00**

7 Enter **Memo: Adjusting entry for accrued interest revenue**

8 Select **Save and close**

9 This completes the chapter activities. **Close** the QBO Sample Company web browser
   window to reset the Sample Company before proceeding to the exercises at the end of this
   chapter.

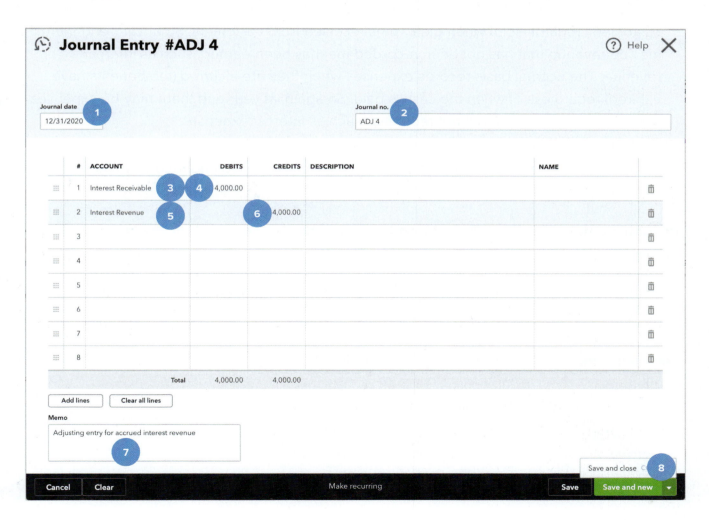

Section 9.11

ACCOUNTING ESSENTIALS
Accounting Adjustments and Corrections

Accounting Essentials summarize important foundational accounting knowledge you may find useful when using QBO

Why are adjusting entries necessary?

- When the accrual basis of accounting is used, adjusting entries are often necessary to bring the accounts up to date at the end of the accounting period. The accrual basis records revenue (income) when it is earned (when products and services are provided to customers) regardless of when the cash is received from customers. So at year-end there may be revenue that has not been recorded that has been earned, such as interest revenue. The accrual basis records expenses when they are incurred (the benefits have expired) regardless of when the cash is paid. So again, at year-end there may be expenses that have been incurred, but not recorded, such as interest expense.

- The accrual basis is often viewed as a better measure of profit than the cash basis. The cash basis records revenue (income) when the cash is received and records expenses when the cash is paid.

In double-entry accounting, how do we know whether to use a debit or credit for adjusting entries?

- Whether a debit or credit increases or decreases an account depends upon the type of account.

Account Type	Debit	Credit
Assets	Increase	Decrease
Liabilities	Decrease	Increase
Equity	Decrease	Increase
Revenues (Income)	Decrease	Increase
Expenses	Increase	Decrease

What are corrections?

- Corrections, or correcting entries, fix mistakes in the accounting system. Adjusting entries, on the other hand, are not mistakes, but updates that are required to bring accounts to their correct balance as of a certain date.

How do we make a correction using journal entries?

- For example, assume the Cash account should have been debited for $200.00 and the Professional Fees Revenue account credited for $200.00. However, the following incorrect entry was made for $2,000.00 instead of $200.00.

Incorrect Entry	Account	Amount
Debit	Cash	$2,000.00
Credit	Professional Fees Revenue	$2,000.00

- Often the easiest way for us to correct an error is to make two correcting entries in the Journal:

1. **Correcting Entry 1: Eliminate the effect of the incorrect entry by making the opposite journal entry.**

Correcting Entry 1	Account	Amount
Debit	Professional Fees Revenue	$2,000.00
Credit	Cash	$2,000.00

2. **Correcting Entry 2: After eliminating the effect of the incorrect entry, make the correct entry that should have been made initially.**

Correcting Entry 2	Account	Amount
Debit	Cash	$200.00
Credit	Professional Fees Revenue	$200.00

How do we correct errors on saved documents, such as Invoices or Purchase Orders?

- Once a document has been saved, we can use one of three approaches to correct the error:
  1. **Display** the document, correct the error, then save the document again.
  2. **Void** the erroneous document, then create a new document. Voiding keeps a record of the document, but changes the amounts to zero.
  3. **Delete** the erroneous document, then create a new document. Deleting the document erases the document from our system.

- Typically, options 1 or 2 are preferable because we have a better audit trail showing changes.

Practice Quiz 9

Q9.1

QuickBooks Online uses which basis of accounting?

a. Accrual

b. Cash

c. Both a and b

d. Neither a nor b

Q9.2

At the end of an accounting period, adjusting entries are made to:

a. To ensure a profit

b. Bring the accounts up to date

c. Debit or credit the checking account

d. Prove that debits equal credits

Q9.3

Accrued revenues are:

a. Revenues that have been earned, but not collected

b. Payment received in advance of receiving the service

c. Revenues that have been collected, but not yet earned

d. Revenues that have been recorded

Q9.4

Sales are recorded under cash basis accounting when:

a. The goods or services are provided regardless of whether the payment is collected from customers

b. The costs are incurred to earn the revenue

c. The cash is collected from customers

d. The bookkeeper has time to record the transactions

Q9.5

Sales are recorded under accrual basis accounting when:

a. The goods or services are provided regardless of whether the payment is collected from customers

b. The costs are incurred to earn the revenue

c. The actual cash is collected from customers

d. The bookkeeper has time to record the transactions

Q9.6

Adjusting entries are typically made:

a. At the beginning of the accounting period

b. Whenever an error is found and a correction is required

c. At the beginning of each month

d. On the last day of the accounting period

Q9.7

The Journal entry to update the Office Supplies account for office supplies used is which of the following types of adjusting entry?

a. Prepaid item

b. Unearned Revenue

c. Accrued Expense

d. Accrued Revenue

e. Not an adjusting entry

Q9.8

The Journal entry to update the accounts for interest expense incurred but not recorded is which of the following types of adjusting entries?

a. Prepaid item

b. Unearned Revenue

c. Accrued Expense

d. Accrued Revenue

e. Not an adjusting entry

Q9.9

The Journal entry to update the accounts for interest earned but not recorded is which of the following types of adjusting entries?

a. Prepaid item

b. Unearned Revenue

c. Accrued Expense

d. Accrued Revenue

e. Not an adjusting entry

Q9.10

The Journal entry to update the accounts for customer subscriptions that are prepaid but not yet earned is which of the following types of adjusting entries?

a. Prepaid item

b. Unearned Revenue

c. Accrued Expense

d. Accrued Revenue

e. Not an adjusting entry

Q9.11

The Journal entry to update the accounts for prepaid insurance that has expired is which of the following types of adjusting entries?

a. Prepaid item

b. Unearned Revenue

c. Accrued Expense

d. Accrued Revenue

e. Not an adjusting entry

Q9.12

The Journal entry to update the accounts for customer services provided but not yet recorded is which of the following types of adjusting entries?

a. Prepaid item

b. Unearned Revenue

c. Accrued Expense

d. Accrued Revenue

e. Not an adjusting entry

Q9.13

The Journal entry to record payment of cash for office supplies is which of the following types of adjusting entries?

a. Prepaid item

b. Unearned Revenue

c.   Accrued Expense

d.   Accrued Revenue

e.   Not an adjusting entry

Q9.14

The Journal entry to update the accounts for rent expense recorded that has not expired is which of the following types of adjusting entries?

a.   Prepaid item

b.   Unearned Revenue

c.   Accrued Expense

d.   Accrued Revenue

e.   Not an adjusting entry

Exercises 9

> We use the QBO Sample Company, Craig's Design and Landscaping Services, for practice throughout the exercises. The Sample Company will reset each time it is reopened. So make certain to allow enough time to complete exercise before closing the Sample Company. Otherwise, you will lose the work you have entered when you reopen the Sample Company.

> ⚠️ Since the Sample Company resets each time it is reopened, be certain to close any web browser windows displaying the QBO Sample Company before starting these exercises. Closing the browser window and starting with a new browser window for the QBO Sample Company resets the data before starting the exercises.

To access the QBO Sample Company, complete the following steps.

1   Open a web browser. (Note: Intuit recommends using Google Chrome.)

2   Go to the https://qbo.intuit.com/redir/testdrive

3   Follow onscreen instructions for security verification

Craig's Design and Landscaping Services should appear on your screen.

E9.1 Debits and Credits

Enter either Increase or Decrease in the following table to complete it.

- **Increase**
- **Decrease**

Account Type	Debit	Credit
Assets	_____	_____
Liabilities	_____	_____
Equity	_____	_____
Revenues (Income)	_____	_____
Expenses	_____	_____

E9.2 Journal

Identify the labels of the following columns in the QBO Journal.

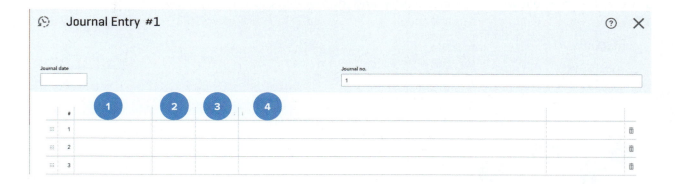

1 _____

2 _____

3 _____

4 _____

E9.3 Adjusting Entry Prepaid Rent

Using the QBO Sample Company, Craig's Design and Landscaping Services, complete the following.

Craig paid $1,800 rent on December 1 for an entire year (12 months). So at the end of the accounting period on December 31, Craig has used 1 month of rent @ $150 ($1,800/12 months = $150 per month). The unused portion of the rent is Prepaid Rent Expense, an asset account with future benefit. Since Craig recorded the entire $1,800 as Rent Expense, an adjusting entry is needed to bring accounts up to date at December 31.

1. Complete the following table.

Account	Account Type	Increase or Decrease?	Debit or Credit?	Amount
Rent Expense	Expense	_____	_____	$_____
Prepaid Rent Expense	Asset	_____	_____	$_____

2. Plan Adjusting Journal Entry.
   a. Complete the following to plan the adjusting journal entry to enter in QBO

Journal Entry #1

Journal date

Journal no.
1

#	ACCOUNT	DEBITS	CREDITS	DESCRIPTION	NAME
1					
2					
3					
4					

1. _____
2. _____
3. _____
4. _____

3. Create Adjusting Journal Entry.
   a. Add a new Subaccount to Prepaid Expenses: **Prepaid Rent Expense**
   b. Select **Create (+) icon > Journal Entry**
   c. Enter the adjusting journal entry in QBO

E9.4 Adjusting Entry Prepaid Insurance

Using the QBO Sample Company, Craig's Design and Landscaping Services, complete the following.

In December, Craig paid $482.46 for insurance to cover a 3-month period. So at the end of the accounting period on December 31, 1 month of insurance had expired @ $160.82 ($482.46/ 3 months = $160.82 per month). The unexpired portion of the insurance is Prepaid Insurance, an asset account with future benefit. Since Craig recorded the entire $482.46 as Insurance Expense, an adjusting entry is needed to bring accounts up to date at December 31.

1. Complete the following table.

Account	Account Type	Increase or Decrease?	Debit or Credit?	Amount
Insurance Expense	Expense	_____	_____	$_____
Prepaid Insurance	Asset	_____	_____	$_____

2. Plan Adjusting Journal Entry.
   a. Complete the following to plan the adjusting journal entry to enter in QBO

3. Create Adjusting Journal Entry.
    a. Add a new Subaccount to Prepaid Expenses: **Prepaid Insurance**
    b. Select **Create (+) icon > Journal Entry**
    c. Enter the adjusting journal entry in QBO

E9.5 Adjusting Entry Prepaid Equipment Rental

Using the QBO Sample Company, Craig's Design and Landscaping Services, complete the following.

In December, Craig paid $224.00 for equipment rental and recorded it as Equipment Rental, an Expenses account. But the $224.00 was prepaid to reserve the equipment for use in January of next year. So at the end of the accounting period on December 31, the benefits of the $224.00 had not expired and would not be Equipment Rental Expense, but Prepaid Rent Expense, an asset with future benefit. Since Craig recorded the entire $224.00 as Equipment Rental Expense, an adjusting entry is needed to bring accounts up to date at December 31.

1. Complete the following table.

Account	Account Type	Increase or Decrease?	Debit or Credit?	Amount
Equipement Rental	Expense	_____	_____	$_____
Prepaid Rent Expense	Asset	_____	_____	$_____

2. Plan Adjusting Journal Entry.
   a. Complete the following to plan the adjusting journal entry to enter in QBO

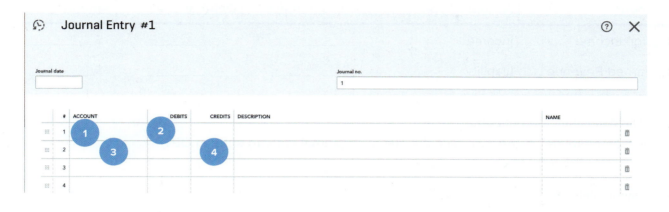

3. Create Adjusting Journal Entry.
   a. Select **Create (+) icon > Journal Entry**
   b. Enter the adjusting journal entry in QBO

E9.6 Adjusting Entry Unearned Revenue

Using the QBO Sample Company, Craig's Design and Landscaping Services, complete the following.

In November, Craig received $450.00 from Kate Whelan as a customer prepayment for design work. Craig recorded the entire $450.00 as Design Income. At the end of the accounting period on December 31, none of the design work had been provided to Kate, so the $450.00 had not been earned as of year end. Since it had not been earned, the $450.00 is a liability because Craig has an obligation to provide the design service or return the $450.00 to the customer. So an adjusting entry is needed to bring accounts up to date at December 31.

1. Complete the following table.

Account	Account Type	Increase or Decrease?	Debit or Credit?	Amount
Design Income	Income	_____	_____	$_____
Unearned Revenue	Liability	_____	_____	$_____

2. Plan Adjusting Journal Entry.
    a. Complete the following to plan the adjusting journal entry to enter in QBO

1 _____

2 _____

3 _____

4 _____

3. Create Adjusting Journal Entry.
    a. Add a new Liability Account to the Chart of Accounts: **Unearned Revenue**
    b. Select **Create (+) icon > Journal Entry**
    c. Enter the adjusting journal entry in QBO

E9.7 Adjusting Entry Accrued Expenses

Using the QBO Sample Company, Craig's Design and Landscaping Services, complete the following.

PG&E will bill Craig on January 1 for the prior year December utility services provided of $198.00. Since the Utilities Expense is incurred in December, the $198.00 must be recorded as an accrued expense and a liability recorded for the amount that Craig is obligated to pay in January. So an adjusting entry is needed to bring accounts up to date at December 31.

1. Complete the following table.

Account	Account Type	Increase or Decrease?	Debit or Credit?	Amount
Utilities: Gas and Electric	Expense	_____	_____	$_____
Accounts Payable (A/P)	Liability	_____	_____	$_____

2. Plan Adjusting Journal Entry.
   a. Complete the following to plan the adjusting journal entry to enter in QBO

1. _____

2. _____

3. _____

4. _____

3. Create Adjusting Journal Entry.
   a. Select **Create (+) icon > Journal Entry**
   b. Enter the adjusting journal entry in QBO. When entering Accounts Payable (A/P), select **Name: PG&E**.

E9.8 Adjusting Entry Accrued Expenses

Using the QBO Sample Company, Craig's Design and Landscaping Services, complete the following.

Interest on Craig's Notes Payable has been incurred, but not recorded or paid. The interest that has been incurred is calculated as principal multiplied by the interest rate multiplied by the time period ($8,000 x 10% x 1/12 = $66.66). Interest Expense of $66.66 must be recorded as an accrued expense and Interest Payable, a liability, recorded for the amount that Craig is obligated to pay later. So an adjusting entry is needed to bring accounts up to date at December 31.

1. Complete the following table.

Account	Account Type	Increase or Decrease?	Debit or Credit?	Amount
Interest Expense	Expense	_____	_____	$_____
Interest Payable	Liability	_____	_____	$_____

2. Plan Adjusting Journal Entry.
   a. Complete the following to plan the adjusting journal entry to enter in QBO

1 _____

2 _____

3 _____

4 _____

3. Create Adjusting Journal Entry.
    a. Add a new Expense Account to the Chart of Accounts: **Interest Expense**
    b. Add a new Other Current Liability Account to the Chart of Accounts: **Interest Payable**
    c. Select **Create (+) icon > Journal Entry**
    d. Enter the adjusting journal entry in QBO

E9.9 Adjusting Entry Accrued Expense

Using the QBO Sample Company, Craig's Design and Landscaping Services, complete the following.

Interest on Craig's Loan Payable has been incurred, but not recorded or paid. The interest that has been incurred is calculated as principal multiplied by the interest rate multiplied by the time period ($50,000 x 12% x 1/12 = $500.00). Interest Expense of $500.00 must be recorded as an accrued expense and Interest Payable, a liability, recorded for the amount that Craig is obligated to pay later. So an adjusting entry is needed to bring accounts up to date at December 31.

1. Complete the following table.

Account	Account Type	Increase or Decrease?	Debit or Credit?	Amount
Interest Expense	Expense	_____	_____	$_____
Interest Payable	Liability	_____	_____	$_____

2. Plan Adjusting Journal Entry.
    a. Complete the following to plan the adjusting journal entry to enter in QBO

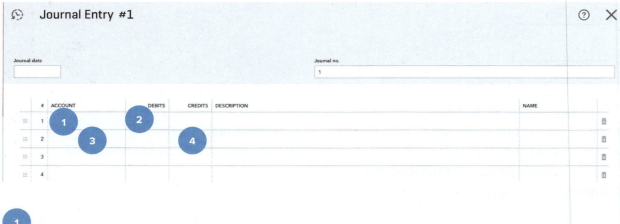

3. Create Adjusting Journal Entry.
    a. If needed, add a new Expense Account to the Chart of Accounts: **Interest Expense**
    b. If needed, add a new Other Current Liability Account to the Chart of Accounts: **Interest Payable**
    c. Select **Create (+) icon > Journal Entry**
    d. Enter the adjusting journal entry in QBO

E9.10 Adjusting Entry Accrued Revenue

Using the QBO Sample Company, Craig's Design and Landscaping Services, complete the following.

Craig has earned interest of $14.40 on its Saving account. This interest has been earned, but not recorded or received. Interest Earned of $14.40 needs to be recorded as an accrued revenue and Accounts Receivable, an asset, recorded for the amount that Craig will receive later. So an adjusting entry is needed to bring accounts up to date at December 31.

1. Complete the following table.

Account	Account Type	Increase or Decrease?	Debit or Credit?	Amount
Interest Earned	Income	_____	_____	$_____
Accounts Receivable (A/R)	Asset	_____	_____	$_____

2. Plan Adjusting Journal Entry.
    a. Complete the following to plan the adjusting journal entry to enter in QBO

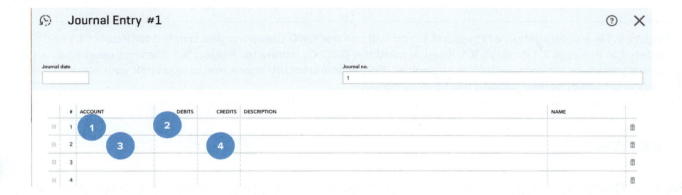

1 _____

2 _____

3 _____

4 _____

3. Create Adjusting Journal Entry.
    a. Select **Create (+) icon > Journal Entry**
    b. Enter the adjusting journal entry in QBO. When entering Accounts Receivable (A/R), select **Name: Weiskopf Consulting**.

4. How can you save this adjusting entry as a recurring transaction?

Project 9.1

Mookie the Beagle™ Concierge

> **Project 9.1 is a continuation of Project 8.1. You will use the QBO Company you created for Project 1.1 and updated in Projects 2.1 through 8.1. Keep in mind the QBO Company for Project 9.1 does not reset and carries your data forward, including any errors. So it is important to check and crosscheck your work to verify it is correct before clicking the Save button.**

BACKSTORY

Mookie The Beagle™ Concierge, a provider of convenient, high-quality pet care, has asked for your assistance in making adjusting entries before preparing financial reports for the first month of operations.

Complete the following for Mookie the Beagle Concierge.

🌐 QBO SATNAV

Project 9.1 focuses on QBO Reports as shown in the following QBO SatNav.

QBO SatNav

⚙ QBO Settings

⚙ Company Settings
⚙ Chart of Accounts

💰 QBO Transactions

💰 Banking
💰 Customers & Sales
💰 Vendors & Expenses
💰 Employees & Payroll

📊 QBO Reports

📊 Reports

HOW TO LOG INTO QBO

To log into QBO, complete the following steps.

1 Using a web browser go to qbo.intuit.com

2 Enter **User ID** (the email address you used to set up your QBO Account)

3 Enter **Password** (the password you used to set up your QBO Account)

4 Select **Sign in**

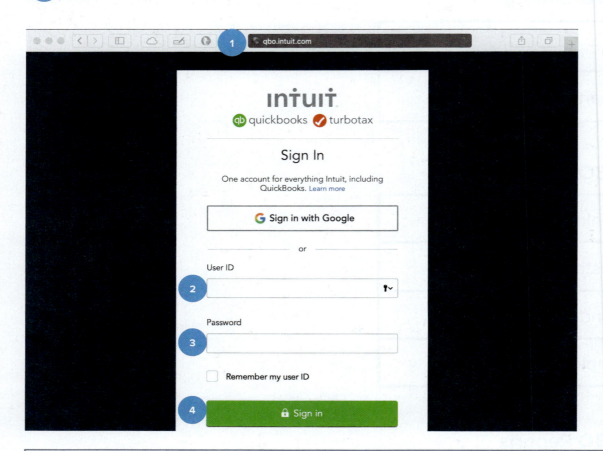

If you are <u>not</u> using a public or shared computer, to speed up login, you can save your login to your desktop and select Remember Me. If you are using a public computer or shared computer, do not save to the desktop and unselect Remember Me.

The new QBO Company we created in Project 1.1 will carry all work forward into future chapters. So it is important to check and crosscheck your work to verify it is correct before clicking the Save button. Any uncorrected errors will be carried forward in your QBO Company for text projects.

P9.1.1 Adjusting Entry Prepaid Insurance

At January 31, 2022 Cy needs to update his accounts before preparing financial statements to review Mookie The Beagle Concierge performance for its first month of operations. Cy has asked for your assistance in preparing the adjusting entries. Mookie The Beagle Concierge will be using the accrual basis of accounting.

In January, Mookie The Beagle Concierge purchased $600 of liability insurance to cover a 3-month period. So at the end of the accounting period on January 31, 1 month of rent had expired @ $200 ($600/3 months = $200 per month). The 2 months of unexpired rent is Prepaid Expenses: Insurance, an asset account with future benefit. Since Mookie The Beagle Concierge recorded the entire $600 as Insurance: Liability Insurance Expense, an adjusting entry is needed to bring accounts up to date at January 31.

1. Complete the following table.

Account	Account Type	Increase or Decrease?	Debit or Credit?	Amount
Insurance: Liability Insurance Expense	Expense	_____	_____	$_____
Prepaid Expenses: Insurance	Asset	_____	_____	$_____

2. Plan Adjusting Journal Entry.
   a. Complete the following to plan the adjusting journal entry to enter in QBO

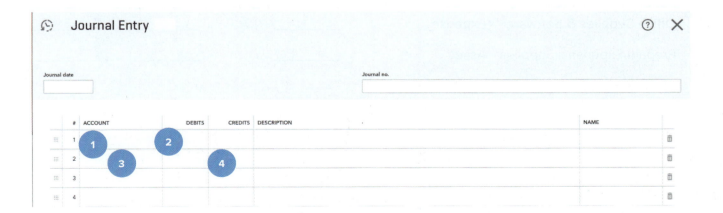

1 _____

2 _____

3 _____

4 _____

3. Enter Adjusting Journal Entry.
    a. Select **Create (+) icon > Journal Entry**
    b. Enter the adjusting journal entry in QBO on January 31, 2022
    c. Enter **Journal No.: ADJ 1**

P9.1.2 Adjusting Entry Supplies

Complete the following adjusting entry for Mookie The Beagle Concierge.

Mookie The Beagle Concierge purchased $852 of office supplies during January 2022. At the end of the accounting period on January 31, Mookie The Beagle Concierge still had $472 of unused supplies on hand. The $472 of supplies is an asset with future benefit. Since Mookie The Beagle Concierge recorded the entire $852 as Office Supplies & Software (Expenses), an adjusting entry is needed to bring accounts up to date at January 31.

1. Complete the following table.

Account	Account Type	Increase or Decrease?	Debit or Credit?	Amount
Office Supplies & Software	Expense	_____	_____	$_____
Prepaid Expenses: Supplies	Asset	_____	_____	$_____

2. Plan Adjusting Journal Entry.

  a. Complete the following to plan the adjusting journal entry to enter in QBO

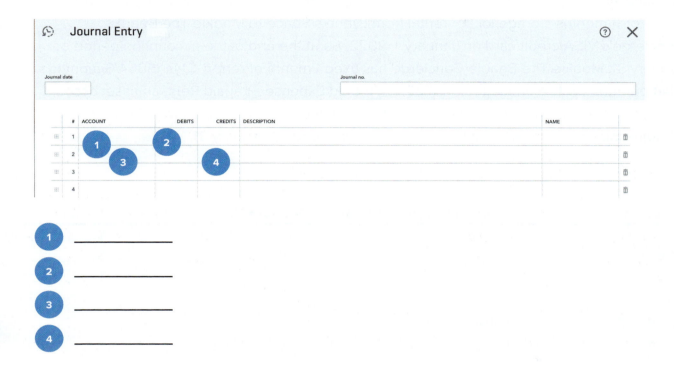

3. Create Adjusting Journal Entry.

  a. Select **Create (+) icon > Journal Entry**

  b. Enter the adjusting journal entry in QBO on January 31, 2022

  c. Enter **Journal No.: ADJ 2**

P9.1.3 Adjusting Entry Prepaid Rental

When Mookie The Beagle Concierge started stocking Mookie The Beagle Concierge branded inventory, Cy rented a centrally located storage locker with digital access. This permits Mookie The Beagle Concierge contractors to access the storage locker for deliveries to customers. Cy has digital surveillance and from his smartphone can electronically permit the contractors access when they arrive at the storage locker. In addition, all inventory has an RFID chip that is automatically read when the contractor passes the storage locker door to exit. This feature improves inventory control in that Cy is immediately notified on his smartphone when any inventory is removed from the storage locker. The storage locker streamlines operations. The only issue is that Cy overlooked recording the storage locker rental in QBO.

Complete the following adjusting entry for Mookie The Beagle Concierge.

In anticipation of stocking Mookie The Beagle Concierge branded inventory, Cy charged $864 for 6 months storage locker rental from Lynne's Space to Mookie The Beagle Concierge's VISA credit card on January 1, 2022. So at the end of the accounting period on January 31, Mookie The Beagle Concierge has used 1 month of rent @ $144 ($864/6 months = $144 per month). The unused rent ($720) is Prepaid Expense: Prepaid Rent, an asset account with future benefit. Since Cy had not recorded anything related to the storage locker rental, an adjusting entry is needed to bring accounts up to date at January 31.

1. Complete the following table.

Account	Account Type	Increase or Decrease?	Debit or Credit?	Amount
Rent & Lease	Expense	_____	_____	$_____
Prepaid Expenses: Rent	Asset	_____	_____	$_____
VISA Credit Card	Liability	_____	_____	$_____

2. Plan Adjusting Journal Entry.
   a. Complete the following to plan the adjusting journal entry to enter in QBO

1. _____

2. _____

3. _____

④ _____

⑤ _____

⑥ _____

3. Create Adjusting Journal Entry.
   a. Select **Create (+) icon > Journal Entry**
   b. Enter the adjusting journal entry in QBO on January 31, 2022
   c. Enter **Journal No.: ADJ 3**

P9.1.4 Adjusting Entry Unearned Revenue
Complete the following adjusting entry for Mookie The Beagle Concierge.

On January 14, 2022, Angel prepaid $3,200 for pet care services to be provided each Friday for 8 weeks for her German Shepherd, Kuno. Mookie The Beagle Concierge recorded the entire $3,200 as Sales. At the end of the accounting period on January 31, 3 weeks (01/14, 01/21, 01/28) of the pet care services had been provided to Kuno, so 5 weeks of services or $2,000 ($3,200/8 = $400 per week) had not been earned as of the end of January. Since $2,000 had not been earned, the $2,000 is a liability because Mookie The Beagle Concierge has an obligation to provide the pet care service or return the $2,000 to the customer. So an adjusting entry is needed to bring accounts up to date at January 31.

1. Complete the following table.

Account	Account Type	Increase or Decrease?	Debit or Credit?	Amount
Sales	Income	_____	_____	$_____
Unearned Revenue	Liability	_____	_____	$_____

2. Plan Adjusting Journal Entry.
   a. Complete the following to plan the adjusting journal entry to enter in QBO

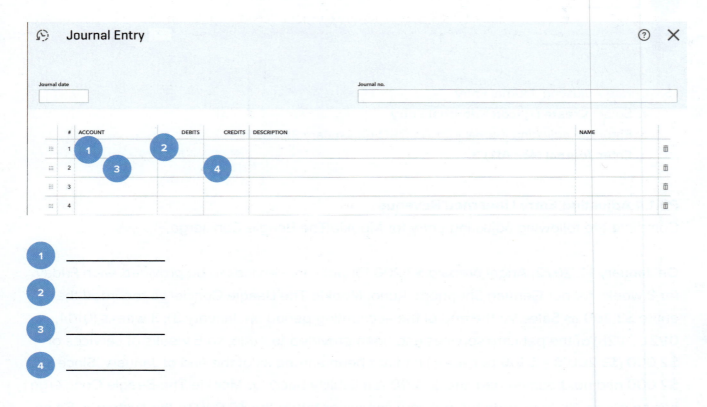

3. Create Adjusting Journal Entry.
   a. Select **Create (+) icon > Journal Entry**
   b. Enter the adjusting journal entry in QBO on January 31, 2022
   c. Enter **Journal No.: ADJ 4**

P9.1.5 Adjusting Entry Accrued Expenses

Complete the following adjusting entry for Mookie The Beagle Concierge.

Interest on Mookie The Beagle Concierge's Loan Payable to Cy has been incurred, but not recorded or paid. The interest that has been incurred is calculated as principal multiplied by the interest rate multiplied by the time period ($2,000 x 6% x 1/12 = $10.00). Interest Expense of $10.00 must be recorded as an accrued expense and Interest Payable, a liability, recorded for the amount that Mookie The Beagle Concierge is obligated to pay later. So an adjusting entry is needed to bring accounts up to date at January 31.

1. Complete the following table.

Account	Account Type	Increase or Decrease?	Debit or Credit?	Amount
Interest Paid	Expense	_____	_____	$_____
Interest Payable	Liability	_____	_____	$_____

2. Plan Adjusting Journal Entry.
   a. Complete the following to plan the adjusting journal entry to enter in QBO

3. Create Adjusting Journal Entry.
   a. Add a new Other Current Liabilities account to the Chart of Accounts: **Interest Payable**
   b. Select **Create (+) icon > Journal Entry**
   c. Enter the adjusting journal entry in QBO on January 31, 2022
   d. Enter **Journal No.: ADJ 5**

P9.1.6 Adjusting Entry Accrued Expenses

Complete the following adjusting entry for Mookie The Beagle Concierge.

During January, Mary Dolan, a contractor, provided pet care services to Angel's Kuno for three Fridays in January, totaling 24 hours @ $20 per hour. Cy overlooked recording this contractor expense since Mary had not been paid for these services yet. So at January 31, an adjusting entry is needed to record Contractors Expense that will be paid later. In the future, Cy is hoping that the QBO time tracking will assist in avoiding this type of oversight going forward.

1. Complete the following table.

Account	Account Type	Increase or Decrease?	Debit or Credit?	Amount
Contractors Expense	Expense	_____	_____	$_____
Accounts Payable (A/P)	Liability	_____	_____	$_____

2. Plan Adjusting Journal Entry.
   a. Complete the following to plan the adjusting journal entry to enter in QBO

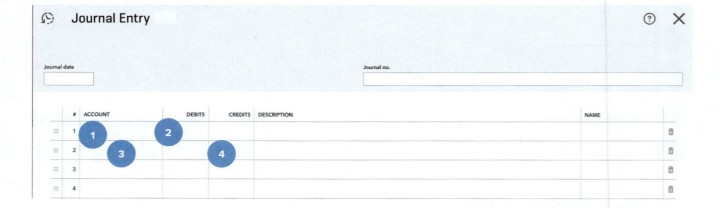

1 _____

2 _____

3 _____

4 _____

3. Create Adjusting Journal Entry.
   a. Select **Create (+) icon** > **Journal Entry**
   b. Enter the adjusting journal entry in QBO on January 31, 2022. If requested, select Mary Dolan for the Name field.
   c. Enter **Journal No.: ADJ 6**

P9.1.7 Adjusting Entry Accrued Expense

Complete the following adjusting entry for Mookie The Beagle Concierge.

At January 31, Mookie The Beagle Concierge has incurred $220 of accounting services for assistance with QBO. This amount has not been paid nor recorded by Mookie The Beagle Concierge, so an adjusting entry is needed to record the expense incurred.

1. Complete the following table.

Account	Account Type	Increase or Decrease?	Debit or Credit?	Amount
Legal & Professional Services	Expense	_____	_____	$_____
Accounts Payable (A/P)	Liability	_____	_____	$_____

2. Plan Adjusting Journal Entry.
   a. Complete the following to plan the adjusting journal entry to enter in QBO

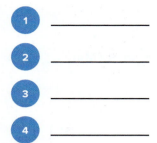

1 _____

2 _____

3 _____

4 _____

3. Create Adjusting Journal Entry.
    a. Select **Create (+) icon > Journal Entry**.
    b. Enter the adjusting journal entry in QBO on January 31, 2022. If requested, enter Your Name in the Vendor Name field.
    c. Enter **Journal No.: ADJ 7**

P9.1.8 Adjusting Entry Renter Insurance

Oops... When cleaning out his jacket pocket, Cy discovers a receipt for renter insurance for the storage locker rental. The renter insurance was purchased from Cyrus Insurance to provide insurance coverage for the inventory that Cy planned to store in the storage locker. Mookie The Beagle Concierge purchased 1 month of renter insurance coverage for the period January 1 through January 31, 2022. Using the company credit card, Mookie The Beagle Concierge paid $16.00 on January 16, 2022 for the 1 month of insurance coverage.

So at the end of the accounting period on January 31, 1 month of rent had expired at $16.00. Since Mookie The Beagle Concierge had not recorded the transaction, the entire $16.00 should be recorded as Renter Insurance Expense with an adjusting entry to bring accounts up to date at January 31.

1. Complete the following table.

Account	Account Type	Increase or Decrease?	Debit or Credit?	Amount
Insurance: Renter Insurance Expense	Expense	_____	_____	$_____
VISA Credit Card	Liability	_____	_____	$_____

2. Plan Adjusting Journal Entry.

   a. Complete the following to plan the adjusting journal entry to enter in QBO

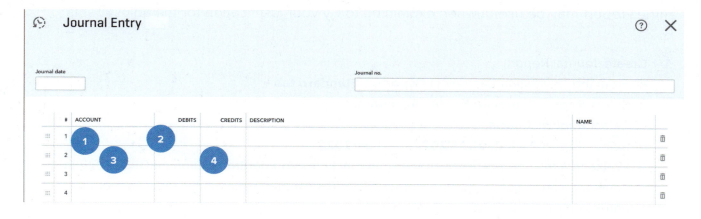

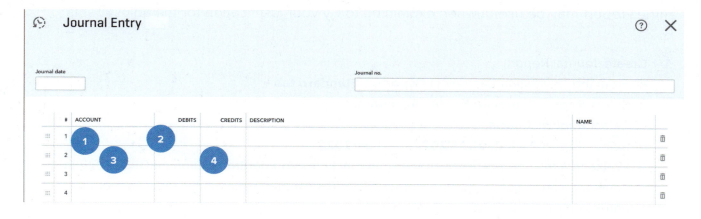

1. _____

2. _____

3. _____

4. _____

3. Create Adjusting Journal Entry.

   a. Select **Create (+) icon > Journal Entry**

   b. Enter the adjusting journal entry in QBO on January 31, 2022

   c. Enter **Journal No.: ADJ 8**

4. Make Recommendations on How to Improve Processes.

   Business owners are busy people, juggling multiple items at once. So occasionally accounting items are not recorded due to an oversight. Suggest two ways that Mookie The Beagle Concierge and Cy could improve processes to ensure that all accounting items are recorded in a timely manner.

   a. _____

   b. _____

P9.1.9 Journal Report

To review for accuracy the adjusting entries you entered for Mookie The Beagle Concierge, you decide to print a report of the adjusting journal entries. In addition, the adjusting journal entries report may be useful when explaining to Cy your justification for the adjustments.

1. Create Journal Report.
   a. From the Navigation Bar, select **Reports > Standard tab**
   b. Select **Report Category: For My Accountant**
   c. Select **Report: Journal**
   d. Select **Report Period: 01/31/2022 to 01/31/2022**
   e. Notice that the Journal report that displays includes another transaction on 01/31/2022 in addition to the adjusting journal entries. To add a filter to display only adjusting journal entries on 01/31/2022, select **Customize**.
   f. Select **Filter**
   g. Check **Transaction Type**
   h. Select **Transaction Type: Journal Entry**
   i. Select **Run report**
   j. Review the adjusting journal entries listed in the report for accuracy

2. Export the Adjusting Journal Entries Report to PDF.
   a. With the Journal report displayed, select the **Export icon**
   b. Select **Export to PDF**
   c. Select **Save as PDF**

3. Export the Adjusting Journal Entries Report to Excel.
   a. With the Journal report displayed, select the **Export icon**
   b. Select **Export to Excel**

Chapter 10

QBO Reports

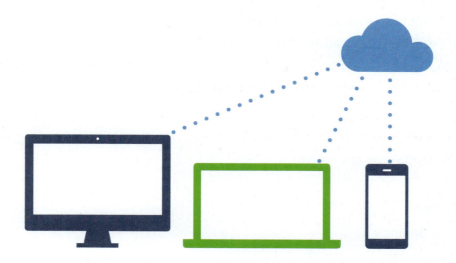

After Mookie the Beagle Concierge completed its first month in business, Cy Walker realizes that he needs information to assess the financial and operating performance of the business. Also, Cy needs more information in order to make sound management decisions going forward. So Cy would like you to learn more about how to create reports using QuickBooks Online and how to use the various QBO reports for better decision making.

Chapter 10

LEARNING OBJECTIVES

Chapter 10 explores some frequently used QBO reports and the reporting process. The objective of financial reports is to provide information to users for decision making. The users of the financial reports include investors, creditors, tax agencies, and management. Different users are focused on different decisions and require different types of reports to provide information related to those decisions. For example, an investor may be deciding whether to invest and a creditor deciding whether to extend credit to a business.

In this chapter, you will learn about the following topics:

- Navigating Reports
- Trial Balance
- Adjusting Entries
- Adjusted Trial Balance
- Financial Statements
  - Profit and Loss
  - Balance Sheet
  - Statement of Cash Flows
- Management Reports
- Who Owes You Reports
  - Accounts Receivable Aging
  - Open Invoices
- Sales and Customer Reports
  - Income by Customer
  - Sales by Product/Service
  - Physical Inventory Worksheet
- What You Owe Reports
  - Accounts Payable Aging
  - Unpaid Bills

- Expenses and Vendors Reports
  - Open Purchase Order List
  - Purchases by Vendor Detail
- For My Accountant Reports
  - Journal
  - Audit Log
- Accounting Essentials: Financial Reports

Section 10.1
 QBO SATNAV

QBO SatNav is our satellite navigation for QuickBooks Online, assisting us in navigating QBO Chapter 10 covers QBO Reports, as shown in the following QBO SatNav.

 **QBO Settings**
⚙ Company Settings
⚙ Chart of Accounts

 **QBO Transactions**
💰 Banking
💰 Customers & Sales
💰 Vendors & Expenses
💰 Employees & Payroll

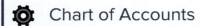 **QBO Reports**
📊 Reports

Section 10.2

QBO SAMPLE COMPANY LOGIN

To log into the QBO Sample Company:

1 Open a web browser. (Note: Intuit recommends using Google Chrome.)

2 Go to the https://qbo.intuit.com/redir/testdrive

3 Follow onscreen instructions for security verification

Craig's Design and Landscaping Services should appear on your screen.

> **Note: Although the Sample Company link should work, if for some reason the previous link for the Sample Company doesn't work with your browser, using Google search type in "qbo.intuit.com Sample Company". Select the entry to Test Drive Sample Company.**

To increase the amount of time from one (1) hour to three (3) hours before the log out for inactivity occurs:

1 From Craig's Design and Landscaping Services QBO Sample Company, select the **Gear** icon

2 Under Your Company section, select **Account and Settings**

3 Select **Advanced**

4 Select **Other preferences**

5 For the option Sign me out if inactive for, select **3 hours**

6 Select **Save**

7 Select **Done**

> ⚠️ **The Sample Company** will reset each time it is reopened. This allows you to explore and practice QBO without concern about carrying forward errors to later chapters. However, you will want to make certain to allow enough time to complete all chapter activities before closing the Sample Company. Otherwise, you will lose the work you have entered when you close and reopen the Sample Company.

To set QBO preferences to display account numbers in the Chart of Accounts:

1 Select the **Gear** icon to display options

2 Select **Account and Settings**

3 Select **Advanced**

4 For Chart of Accounts, select the **Edit Pencil**, then select **Enable account numbers**

5 Select **Show account numbers**

6 Select **Save**

7 Select **Done** to close Account and Settings

Section 10.3

NAVIGATING REPORTS

Most QBO reports are accessed from the Navigation Bar. Don't be overwhelmed by the number of reports offered by QBO. QBO offers a wide variety of reports to meet the needs of different QBO users. We will explore some of the more frequently used reports in this chapter.

To navigate QBO reports:

1. From the Navigation Bar, select **Dashboard** to view a financial dashboard for the company. This dashboard summarizes key financial metrics. The dashboard includes bank account summaries, and charts for expenses, sales, and income. Select **Edit** or **drop-down arrows** to customize the dashboard.

2. From the Navigation Bar, select **Reports**

3. To search for a specific report, in the **Find report by name** field, enter the **report name** and click the magnifying glass

4. Select **Standard** report tab to view QBO reports, grouped by category, such as Favorites, Business Overview, Sales and Customers, and Expenses and Vendors

5. Under Standard report tab, **Favorites** are listed first

6. To list a report in the Favorites category, click the **star** by the report. Then the report is also listed in the Favorites section for easier access. For example, the star by the Balance Sheet is selected, and the Balance Sheet then also appears in the Favorites category.

7. **Business Overview** reports include financial statements, such as Profit and Loss reports, Balance Sheet reports, and Statement of Cash Flows

8. **Who Owes You** reports are used to track amounts that customers owe your business, including Accounts Receivable Aging reports, Collection reports, and Open Invoices

9. **Sales and Customers** reports provide detailed information about customers and sales transactions, including Customers List, Products and Services List, Deposit Detail, Income by Customer, Sales by Customer, and Sales by Product/Service

10. **What You Owe** reports are used to track amounts that your business owes others, including Accounts Payable reports, Unpaid Bills reports, and Vendor Balance reports

11. **Expenses and Vendors** reports provide detail information about vendors and expenses transactions, including Check Detail report, Expenses by Vendor report, Open Purchase Order Lists, and Vendors List

12 **Sales Tax** reports include reports about Sales Tax Liabilities and Taxable Sales

13 **Employees** reports include the Employees List and Time Activities reports

14 **For My Accountant** reports include the Account List (Chart of Accounts), General Ledger, Journal, and Trial Balance

15 **Payroll** reports are the same reports as the Employees reports, including the Employees List and Time Activities reports

16 Select the **Custom Reports** tab to view saved customized reports. These are reports that you have created, customized, and then saved for reuse. To save a customized report, after preparing the report, select Save Customization.

17 Select the **Management Reports** tab to view management reports that QBO has prepared for you

18 Select the **drop-down arrow** to view report options to Edit, Send, Export as PDF, Export as DOCX or Copy

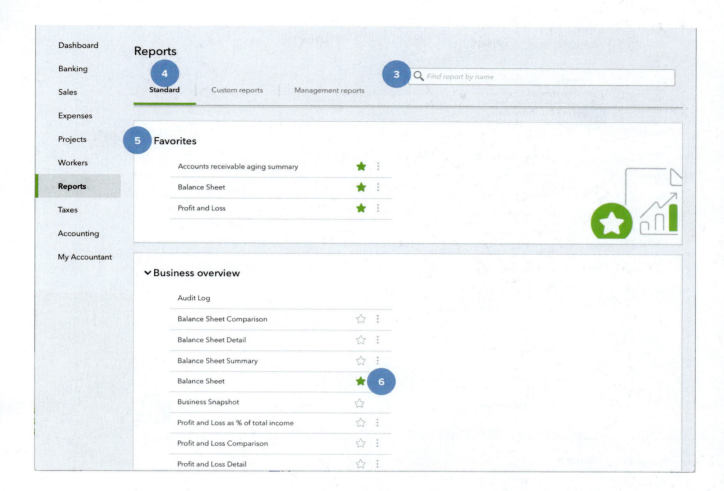

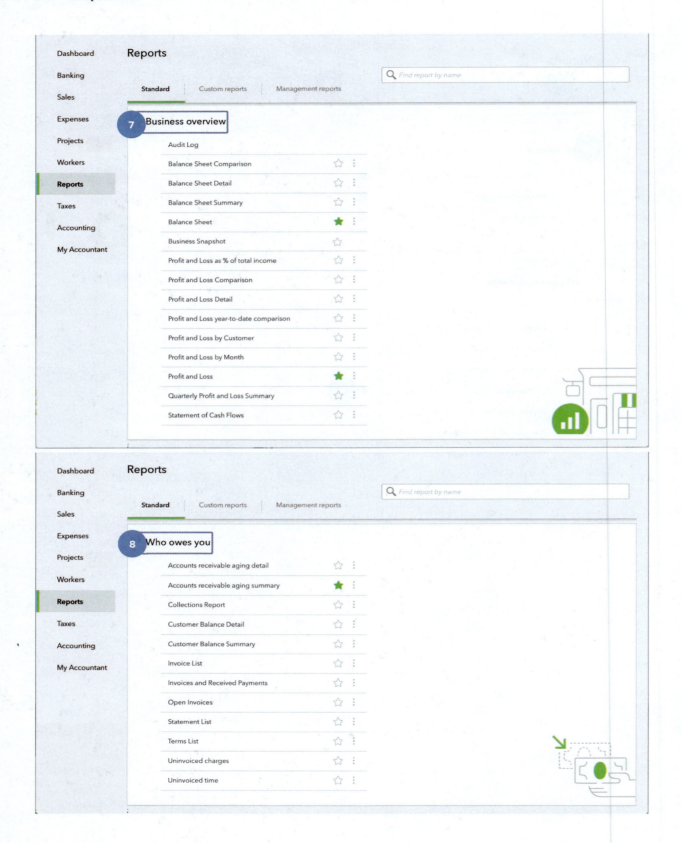

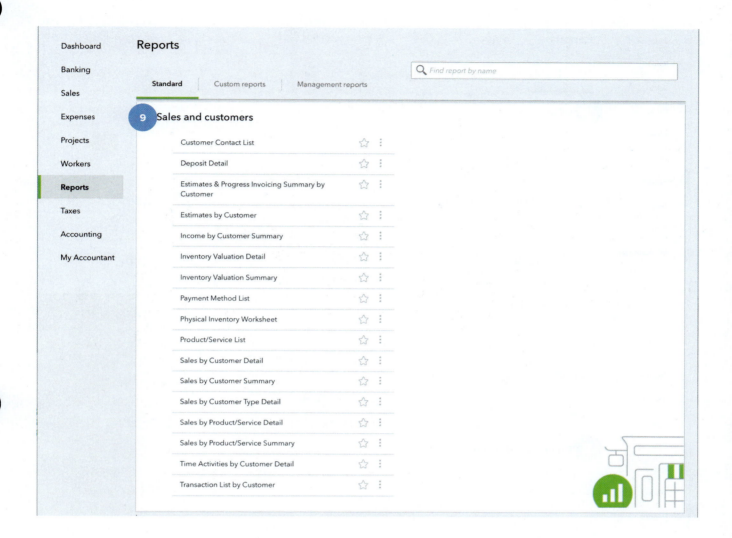

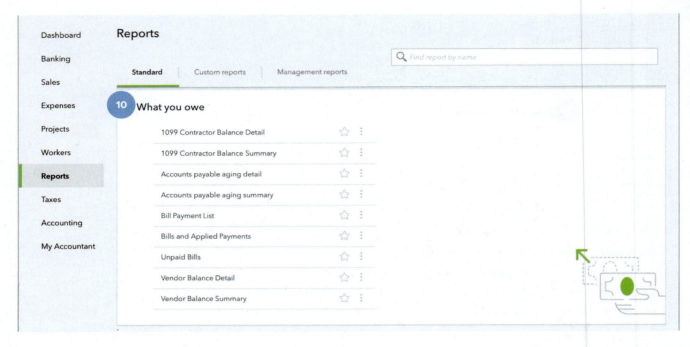

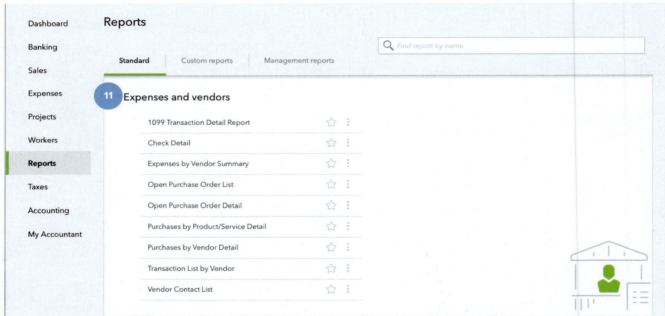

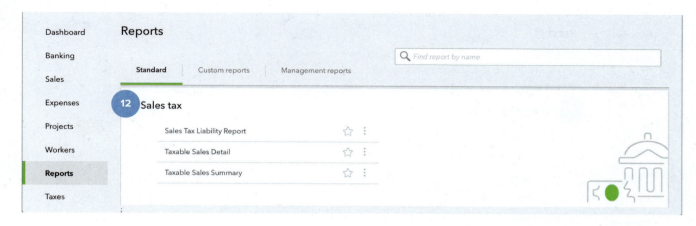

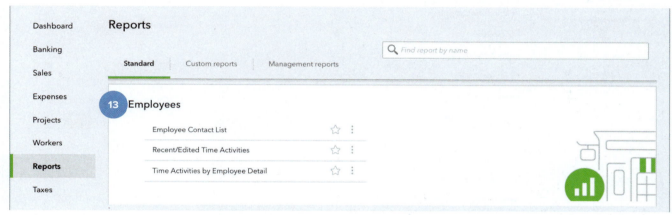

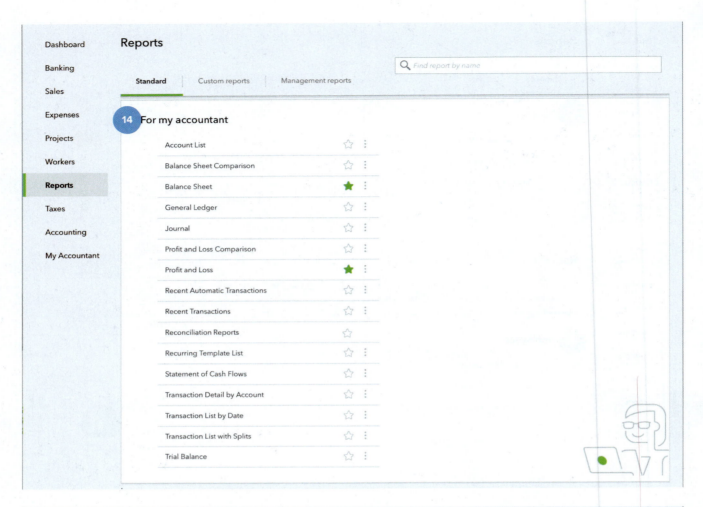

Reports

Dashboard		
Banking	Standard	Custom reports	Management reports
Sales		

(14) For my accountant

Account List	☆	⋮
Balance Sheet Comparison	☆	⋮
Balance Sheet	★	⋮
General Ledger	☆	⋮
Journal	☆	⋮
Profit and Loss Comparison	☆	⋮
Profit and Loss	★	⋮
Recent Automatic Transactions	☆	⋮
Recent Transactions	☆	⋮
Reconciliation Reports	☆	
Recurring Template List	☆	⋮
Statement of Cash Flows	☆	⋮
Transaction Detail by Account	☆	⋮
Transaction List by Date	☆	⋮
Transaction List with Splits	☆	⋮
Trial Balance	☆	⋮

Left navigation: Dashboard, Banking, Sales, Expenses, Projects, Workers, **Reports**, Taxes, Accounting, My Accountant

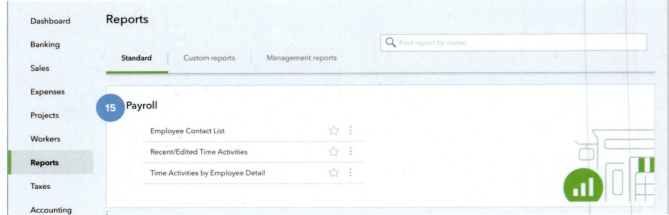

Reports

Left navigation: Dashboard, Banking, Sales, Expenses, Projects, Workers, **Reports**, Taxes, Accounting

Standard | Custom reports | Management reports

(15) Payroll

Employee Contact List	☆	⋮
Recent/Edited Time Activities	☆	⋮
Time Activities by Employee Detail	☆	⋮

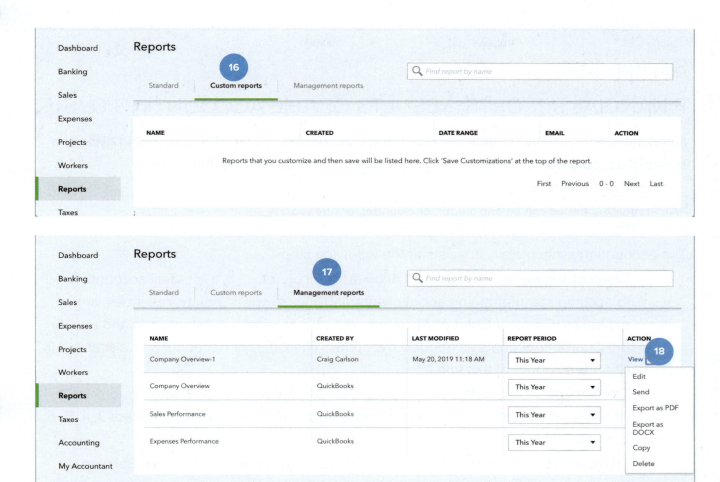

Next, we will explore the process used to prepare QBO financial reports.

Section 10.4

FINANCIAL REPORTS: RESULTS OF THE ACCOUNTING CYCLE

Financial reports are the results or output of the accounting cycle. The accounting cycle is a series of accounting activities that a business performs each accounting period.

> **An accounting period** can be one month, one quarter, or one year.

The accounting cycle usually consists of the following steps.

- **Chart of Accounts.** The Chart of Accounts (Account List) is a list of all accounts used to accumulate information about assets, liabilities, owners' equity, revenues, and expenses. Create a Chart of Accounts when the business is established and modify the Chart of Accounts as needed over time. (The Chart of Accounts was discussed in Chapters 1 and 2 of this text.)

- **Transactions.** During the accounting period, record transactions with customers, vendors, employees, and owners. (Transactions were explored in Chapters 3, 4, 5, 6, 7, and 8 of this text.)

- **Trial Balance.** A Trial Balance is also referred to as an unadjusted Trial Balance because it is prepared before adjustments. A Trial Balance lists each account and the account balance at the end of the accounting period. Prepare a Trial Balance to verify that the accounting system is in balance—total debits should equal total credits.

- **Adjustments.** At the end of the accounting period before preparing financial statements, make any adjustments necessary to bring the accounts up to date. Adjustments are entered in the Journal using debits and credits. (Adjustments were covered in Chapter 9.)

- **Adjusted Trial Balance.** Prepare an Adjusted Trial Balance (a Trial Balance after adjustments) to verify that the accounting system still balances. If additional account detail is required, view the General Ledger (the collection of all the accounts listing the transactions that affected the accounts).

- **Financial Statements.** Prepare financial statements (Profit and Loss, Balance Sheet, and Statement of Cash Flows) for external users and internal users. Prepare management reports.

Section 10.5

TRIAL BALANCE

Trial Balance is a listing of all of a company's accounts and the ending account balances. A Trial Balance is often prepared both before and after making adjustments. The purpose of the Trial Balance is to verify account balances and that the accounting system balances. On a Trial Balance, all debit ending account balances are listed in the debit column and credit ending balances are listed in the credit column. If the accounting system balances, total debits equal total credits.

To view the Trial Balance in QBO:

1. From the Navigation Bar, select **Reports**

2. Select **Standard** tab

3. Select **Report Category: For My Accountant**

4. Select **Trial Balance**

5. From the drop-down menu, select **Report Period: This Year**

6. **Dates** should autofill

7. Select **Active rows/active columns**

8. Select **Accounting Method: Accrual**

9. Select **Run report**

10. To customize the report further, select **Customize**

11. From the Customize report slide out drawer, make **customization selections**

12. Select **Run report**

13. Notice on the Trial Balance report that **Total Debits equal Total Credits**

14 Select **Export** icon to display the export options: Export to Excel and Export to PDF

15 Select **Save Customization** and follow onscreen instructions to save so the customized report appears under the Custom Reports tab

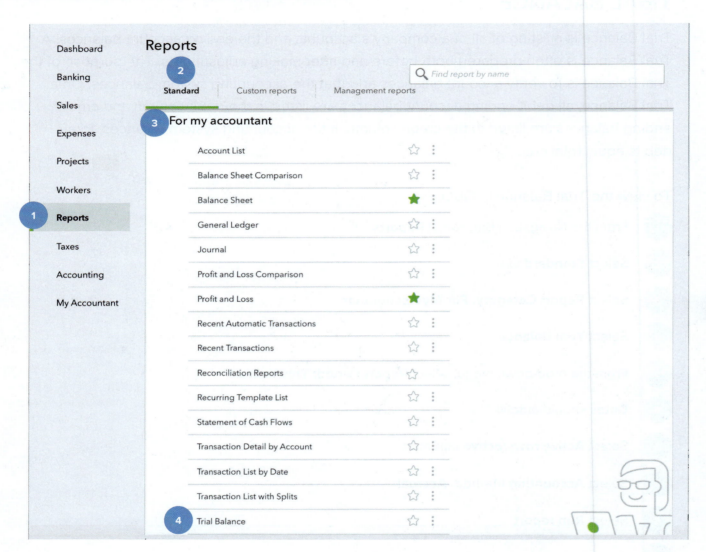

Trial Balance Report

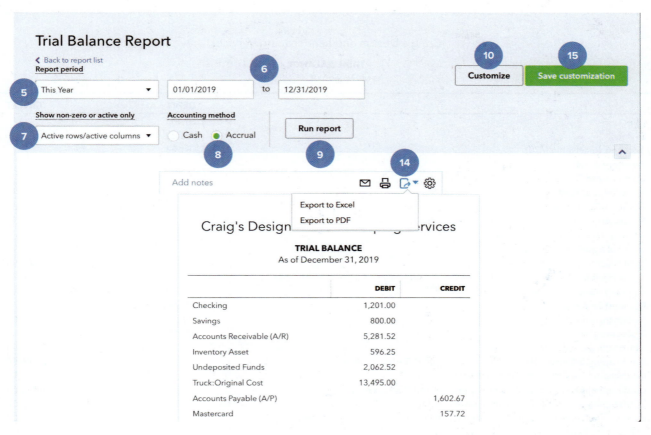

‹ Back to report list

Report period

⑤ This Year ⑥ 01/01/2019 to 12/31/2019

⑩ Customize ⑮ Save customization

Show non-zero or active only

⑦ Active rows/active columns

Accounting method

⑧ ○ Cash ● Accrual ⑨ Run report

Add notes ✉ 🖨 ⑭ ⚙

Export to Excel
Export to PDF

Craig's Design ... ervices

TRIAL BALANCE
As of December 31, 2019

	DEBIT	CREDIT
Checking	1,201.00	
Savings	800.00	
Accounts Receivable (A/R)	5,281.52	
Inventory Asset	596.25	
Undeposited Funds	2,062.52	
Truck:Original Cost	13,495.00	
Accounts Payable (A/P)		1,602.67
Mastercard		157.72

Customize report ×

⑪ ▼ General

Report period

This Year ▾ 01/01/2019 to 12/31/2019

Accounting method

○ Cash ● Accrual

Number format **Negative numbers**

☐ Divide by 1000 -100 ▾

☐ Without cents

☑ Except zero amount ☐ Show in red

▼ Rows/Columns

Show non-zero or active only

Active rows/active c ▾

▼ Header/Footer

Header

☑ Company name Craig's Design and Land

☑ Report title Trial Balance

☑ Report period

Footer

☑ Date prepared

☑ Time prepared

☑ Report basis (cash vs. accrual)

Alignment

Header Center ▾

Footer Center ▾

⑫ Run report

Craig's Design and Landscaping Services

TRIAL BALANCE

As of December 31, 2019

	DEBIT	CREDIT
Checking	1,201.00	
Savings	800.00	
Accounts Receivable (A/R)	5,281.52	
Inventory Asset	596.25	
Undeposited Funds	2,062.52	
Truck:Original Cost	13,495.00	
Accounts Payable (A/P)		1,602.67
Mastercard		157.72
Arizona Dept. of Revenue Payable		0.00
Board of Equalization Payable		370.94
Loan Payable		4,000.00
Notes Payable		25,000.00
Opening Balance Equity	9,337.50	
Retained Earnings	300.00	
Design income		2,250.00
Discounts given	89.50	
Landscaping Services		1,477.50
Landscaping Services:Job Materials:Fountains and Garden Lighting		2,246.50
Landscaping Services:Job Materials:Plants and Soil		2,351.97
Landscaping Services:Job Materials:Sprinklers and Drip Systems		138.00
Landscaping Services:Labor:Installation		250.00
Landscaping Services:Labor:Maintenance and Repair		50.00
Pest Control Services		110.00
Sales of Product Income		912.75
Services		503.55
Cost of Goods Sold	405.00	
Advertising	74.86	
Automobile	113.96	
Automobile:Fuel	349.41	
Equipment Rental	112.00	
Insurance	241.23	
Job Expenses	155.07	
Job Expenses:Job Materials:Decks and Patios	234.04	
Job Expenses:Job Materials:Plants and Soil	353.12	
Job Expenses:Job Materials:Sprinklers and Drip Systems	215.66	
Legal & Professional Fees	75.00	
Legal & Professional Fees:Accounting	640.00	
Legal & Professional Fees:Bookkeeper	55.00	
Legal & Professional Fees:Lawyer	100.00	
Maintenance and Repair	185.00	
Maintenance and Repair:Equipment Repairs	755.00	
Meals and Entertainment	28.49	
Office Expenses	18.08	
Rent or Lease	900.00	
Utilities:Gas and Electric	200.53	
Utilities:Telephone	130.86	
Miscellaneous	2,916.00	
TOTAL	$41,421.60	$41,421.60

Section 10.6

ADJUSTING ENTRIES

The QBO Journal is used to record adjustments (and corrections). Adjustments are often necessary to bring the accounts up to date at the end of the accounting period.

To make adjusting entries using the Journal:

1   Select **Create (+)** icon

2   Select **Journal Entry** to access the onscreen Journal

3   Enter **Journal Date**

4   Enter **Journal No.** QBO will automatically number Journal entries consecutively unless we modify the Journal No. Often we label adjusting entries as ADJ 1, ADJ 2, and so on. Then we can clearly see which Journal entries are adjusting entries.

5   On Line 1, from the drop-down list of accounts, select the **Account** to debit

6   Enter **Debit Amount**

7   Enter **Description**

8   On Line 2, select **Account** to credit

9   Enter **Credit Amount**

10   Enter **Description**

11   Enter **Memo,** such as Adjusting entry to record amount of insurance expired. If we had to make any calculations to determine the adjusting entry amounts, then we should include those calculations in the Memo field.

12   Add **Attachments** that are source documents related to the adjusting entry

13   Normally we would select Save and new or Save and close, but in this case, select **Cancel**

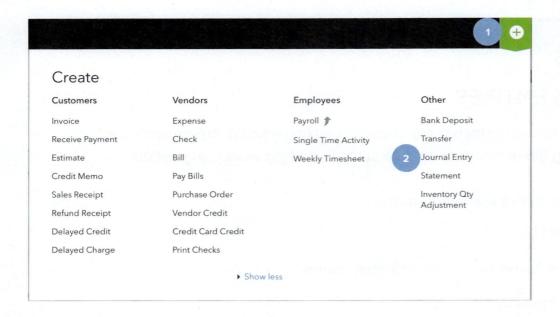

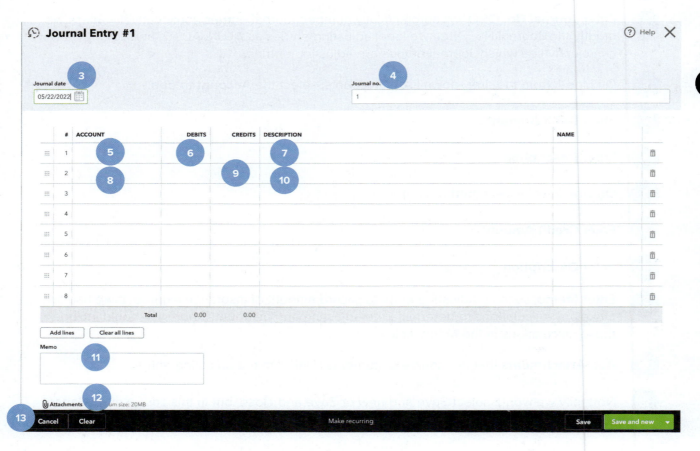

If we use the accrual basis of accounting to calculate profits, the following four types of adjusting entries may be necessary.

1. **Prepaid items.** Items that are prepaid, such as prepaid insurance or prepaid rent.
2. **Unearned items.** Items that a customer has paid us for, but we have not provided the product or service.
3. **Accrued expenses.** Expenses that are incurred but not yet paid or recorded.
4. **Accrued revenues.** Revenues that have been earned but not yet collected or recorded.

For more detailed information about adjusting entries, see Chapter 9.

Section 10.7

ADJUSTED TRIAL BALANCE

The Adjusted Trial Balance is prepared after adjusting entries are made to view updated account balances and verify that the accounting system still balances.

To view an Adjusted Trial Balance in QBO simply run the Trial Balance report again after adjusting entries have been entered in QBO.

1   From the Navigation Bar, select **Reports**

2   Select **Standard** report tab

3   Select **Report Category: For My Accountant**

4   Select **Trial Balance**, then complete steps to run the Trial Balance again after adjusting entries are entered

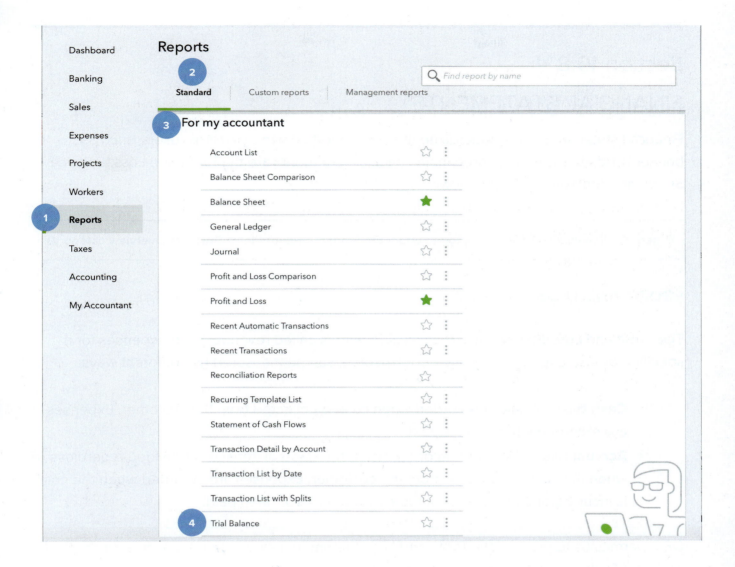

Section 10.8

FINANCIAL STATEMENTS

Financial statements are standardized financial reports given to external users, such as bankers and investors. The three main financial statements are the Profit and Loss, Balance Sheet, and Statement of Cash Flows.

> **In general, financial statements are found under the Standard reports tab > Business Overview category.**

PROFIT AND LOSS

The Profit and Loss Statement lists sales (sometimes called revenues) and expenses for a specified accounting period. Profit, or net income, can be measured two different ways:

- **Cash basis.** A sale is recorded when cash is collected from the customer. Expenses are recorded when cash is paid.
- **Accrual basis.** Sales are recorded when the good or service is provided regardless of when the cash is collected from the customer. Expenses are recorded when the cost is incurred or expires, even if the expense has not been paid.

QBO permits us to prepare the Profit and Loss Statement using either the accrual or the cash basis. QBO also permits us to prepare Profit and Loss Statements monthly, quarterly, or annually.

To prepare a Profit and Loss Statement using the accrual basis:

1. From the Navigation Bar, select **Reports**

2. Select **Standard** tab

3. Select **Business Overview**

4. Select **Profit and Loss**

5 Select **Customize**

6 Select **Report Period: This Year**

7 Select **Accounting Method: Accrual**

8 Select **Negative Numbers: (100)**

9 Select **Run report**

10 Select **Save Customization** and follow onscreen instructions to save so the customized report will now appear under the Custom Reports tab

11 Select **Export** icon to display the export options: Export to Excel and Export to PDF

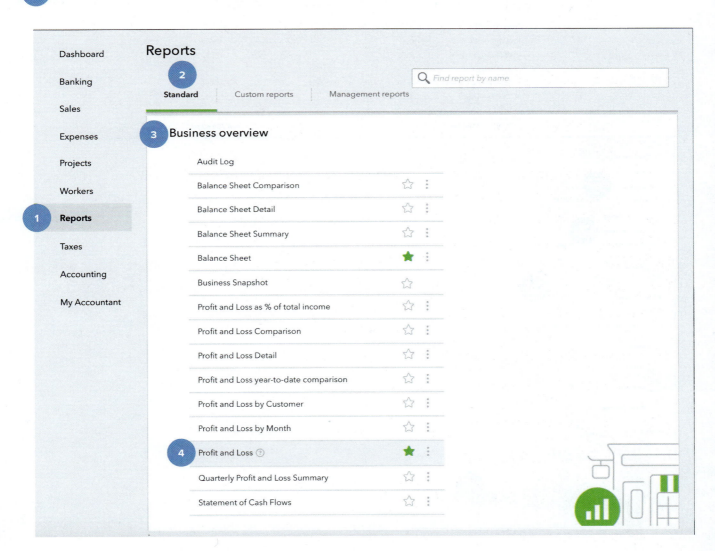

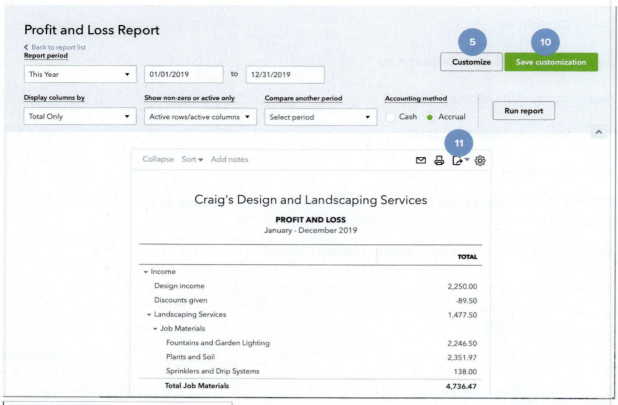

BALANCE SHEET

The Balance Sheet presents a company's financial position on a specific date. The Balance Sheet can be prepared at the end of a month, quarter, or year. The Balance Sheet lists:

1. **Assets**. What a company owns. On the Balance Sheet, assets are recorded at their historical cost, the amount we paid for the asset when we purchased it. Note that historical cost can be different from the market value of the asset, which is the amount the asset is worth now.
2. **Liabilities**. What a company owes. Liabilities are obligations that include amounts owed vendors (accounts payable) and bank loans (notes payable).
3. **Owners' equity.** The residual that is left after liabilities are satisfied. Also called net worth, owners' equity is increased by owners' contributions and net income. Owners' equity is decreased by owners' withdrawals (or dividends) and net losses.

To prepare a Balance Sheet:

1. From the Navigation Bar, select **Reports**
2. Select **Standard** tab
3. Select **Business Overview**
4. Select **Balance Sheet**
5. Enter **Customize** features using the Customization Bar across the top of the report or using the Customize button
6. Select **Save Customization** and follow onscreen instructions to save so the customized report will now appear under the Custom Reports tab
7. Select **Export** icon to display the export options: Export to Excel and Export to PDF

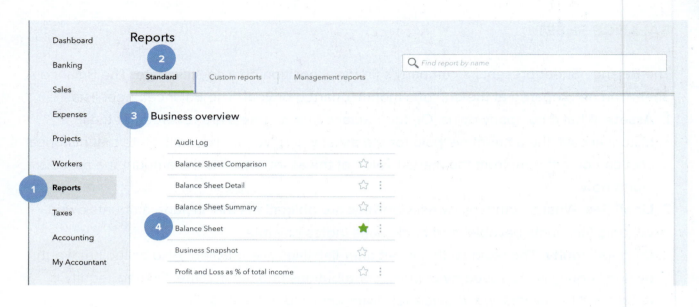

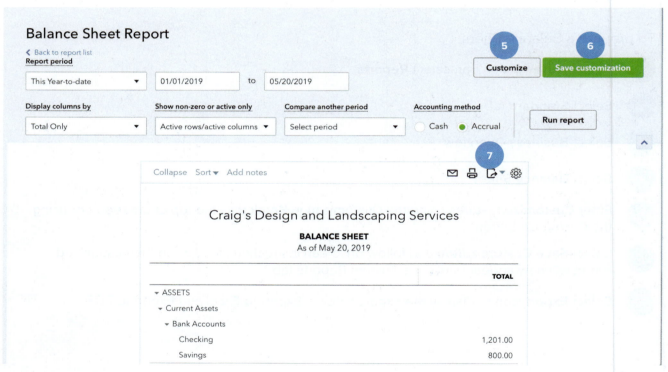

STATEMENT OF CASH FLOWS

The Statement of Cash Flows summarizes cash inflows and cash outflows for a business over a period of time. Cash flows are grouped into three categories:

1. **Cash flows from operating activities.** Cash inflows and outflows related to the company's primary business, such as cash flows from sales and operating expenses.
2. **Cash flows from investing activities.** Cash inflows and outflows related to acquisition and disposal of long-term assets.
3. **Cash flows from financing activities.** Cash inflows and outflows to and from investors and creditors (except for interest payments). Examples include: loan principal repayments and investments by owners.

To prepare the Statement of Cash Flows:

1. From the Navigation Bar, select **Reports**

2. Select **Standard** tab

3. Select **Business Overview**

4. Select **Statement of Cash Flows**

5. Enter **Customize** features using the Customization Bar across the top of the report or using the Customize button

6. Select **Save Customization** and follow onscreen instructions to save so the customized report will now appear under the Custom Reports tab

7. Select **Export** icon to display the export options: Export to Excel and Export to PDF

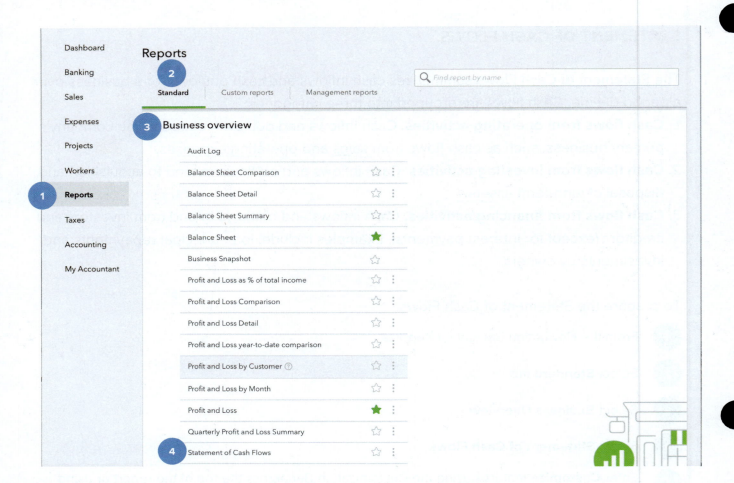

Statement of Cash Flows Report

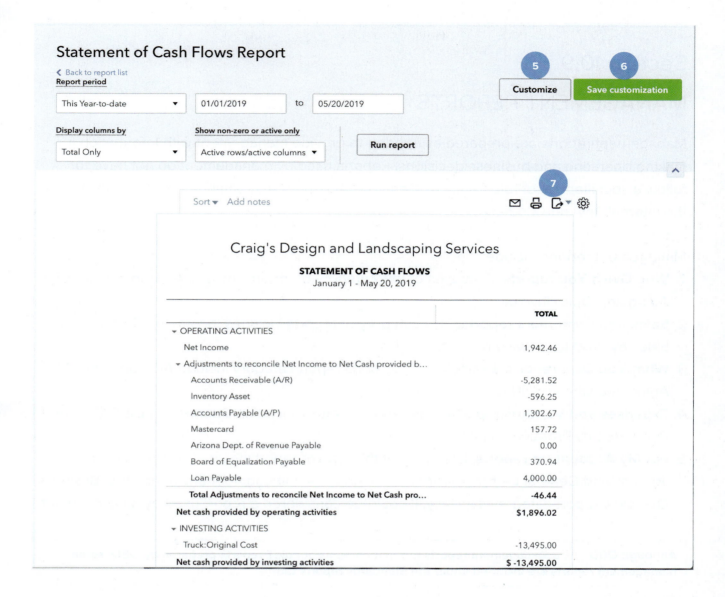

‹ Back to report list

Report period

| This Year-to-date ▼ | 01/01/2019 | to | 05/20/2019 |

Display columns by

| Total Only ▼ |

Show non-zero or active only

| Active rows/active columns ▼ |

Run report

⑤ Customize   ⑥ **Save customization**

Sort ▼   Add notes   ✉ 🖨 ➦▼ ⑦ ⚙

Craig's Design and Landscaping Services

STATEMENT OF CASH FLOWS
January 1 - May 20, 2019

	TOTAL
▾ OPERATING ACTIVITIES	
Net Income	1,942.46
▾ Adjustments to reconcile Net Income to Net Cash provided b...	
Accounts Receivable (A/R)	-5,281.52
Inventory Asset	-596.25
Accounts Payable (A/P)	1,302.67
Mastercard	157.72
Arizona Dept. of Revenue Payable	0.00
Board of Equalization Payable	370.94
Loan Payable	4,000.00
Total Adjustments to reconcile Net Income to Net Cash pro...	-46.44
Net cash provided by operating activities	**$1,896.02**
▾ INVESTING ACTIVITIES	
Truck:Original Cost	-13,495.00
Net cash provided by investing activities	**$ -13,495.00**

Section 10.9

MANAGEMENT REPORTS

Management reports are prepared as needed to provide management with information for making operating and business decisions. Reports used by management do not have to follow a specified set of rules, such as Generally Accepted Accounting Principles (GAAP) or the Internal Revenue Code.

Management reports include:

1. **Who Owes You reports.** Examples of this category of reports include Accounts Receivable Aging and Open Invoices.
2. **Sales and Customers reports.** This category of reports includes Income by Customer and Sales by Product/Service reports.
3. **What You Owe reports.** Examples of this QBO report category include Accounts Payable Aging and Unpaid Bills.
4. **Expenses and Vendors reports**. This report category includes Open Purchase Orders and Purchases by Product/Service.
5. **For My Accountant reports.** Examples of this type of report include the Trial Balance, Journal, and General Ledger reports. Although the Audit Log appears in the QBO Business Overview report category, typically, it could be considered a report used by an accountant.

> Although QBO has a **Management reports tab that contains bundled reports prepared by QBO, some management reports are included under the Standards reports tab.**

Section 10.10

WHO OWES YOU REPORTS

Who Owes You reports are used to track amounts that customers owe your business. Examples of this type of report includes Accounts Receivable Aging report, Collection reports, and Open Invoices.

ACCOUNTS RECEIVABLE (A/R) AGING

Accounts Receivable reports provide information about which customers owe our business money. When we make a credit sale, our company provides products and services to a customer in exchange for a promise that the customer will pay us later. Sometimes the customer breaks the promise and does not pay. Therefore, a business should have a credit policy to ensure that credit is extended only to customers who are likely to keep their promise and pay their bills.

After credit has been extended, a business needs to track accounts receivable to determine if accounts are being collected in a timely manner.

The Accounts Receivable Aging report provides information useful in tracking accounts receivable by providing information about the age of customer accounts. This report lists the age of accounts receivable balances. In general, the older an account, the less likely the customer will pay the bill. So it is important to monitor the age of accounts receivable and take action to collect old accounts.

To prepare the Accounts Receivable Aging report:

1. From the Navigation Bar, select **Reports**

2. Select **Standard** tab

3. Select **Report Category: Who Owes You**

4. Select **Accounts Receivable Aging Summary**

5. Enter **Customize** features using the Customization Bar across the top of the report or using the Customize button

6 Select **Save Customization** and follow onscreen instructions to save so the customized report will now appear under the Custom Reports tab

7 Select **Export** icon to display the export options: Export to Excel and Export to PDF

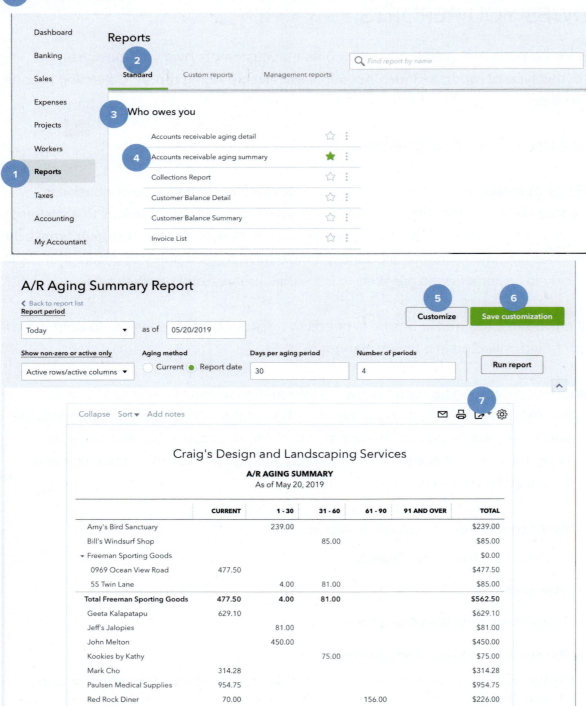

OPEN INVOICES

The Open Invoices report lists all unpaid invoices, displaying totals by customer. A report of this type provides information about invoices that have not been paid so collection efforts can be focused on these invoices.

To prepare the Open Invoices report:

1 From the Navigation Bar, select **Reports**

2 Select **Standard** tab

3 Select **Report Category: Who Owes You**

4 Select **Open Invoices**

5 Enter **Customize** features using the Customization Bar across the top of the report or using the Customize button

6 Select **Save Customization** and follow onscreen instructions to save so the customized report will now appear under the Custom Reports tab

7 Select **Export** icon to display the export options: Export to Excel and Export to PDF

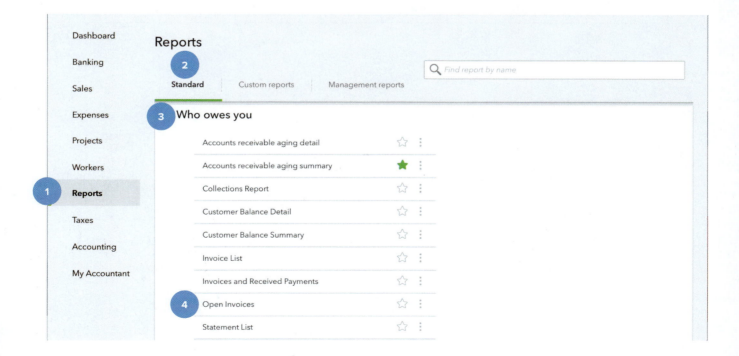

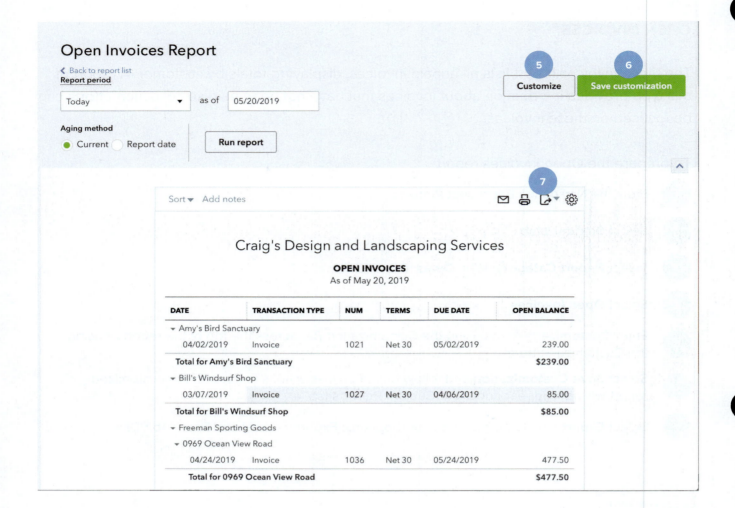

Section 10.11

SALES AND CUSTOMERS REPORTS

Sales and Customers reports provide detailed information about customers and sales transactions, including Customers List, Products and Services List, Deposit Detail, Income by Customer, Sales by Customer, and Sales by Product/Service reports.

INCOME BY CUSTOMER SUMMARY

To improve profitability in the future, a business may evaluate which customers have been profitable in the past. This information permits a business to improve profitability by:

- Increasing business in profitable areas
- Improving performance in unprofitable areas
- Discontinuing unprofitable areas

To determine which customers are generating the most profit for our business, it is necessary to look at both the sales for the customer and associated costs.

To prepare the Income by Customer Summary report:

1 From the Navigation Bar, select **Reports**

2 Select **Standard** tab

3 Select **Report Category: Sales and Customers**

4 Select **Income by Customer Summary**

5 Enter **Customize** features using the Customization Bar across the top of the report or using the Customize button

6 Select **Save Customization** and follow onscreen instructions to save so the customized report will now appear under the Custom Reports tab

7 Select **Export** icon to display the export options: Export to Excel and Export to PDF

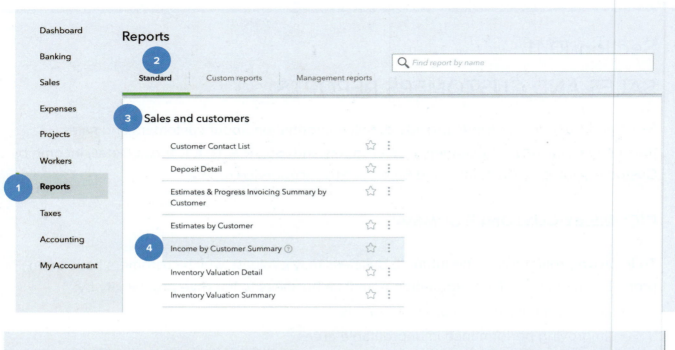

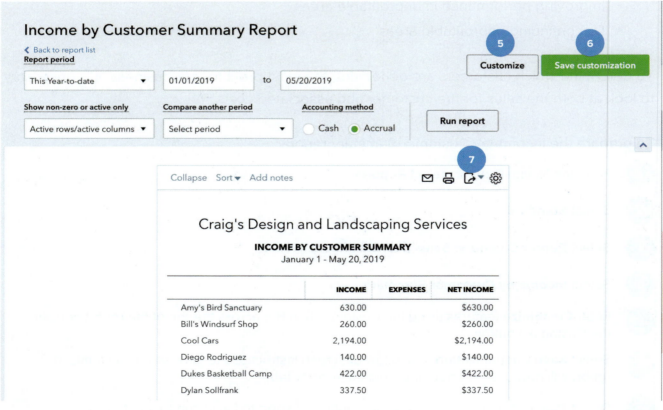

SALES BY PRODUCT/SERVICE SUMMARY

The Sales by Product/Service Summary report shows us which products are selling the most and which products are the most profitable. This information is useful for planning which products to order.

To prepare the Sales by Product/Service Summary report:

1 From the Navigation Bar, select **Reports**

2 Select **Standard** tab

3 Select **Report Category: Sales and Customers**

4 Select **Sales by Product/Service Summary**

5 Enter **Customize** features using the Customization Bar across the top of the report or using the Customize button

6 Select **Save Customization** and follow onscreen instructions to save so the customized report will now appear under the Custom Reports tab.

7 Select **Export** icon to display the export options: Export to Excel and Export to PDF

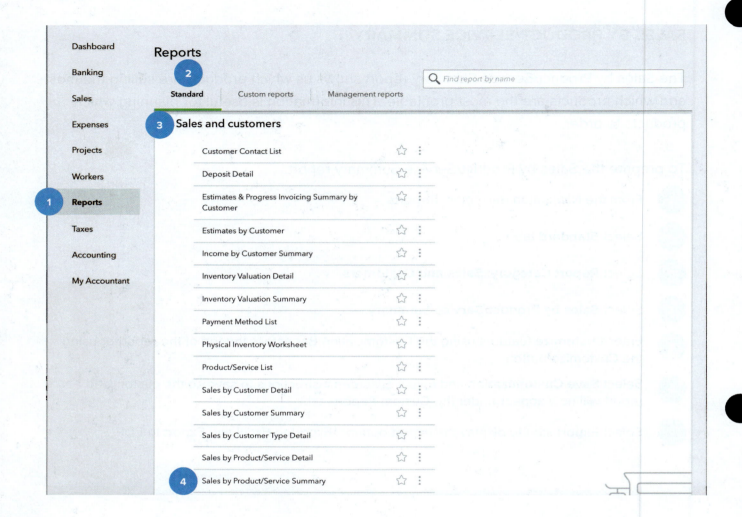

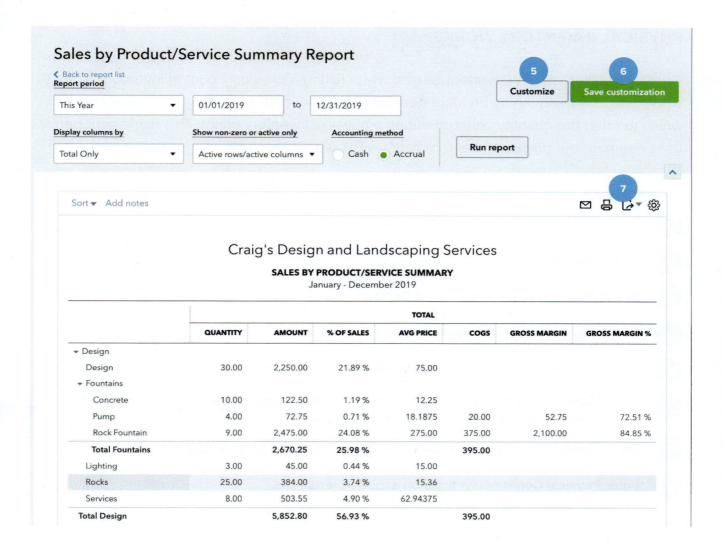

Sales by Product/Service Summary Report

‹ Back to report list

Report period

| This Year ▾ | 01/01/2019 | to | 12/31/2019 |

5 Customize   **6** Save customization

| **Display columns by** | **Show non-zero or active only** | **Accounting method** |
| Total Only ▾ | Active rows/active columns ▾ | ○ Cash ● Accrual |

Run report

Sort ▾   Add notes

7

Craig's Design and Landscaping Services

SALES BY PRODUCT/SERVICE SUMMARY

January - December 2019

	TOTAL						
	QUANTITY	AMOUNT	% OF SALES	AVG PRICE	COGS	GROSS MARGIN	GROSS MARGIN %
▾ Design							
Design	30.00	2,250.00	21.89 %	75.00			
▾ Fountains							
Concrete	10.00	122.50	1.19 %	12.25			
Pump	4.00	72.75	0.71 %	18.1875	20.00	52.75	72.51 %
Rock Fountain	9.00	2,475.00	24.08 %	275.00	375.00	2,100.00	84.85 %
Total Fountains		**2,670.25**	**25.98 %**		**395.00**		
Lighting	3.00	45.00	0.44 %	15.00			
Rocks	25.00	384.00	3.74 %	15.36			
Services	8.00	503.55	4.90 %	62.94375			
Total Design		**5,852.80**	**56.93 %**		**395.00**		

PHYSICAL INVENTORY WORKSHEET

The Physical Inventory Worksheet is used when taking a physical count of inventory. The worksheet lists the quantity on hand per QBO inventory data and provides a blank column in which to enter the quantity counted during a physical inventory count. This worksheet permits us to compare our physical inventory count with our QBO records.

To prepare the Physical Inventory Worksheet:

1 From the Navigation Bar, select **Reports**

2 Select **Standard** tab

3 Select **Report Category: Sales and Customers**

4 Select **Physical Inventory Worksheet**

5 To customize the report, select **Customize**

6 Select **Save Customization** and follow onscreen instructions to save so the customized report will now appear under the Custom Reports tab.

7 Select **Export** icon to display the export options: Export to Excel or Export to PDF

8 Enter **Physical Count** of inventory on exported report

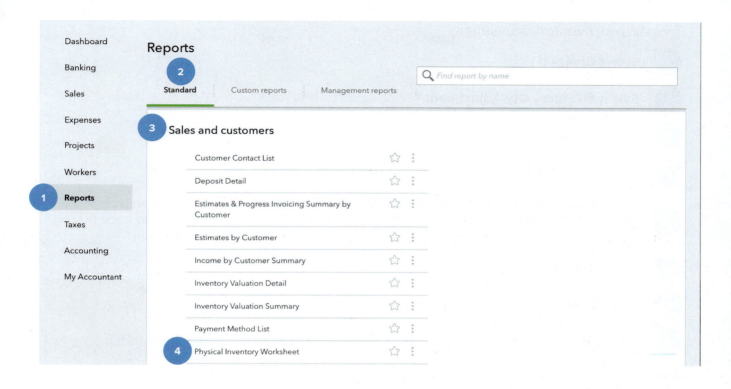

After completing the worksheet if we have any unresolved discrepancies, we can use the Inventory Adjustment feature to update our inventory records.

To make an inventory adjustment:

1 Select **Create (+)** icon

2 Select **Inventory Qty Adjustment**

3 Enter **Adjustment Date**

4 Enter **Reference No.** or use the Reference No. that QBO automatically assigns

5 Select **Inventory Adjustment Account**. We can adjust Cost of Goods Sold or we can add a new account entitled Inventory Shrinkage as an Expense account If we want to track the amount of inventory shrinkage separately from our Cost of Goods Sold account.

6 Select **Product** from the drop-down list

7 Verify **Description** which QBO should autofill from the Products and Services List

8 Verify **QTY on Hand** which QBO should autofill from our inventory tracking records

9 Enter **New QTY** from physical inventory worksheet

10 Verify **Change in QTY** which QBO will automatically calculate for us

11 Enter **Memo** to document the inventory adjustment

12 Normally we would select Save and new or Save and close, but in this case select **Cancel**

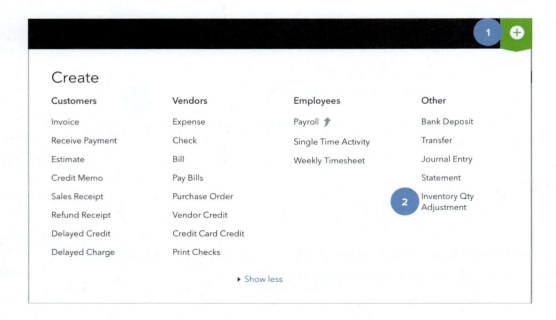

Section 10.12

WHAT YOU OWE REPORTS

What You Owe reports are used to track amounts that your business owes others, including Accounts Payable reports, Unpaid Bills report, and Vendor Balance reports.

ACCOUNTS PAYABLE (A/P) AGING

Accounts payable consists of amounts that our company is obligated to pay in the future. Accounts Payable reports tell us how much we owe vendors and when amounts are due.

The Accounts Payable Aging Summary summarizes accounts payable balances by the age of the account. This report helps to track any past due bills as well as provides information about bills that will be due shortly.

To prepare the Accounts Payable Aging Summary report:

1. From the Navigation Bar, select **Reports**

2. Select **Standard** tab

3. Select **Report Category: What You Owe**

4. Select **Accounts Payable Aging Summary**

5. Enter **Customize** features using the Customization Bar across the top of the report or using the Customize button

6. Select **Save Customization** and follow onscreen instructions to save so the customized report will now appear under the Custom Reports tab.

7. Select **Export** icon to display the export options: Export to Excel and Export to PDF

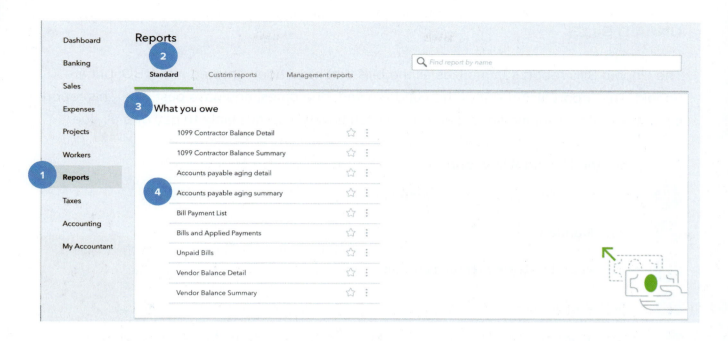

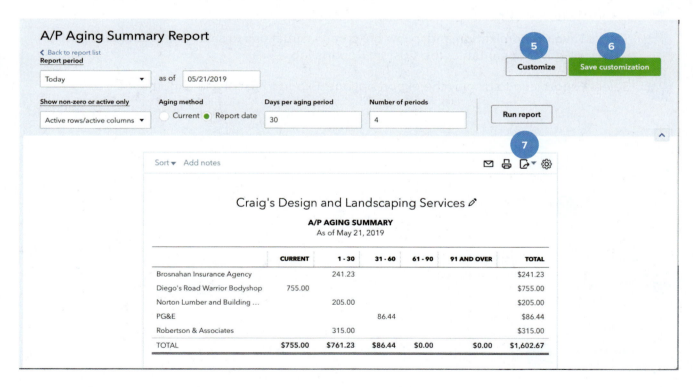

UNPAID BILLS

The Unpaid Bills report summarizes all the bills that have been entered into QBO, but are unpaid. The report also displays the vendor owed, due dates, and days past due. This report can be useful in planning so that adequate cash flow will be available to pay bills as due.

To prepare the Unpaid Bills report:

1   From the Navigation Bar, select **Reports**

2   Select **Standard** tab

3   Select **Report Category: What You Owe**

4   Select **Unpaid Bills**

5   Enter **Customize** features using the Customization Bar across the top of the report or using the Customize button

6   Select **Save Customization** and follow onscreen instructions to save so the customized report will now appear under the Custom Reports tab.

7   Select **Export** icon to display the export options: Export to Excel and Export to PDF

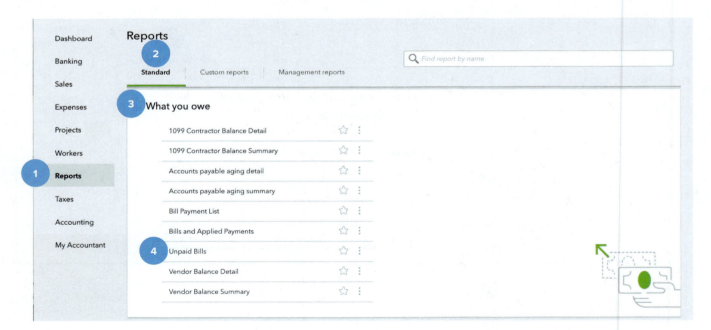

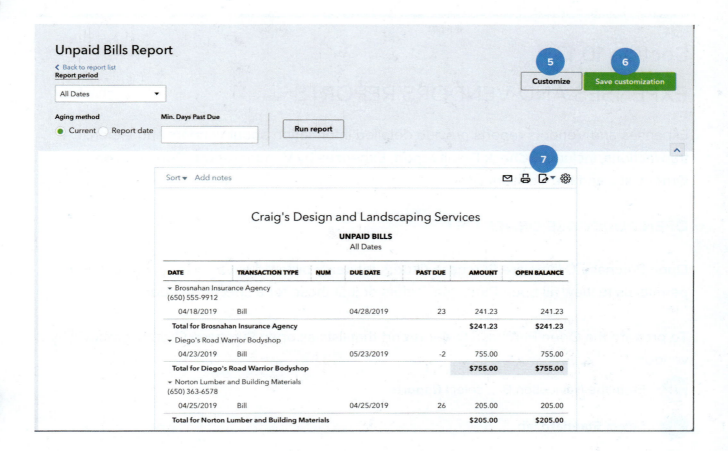

Section 10.13

EXPENSES AND VENDORS REPORTS

Expenses and Vendors reports provide detailed information about vendors and expenses transactions, including Check Detail report, Expenses by Vendor report, Open Purchase Order Lists, and the Vendors List.

OPEN PURCHASE ORDER LIST

Open Purchase Orders are Purchase Orders for items ordered but not yet received. QBO permits us to view all open Purchase Orders or just those for a specific vendor.

To prepare the Open Purchase Order report that lists all open Purchase Orders, grouped by vendor:

1. From the Navigation Bar, select **Reports**

2. Select **Standard** tab

3. Select **Report Category: Expenses and Vendors**

4. Select **Open Purchase Order List**

5. Enter **Customize** features using the Customization Bar across the top of the report or using the Customize button

6. Select **Save Customization** and follow onscreen instructions to save so the customized report will now appear under the Custom Reports tab.

7. Select **Export** icon to display the export options: Export to Excel and Export to PDF

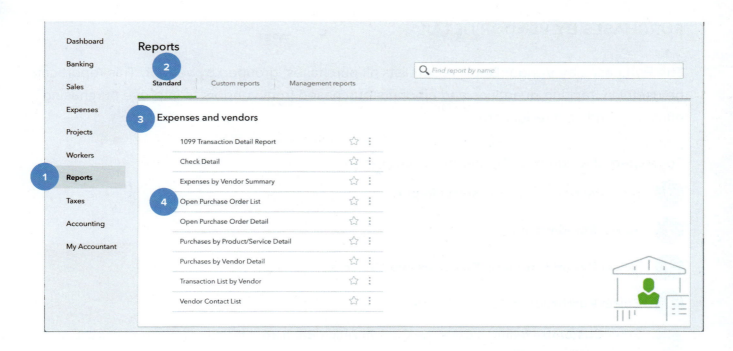

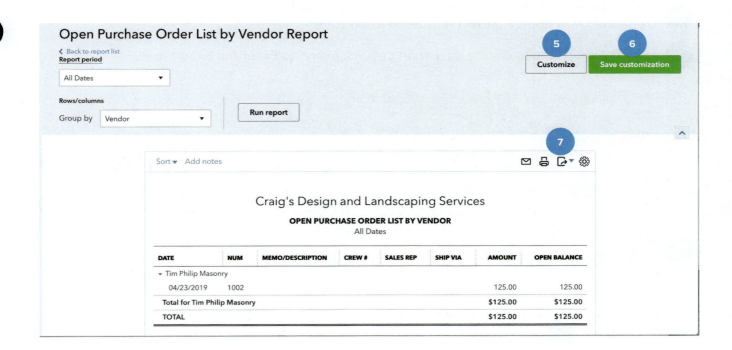

PURCHASES BY VENDOR DETAIL

The Purchases by Vendor Detail report lists all purchases, grouped by vendor. This report can be useful in tracking quantities and amounts purchased from vendors to improve purchasing efficiency and cost reductions.

To prepare the Purchase by Vendor Detail report:

1 From the Navigation Bar, select **Reports**

2 Select **Standard** tab

3 Select **Report Category: Expenses and Vendors**

4 Select **Purchases by Vendor Detail**

5 Enter **Customize** features using the Customization Bar across the top of the report or using the Customize button

6 Select **Save Customization** and follow onscreen instructions to save so the customized report will now appear under the Custom Reports tab.

7 Select **Export** icon to display the export options: Export to Excel and Export to PDF

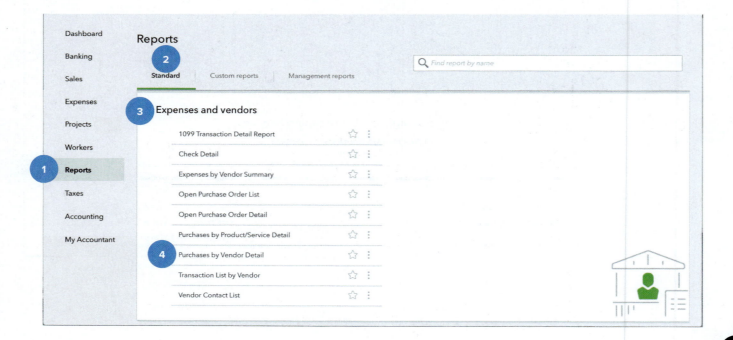

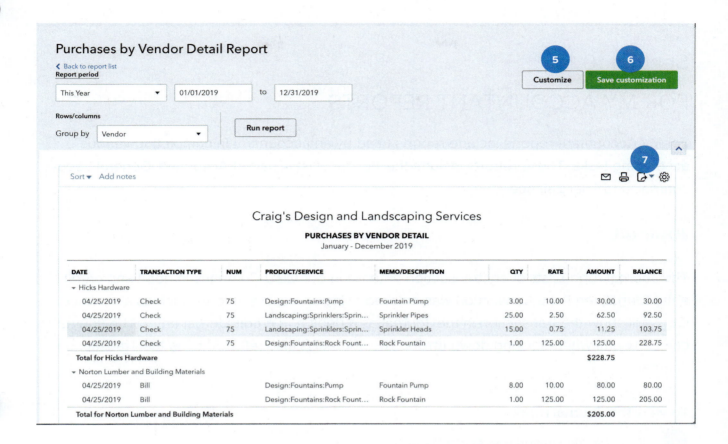

Purchases by Vendor Detail Report

< Back to report list

Report period

| This Year ▼ | 01/01/2019 | to | 12/31/2019 |

Rows/columns

Group by Vendor ▼ | Run report |

5 Customize   6 Save customization

7

Sort ▼ Add notes

Craig's Design and Landscaping Services

PURCHASES BY VENDOR DETAIL
January - December 2019

DATE	TRANSACTION TYPE	NUM	PRODUCT/SERVICE	MEMO/DESCRIPTION	QTY	RATE	AMOUNT	BALANCE
▼ Hicks Hardware								
04/25/2019	Check	75	Design:Fountains:Pump	Fountain Pump	3.00	10.00	30.00	30.00
04/25/2019	Check	75	Landscaping:Sprinklers:Sprin...	Sprinkler Pipes	25.00	2.50	62.50	92.50
04/25/2019	Check	75	Landscaping:Sprinklers:Sprin...	Sprinkler Heads	15.00	0.75	11.25	103.75
04/25/2019	Check	75	Design:Fountains:Rock Fount...	Rock Fountain	1.00	125.00	125.00	228.75
Total for Hicks Hardware							**$228.75**	
▼ Norton Lumber and Building Materials								
04/25/2019	Bill		Design:Fountains:Pump	Fountain Pump	8.00	10.00	80.00	80.00
04/25/2019	Bill		Design:Fountains:Rock Fount...	Rock Fountain	1.00	125.00	125.00	205.00
Total for Norton Lumber and Building Materials							**$205.00**	

Section 10.14

FOR MY ACCOUNTANT REPORTS

For My Accountant reports include reports used by an accountant in completing various accounting tasks. These reports include the Account List (Chart of Accounts), General Ledger, Journal, and Trial Balance.

JOURNAL

The Journal report lists every transaction entered in our QBO Company in debit and credit entry form. Even if the transaction was entered using an onscreen form, such as an Invoice, QBO will show the transaction in the Journal as a debit and credit journal entry. The Journal can be useful when tracking down errors. The Journal is also referred to as the Transaction Journal.

To view the Journal report:

1. From the Navigation Bar, select **Reports**

2. Select **Standard** tab

3. Select **Report Category: For My Accountant**

4. Select **Journal**

5. Select **Report Period**

6. To customize the report further, select **Customize**

7. Select **Save Customization** and follow onscreen instructions to save so the customized report will now appear under the Custom Reports tab.

8. Select **Export** icon to display the export options: Export to Excel or Export to PDF

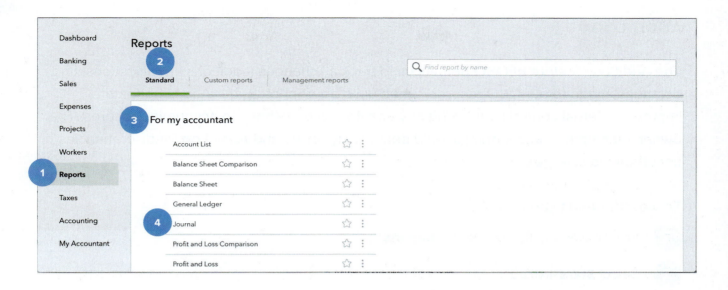

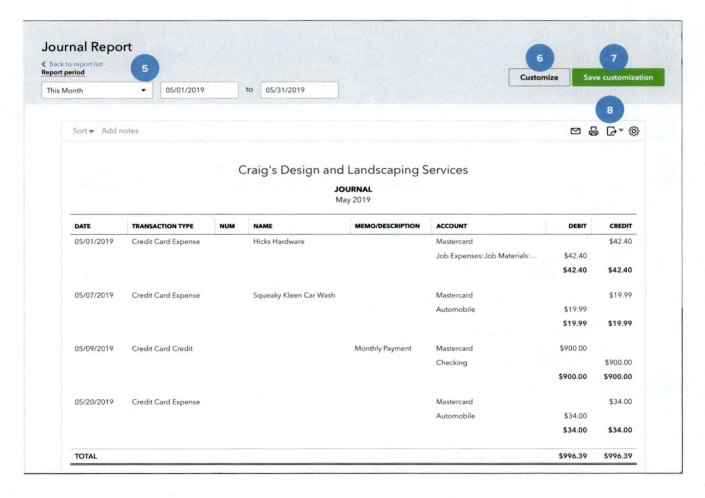

AUDIT LOG

The Audit Log feature of QBO permits us to track all changes (additions, modifications, and deletions) made to our QBO records. When used appropriately, the Audit Log feature improves internal control by tracking any unauthorized changes to accounting records. The owner, manager, or accountant should periodically review the Audit Log for discrepancies or unauthorized changes.

To view the Audit Log in QBO:

1 From the Navigation Bar, select **Reports**

2 Select **Standard** tab

3 Select **Report Category: Business Overview**

4 Select **Audit Log**

5 Select **Filter** to filter for specific dates and entries, such as Transactions

6 Select **View** to view the History of the log entry with a record of changes made by specific users

7 This completes the chapter activities. **Close** the QBO Sample Company web browser window to reset the Sample Company before proceeding to the exercises at the end of this chapter.

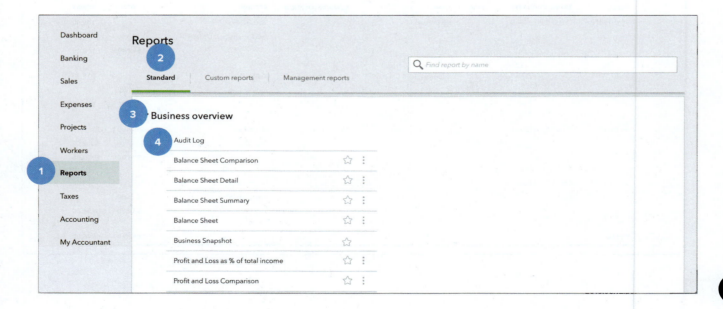

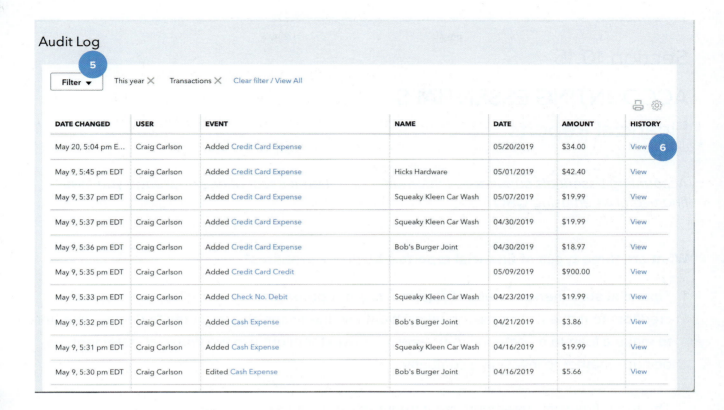

The Audit Log is especially useful if we have more than one QBO user. The Audit Log permits us to determine which user made which changes.

> **Although the Audit Log appears in the Business Overview report category in QBO, an Audit Log is a useful tool used by accountants.**

> **The Audit Log can also be accessed by selecting the Gear icon > Audit Log.**

This chapter provided an overview of some frequently used reports. QBO offers many more reports that provide useful information to a business. These additional reports can be accessed from the Reports screen.

Section 10.15

ACCOUNTING ESSENTIALS
Financial Reports

Accounting Essentials summarize important foundational accounting knowledge you may find useful when using QBO

What are three types of financial reports a business prepares?

1. **Financial statements.** Financial statements are reports used by investors, owners, and creditors to make decisions. A banker might use the financial statements to decide whether to make a loan to a company. A prospective investor might use the financial statements to decide whether to invest in a company.

   The three financial statements most frequently used by external users are:
   - **Profit and Loss** (also referred to as the P & L or Income Statement) lists income and expenses, summarizing the income a company has earned and the expenses incurred to earn the income.
   - **Balance Sheet** lists assets, liabilities, and owners' equity, summarizing what a company *owns* and *owes* on a particular date.
   - **Statement of Cash Flows** lists cash flows from operating, investing, and financing activities of a business.

2. **Tax forms.** The objective of the tax form is to provide information to federal and state tax authorities. When preparing tax returns, a company uses different rules from those used to prepare financial statements. When preparing a federal tax return, use the Internal Revenue Code.

   Tax forms include the following:
   - Federal income tax return
   - State income tax return

- Federal Payroll Forms 940, 941/944, W-2, W-3
- Federal Form 1099

3. Management reports. Management reports are used by internal users (managers) to make decisions regarding company operations. These reports are created to satisfy a manager's information needs.

Examples of reports that managers use include:

- Cash budget that projects amounts of cash that will be collected and spent in the future. (Note a Statement of Cash Flows focuses on cash inflows and outflows in the *past*. A Cash Budget focuses on expected cash flows in the *future.)*
- Accounts receivable aging report that lists the age and balance of customer accounts receivable so accounts are collected in a timely manner.

Practice Quiz 10

Q10.1

The physical inventory worksheet is used when:

a. Inventory items are physically placed in the warehouse

b. The computer network goes down

c. Taking a physical count of inventory on hand

d. All of the above

Q10.2

Which one of the following is not a financial statement?

a. Statement of Cash Flows

b. Profit & Loss

c. Trial Balance

d. Balance Sheet

Q10.3

The Chart of Accounts displays:

a. Account Name

b. Type

c. Detail Type

d. All of the above

Q10.4

The Balance Sheet lists:

a.   Assets, Revenues, and Owners' Equity

b.   Assets, Liabilities, and Owners' Equity

c.   Revenues, Expenses, and Net Income

d.   Revenues, Liabilities, and Net Income

Q10.5

Which one of the following classifications is not found on the Statement of Cash Flows?

a.   Cash Flows from Selling Activities

b.   Cash Flows from Financing Activities

c.   Cash Flows from Investing Activities

d.   Cash Flows from Operating Activities

Q10.6

Which of the following is correct?

a.   Statement of Cash Flows is reported on a particular date

b.   Income Statement is reported on a particular date

c.   Balance Sheet is reported on a particular date

d.   Balance Sheet is reported for a specific time period

Q10.7

QuickBooks Online uses which basis of accounting?

a.   Accrual

b.   Cash

c.   Both a and b

d.   Neither a nor b

Q10.8

The Profit and Loss Statement lists:

a.   Assets, Revenues, and Owners' Equity

b.   Assets, Liabilities, and Owners' Equity

c.   Revenues, Expenses, and Net Income

d.   Revenues, Liabilities, and Net Income

Q10.9

Management reports:

a.   Must follow a set of rules specified by Generally Accepted Accounting Principles

b.   Must follow the rules specified by the Internal Revenue Service

c.   Must follow the rules specified by vendors

d.   Do not have to follow a specified set of rules

Q10.10

Management reports include:

a.   Customer Profitability reports

b.   Accounts Receivable Aging reports

c. Accounts Payable Aging reports

d. Inventory reports

e. All of the above

Q10.11

Which of the following is a Customer report:

a. Accounts Receivable (A/R) Aging

b. Accounts Payable (A/P) Aging

c. Open Purchase Orders

d. None of the above

Q10.12

The Journal:

a. Lists every journal entry made only through the onscreen journal

b. Is also called the Audit Log

c. Lists every transaction entered in QBO through a journal or onscreen form, as a debit and credit entry

d. None the above

Q10.13

The Audit Log tracks:

a. Additions to our QBO records

b. Modifications to our QBO records

c. Deletions to our QBO records

d. All of the above

Q10.14

Which of the following reports can improve internal control by tracking unauthorized changes to accounting records?

a. Cash Budget

b. Cash Forecast

c. Audit Log

d. Journal

Exercises 10

> We use the QBO Sample Company, Craig's Design and Landscaping Services, **for practice throughout the exercises. The Sample Company will reset each time it is reopened. So make certain to allow enough time to complete exercise before closing the Sample Company. Otherwise, you will lose the work you have entered when you reopen the Sample Company.**

> ⚠️ **Since the Sample Company** resets each time it is reopened, be certain to close any web browser windows displaying the QBO Sample Company before starting these exercises. Closing the browser window and starting with a new browser window for the QBO Sample Company resets the data before starting the exercises.

To access the QBO Sample Company, complete the following steps.

1. Open a web browser. (Note: Intuit recommends using Google Chrome.)

2. Go to the https://qbo.intuit.com/redir/testdrive

3. Follow onscreen instructions for security verification

Craig's Design and Landscaping Services should appear on your screen.

E10.1 Accounting Cycle
Match the following accounting cycle steps with the appropriate description.

Accounting Cycle Descriptions

a. Prepared at the end of the accounting period before preparing financial statements to bring the accounts up to date.

b. Prepared during the accounting period to record exchanges with customers, vendors, employees, and owners.

c. A list of all accounts used to accumulate information about assets, liabilities, owners' equity, revenues, and expenses.

d. Prepared for external users and includes the Profit and Loss, Balance Sheet, and Statement of Cash Flows.

e. Prepared after adjustments to verify that the accounting system still balances.

f. Lists each account and the account balance at the end of the accounting period to verify that the accounting system is in balance—total debits should equal total credits.

Accounting Cycle Steps	Accounting Cycle Descriptions
1. Chart of Accounts	_____
2. Transactions	_____
3. Trial Balance	_____
4. Adjustments	_____
5. Adjusted Trial Balance	_____
6. Financial Statements	_____

E10.2

For the following accounts on Craig's Design and Landscaping Services Chart of Accounts, identify Account Type and Financial Statement on which it appears.

Account Types

- **Asset**
- **Liability**
- **Equity**
- **Income**
- **Expense**

Financial Statements

- **Balance Sheet**
- **Profit and Loss**

Account	Account Type	Financial Statement
1. Design Income		
2. Savings		
3. Accounts Receivable (A/R)		
4. Rent or Lease		
5. Prepaid Expenses		
6. Notes Payable		
7. Inventory Asset		
8. Opening Balance Equity		
9. Utilities		
10. Undeposited Funds		
11. Accounts Payable (A/P)		
12. Mastercard		
13. Visa		
14. Loan Payable		
15. Sales of Product Income		
16. Legal & Professional Fees		
17. Advertising		
18. Meals and Entertainment		
19. Retained Earnings		
20. Checking		
21. Landscaping Services		
22. Pest Control Services		
23. Cost of Goods Sold		
24. Automobile: Fuel		
25. Bank Charges		
26. Interest Earned		

E10.3 Statement of Cash Flows

For each of the following, identify the appropriate classification on the Statement of Cash Flows.

Statement of Cash Flows Classifications

a. Cash Flows from Operating Activities

b. Cash Flows from Investing Activities

c. Cash Flows from Financing Activities

Activity	Statement of Cash Flows Classification
1. Cash flows related to sales	
2. Cash paid to repay a long term loan	
3. Cash flows related to purchasing inventory to resell	
4. Cash flow from issuance of capital stock	
5. Cash paid to purchase new equipment	
6. Cash from sale of a warehouse	

E10.4 Trial Balance (Adjusted)

Using the QBO Sample Company, Craig's Design and Landscaping Services, complete the following.

Match the following steps to prepare a QBO Trial Balance with the order in which the steps should occur.

Steps to Prepare a QBO Trial Balance

- Select For My Accountant Reports
- Select Accrual
- Select Navigation Bar Reports
- Select Run Report
- Select Standard Tab
- Select Trial Balance
- Select Report Period

1. _____
2. _____
3. _____
4. _____
5. _____
6. _____
7. _____

E10.5 Profit and Loss Statement

Using the QBO Sample Company, Craig's Design and Landscaping Services, complete the following.

Match the following steps to prepare a QBO Profit and Loss Statement with the order in which the steps should occur.

Steps to Prepare a QBO Profit and Loss Statement

- Select Navigation Bar Reports
- Select Profit and Loss
- Select Report Period
- Select Run Report
- Select Standard Tab
- Select Business Overview
- Select Accrual

1. _____

2. _____

3. _____

4. _____

5. _____

6. _____

7. _____

E10.6 Balance Sheet

Using the QBO Sample Company, Craig's Design and Landscaping Services, complete the following.

Match the following steps to prepare a QBO Balance Sheet with the order in which the steps should occur.

Steps to Prepare a QBO Balance Sheet

- Select Business Overview
- Select Accrual
- Select Navigation Bar Reports
- Select Balance Sheet
- Select Standard Tab
- Select Run Report
- Select Report Period

1. _____

2. _____

3. _____

4. _____

5. _____

6. _____

7. _____

E10.7 Statement of Cash Flows

Using the QBO Sample Company, Craig's Design and Landscaping Services, complete the following.

Match the following steps to prepare a QBO Statement of Cash Flows with the order in which the steps should occur.

Steps to Prepare a QBO Statement of Cash Flows
- Select Business Overview
- Select Statement of Cash Flows Select
- Select Run Report
- Select Standard Tab
- Select Navigation Bar Reports
- Select Report Period

1. _____

2. _____

3. _____

4. _____

5. _____

6. _____

E10.8 Accounts Receivable (A/R) Aging

Using the QBO Sample Company, Craig's Design and Landscaping Services, complete the following.

Match the following steps to prepare a QBO A/R Aging Summary report with the order in which the steps should occur.

Steps to Prepare a QBO A/R Aging Summary Report
- Select Standard Tab
- Select Navigation Bar Reports

- Select Accounts Receivable Aging Summary
- Select Days Per Aging Period
- Select Who Owes You
- Select Run Report
- Select Report Period
- Select Aging Method
- Select Number of Periods

1. _____
2. _____
3. _____
4. _____
5. _____
6. _____
7. _____
8. _____
9. _____

E10.9 Open Purchase Orders

Using the QBO Sample Company, Craig's Design and Landscaping Services, complete the following.

Match the following steps to prepare a QBO Open Purchase Orders report with the order in which the steps should occur.

Steps to Prepare a QBO Open Purchase Orders Report

- Select Report Period
- Select Open Purchase Order List
- Select Navigation Bar Reports
- Select Run Report
- Select Standard Tab
- Select Expenses and Vendors

1. _____
2. _____
3. _____
4. _____
5. _____
6. _____

E10.10 Accounts Payable (A/P) Aging

Using the QBO Sample Company, Craig's Design and Landscaping Services, complete the following.

Match the following steps to prepare a QBO A/P Aging report with the order in which the steps should occur.

Steps to Prepare a QBO A/P Aging Report

- Select Navigation Bar Reports
- Select Standard Tab
- Select Number of Periods
- Select What You Owe
- Select Report Period
- Select Aging Method
- Select Days Per Aging Period
- Select Accounts Payable Aging Summary
- Select Run Report

1. _____
2. _____
3. _____
4. _____
5. _____
6. _____
7. _____
8. _____
9. _____

Project 10.1

Mookie the Beagle™ Concierge

> **Project 10.1 is a continuation of Project 9.1. You will use the QBO Company you created for Project 1.1 and updated in Projects 2.1 through 9.1. Keep in mind the QBO Company for Project 10.1 does not reset and carries your data forward, including any errors.**

BACKSTORY

Mookie The Beagle™ Concierge, the provider of convenient, high-quality pet care, has asked for your assistance in preparing QBO financial reports for the first month of its operations.

Complete the following for Mookie The Beagle Concierge.

 QBO SatNav

Project 10.1 focuses on QBO Reports as shown in the following QBO SatNav.

🌐 **QBO SatNav**

⚙️ **QBO Settings**

⚙️ Company Settings
⚙️ Chart of Accounts

💰 **QBO Transactions**

💰 Banking
💰 Customers & Sales
💰 Vendors & Expenses
💰 Employees & Payroll

📊 **QBO Reports**

📊 Reports

HOW TO LOG INTO QBO

To log into QBO, complete the following steps.

1 Using a web browser go to qbo.intuit.com

2 Enter **User ID** (the email address you used to set up your QBO Account)

3 Enter **Password** (the password you used to set up your QBO Account)

4 Select **Sign in**

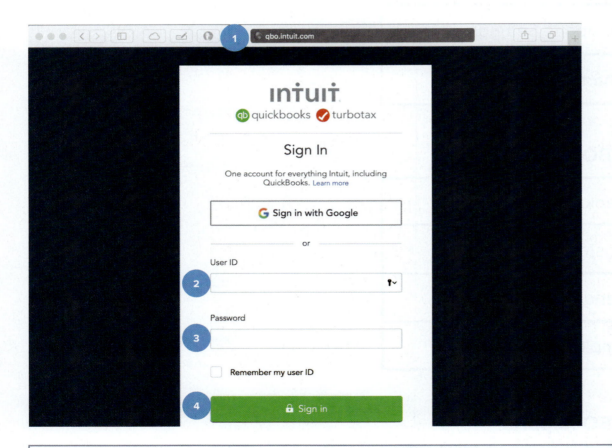

> **If you are <u>not</u> using a public or shared computer, to speed up login, you can save your login to your desktop and select Remember Me. If you are using a public computer or shared computer, do not save to the desktop and unselect Remember Me.**

QBO EXCEL TEMPLATE

For your convenience, a QBO Excel Template is provided with your text to organize your Project 10.1 Excel reports. Download the QBO Excel Template as follows:

- Go to www.my-quickbooksonline.com
- Select QBO 2e link
- Scroll down to QBO Excel Template
- Download the template

The QBO Excel Template can also be downloaded from www.mhhe.com/KayQBO2e.

Select the Instructions sheet in the QBO Excel Template to view the steps to copy your exported Excel reports to the Excel Template.

CHECK YOUR PROJECT 10.1 ACCOUNT BALANCES

We already made adjusting entries for Mookie The Beagle Concierge in Project 9.1, so we will start the Accounting Cycle in Project 10.1 with the Adjusted Trial Balance, a Trial Balance prepared after adjusting entries have been made.

Since any errors in your Mookie The Beagle Concierge QBO Company will be carried forward from prior Projects 1.1 through 9.1, in the following Project 10.1.1 make sure your Adjusted Trial Balance has the correct balances. Update account balances as needed to obtain the correct balances before proceeding to prepare other reports.

P10.1.1 Trial Balance (Adjusted)
Complete the following to prepare an Adjusted Trial Balance for Mookie The Beagle Concierge.

1. Create a Trial Balance (Adjusted).
   a. From the Navigation Bar, select **Reports > Standard tab > For My Accountant Reports > Trial Balance**
   b. Enter **Report Period: 01/31/2022 to 01/31/2022**
   c. Select **Active rows/active columns**
   d. Select **Accounting Method: Accrual**
   e. Select **Run report**

2. Verify Account Balances.

   Before creating QBO reports, verify that your QBO account balances are the same as the balances in the following Trial Balance (Adjusted) report. If your account balances are the same as the following Trial Balance, proceed to Step 3.

   If any of your QBO account balances differ from the following Trial Balance, then there must be one or more errors in your accounts.

TROUBLESHOOTING TIPS

If your QBO account balances differ from the following Trial Balance, try these troubleshooting tips:

- From your Trial Balance (Adjusted) report, drill down on any account balances that differ from the following Trial Balance amounts. Review the account for errors.

- Create a Journal report for the period from 01/01/2022 to 01/31/2022. Review the Journal for apparent discrepancies. In the Journal, you can drill down to the source document and correct any errors on the source document, such as a Check or Invoice.

- If necessary, make correcting journal entries as needed to update your accounts to the correct balances. See Chapter 9 Accounting Essentials for more information about correcting entries. To use the Journal to make any necessary correcting entries, select Create (+) icon > Journal Entry.

3. Trial Balance (Adjusted) Totals.
   a. What is the amount of Total Debits on the Trial Balance?
   b. What is the amount of Total Credits on the Trial Balance?

4. **Export** the Trial Balance (Adjusted) to PDF.

5. **Export** the Trial Balance (Adjusted) to Excel.
   a. With the Trial Balance report displayed, select the **Export icon**
   b. Select **Export to Excel**
   c. Download the QBO Excel Template to consolidate your Excel reports for Project 10.1. (See the preceding section entitled, QBO Excel Template, for instructions on how to download the template.)
   d. Select the Instructions sheet in the Excel Template. Complete the steps listed in the instructions to copy your Trial Balance Excel export to the Excel Template.

Mookie The Beagle Concierge [Your Name]

TRIAL BALANCE

As of January 31, 2022

	DEBIT	CREDIT
1001 Checking	16,367.80	
1002 Accounts Receivable (A/R)	1,372.76	
1005 Prepaid Expenses:Insurance	400.00	
1006 Prepaid Expenses:Rent	720.00	
1007 Prepaid Expenses:Supplies	472.00	
1009 Undeposited Funds	0.00	
Inventory Asset	780.00	
2001 Accounts Payable (A/P)		990.00
2002 VISA Credit Card		2,456.00
2003 Unearned Revenue		2,000.00
California Department of Tax and Fee Administration Payable		106.56
Interest Payable		10.00
Loan Payable		2,000.00
3001 Opening Balance Equity		0.00
3003 Owner's Investment		10,000.00
4002 Sales		7,770.00
Sales of Product Income		1,184.00
5001 Cost of Goods Sold	450.00	
5003 Advertising & Marketing	2,000.00	
5007 Contractors	2,640.00	
5010 Insurance:Liability Insurance Expense	200.00	
5011 Insurance:Renter Insurance Expense	16.00	
5012 Interest Paid	10.00	
5014 Legal & Professional Services	220.00	
5016 Office Supplies & Software	380.00	
5019 Rent & Lease	144.00	
5025 Utilities	344.00	

P10.1.2 Profit and Loss Statement

Complete the following to prepare a Profit and Loss Statement for Mookie The Beagle Concierge.

1. Create a Profit and Loss Statement.
   a. From the Navigation Bar, select **Reports > Standard tab > Business Overview > Profit and Loss**
   b. Enter **Report Period: 01/01/2022 to 01/31/2022**
   c. Select **Active rows/active columns**
   d. Select **Accounting Method: Accrual**
   e. Select **Run report**
   f. On the Profit and Loss Statement, what is Gross Profit?
   g. On the Profit and Loss Statement, what are Total Expenses?
   h. On the Profit and Loss Statement, what is Net Income?

2. **Export** the Profit and Loss Statement to PDF.

3. **Export** the Profit and Loss Statement to Excel.
   a. With the Profit and Loss report displayed, select the **Export icon**
   b. Select **Export to Excel**
   c. Complete the steps listed in the Instructions sheet of the QBO Excel Template to copy your Profit and Loss Statement Excel export to the Excel Template.

P10.1.3 Balance Sheet

Complete the following to prepare a Balance Sheet for Mookie The Beagle Concierge.

1. Create a Balance Sheet.
   a. From the Navigation Bar, select **Reports > Standard tab > Business Overview > Balance Sheet**
   b. Enter **Report Period: 01/31/2022 to 01/31/2022**
   c. Select **Active rows/active columns**
   d. Select **Accounting Method: Accrual**
   e. Select **Run report**
   f. On the Balance Sheet, what are Total Assets?
   g. On the Balance Sheet, what are Total Liabilities?

2. **Export** the Balance Sheet to PDF.

3. **Export** the Balance Sheet to Excel.
   a. With the Balance Sheet report displayed, select the **Export icon**
   b. Select **Export to Excel**
   c. Complete the steps listed in the Instructions sheet of the QBO Excel Template to copy your Balance Sheet Excel export to the Excel Template.

P10.1.4 Statement of Cash Flows

Complete the following to prepare a Statement of Cash Flows for Mookie The Beagle Concierge.

1. Create a Statement of Cash Flows.
   a. From the Navigation Bar, select **Reports > Standard tab > Business Overview > Statement of Cash Flows**
   b. Enter **Report Period: 01/01/2022 to 01/31/2022**
   c. Select **Active rows/active columns**
   d. Select **Run report**
   e. On the Statement of Cash Flows, what is the Net Cash Provided by Operating Activities?
   f. On the Statement of Cash Flows, what is the Net Cash Provided by Investing Activities?
   g. On the Statement of Cash Flows, what is the Net Cash Provided by Financing Activities?
   h. What was Cash at the end of the period?

2. **Export** the Statement of Cash Flows to PDF.

3. **Export** the Statement of Cash Flows to Excel.
   a. With the Statement of Cash Flows report displayed, select the **Export icon**
   b. Select **Export to Excel**
   c. Complete the steps listed in the Instructions sheet of the QBO Excel Template to copy your Statement of Cash Flows Excel export to the Excel Template.

P10.1.5 Accounts Receivable (A/R) Aging

Complete the following to prepare an Accounts Receivable (A/R) Aging report for Mookie The Beagle Concierge.

1. Create Accounts Receivable (A/R) Aging Report.
   a. From the Navigation Bar, select **Reports > Standard tab > Who Owes You Reports > Accounts Receivable Aging Summary**
   b. Enter **Report Period: 01/31/2022**
   c. Select **Active rows/active columns**
   d. Select **Aging Method: Report Date**
   e. Select **Days per Aging Period: 30**

    f. Select **Number of Periods: 4**

    g. Select **Run report**

    h. On the Accounts Receivable (A/R) Aging Summary, what is the amount of A/R that is Current?

    i. On the A/R Aging Summary, what is the amount of A/R that is 1-30 days past due?

2. **Export** the Accounts Receivable (A/R) Aging Summary to PDF.

3. **Export** the Accounts Receivable (A/R) Aging Summary to Excel.

    a. With the Accounts Receivable (A/R) Aging Summary report displayed, select the **Export icon**

    b. Select **Export to Excel**

    c. Complete the steps listed in the Instructions sheet of the QBO Excel Template to copy your Accounts Receivable (A/R) Aging Summary Excel export to the Excel Template.

P10.1.6 Accounts Payable (A/P) Aging

Complete the following to prepare an Accounts Payable (A/P) Aging report for Mookie The Beagle Concierge.

1.   Create Accounts Payable (A/P) Aging Report.

    a. From the Navigation Bar, select **Reports > Standard tab > What You Owe Reports > Accounts Payable Aging Summary**

    b. Enter **Report Period: 01/31/2022**

    c. Select **Active rows/active columns**

    d. Select **Aging Method: Report Date**

    e. Select **Days per Aging Period: 30**

    f. Select **Number of Periods: 4**

    g. Select **Run report**

    h. On the Accounts Payable (A/P) Aging Summary Report, what is the amount of A/P that is Current?

    i. On the A/P Aging Summary, what is the amount of A/P that is 1-30 days past due?

    j. On the A/P Aging Summary, what is the amount of A/P that is 31-60 days past due?

2. **Export** the Accounts Payable (A/P) Aging Summary to PDF.

3. **Export** the Accounts Payable (A/P) Aging Summary to Excel.

    a. With the Accounts Payable (A/P) Aging Summary report displayed, select the **Export icon**

    b. Select **Export to Excel**

    c. Complete the steps listed in the Instructions sheet of the QBO Excel Template to copy your Accounts Payable (A/P) Aging Summary Excel export to the Excel Template.

QBO Apps: Mac, Windows, and Mobile

QBO MAC OR WINDOWS APP

Whether using a Mac or Windows-based desktop or laptop, we can access QuickBooks Online using a browser and the Internet. In addition, QuickBooks Online also offers the option to download and install a QBO Mac App or a QBO Windows App on our desktop or laptop. The Mac and Windows Apps provide additional features. First, we must determine whether we will use the App with Mac or Windows. Then download either the QBO Mac App or the QBO Windows App to our desktop or laptop. After installing the App, use our QBO Company sign in.

The QBO Mac and Windows Apps provide a blended approach. We can still access our QBO company from anywhere, anytime through a browser. In addition, if we have the desktop QBO Mac or Windows App installed, we have additional features available, including a menu bar (similar to the QuickBooks Desktop version), the functionality to open multiple windows at the same time, and the ability to enter QBO data without an active Internet connection. Later, when you establish an Internet connection, the data will sync with QBO in the cloud. The QBO Mac and Windows Apps are available free with a QBO subscription.

Open multiple windows at the same time

- Drag and drop them anywhere, even across screens and side by side
- Switch quickly between multiple tasks
- Save time with automatic refresh of open windows

QBO MOBILE APP

In addition to the QBO Mac and Windows Apps, there is also a QBO Mobile App available for smartphones and tablets. The QBO mobile app permits us to add transactions, such as credit card expenses, on the go. Snap a picture of our credit card receipt and input the data into the QBO mobile app. When set up to sync with our QBO, the credit card expense then is updated in our QBO system.

QuickBooks Online versus QuickBooks Desktop

ASK MY ACCOUNTANT: WHICH QUICKBOOKS SHOULD I USE?

To meet different QuickBooks users' needs, Intuit offers several different versions of QuickBooks. If we are advising different clients on the best fit between their needs and QuickBooks version, then a general knowledge of the different types of QuickBooks available becomes vital to provide sound client advice.

In general, QuickBooks versions can be divided into two broad categories:

- **QuickBooks Client.** Businesses and organizations that use QuickBooks to maintain their accounting and financial records.
- **QuickBooks Accountant.** Accountants who provide accounting and financial services to multiple clients who use QuickBooks.

Since QuickBooks offers several different options (summarized in the following table), QuickBooks users often turn to their accountants for recommendations about which QuickBooks to use. The QuickBooks version that the client uses dictates which QuickBooks version the client's accountant must use. As the accountant making recommendations, we need to consider not only how the recommendation affects our client, but also how the recommendation will impact our client services.

	QuickBooks Online (QBO)	**QuickBooks Desktop (QBDT)**
Client	• QuickBooks Online (QBO) Simple Start • QuickBooks Online (QBO) Essentials • QuickBooks Online (QBO+) Plus • QuickBooks Online (QBO) Advanced	• QuickBooks Desktop (QBDT) Pro • QuickBooks Desktop (QBDT) Premier • QuickBooks Enterprise
Accountant	• QuickBooks Online Accountant (QBOA)	• QuickBooks Desktop Accountant (QBDTA)

Although features and functionality of QuickBooks options can be expected to change over time, the following sections summarize information about some of the QuickBooks options for clients and accountants. For additional updates about each of these options, see www.Intuit.com.

WHAT ARE MY QUICKBOOKS CLIENT OPTIONS?

A QuickBooks client is a business, entrepreneur, or not-for-profit organization that uses QuickBooks to maintain accounting and financial records for that entity. A QuickBooks client has two basic options:

- QuickBooks Desktop (QBDT)
- QuickBooks Online (QBO)

If the QuickBooks client selects the QuickBooks Desktop option, then there are several additional choices to consider that are summarized next.

QUICKBOOKS DESKTOP (QBDT)

QuickBooks Desktop software can be installed on the hard drive of desktop computers, laptops, or servers controlled by the client. If QuickBooks is installed on a network, it can be accessed by multiple QuickBooks users. QuickBooks Desktop can also be hosted in the cloud by Intuit authorized providers. QuickBooks Desktop software can be purchased using three different approaches:

1. CD. QuickBooks software is installed from a CD.
2. Software Download. Since new desktop computers and laptops increasingly do not have CD drives, users can purchase a QuickBooks software key code and download the QuickBooks software using an Internet browser.

3. Subscription. Instead of purchasing QuickBooks software, the user can choose to pay a monthly subscription fee to use the software. The QuickBooks software is still downloaded to the desktop computer or laptop, but when the user decides to stop paying the monthly fee, the user's access to the QuickBooks software is blocked.

In general, QuickBooks Desktop offers several advantages including:
-   Additional features and functionality not offered by QuickBooks Online
-   User control over desktop computer access and security
-   User control over backups and access to backup data files
-   Portability of backup and portable QuickBooks files
-   Navigation features to streamline use, such as the Home Page with flowcharts
-   Intuit offers the following different editions of the QuickBooks Desktop software to meet specific user needs, including:
    -   QuickBooks Pro
    -   QuickBooks Premier
    -   QuickBooks Enterprise

QuickBooks Desktop Pro is a good option for small businesses that do not require industry-specific features because it is less expensive.

QuickBooks Desktop Premier offers more advanced features than QuickBooks Pro and permits you to customize QuickBooks by selecting a version with industry-specific features. QuickBooks Premier has different industry versions from which you can choose including the following.
-   Contractor
-   Manufacturing and Wholesale
-   Nonprofit
-   Professional Services
-   Retailers
-   General Business

QuickBooks Enterprise is designed for mid-size companies that have outgrown QuickBooks Premier. QuickBooks Enterprise can be used to track inventory at multiple locations and consolidate reports from multiple companies.

QUICKBOOKS ONLINE (QBO)

Accessed using a browser and the Internet, with QuickBooks Online, there is no need to install software on a computer hard drive or local server. (See Appendix A for the QBO App that can be installed on a computer to enhance the features of QBO.) The main advantage to QuickBooks Online is its anytime, anywhere use, so long as Internet access is available. Factors to consider when using QuickBooks Online include:

- Internet connection needs to be a secure connection with data in transit encrypted. Using an open WiFi at a café or a hotel when traveling to access QuickBooks Online, while convenient, places data in transit at risk. Our login, password, and confidential financial data could be viewed by others.

- Fewer features and functionality than QuickBooks Desktop with features that will continue to change as QuickBooks Online is dynamically updated.

- The convenience of dynamic updates that occur automatically without needing to download and install.

- Loss of control over when updates occur, which may result in the need to learn new updates at unplanned times.

- Backups are performed automatically by Intuit.

- QBO Mobile app that makes it easier to stay up to date while on the go.

WHAT ARE MY QUICKBOOKS ACCOUNTANT OPTIONS?

Designed for accountants serving multiple clients, Intuit offers two QuickBooks Accountant options:

- QuickBooks Desktop Accountant (QBDTA)
- QuickBooks Online Accountant (QBOA)

Which option the accountant chooses is typically dictated by client use because QuickBooks Desktop files, in general, are not compatible with QuickBooks Online. For example, if all the accounting firm's clients use QuickBooks Desktop software, then the accounting firm would use QuickBooks Desktop Accountant version. If the clients use QuickBooks Online, then the accountant needs to use QuickBooks Online Accountant. Some accounting firms have clients using QuickBooks Desktop versions and other clients using QuickBooks Online, so those accounting firms must use both QuickBooks Desktop Accountant and QuickBooks Online Accountant to be able to work with both types of clients.

QUICKBOOKS DESKTOP ACCOUNTANT (QBDTA)

QuickBooks Desktop Accountant is the software used with Kay's *Computer Accounting with QuickBooks* text. Like QuickBooks Desktop software, QuickBooks Desktop Accountant is installed on the hard drive of desktop computers, laptops, or network servers. The QuickBooks Desktop Accountant edition permits the accountant to toggle between different desktop user editions of QuickBooks. This permits the accountant to view whatever edition of QuickBooks (QuickBooks Pro, QuickBooks Premier, and so on) that a particular client uses.

For more information about using QuickBooks Desktop, see Kay's *Computer Accounting with QuickBooks* at www.My-QuickBooks.com

How Can Our Accounting Firm Streamline Our QuickBooks Desktop Consulting?

Which QuickBooks version our clients use affects our consulting services operations. Some accounting firms relate nightmarish stories about clients using an array of QuickBooks Desktop software from the 2002 edition and every year to the present edition. This approach to QuickBooks consulting requires the accounting firm to maintain all the various versions of the client software and track which clients use which versions. This can become a logistical nightmare for an accounting firm since it must have not only all the QuickBooks editions operational but also staff trained on the multiple versions.

Other accounting firms take a more streamlined, proactive approach when working with multiple clients that use QuickBooks. These firms recommend to clients which QuickBooks edition to use based on the best fit for the client while still keeping it manageable for the firm. Some accountants move all their clients to the next edition of QuickBooks at the same time. For example, after the 2020 QuickBooks edition is released, the accounting firm thoroughly tests the new edition, and then the firm moves all clients to QuickBooks 2020 on January 1, 2020. This approach permits the accounting firm to test the new software for possible issues, install updates, and create workarounds before moving clients to the new edition. Since many clients are on a calendar year starting January 1, this timeline permits a nice cutoff. Also, this approach streamlines firm operations since now all clients and the firm are in sync, using the same version of QuickBooks.

This proactive approach requires the accounting firm to communicate clearly with clients, working as a team with clients to prepare and transition them to the new version. Firms that use this proactive approach often state that it requires time and effort to do so, but much less time than trying to maintain multiple versions of QuickBooks for multiple clients. If clients start moving to the new edition as soon as it is released, clients may encounter unexpected issues that the accounting firm has not had time to thoroughly investigate and resolve. Some firms even provide training for clients as they transition them to the new version, summarizing differences and new features to proactively prepare clients for what to expect. This can minimize client errors in working with the new version and save the firm from unexpected disruptions and surprises.

QUICKBOOKS ONLINE ACCOUNTANT (QBOA)

QuickBooks Online Accountant is designed for accounting firms that provide services to multiple clients who use QuickBooks Online. QuickBooks Online Accountant is accessed using the Internet and a browser and permits the accountant to collaborate with several different clients, viewing their QuickBooks Online company files. At this time QuickBooks Online Accountant does not use the Home Page navigational feature. In addition, there are fewer features and functionality with the QuickBooks Online Accountant version than the QuickBooks Desktop Accountant version.

QBOA offers more features than QBO for clients. For example, QBOA has Adjusted Trial Balance and Adjusting Journal Entry features. In addition, there are other Accountant Tools in QBOA.

The main advantage to QuickBooks Online Accountant is the anytime, anywhere access when an Internet connection is available. Of course, since the accountant is responsible for maintaining the confidentiality of client financial data, the Internet connection needs to be a secure connection with data in transit encrypted. Using an open WiFi connection risks data in transit (such as login, password, and confidential client financial data) being viewed by others. Since accounting firms have a responsibility to maintain client data confidentiality and security, this is a serious concern.

For more information about QuickBooks Online, go to www.my-quickbooksonline.com.

Index

A

access code, QBO+, P1.1
account(s)
    Account and Settings screen, 1.6
    adding, 2.5, P2.1.2–P2.1.5
    deleting/inactivating, 2.5
    editing, 2.5
    permanent, 2.6
    reasons for using, 2.6
    subaccounts, 2.3, 2.5, 2.6, P2.1.4–P2.1.5, 9.7,
        P9.1.1–P9.1.3
    temporary, 2.6
    types of, P1.1.5, 2.3, 2.6, P2.1.7–P2.1.8
    uncollectible, 5.10
Account and Settings screen, 1.6
accountants
    adjusting entry preparation, 9.4
    best QuickBooks version for clients, App. B
    For My Accountant reports, 10.3, 10.9, 10.14
    My Accountant (instructor) screen, 1.3, P1.1
    QuickBooks versions for, App. B
accounting
    accrual basis. *See* accrual basis accounting
    banking *vs.* accounting records, 4.7
    cash basis. *See* cash basis accounting
    corrections/correcting entries, 9.11
    double-entry, 3.12, P3.1.8, 9.7–9.10, 9.11
    Generally Accepted Accounting Principles
        (GAAP), 10.9
    primary objective, 2.6
accounting cycle, 9.3, 9.4, 10.4
Accounting Essentials
    accounting adjustments and corrections, 9.11
    banking for business, 4.7
    business tax returns and filing requirements, 1.7
    Chart of Accounts (COA), 2.6
    customer sales and accounts receivable, 5.10
    double-entry accounting, 3.12, 9.11

    financial reports overview, 10.15
    inventory and internal control, 7.11
    legal entity types, 1.7
    payroll liabilities and payroll taxes, 8.10
    vendor transactions, accounts payable, and
        1099s, 6.10
accounting periods, 4.7
    timing of adjusting entries, 9.4
Accounting screen overview, 1.3
account numbers, entering and displaying, 2.3, 2.1.6
accounts payable (A/P)
    Accounts Payable Aging report, 6.10, 10.12,
        P10.1.6
    adding account, P2.1.3
    adjusting entries, P9.1.5–P9.1.7
    recording bills, 7.6.P7.1.5–P7.1.7
    Unpaid Bills report, 10.12
accounts receivable (A/R)
    Accounts Receivable Aging report, 5.10, 10.10,
        10.15, P10.1.5
    adding accounts, P2.1.2
    bad debts, 5.10
    defined, 5.10
    Open Invoices report, 10.10
    Receive Payments and, 5.4, 5.9, P5.1.4–P5.1.7,
        7.3, 7.9, P7.1.12
account types, P1.1.5, 2.3, 2.6, P2.1.7–P2.1.8
accrual basis accounting
    accrued expenses, 9.6, 9.9, P9.1.5–P9.1.7
    accrued revenues, 9.6, 9.10
    cash basis accounting *vs.,* 9/6, 9.11, 10.8
    described, 9.6, 10.8
    measuring profit and loss, 10.8
    prepaid items, 9.6, 9.7, P9.1.1–P9.1.3
    unearned items, 9.6, 9.8, P9.1.4
Adjusted Trial Balance
    in accounting cycle, 9.3, 9.4, 10.4
    preparing, 10.7, P10.1.1

adjustments/adjusting entries, 9.3–9.11
  in accounting cycle, 9.3, 10.4
  methods of preparing, 9.4
    Journal, 9.4, 9.5, 9.7–9.10, 9.11,
      P9.1.1–P9.1.9, 10.6
    recurring transactions, 9.5
  as Other transactions, 3.10
  reason to use, 9.4, 9.11
  types, 9.6–9.10
    accrued expenses, 9.6, 9.9, P9.1.5–P9.1.7
    accrued revenues, 9.6, 9.10
    prepaid items, 9.6, 9.7, P9.1.1–P9.1.3
    unearned items, 9.6, 9.8, P9.1.4
Advanced settings, 1.1, P1.1.4
  automatic log out prevention, 1.1, 2.2
aging reports
  accounts payable, 6.10, 10.12, P10.1.6
  accounts receivable, 5.10, 10.10, 10.15, P10.1.5
allowance method, bad debt, 5.10
Apple, QBO app for, App. A
apps, QBO mobile, 8.7, App A.
assets and asset accounts
  accrued revenues and, 9.6, 9.10
  adding, P2.1.2, P2.1.4
  adjusting entries, 9.7, 9.10
  assets, defined, 2.6
  as Balance Sheet accounts, 2.6
  depreciation, 9.6
  double-entry accounting, 3.12, 9.7, 9.10
  entering and displaying numbers, P2.1.6
  prepaid items and, 9.7
  types of, 2.6
Audit Log, 10.14
automatic downloads, bank or credit card account, 4.6

B

bad debts
  allowance method, 5.10
  direct write-off method, 5.10
  uncollectible accounts, 5.10
Balance Sheet
  account types, 2.6
  described, 1.2, 2.6, 10.15
  preparing, 10.8, P10.1.3
  as primary financial statement, 1.2, 2.6

Banking screen, 1.3
Banking transactions, 3.5, 4.1–4.7, P4.1.1–P4.1.7.
    See also credit cards
  accessing, 1.3
  accounting records *vs.* bank statements, 4.7
  adding accounts, P2.1.2
  automatic downloads, 4.6
  bank accounts as Balance Sheet accounts, 2.6
  bank deposits
    from customer sales, 4.4, 5.8–5.9, P5.1.8, 7.3,
      7.10
    recording, 3.6, P3.1.2, 4.4, P4.1.1
    in transit, 4.7
    undeposited funds, P2.1.2, 3.6,
      5.8–5.9, 7.10
    unrecorded charges, 4.7
    unrelated to customer sales, 4.4, P4.1.1
Banking screen, 1.3
banking *vs.* accounting records, 4.7
bank reconciliation, 4.7
checking accounts
  bank reconciliation, 4.7
  Check form, 4.5, 6.4, 6.6, 6.8
  Check Register, 2.3, 4.3
  debit card vendor transaction, P6.1.4
  expense paid with check, P3.1.3,
    P4.1.4–P4.1.5, P6.1.3
  match credit card transactions, 4.6,
    P4.1.6–P4.1.7
  number of accounts needed, 4.7
  outstanding checks, 4.7
  recording checks, 4.5, P4.1.4–P4.1.5
connecting with credit card accounts, 4.6,
  P4.1.6–P4.1.7
creating, 3.6
double-entry accounting, 3.12
interest earned on the account, 4.7
money in, 4.4
money out, 4.5
Navigation Bar access, 1.3
number of accounts needed for business, 4.7
overview, 1.3
payroll. *See* Employees & Payroll transactions
sales receipts and, 5.4, 5.8, P5.1.1–P5.1.2
SatNav overview, 1.2, 3.1, 3.6, 4.1

Banking transactions—*Cont.*
　Undeposited Funds account, P2.1.2, 3.6,
　　5.8–5.9, 7.10
　unrecorded charges, 4.7
bank reconciliation, 4.7
bills. *See also* invoices and invoicing
　Bill form, 6.4, 6.6, 6.9, P6.1.6, 7.6, 7.7
　creating bills, 6.9, P6.1.6
　recording, 7.6, P7.1.5–P7.1.7
　vendor transactions, 6.4, 6.6, 6.9, P6.1.6, 7.3,
　　7.6, 7.7, P7.1.5–P7.1.7
budgets, cash, 10.15
bundle, Products and Services List, 5.6, 7.4
business tax returns. *See* taxes and tax forms

C

capital stock account, double-entry
　　accounting, 3.12
cash basis accounting
　accrual basis accounting *vs.,* 9.6, 9.11, 10.8
　described, 9.6, 10.8
　measuring profit and loss, 10.8
cash budgets, 10.15
cash flows. *See also* Statement of Cash Flows
　sources of, 10.8
C corporations, tax return forms, 1.7, 2.4
Chart of Accounts (COA)
　accessing, 1.3
　in accounting cycle, 9.3, 10.4
　adding accounts, 2.5, P2.1.2–P2.1.5
　creating, 1.6
　customizing, P2.1
　deleting/deactivating accounts, 2.5
　described, 1.2, 2.6, 3.3
　displaying account numbers, 2.3, P2.1.6
　double-entry accounting, P3.1.8
　editing accounts, 2.5
　entering account numbers, 2.3, P2.1.6
　Navigation Bar access, 1.3
　run report, 1.6
　SatNav overview, 1.2, 2.1
　tax return alignment with, 2.4, P2.1.1
　updating, 3.3
　viewing, 1.6, P1.1.5, 2.3, 3.3
Check form, 4.5, 6.4, 6.6, 6.8
checking accounts. *See* Banking transactions

Check Register
　adding new transactions, 4.3
　drill down, 4.3
　viewing, 2.3, 4.3
Client List. *See* Customers List
Company Settings
　accessing, 1.6
　described, 1.2
　overview, 1.6, P1.1.1–P1.1.4
　SatNav overview, 1.2
corporations
　C corporation tax return forms, 1.7, 2.4
　defined, 2.6
　nonprofit tax filings, 1.7
　S corporation tax return forms, 1.7, 2.4
corrections/correcting entries, 9.11
Craig's Design and Landscaping Services. *See*
　　Sample Company (Craig's Design and
　　Landscaping Services)
Create (+) icon, 1.4
　entering transactions by, 3.4
　　expense transactions, 6.3
　　sales transactions, 5.3
creating lists, 3.3
credit cards. *See also* Banking transactions
　adding credit card account, P2.1.3
　automatic downloads, 4.6
　connecting with bank accounts, 4.6, P4.1.6–P4.1.7
　expense transactions, P3.1.4, 4.5, P4.1.2–P4.1.3
　match bank transactions, 4.6, P4.1.6–P4.1.7
Credit Memo form, 5.4
credit transactions
　for adjusting entries, 9.7–9.10, 9.11,
　　P9.1.1–P9.1.9
　Chart of Accounts, P3.1.8
　double-entry accounting, 3.12, P3.1.8,
　　9.7–9–10, 9.11
Customers List, 7.4
　described, 3.3
　exporting, P5.1.9
　updating, 3.3, 5.5
　viewing, 3.3
Customers & Sales transactions, 3.5, 5.1–5.10,
　　P5.1.1–P5.1.9. *See also* revenue and revenue
　　(income) accounts
　accessing, 1.3

Company Settings, P1.1.2
inventory. *See* inventory transactions, customers transactions
Navigation Bar access, 1.3
sales
    accounts receivable and, 5.4, 5.9, 5.10
    bank deposits from, 4.4, 5.8–5.9, P5.1.8, 7.3
    Credit Memo form, 5.4
    Delayed Charge form, 5.4
    Delayed Credit form, 5.4
    Estimate form, 5.4
    invoices, 3.7, 5.4, 5.7, P5.1.3–P5.1.4
    navigating, 5.3
    Receive Payment form, 5.4, 5.9, P5.1.5–P5.1.7, 7.3, 7.9, P7.1.2
    recording, 5.7
    Refund Receipt form, 5.4
    sales receipts, 5.4, 5.7, 5.8, P5.1.1–P5.1.2
    transaction types, 5.4
Sales and Customers reports, 10.3, 10.9, 10.11
Sales screen overview, 1.3
SatNav overview, 1.2, 3.1, 3.7, 5.1, 7.1

D

Dashboard screen, 1.3, P1.1
debit card, vendor transaction, P6.1.4
debit transactions
    for adjusting entries, 9.7–9–10, 9.11, P9.1.1–P9.1.9
    Chart of Accounts, P3.1.8
    double-entry accounting, 3.12, P3.1.8, 9.7–9.10, 9.11
Delayed Charge form, 5.4
Delayed Credit form, 5.4
deleting/inactivating accounts, 2.5
deposits. *See* Banking transactions, bank deposits
depreciation, 9.6
direct deposit, paying employees by, 8.7
direct write-off method, bad debt, 5.10
double-entry accounting
    adjusting entries, 9.7–9.10, 9.11
    Chart of Accounts (COA), 3.12, P3.1.8
    described, 3.12

E

editing accounts, 2.5
employee paychecks, 8.5, 8.7. *See also* Employees & Payroll transactions
Employees List, 3.3, 8.4
Employees & Payroll transactions, 3.5, 8.1–8.10
    accessing, 1.3
    Employees List, 3.3, 8.4
    Employees report, 10.3
    Navigation Bar access, 1.3
    payroll, 8.1–8.10, P8.1.1–P8.1.7
        accessing, 3.9
        creating, 3.9
        direct deposit payments to employees, 8.7
        employee paychecks, 8.5, 8.7
        employee time tracking, 8.3, 8.5, P8.1.1–8.1.7
        mobile payroll app, 8.7
        payroll tax forms and filing requirements, 8.3, 8.9–8.10
        payroll tax liabilities, 8.3, 8.8–8.10
        processing, 8.3
        setup, 8.3, 8.6
        Taxes screen overview, 1.3
    Payroll report, 10.3
    SatNav overview, 1.2, 3.1, 3.9, 8.1
    Workers screen overview, 1.3
equity accounts
    adding owner distributions account, P2.1.3
    as Balance Sheet accounts, 2.6
    calculating equity, 2.6
    defined, 2.6
    double-entry accounting, 3.12
    entering and displaying numbers, P2.1.6
    increases/decreases in owners' equity, 2.6
    types of, 2.6
errors
    bank account, 4.7
    corrections/correcting entries, 9.11
    error message, invite accountant (instructor), P1.1
Estimate form, 5.4
Excel Template, P10.1
Expense form
    vendor transaction, 3.8, 6.4, 6.6, 6.7, P6.1.1
    viewing, 3.4, 4.5

expenses and expense accounts. *See also* Vendors
    & Expenses transactions
    accrued expenses, 9.6, 9.9, P9.1.5–P9.1.7
    adjusting entries and, 9.7, 9.9, P9.1.1,
        P9.1.5–P9.1.8
    check payment transactions, P3.1.3,
        P4.1.4–P4.1.5, P6.1.3
    Company Settings, P1.1.3
    creating expense transactions, 3.8
    credit card payment transactions, P3.1.4, 4.5,
        P4.1.2–P4.1.3
    double-entry accounting, 3.12, 9.7, 9.9
    entering and displaying numbers, P2.1.6
    examples, 2.6
    expense accounts, defined, 2.6
    Expense form to record expenses, 3.8, 6.4, 6.6,
        6.7, P6.1.1
    money out, 4.5
    navigating, 6.3
    Navigation Bar access, 1.3
    payroll. *See* Employees & Payroll transactions
    prepaid items
        adding accounts, P2.1.2
        adjusting entries, 9.7
        insurance subaccount, P2.1.4, 9.7, P9.1.1
        rent subaccount, P2.1.4, 9.7, P9.1.3
        supplies subaccount, P2.1.4, 9.7, P9.1.2
    as Profit and Loss accounts, 2.6
    recurring expenses, P6.1.5
Expenses and Vendors reports, 10.3, 10.9, 10.13
Expenses screen, 1.3
exporting lists
    Customers List, P5.1.9
    Products and Services List, 3.3
    Vendors List, P6.1.8
external users, 2.6

F

FICA taxes, 8.3, 8.8, 8.9, 8.10
financial reports. *See* financial statements; manage-
    ment reports; taxes and tax forms
financial statements, P2.1.8
    in accounting cycle, 9.3, 10.4
    Balance Sheet, 1.2, 2.6, 10.8, 10.15, P10.1.3
    described, 1.2, 10.15

    management reports *vs.*, 1.2, 2.6, 10.15
    navigating Reports, 10.3
    overview, 1.2
    preparing, 10.8
    primary, 1.2, 2.6
    Profit and Loss Statement (P&L), 1.2, 2.6, 10.8,
        10.15, P10.1.2
    QBO reports for, 1.6
    Statement of Cash Flows, 1.2, 2.6, 10.8, 10.15,
        P10.1.4
financing activities, cash flows from, 10.8
For My Accountant reports, 10.3, 10.9, 10.14
forms
    business tax returns, 1.7, 2.4, P2.1.1, 8.9–8.10
    Check form, 4.5, 6.4, 6.6, 6.8
    Expense form, 3.4, 4.5
    Journal form, 3.4
    paychecks, 8.5

G

Gear icon, 1.4, 1.6
    entering transactions by, 3.4
    Lists section, 3.3
Generally Accepted Accounting Principles (GAAP),
    10.9

H

Help and Support feature, 1.5

I

income accounts. *See* revenue and revenue (income)
    accounts
Income by Customer Summary report, 10.11
Income Statement. *See* Profit & Loss Statement (P&L)
input, transactions as, 1.2
interest expense, adjusting entries, P9.1.5
interest income, bank account, 4.7
internal control, inventory and, 7.11
internal users, 2.6
inventory transactions, 7.1–7.10, P7.1.1–P7.1.12
    customers transactions
        bank deposit from sale, 7.3, 7.10
        Customers List. *See* Customers List
        invoice from sale, 7.3, 7.8, P7.1.9–7.1.11
        receive payment from sale, 7.3, 7.9, 7P.1.12

defined, 5.6, 7.4

internal control and, 7.11

inventory records, 7.3

navigating inventory tasks, 7.3

Physical Inventory Worksheet, 10.11

as product or service, 5.6, 7.4. *See also* Products and Services List

SatNav overview, 7.1

tracking, turning on, P7.1.1

vendors transactions

    bill, 7.3, 7.6, P7.1.5–P7.1.7

    pay bills, 7.3, 7.7, P7.1.8

    purchase order, 7.3, 7.5, P7.1.2–P7.1.4

    Vendors List. *See* Vendors List

investing activities, cash flows from, 10.8

invite accountant (instructor), 1.3, P1.1

invoices and invoicing

    accounts receivable, 5.4, 5.9, 5.10

    creating bank deposit for undeposited funds from Receive Payments, 3.6, 5.9, 7.10

    creating invoices, 3.7, P3.1.5–P3.1.6, 5.9, P5.1.3–P5.1.4, 7.3

    customer transactions, 7.3, 7.8, P7.1.9–P7.1.11

    Invoice form, 5.4

    Invoices tab, 1.3

    sales transactions, 3.7, 5.4, 5.7, P5.1.3–P5.1.4

    tracked time and, P8.1.7

    creating Receive Payments, 5.9, 7.9

    Open Invoices report, 10.10

IRS Form 940: Employer's Annual Federal Unemployment (FUTA) Tax Return, 8.9–8.10

IRS Form 941: Employer's Quarterly Federal Tax Return, 8.9–8.10

IRS Form 944: Employer's Annual Federal Tax Return, 8.9–8.10

IRS Form 1040: U.S. Individual Income Tax Return, Schedule C, 1.7, 2.4

IRS Form 1065: U.S. Return of Partnership Income, 1.7, 2.4

IRS Form 1099-MISC, Miscellaneous Income, 6.10

IRS Form 1120: U. S. Corporation Income Tax Return, 1.7, 2.4

IRS Form 1120S: U.S. Income Tax Return for an S Corporation, 1.7, 2.4

IRS Form W-2: Wage and Tax Statement, 8.9–8.10

IRS Form W-3: Transmittal of Wage and Tax Statements, 8.9–8.10

J

Journal, QBO

    for adjusting entries, 9.4, 9.5, 9.7–9.10, 9.11, P9–1.1–P9–1.9, 10.6

    for corrections/correcting entries, 9.11

    double-entry accounting, 3.12, P3.1.8, 9.7–9.10, 9.11

    Journal Report, P9.1.9, 10.14

    onscreen Journal form, 3.4

    viewing journal entry, 3.4

Journal Report, P9.1.9, 10.14

L

legal entities

    QBO settings, 1.6

    tax returns and filing requirements, 1.7, 2.4

    types, 1.7

liabilities and liability accounts

    accrued expenses and, 9.6, 9.9, P9.1.5–P9.1.7

    adding, P2.1.3

    adjusting entries and, 9.8, 9.9, P9.1.4–P9.1.8

    as Balance Sheet accounts, 2.6

    double-entry accounting, 3.12, 9.8, 9.9, P9.1.4

    entering and displaying numbers, P2.1.6

    liabilities, defined, 2.6

    payroll, 8.3, 8.8–8.10

    types of, 2.6

    unearned items, 9.6, 9.8, P9.1.4

limited liability companies (LLCs), 1.7

limited liability partnerships (LLPs), 1.7

Lists, QBO

    Chart of Accounts, 3.3. *See also* Chart of Accounts (COA)

    creating, 3.3

    Customers List, 3.3, 5.5, P5.1.9, 7.4

    Employees List, 3.3, 8.4

    exporting, 3.3, P5.1.9, P6.1.8

    overview, 3.3

    Products and Services List, 3.3, P3.1.1, 5.6, 7.4, P7.1.1

    updating, 3.3, 3.4, 5.5–5.6, 6.5, 7.4

Lists, QBO—*Cont.*
　　Vendors List, 3.3, 6.5, P6.1.8, 7.4
　　viewing, 3.3
LLCs (limited liability companies), 1.7
LLPs (limited liability partnerships), 1.7
loan payable, recording, P4.1.1
login instructions
　　Mookie the Beagle™ Concierge (QBO Project
　　　　Company), P1.1.1
　　preventing log out for inactivity, 1.1, 2.2
　　Remember Me, P1.1
　　Sample Company (Craig's Design and
　　　　Landscaping Services), 2.2
logout due to inactivity, 1.1, 2.2

M

Mac, QBO app for, App. A
management reports, 1.6, 10.9–10.14
　　cash budgets, 10.15
　　described, 1.2, 10.15
　　Expenses and Vendors, 10.3, 10.9, 10.13
　　financial statements *vs.*, 1.2, 2.6, 10.15
　　For My Accountant, 10.3, 10.9, 10.14
　　list, 10.9
　　preparing, 10.9–10.14
　　Sales and Customers, 10.3, 10.9, 10.11
　　What You Owe, 10.3, 10.9, 10.12
　　Who Owes You, 10.3, 10.9, 10.10
mastery project company. *See* Mookie the Beagle™
　　　　Concierge (QBO Project Company)
Medicare taxes, 8.3, 8.8, 8.9, 8.10
mobile apps, 8.7, App A.
money in, 4.4
money out, 4.5
Mookie the Beagle™ Concierge (QBO Project
　　　　Company)
　　adjusting entries, P9.1.1–P9.1.9
　　backstory and instructions, P1.1, P2.1, P3.1,
　　　　P4.1, P5.1, P6.1, P7.1, P8.1, 9.1, P10.1
　　Banking transactions, P4.1.1–P4.1.7
　　Chart of Accounts (COA), P1.1.5, P2.1.1–P2.1.8,
　　　　P3.1.8
　　Company Settings, P1.1.1–P1.1.4
　　Customers & Sales transactions, 5P1.1–P5.1.1.9
　　Employees & Payroll transactions, P8.1.1–P8.1.7
　　inventory transactions, P7.1.1–P7.1.12

lists, P3.1.1
login, P1.1.1
QBO+ access code, P1.1
Reports, P10.1
setup, P1.1.1
transaction entry, P3.1.2–P3.1.7
Vendors & Expenses transactions, P6.1.1–P6.1.8
My Accountant screen
　　accessing, 1.3
　　invite your accountant (instructor), P1.1

N

Navigation Bar
　　entering transactions by, 3.4, 5.3, 6.3
　　overview, 1.3
net income, calculating, 2.6
non-inventory items, 5.6, 7.4
nonprofit organization tax filings, 1.7

O

Open Invoices report, 10.10
Open Purchase Orders report, 10.13
operating activities, cash flows from, 10.8
Other transactions, 3.10
output, reports as, 1.2
owner's equity. *See* equity accounts

P

partnerships
　　defined, 2.6
　　IRS Form 1099-MISC, Miscellaneous Income,
　　　　6.10
　　tax return forms, 1.7, 2.4
Pay Bills form
　　inventory transactions, 7.3, 7.7, P7.1.8
　　vendors transactions, 6.4, 6.6, 6.9, P6.1.7
payroll. *See* Employees & Payroll transactions, payroll
permanent accounts, 2.6
Physical Inventory Worksheet, 10.11
prepaid items
　　adding accounts, P2.1.2
　　adjusting entries, 9.7
　　　　prepaid insurance, 9.7, P9.1.1
　　　　prepaid rent, 9.7, P9.1.3
　　　　prepaid supplies, 9.7, P9.1.2

defined, 9.6, 9.7

subaccounts

insurance, P2.1.4, 9.7, P9.1.1

rent, P2.1.4, 9.1.3, 9.7

supplies, P2.1.4, 9.7, P9.1.2

Products and Services List

creating, 3.3

described, 3.3

exporting, 3.3

inventory transactions, 7.4, P7.1.1

types of products and services, 5.6, 7.4

updating, 3.3, P3.1.1, 5.6, 7.4, P7.1.1

viewing, 3.3

profit and loss accounts. *See* revenue and revenue (income) accounts

expenses and expense accounts

Profit & Loss Statement (P&L)

account types, 2.6

described, 1.2, 2.6, 10.15

preparing, 10.8, P10.1.2

as primary financial statement, 1.2, 2.6

Profit and Loss screen, 1.3

Projects screen overview, 1.3

Purchase Orders

creating, 7.5, P7.1.2–P7.1.4

Open Purchase Orders report, 10.13

vendor transactions, 6.4, 6.6, 7.3, 7.5, P7.1.2–P7–1.4

Purchases by Vendor Detail report, 10.13

Q

QBO Apps (Mac, Windows, and Mobile), 8.7, App. A

QBO Excel Template, P10.1

QBO lists. *See* lists, QBO

QBO+, access code, P1.1

QBO Project Company. *See* Mookie the Beagle™ Concierge (QBO Project Company)

QBO Sample Company. *See* Sample Company (Craig's Design and Landscaping Services)

QBO SatNav. *See* SatNav (satellite navigation)

QuickBooks® Desktop (QBDT)

described, 1.1

QuickBooks® Online (QBO) *vs.,* 1.1, App. B

QuickBooks Desktop Accountant (QBTA), App. B

QuickBooks® Online (QBO)

dashboard overview, 1.3

described, 1.1

Help and Support feature, 1.5

login instructions, P1.1, 2.2

mastery project company, 1.1. *See also* Mookie the Beagle™ Concierge (QBO Project Company)

mobile apps, 8.7, App. A

navigation (QBO SatNav), 1.2. *See also* SatNav (satellite navigation)

Navigation Bar overview, 1.3

online learning resources, App B

QBO+ access code, P1.1

QuickBooks® Desktop (QBDT) *vs.,* 1.1, App. B

Sample Company, 1.1. *See also* Sample Company (Craig's Design and Landscaping Services)

settings overview, 1.6

software updates, 1.1, 1.3, P1.1

tips for learning, 1.1

tools overview, 1.4

QuickBooks Online Accountant (QBOA), App B

R

Receive Payment

creating, 5.9, P5.1.5–P5.1.7, 7.9

creating bank deposit for undeposited funds from, 3.6, 5.9, 7.10

customers transaction, 7.3, 7.9, P7.1.12

Receive Payment form, 5.4, 5.9, P5.1.5–P5.1.7, 7.3, 7.9, P7.1.2

Undeposited Funds selected on, 5.9, 7.10

recurring transactions, 1.4, 3.4, 3.11, P3.1.7

expense, P6.1.5

recording adjustments, 9.5

Reminder option, 3.11, 9.5

scheduled/unscheduled, 3.11, 9.5

unscheduled, 3.11

Refund Receipt form, 5.4

registers. *See also* Check Register

QBO account, 2.3

Remember Me, P1.1

Reminder option, recurring transactions, 3.11, 9.5

renter insurance, adjusting entry for, P9.1.8

Reports, QBO

accessing, 1.3

Reports, QBO—*Cont.*

adjustments. *See* adjustments/adjusting entries

Business Overview, 10.3

Custom Reports, 10.3

Employees, 10.3

financial statements. *See also* financial statements

Balance Sheet, 1.2, 2.6, 10.8, 10.15, P10.1.3

Profit & Loss (P&L), 1.2, 2.6, 10.8, 10.15, P10.1.2

Statement of Cash Flows, 1.2, 2.6, 10.8, 10.15, P10.1.4

Journal Report, P9.1.9, 10.14

management reports. *See also* management reports

Expenses and Vendors, 10.3, 10.9, 10.13

For My Accountant, 10.3, 10.9, 10.14

Sales and Customers, 10.3, 10.9, 10.11

What You Owe, 10.3, 10.9, 10.12

Who Owes You, 10.3, 10.9, 10.10

navigating, 1.3, 10.3

Navigation Bar access, 1.3

Payroll, 10.3

Reports screen, 1.3, 10.3

run reports, 1.6

SatNav overview, 1.2, 9.1, 10.1

tax returns, 1.2. *See also* taxes and tax forms

Trial Balance, 9.3, 9.4, 10.4, 10.5

Reports screen, 1.3, 10.3

revenue and revenue (income) accounts. *See also* Customers & Sales transactions

accrued revenue, 9.6, 9.10

adjusting entries, 9.8, 9.10, P9.1.4

calculating net income, 2.6

double-entry accounting, 3.12, 9.8, 9.10

entering and displaying numbers, P2.1.6

examples, 2.6

as Profit and Loss accounts, 2.6

revenue, defined, 2.6

unearned items

adding account, P2.1.3

adjusting entries, 9.6, 9.8, P9.1.4

run reports, 1.6

S

Sales and Customers reports, 10.3, 10.9, 10.11

sales and sales transactions. *See* Customers & Sales transactions

Sales by Product/Service Summary report, 10.11

sales receipts

creating, 5.8, P5.1.1–P5.1.2

creating bank deposits for undeposited funds from, 3.6, 7.10

in recording sales transactions, 5.7

Sales Receipt form, 5.4, 5.8

Sales screen, 1.3

sales taxes, 1.3

on invoice, 7.8, P7.1.9

liability accounts, 2.6

on Products and Services List, 3.3, 5.6

reports, 10.3

Sample Company (Craig's Design and Landscaping Services)

access/reset, 1.1

adjusting entries, 9.4–9.11

Banking transactions, 3.6, 4.1–4.7

Chart of Accounts (COA), 1.6, 2.3

Company Settings, 1.6

Customers & Sales transactions, 3.7, 5.1–5.10

Employees & Payroll transactions, 3.9, 8.1–8.9

inventory transactions, 7.1–7.10

lists, 3.3

login, 2.2

logout due to inactivity, 1.1, 2.2

mastery project companies *vs.,* 1.1

recurring transactions, 3.11, 9.5

Reports, 10.2–10.14

tools, 1.4, 3.4, 5.3, 6.3

Vendors & Expenses transactions, 3.8, 6.1–6.10

SatNav (satellite navigation)

overview, 1.2

QBO Reports, 1.2, 9.1, 10.1. *See also* Reports, QBO

QBO Settings

Chart of Accounts, 1.2, 2.1. *See also* Chart of Accounts (COA)

Company Settings, 1.2. *See also* Company Settings

QBO Transactions

Banking, 1.2, 3.1, 3.6, 4.1. *See also* Banking transactions

Customers & Sales, 1.2, 3.1, 3.7, 5.1, 7.1. *See also* Customers & Sales transactions

Employees & Payroll, 1.2, 3.1, 3.9, 8.1. *See also* Employees & Payroll transactions

Vendors & Expenses, 1.2, 6.1, 7.1. *See also*
    Vendors & Expenses transactions
S corporation tax return forms, 1.7, 2.4
Search icon, 1.4
services, 5.6, 7.4. *See also* Products and Services List
Settings, QBO
    Advanced, 1.1, P1.1.4, 2.2
    Chart of Accounts (COA), 1.2, 1.6. *See also* Chart
        of Accounts (COA)
    Company Settings, 1.2, 1.6, P1.1.1–P1.1.4
    overview, 1.6
    SatNav overview, 1.2
setup, P1.1.1
single time activity, 8.5, P8.1.1–P8.1.7
Social Security taxes, 8.3, 8.8, 8.9, 8.10
sole proprietorships
    defined, 2.6
    IRS Form 1099-MISC, Miscellaneous Income, 6.10
    tax return forms, 1.7, 2.4
Statement of Cash Flows
    described, 1.2, 2.6, 10.15
    prepaid items, P2.1.4, P9.1.1–P9.1.4
    preparing, 10.8, P10.1.4
    as primary financial statement, 1.2, 2.6
subaccounts, 2.3, 2.5, 2.6, P2.1.4–P2.1.5, 9.7,
    P9.1.1–P9.1.3
Support and Help feature, 1.5

T

tasks, Gear icon to access, 1.4
taxes and tax forms
    aligning with Chart of Accounts, 2.4, P2.1.1
    C corporation, 1.7, 2.4
    form types
        IRS Form 940: Employer's Annual Federal
            Unemployment (FUTA) Tax Return, 8.9–8.10
        IRS Form 941: Employer's Quarterly Federal
            Tax Return, 8.9–8.10
        IRS Form 944: Employer's Annual Federal Tax
            Return, 8.9–8.10
        IRS Form 1040: U.S. Individual Income Tax
            Return, Schedule C, 1.7, 2.4
        IRS Form 1065: U.S. Return of Partnership
            Income, 1.7, 2.4
        IRS Form 1099-MISC, Miscellaneous Income,
            6.10

        IRS Form 1120: U. S. Corporation Income Tax
            Return, 1.7, 2.4
        IRS Form 1120S: U.S. Income Tax Return for
            an S Corporation, 1.7, 2.4
        IRS Form W-2: Wage and Tax Statement,
            8.9–8.10
        IRS Form W-3: Transmittal of Wage and Tax
            Statements, 8.9–8.10
        overview, 10.15
    impact on financial system, 1.7
    legal business entity types, 1.7, 2.4
    LLC (limited liability company), 1.7
    LLP (limited liability partnership), 1.7
    partnership, 1.7, 2.4
    payroll tax liabilities, 8.3, 8.8–8.10
    QBO report for, 1.6
    QBO settings, 1.6
    sales taxes. *See* sales taxes
    SatNav overview, 1.2
    S corporation, 1.7, 2.4
    sole proprietorship, 1.7, 2.4
    Tax screen overview, 1.3
Taxes screen, 1.3
temporary accounts, 2.6
timesheet, weekly, 8.3, 8.5, P8.1.1–P8.1.7
time tracking
    employee timesheet, 8.3, 8.5, P8.1.1–P8.1.7
    invoices and, P8.1.7
    preferences, 8.5
Tools, QBO, 1.4
    Create (+) icon, 1.4
        entering transactions by, 3.4, 5.3, 6.3
    Gear icon, 1.4, 1.6
        entering transactions by, 3.4
        Lists section, 3.3
    Navigation Bar
        entering transactions by, 3.4, 5.3, 6.3
        overview, 1.3
    Search icon, 1.4
Transactions, QBO
    in accounting cycle, 9.3, 10.4
    banking and credit card. *See* Banking
        transactions
    customers and sales. *See* Customers & Sales
        transactions
    described, 1.2, 3.4

Transactions, QBO—*Cont.*
employees and payroll. *See* Employees & Payroll transactions
entering, tools for, 1.4, 3.4
inventory. *See* inventory transactions
lists and, 3.3. *See also* lists, QBO
Other, 3.5, 3.10
payroll. *See* Employees & Payroll transactions
as QBO process, 1.6
recurring. *See* recurring transactions
sales. *See* Customers & Sales transactions
SatNav overview, 1.2, 3.1
types, 3.5
vendor and expense. *See* Vendors & Expenses transactions
Trial Balance, 10.5
in accounting cycle, 9.3, 9.4, 10.4
adjusted, 9.3, 9.4, 10.4, 10.7, P10.1.1

U

uncollectible accounts, 5.10
undeposited funds
adding account, P2.1.2
create bank deposit for, 3.6, 5.8–5.9, 7.10
transferring via bank deposit, 5.9, 7.10
unearned items
adding account, P2.1.3
adjusting entries, 9.6, 9.8, P9.1.4
defined, 9.6, 9.8
unemployment taxes, 8.3, 8.8, 8.9–8.10
Unpaid Bills report, 10.12
updates, QBO software, 1.1, 1.3, P1.1
updating lists
before entering transactions, 3.3, 5.5–5–6, 6.5, 7.4
Chart of Accounts, 3.3
Customers List, 3.3, 5.5
Employees List, 3.3
Products and Services List, 3.3, P3.1.1, 5.6, 7.4, P7.1.1
Vendors List, 3.3, 6.5
while entering transactions, 3.3, 5.5–5.6, 6.5, 7.4
Usage limits, Account and Settings, 1.6

V

Vendor Credit form, 6.4
Vendors & Expenses transactions, 3.5, 6.1–6.10, P6.1.1–P6.1.8

accessing, 1.3
accounts payable. *See* accounts payable (A/P)
Bill form, 6.4, 6.6, 6.9, P6.1.6–P6.1.7, 7.6, 7.7
Check form, 4.5, 6.4, 6.6, 6.8
checking debit card, P6.1.4
creating, 3.8
Credit Card Credit form, 6.4, P6.1.2
expense checking, P6.1.3
Expense form, 3.4, 3.8, 4.5, 6.4, 6.6, 6.7, P6.1.1
Expenses and Vendors reports, 10.3, 10.9, 10.13
Expenses screen, 1.3, P1.1.3
inventory. *See* inventory transactions, vendors transactions
IRS Form 1099-MISC, Miscellaneous Income, 6.10
navigating, 1.3, 6.3
Navigation Bar access, 1.3
Pay Bills form, 6.4, 6.6, 6.9, P6.1.7
purchase order, 6.4, 6.6, 7.3, 7.5
recording, 6.6
recurring transaction expense, P6.1.5
SatNav overview, 1.2, 3.1, 3.8, 6.1, 7.1
types, 6.4, 6.6
Vendor Credit form, 6.4
Vendors List. *See* Vendors List
Vendors List, 7.4
described, 3.3, 6.5
exporting, P6.1.8
updating, 3.3, 6.5
vendor, defined, 6.5
viewing, 3.3
Vendors tab, 1.3
view register, 1.6

W

weekly timesheet, 8.5
What You Owe reports, 10.3, 10.9, 10.12
Who Owes You reports, 10.3, 10.9, 10.10
Windows, QBO App for, App A
withdrawals/money out, 4.5
Workers screen overview, 1.3. *See also* Employees & Payroll transactions